Can’t Stop Won’t Stop

Also by Jeff Chang

We Gon' Be Alright:
Notes on Race and Resegregation

Who We Be: A Cultural History of Race
in Post–Civil Rights America

Can't Stop Won't Stop:
A History of the Hip-Hop Generation

Can't Stop Won't Stop

A Hip-Hop History

Jeff Chang with
Dave "Davey D" Cook

WEDNESDAY BOOKS
NEW YORK

First published in the United States by Wednesday Books, an imprint of St. Martin's Publishing Group

www.wednesdaybooks.com

Cover and section inserts designed by Brent Rollins

Photography credits: photograph of Cold Crush Brothers © Joe Conzo; photograph of D.M.C. at debutante ball © Josh Cheuse; photograph of National Guard, Los Angeles, 1992 © Ben Higa

The Library of Congress Cataloging-in-Publication Data is available upon request.

ISBN 978-1-250-79051-4 (hardcover)
ISBN 978-1-250-19855-6 (ebook)

Our books may be purchased in bulk for promotional, educational, or business use. Please contact your local bookseller or the Macmillan Corporate and Premium Sales Department at 1-800-221-7945, extension 5442, or by email at MacmillanSpecialMarkets@macmillan.com.

First Edition: 2021

10 9 8 7 6 5 4 3 2 1

To Connie Divack, Robin Cee, Professor Roy Thomas,
Soluna, Akire, and Erika

D.D.

To the memories of Eugene Chang, Carlos Suarez,
Benjamin Melendez, Zulu King Lucky Strike, Tony Silver,
and all of those who made the road for us

J.C.

Contents

A Note from the Authors

As writers, we are constantly choosing the words to use. We are deeply aware of their meaning and their power. We also know that word usages change over time. We always strive to recognize and be intentional about words' impact, knowing the contexts in which they are being read.

We present *Can't Stop Won't Stop* now for a different set of readers than in 2005. In this context, we have chosen to bowdlerize some words that may be considered offensive. We do not do this to censor or to appease—quite the opposite. We hope that by calling attention to these words in this way, readers might think about, ask, and discuss questions of for whom and how these words may be used, what their impacts are, and what meanings they may hold for different audiences. We hope that these discussions may prove productive.

We also recognize that history keeps moving, and that new facts are coming to light all the time that change our way of understanding the past. The text we present now, however, is fixed in time at a moment when the nation is undergoing a historic reckoning around issues of race, class, and gender. We sincerely hope that this edition of *Can't Stop Won't Stop* will contribute to ongoing discussions toward justice and that it will be read in that light.

Jeff Chang and Dave "Davey D" Cook
Berkeley and Oakland, California
December 2020

Introduction

by DJ Kool Herc

When I started DJing back in the early '70s, it was just something that we were doing for fun. I came from "the people's choice," from the street. If the people like you, they will support you, and your work will speak for itself.

We threw our first party at 1520 Sedgwick Avenue in the West Bronx. We were hoping for new housing after we got burned out of the South Bronx. We got a call and went to check out this apartment over by the Major Deegan Expressway.

When we got there we looked at it and it blew us away because we had two bathrooms. It was like *The Jeffersons*—we were moving on up! We were on the second floor and that's how I really was able to do this. I could get my equipment in and out. If it was more than a couple of floors up, we would've never got our equipment in and out of there.

My father helped us out. He said, "This is what you wanna do? You love music?" I said, I love it. And my mom helped us out when we gave the party. I asked my friends to not start any trouble around here. We have always been about respect. Because the management, they wanted something bad to happen. But nothing bad ever happened.

Instead, the parties I gave happened to catch on. They became a rite of passage for young people in the Bronx. Then the younger generation came in and started putting their spin on what I had started. I set down the blueprint, and all the architects started adding on this level and that level. Pretty soon, before we even knew it, it had started to evolve.

Most people know me as DJ Kool Herc. But sometimes when I introduce myself to people, I just tell them that my friends call me Herc. Later on, they might ask, "Are you *that* Herc?" My thing is: Come and meet me as who I am. My head is not swollen, I don't try to front on people. If you like what I do, if you like me playing music or giving parties, hey, that's what I do for my friends and people. It's what I've always done.

To me, hip-hop says, "Come as you are." We are a family. It ain't about security. It ain't about bling-bling. It ain't about how much your gun can shoot. It ain't about two-hundred-dollar sneakers. It is not about me being better than you or you being better than me. It's about you and me, connecting one-to-one. That's why it has universal appeal. It has given young people a way to understand their world, whether they are from the suburbs or the city or wherever.

Hip-hop has also created a lot of jobs that otherwise wouldn't exist. But even more important, I think hip-hop has bridged the culture gap. It brings white kids together with Black kids, brown kids with Asian kids. They all have something in common that they love. It gets past the stereotypes and people hating each other because of those stereotypes.

People talk about the four hip-hop elements: DJing, b-boying, MCing, and graffiti. I think that there are far more than those: the way you walk, the way you talk, the way you look, the way you communicate. Back in my era, we had James Brown and civil rights and Black Power; then you have people calling themselves hip-hop activists. Now we have Black Lives Matter. These young people today are talking about their era. They have a right to speak on it the way they see it coming up.

Hip-hop is the voice of this generation. Even if you didn't grow up in the Bronx in the '70s, hip-hop is there for you. It has become a powerful force. Hip-hop binds all of these people, all of these nationalities, all over the world together.

But we are not making the best use of the recognition and the position that it has. Do we realize how much power hip-hop has? There are lot of people who are doing something positive, who are doing hip-hop the way it was meant to be done. They are reaching young people, showing them what the world could be—people living together and having fun.

But too often, the ones that get the most recognition are those emphasizing the negative. Music is sometimes a medication from reality, and the only time you get a dialogue is when tragedy happens. When Tupac or Biggie or Jam Master Jay died, that's when people wanted to have a dialogue. It was too late. Not enough people are taking advantage of using hip-hop as a way to deal with serious issues, as a way to try to change things before tragedy strikes.

I lost my son to gun violence. We have to be aware of what's going on right now. Hip-hop did not create the violence. You don't need the gun to prevail. What you have to do is master your craft that you love. You don't have to go astray from that.

We have the power to change things. If Jay-Z comes out one day with his shirt hanging this way or LL Cool J comes out with one leg of his pants rolled up, the next day everyone is doing the same thing. If we decide one day to say that we're not gonna kill somebody senselessly, everyone will follow.

I don't want to hear people saying that they don't want to be role models. Cut the crap. That's escape. That's the easy way out. You might be living lovely. But if you came out of the neighborhood, there was somebody who was there to guide you when you needed it, someone that said, "Son, here's two dollars." You might have beat up on the ghetto to get out of it, but what have you done for the ghetto lately? How can you come from nothing to get something, but at the same time, still do dirt to tear it all down?

Hip-hop has always been about having fun, but it's also about taking responsibility. And now we have a platform to speak our minds. Millions of people are watching us. Let's hear something powerful. Tell people what they need to hear. How will we help the community? What do we stand for? What can we change if we get organized? We can see how powerful we really can be.

Hip-hop is a family, so everybody has got to pitch in. East, west, north, or south—we come from one coast and that coast was Africa. This culture was born in the ghetto. We were born here to die. We're surviving now, but we're not yet rising up. If we've got a problem, we've got to correct it. We can't be hypocrites. That's what I hope the hip-hop generation can do, to take us all to the next level by always reminding us: It ain't about keeping it real, it's about keeping it right.

For the younger generation—here's what I want you to know about hip-hop and where we come from. Every five years or so somebody pops up with something brand new and that's what I see going on right now. You're a whole different generation. You all have created a whole world of ideas with your art, music, and I love you for it. Hip-hop is endless. I'm surprised and I'm glad it's come such a long way. This culture is yours. Make something of it.

LOOP 1

1969-

1982

1
Babylon Is Burning

In 1977, President Jimmy Carter emerged from a state motorcade at Charlotte Street in the heart of the South Bronx—three helicopters overhead, Secret Service agents at his side—to gaze silently upon four square blocks of dead city.

The president stood amid the smashed brick and concrete, stripped cars, rotting vermin, and garbage—his secretary of Housing and Urban Development Patricia Harris, Mayor Abraham Beame, and a small army of reporters, photographers, and cameramen tailing behind. For miles and miles, apartment buildings that had once been proud homes for thousands lay in ruins. The Bronx had become a national symbol of urban decay.

Decades before, a powerful urban planner named Robert Moses had decided to build a highway right through the heart of the Bronx. That's how an unbroken continuum of cohesive, diverse communities was cleared for the Cross Bronx Expressway, which Moses hoped would get people from the suburbs of New Jersey to the suburbs of Queens in just fifteen minutes. It was as if the million people living in the Bronx in between didn't matter at all.

Sixty thousand Bronx residents were caught directly in the crosshairs of the Expressway. Moses bulldozed right through them. As the historian Robert Caro wrote, "where once apartment buildings or private homes had stood were now hills of rubble, decorated with ripped-open bags of rotting garbage that had been flung atop them."[1]

When the sound of automobiles replaced the sound of jackhammers on the length of the Expressway, the fuel was in place for the Bronx to burn. Apartment buildings passed into the hands of slumlords, who figured out that they could make more money by destroying their own buildings than by collecting rent.

A fireman described the scheme. First the slumlords refused to provide heat and water to the tenants. Frustrated residents moved out. Then the slumlords hired thugs to burn down their own buildings, so that they could collect sums of up to $150,000 in insurance money. "Before you know it," the fireman said, "you have a block with no one living there."[2] Between 1970 and 1975, the Bronx lost 43,000 apartments, almost one sixth of all its stock.[3] Thousands of vacant, devastated lots and empty buildings littered the borough. In the streets, heroin dealers and junkie thieves followed the contract arsonists like vultures.

During the 1960s, half of the white residents left the Bronx. With them went the businesses and the jobs. The official youth unemployment rate hit 60 percent. If blues culture developed under the conditions of forced labor, hip-hop culture would arise from the conditions of no work at all.

In the words of one Dr. Wise, a neighborhood clinic director, the Bronx was nothing less than "a Necropolis—a city of death."

The Ghetto Brothers

When African American, Afro-Caribbean, and Latinx families moved into formerly Jewish, Irish, and Italian neighborhoods, white youth gangs preyed on the new arrivals. Black and brown youths formed gangs, first in self-defense, then sometimes for power, sometimes for kicks.

By the late 1960s, the Bronx had thickened with gangs. East of the Bronx River, a small band of hardrocks at the Bronxdale Houses called the Savage Seven grew and adopted a new name, the Black Spades. Uniting African American youths, they became the biggest gang in the city. To the north, across Fordham Road, there were white gangs like the Arthur Avenue Boys, Golden Guineas, War Pigs, the Ministers, and the Grateful Dead.

Third Avenue, the main thoroughfare shooting down from Little Italy through the Hub to the bridge into Manhattan, was hot with action—the Chingalings and the Savage Nomads on one side, the Black Falcons nearby. Below Crotona Park, in the heart of the burnt-out South Bronx, were the turfs of the Turbans, the Peacemakers, the Mongols, the Roman Kings, the Seven Immortals, and the Dirty Dozens. Two of the most feared were the Savage Skulls and the Ghetto Brothers. Most of these gangs were predominantly Puerto Rican. The Bronx had been resegregated along race, class, and ethnic lines.

Some of the gangs partnered with each other, and others preyed on each other. Often when one neighborhood got organized into a gang, another sprang up in self-defense. "If you went through someone's neighborhood, you were a target. Or you had to take off your jacket," Carlos "Karate Charlie" Suarez, the president of the Ghetto Brothers, recalled. "If you got caught, they beat the hell out of you."

By the end of the 1960s, the police and the media realized that gangs had divided up the Bronx. They estimated that there were a hundred different gangs claiming eleven thousand members. Gang members figured those numbers were too low.[4] For immigrant latchkey kids, foster children outside the system, girls running away from abusive environments, and thousands of others in the abandoned Bronx, the gangs provided shelter, comfort, and protection. But they also preyed on the weak: the elderly, drug pushers and addicts, store owners, unaffiliated youths.

The gangs warded off boredom and gave meaning to the hours. They turned the wasteland into a playground. They felt like a family. "You know that one percent that don't fit in and don't care? We were living our lifestyle," said Felipe "Blackie" Mercado, the president of the Savage Skulls. "We don't want to be dealing with society's bullshit. This is what we are, this is what we be. You give me respect I give you respect. Simple."

"We like to ride and we like to stay together so we all do the same things and we're happy that way," said Tata, a Savage Skull girl. "That's the only way we can survive out here, because if we all go our own ways, one by one, we're gone."[5]

The Savage Skulls had gotten their name from Benjy Melendez of the Ghetto Brothers, who had formed at 162nd and Westchester in the Hunts Point section of the South Bronx. Through their powerful leadership, the Ghetto Brothers would grow to more than a thousand members, with divisions as far away as New Jersey and Connecticut.[6]

Melendez was the gang's vice president. The skinny, whip-smart nineteen-year-old had founded the gang. If other gangs spoke of themselves as "families," the Ghetto Brothers actually began as one. Benjy, Ulpiano, Victor, and Robert Melendez were brothers whose family was forced by Robert Moses's urban renewal projects to leave Manhattan for the Bronx. Settling near the Cross Bronx Expressway, Benjy joined a small gang called the Cofon Cats. When the Melendezes moved south of Crotona Park, Benjy formed a new clique with his brothers and friends. Benjy came up with a number of names—including the Seven Immortals and the Savage Nomads. He eventually gave those away to his friends' cliques, and they settled on the Ghetto Brothers.

"Yellow Benjy," as he was called, was a gifted organizer and orator. The gang half-mockingly called him "The Preacher." He could fight as well as anyone, but his real love was music. As children, the Melendezes had won a talent contest singing Beatles songs for Tito Puente. Benjy led the Ghetto Brothers' Latin-rock band and was at the center of any clubhouse party.

Carlos Suarez was the Ghetto Brothers president, a handsome twenty-one-year-old martial arts expert with dark, curly locks and a coy smile. On the street, he was known as the short-tempered, street fighting "Karate Charlie," but to women and outsiders, he conveyed a boyish curiosity and a shy charm. He had joined a gang called the Egyptians at the age of twelve, but left as its members all became strung out on heroin, joining other gangs until he befriended Benjamin Melendez.

At eighteen, Suarez's grandmother kicked him out of the house, so he enrolled in the Marines. On Christmas break in 1970, he went AWOL and came back to the gang. Benjy conspired to make him president. Suarez brought discipline and battle-readiness to the gang. He said, "I tried to teach them hand-to-hand combat. I tried to teach them how to throw a Molotov cocktail."

The two became a formidable core. Suarez says, "Benjy was my yin and I was the yang. Good cop, bad cop. I was the one that grabbed them by the throat and administered punishment. Benjy was the one that intervened."

With Yellow Benjy's leadership, the Ghetto Brothers had begun to take community leadership. They criticized the quality of health care at Lincoln Hospital, a place they called "The Butcher Shop," questioned why youths had no jobs or recreation available to them, and decried heavy-handed policing. They cleaned the tenements, and set up a free-breakfast program and free-clothing drive. They became security for prominent Puerto Rican activists. They referred to themselves as "the people's army." By the summer of 1971, Yellow Benjy had come up with another name that described their new activities: The South Bronx Defensive Unit. He told Charlie, "Let's stop this gang stuff and form an organization for peace."

A charismatic twenty-five-year-old, half African American, half Puerto Rican ex-junkie named Cornell Benjamin had come into the fold. Known as "Black Benjie," he became the third staff leader of the Ghetto Brothers. Most gangs had "warlords," whose chief duties involved stockpiling the arsenal, training the members in fighting skills and military techniques, and negotiating times and places for rumbles. But at Melendez's suggestion, Black Benjie became Peace Counselor.

1971 would be a crucial year. The government was cracking down on political activist groups like the Young Lords, a group that advocated for the rights of Puerto Ricans, and the Black Panther Party, which included a young mother-to-be named Afeni Shakur who was imprisoned for her political activities. Both those organizations were trying to recruit gang members to do more positive things for their communities. But the police never thought that the gang members themselves might organize.

All the changes the Ghetto Brothers made put them in an important place at an important moment. The Bronx gangs were quickly burning down two tracks—one toward peace, the other toward more blood. If there was a gang that could end the violence in the Bronx, perhaps it would be the Ghetto Brothers.

The War

Dwyer Junior High was at the center of a number of gang turfs. Its halls were crowded with rival gangbangers. In March, a boy at Dwyer harassed a Savage Nomad sister. She called on Suarez and Savage Nomad president Ben Buxton to back her up. It became an event. Hundreds gathered to see the perpetrator beat down, then they followed as the gangs marched triumphantly through the schoolyard.

Two concerned Dwyer teachers, Rita Fecher and her husband, Manny Dominguez, secured the Ghetto Brothers a storefront clubhouse on 163rd and Stebbins, fully funded by the city's Youth Services Agency. They provided the gang with musical instruments. They brought members of the media to the Bronx to report on the gangs. TV producers and filmmakers flocked to the Ghetto Brothers' storefront to capture their transformation from a gang into "an organization."

But as the days grew hotter, the violence in the South Bronx escalated. Even as the Ghetto Brothers moved publicly toward peace, they became more embroiled in violence. In May, three

Ghetto Brothers were shot in the clubhouse, leaving one paralyzed. Victor Melendez—Benjy's brother, the musical heart of the Ghetto Brothers band, and the then-president of the Savage Nomads—was stabbed. The Ghetto Brothers and the Savage Nomads figured that the Mongols were behind the hits. For weeks, Suarez and Buxton handed out beatings to any with the bad luck to wander near them.

By November, the Ghetto Brothers were beefing with the Javelins, the Dirty Dozens, and the Turbans. The Black Spades and the Savage Skulls, the two largest gangs in the Bronx, erupted into a rumble at a South Bronx movie theater. There were reports that heavy artillery was pouring into the streets—handguns, machine guns, even grenades and bombs.[7]

"It was catastrophe after catastrophe," says Suarez. "Just hate on hate on hate on hate."

Social workers urgently pressed for a peace treaty. One peace organizer, Eduardo Vincenty, secured truce commitments from dozens of gangs, including the Javelins, the Peacemakers, the Reapers, the Young Sinners, and the Black Spades.[8] Separately, Suarez and Melendez met with gang leadership, hosting Friday-night gatherings, where they partied, then turned off the music to talk.

On December 2, word reached the Ghetto Brothers clubhouse that three gangs—the Mongols, the Seven Immortals, and the Black Spades—were in their neighborhood jumping kids. Earlier that day, the Immortals and the Spades had scuffled with some Roman Kings at the Dwyer handball courts, sending one to the hospital. The Mongols had joined them and they were all coming down Southern Boulevard to rumble with the Savage Skulls. With a group of Ghetto Brothers, Black Benjie headed up to Horseshoe Park where the gangs were massing, hoping to mediate.

As Black Benjie descended the park's long staircase, the park was filling up with dozens of bangers, wire-taut and waiting for something to happen.

"Listen, brothers," Black Benjie said, holding up his hands to show he had no weapons, "we're here to talk peace." The Spades, the Mongols, and the Immortals surrounded Black Benjie and the Ghetto Brothers. "Peace, shit," said one of the Immortals, taking out a pipe. Another pulled out a machete. In desperation, a Ghetto Brother whipped out his garrison belt and began swinging it.

"Tip, brothers, tip!" Black Benjie said, and most of the Ghetto Brothers scattered. Then the pipe came crashing down on Black Benjie's head, and he fell to the ground. The gangbangers closed the cipher around him, stomping, cutting, and beating him to death.

Hours later, with Black Benjie's body lying in Lincoln Hospital, police patrols circled Dwyer Junior High and reporters descended on the Ghetto Brothers' clubhouse. "What are you going to do?" they asked the gang members. "Will you retaliate?"

The *Daily News* headline the next day read, BRONX TEEN WAR: PEACEMAKER KILLED IN MELEE. The future lay in the Ghetto Brothers' hands. They could lead the Bronx into a bloodier war than had ever been imagined, or toward a peace the borough had never seen.

As the word spread across the borough on the afternoon of December 2, Suarez called in all his division leaders, some from as far away as Queens and New Jersey. He says, "We were going to find the presidents and we were going to destroy everybody."

By dusk, the Bronx police had mobilized their special operations teams at a state of high alert. They had arrested a teen Black Spade in connection with Black Benjie's murder. But Bam Bam, the president of the Spades, hoping to avoid bigger problems, came to the Ghetto Brothers clubhouse to declare that they had not been involved in the murder. Word on the street was that the killer was a guy named Julio, a leader of the Seven Immortals. He had once been a Ghetto Brother.

Suarez was getting ready for war. The Ghetto Brothers were stacking guns, knives, machetes, bows and arrows, and Molotovs. They went out looking for the Seven Immortals and the Mongols.

Melendez wanted to keep the peace. He told them not to retaliate: "When Black Benjie died, he went for peace and if you go out there to declare war, it will make his mission in vain."

Suarez and his group returned to the clubhouse empty-handed. But Benjy and the other Ghetto Brothers and their allies, the Roman Kings, were there and they had Julio and four other members of the Seven Immortals and the Mongols. They were sitting on the ground, their legs tied and their arms bound behind their backs.

Suarez took a .45 and pressed the gun to Julio's head, and then into Julio's mouth. "I'm gonna blow your brains out," he said. But Melendez stepped up to stop him.

"You want to save this stupid son of a b---h who killed one of us?" Suarez said.

"We're all 'one of us,'" Melendez said.

Finally Suarez wheeled around and kicked Julio. The rest of the clubhouse descended on the Immortals and Mongols and beat them bloody. Then Suarez ended it, pulled the accused up, and pushed them out into the winter night.

Later that evening, Suarez and Melendez went to Black Benjie's apartment to comfort Gwendolyn Benjamin, his mother. "Everyone loved Benjie," Suarez told her. "If something's not done all hell is gonna break loose."

Mrs. Benjamin was clear: "No revenge. Benjie lived for peace."[9]

The next morning, reporters gathered at the Ghetto Brothers clubhouse. Yellow Benjy Melendez was the designated spokesperson. "All the gangs are waiting for one word—'fire'—but I'm not going to say it because that won't bring Benjie back," he said. "I notice you reporters look disappointed because you didn't want to hear that, right? You wanted to hear about these South Bronx savages. But I'm not going to give you the pleasure."

After Black Benjie was buried in an emotional ceremony, the Ghetto Brothers issued a call for the truce meeting to be held on the evening of December 8 at the Bronx Boys Club.

Peace Treaty

Sniper cops perched on the roofs of nearby buildings. Television cameras, photographers, and reporters filed into the gym. Into the gym came the Black and brown boy gangs of the Bronx. The smaller families, the young, hungry bangers, the established gangs, and the major families—the Ghetto Brothers, the Savage Nomads, the Savage Skulls, the Black Spades, and the Seven Immortals.[10] The girl gangs were excluded from the meeting, locked outside in the December freeze.

The tension was thick. The presidents, vice presidents, and warlords filled the folding chairs set in a circle in the middle of the gym floor. Social workers, school teachers, and other gang members filled the bleachers. The unprecedented gathering threatened to explode from the accumulation of unresolved slights and unpaid blood debts.

Charlie, wearing a black beret with a red star, black vest, and denims instead of his Ghetto Brothers colors, reminded the gang leaders that they were there because Black Benjie had died for peace, and then opened the floor. Marvin "Hollywood" Harper, a Vietnam vet and a slim Black member of the Savage Skulls wearing a beret and a gray combat shirt under his colors, began talking. "When I heard about Benjie dying, I told Brother Charlie of the Ghetto Brothers that I would take a life for Benjie. Charlie told me no, so I won't. If the Ghetto Brothers want peace, then there will be peace."

Then he pointed at the Seven Immortals, the Mongols, and the Black Spades, and accused them of attacking his fellow Skulls and taking their colors. He blamed them for the death of Black Benjie. Bam Bam, the leader of the Black Spades, rose to blame the Skulls for invading Spades turf with shotguns. Gang members stood up in the bleachers, as if they were ready to set something off. Suarez silenced them all with a word: "Peace."

Hollywood stepped back up to address the Spades. He gestured angrily with his cigarette. "All we did is ask you people for the colors and you people didn't give us our colors back."

He continued, "When we have static, we settle it among ourselves, man, because, like wow, we have to *live* in this district."

And here the meeting turned. "The whitey don't come down here and live in the fucked-up houses, man," Hollywood said. "The whitey don't come down here, man, and have all the, the fucked-up, fucking no heat in the wintertime. You understand? We do, *jack,* so therefore we got to make it a better place to live."

Now the crowd, even the Spades, jumped to their feet and cheered. Hollywood called for an end to rumors, for a step toward peace. "If we don't have peace now, whitey will come in and stomp us," he shouted.[11] The gangs roared in agreement, holding up peace signs and Black Power salutes.

Then Benjy Melendez stepped forward. He looked Black Benjie's killer in the eye. "You took away one of our brothers' lives, man," Melendez said. "You don't want us to become a gang anymore, right? Because I *know* you. You was up in the meeting and you told me, 'Benjy, I want to get out alive.'"

Melendez concluded, "The thing is, we're not a gang anymore. We're an *organization.* We want to help Blacks and Puerto Ricans to live in a better environment."

Suarez and Vincenty directed the gangs into smaller caucuses to discuss the fine points of the Peace Treaty. It read, "We realize that we are all brothers living in the same neighborhoods and having the same problems. We also realize that fighting amongst ourselves will not solve our common problems." It continued, "All groups are to respect each other—cliques individual members and their women. Each member clique of the Family will be able to wear their colors in other member cliques' turf without being bothered." The Treaty set terms for dealing with rumors and beefs. "If one member of a clique has a beef with a member of another clique, the two are to talk it over. If that does not solve it then they will both fight it out between themselves, after that it is considered finished." Gangs not covered by the Peace Treaty would be given the option of joining, disbanding, or being forced to disband. It concluded, "This is the Peace we pledge to keep. PEACE BETWEEN ALL GANGS AND A POWERFUL UNITY."

Suarez and the Boys Club director, a young priest named Mario Barbell, summoned the presidents into the center of the floor to have them put their hands together as if they were in a huddle. As the photographers and cameramen jockeyed for position, they said "Peace!" and strode out.

News reports would be glowing. But the girl gang members who had played a crucial role in bringing the gangs to the peace table were not even represented, while the media and the social workers were. Many of the gang leaders left the meeting feeling it was some sort of an elaborate charade.

That weekend, the Ghetto Brothers again gathered the presidents, this time privately in their clubhouse. The two-hour meeting at the Boys Club, Melendez told the gang leaders, "was a big show. It was just for the media to see, 'Oh see, the city got the gangs together.' But people went out of there feeling angry, feeling pissed off, and it wasn't genuine. Let's speak for real, because a lot of us here are still holding anger inside."

The presidents talked about how their members still wanted to war over the death of Black Benjie. Julio of the Seven Immortals admitted he knew the gang was marked. He broke down as he apologized. Melendez pointed at Julio. "Attacking these guys is not gonna bring Black Benjie back again," he said. "It never should have happened, but it happened. Let it never, never happen again."

That night, the truce was sealed.

A New World

But even as the community celebrated the peace treaty, many did not want to see change. Afeni Shakur and her fellow Black Panthers were freed after they were acquitted in court. She gave birth to a son she named Tupac Amaru Shakur. But the NYPD continued to pursue Black activists, including Tupac's aunt, Assata Shakur. President Nixon had declared a War on Drugs, which would result in the passage of a number of broad laws that would profile and capture many innocent people of color and progressive organizers in its dragnet.

And just days after the Boys Club meeting, NYPD's Bronx Youth Gang Task Force quietly opened for business. An officer bluntly outlined their message: "We talk to the gangs. We tell 'em,' With some thirty thousand cops, we got the biggest gang in the city. You're going to lose.'"[12]

In just over a year,[13] they compiled three thousand dossiers on gangs and gang members. Many of the leaders were arrested and hauled off to prison. "The enemy around the Bronx now at this very moment," said one gang member, "is the policemen."[14] With each succession in leadership, the truce eroded just a little bit more.

But the peace treaty had been momentous in a wholly unexpected way. Sometime shortly after the treaty, the Ghetto Brothers were approached by the owner of a small Latin music record label. Benjy and Victor Melendez jumped at the chance to record their original compositions in a real studio, and quickly signed the five-hundred-dollar contract. They made an eight-song album, *Ghetto Brothers Power Fuerza.*

The music everyone was listening and dancing to at the time was changing. James Brown led the way. In so many ways, he laid the foundation for hip-hop.

In 1967, he had introduced the sound that would become known as funk on "Cold Sweat," shifting the focus to the rhythms and drums. The following year, just four months after Martin Luther King, Jr. was assassinated, he created an anthem for a new generation: "Say It Loud—I'm Black and I'm Proud." It was an invitation for African Americans and Puerto Ricans alike to come together to celebrate their shared Blackness.

By 1970, Brown was regularly merging African, African American, and Afro Cuban sounds and rhythms into impossibly funky songs with long breaks for the dancers—grooves like "Give It Up

Turnit a Loose," "Get Up (I Feel Like Being a) Sex Machine," and "Get Up, Get Into It, Get Involved." He sang less and rapped more, leading his crowds into a lively trance state. White pop radio played James Brown less, figuring the music was too Black.

But the kids in the Bronx loved it. They gathered around their TV sets to watch James and his band play, and then they practiced imitating his dances. Later, they would aspire to his complete showmanship, that give-it-all-you-got energy. Brown's unabashed Blackness also helped inspire Afro Latino musicians to proudly explore their own African musical roots and mix them with African American styles in *bugalú* and salsa.

While other Bronx Puerto Ricans—like Willie Colón, Ray Barretto, Joe Cuba, and Eddie Palmieri—were creating a new Afro Latino sound, the Melendezes mixed in additional influences like the Beatles, the Beach Boys, and doo-wop. With their sweet melodies and wicked backbeat informed by James Brown, the Ghetto Brothers sounded more like California Latin-rock bands like Santana. Benjy, Victor, and the band recorded their album in one take—lo-fi, raw, brimming with enthusiasm, a feeling that all their pent-up creativity could finally be released.

"This album contains a message; a message to the world, from the Ghetto Brothers," the handwritten liner notes read. "If the Ghetto Brothers' dream comes true, the 'little people' will be 'little people' no more, and make their own mark in this world."

After the truce, the Ghetto Brothers band played Friday block parties, plugging their amps into the lampposts and inviting all the gangs to their turf to party. In the band's signature song, "Ghetto Brothers Power," Benjy called out, "If you want to get your thing together, brothers and sisters, let's do it Ghetto Brother style." Then they launched into the kind of blazing drum-and-conga breakdown that drove the Bronx kids crazy. The song climaxed with a promise: "We are gonna take you higher with Ghetto Brother Power!"

Youthful energies had turned. Gangs had begun dissolving, turfs were disintegrating. The new kids coming up were obsessed with flash, style, *sabor.* If the gangs once had made people afraid of being on the street, a new generation would find their release in block parties under the afternoon sun or evening moonlight. Give them an apocalypse, and they would dance.

2
How DJ Kool Herc Lost His Accent

The plan was simple enough, according to the party's host, Cindy Campbell. "I was saving my money, because what you want to do for back to school is go down to Delancey Street instead of going to Fordham Road, because you can get the newest things that a lot of people don't have. And when you go back to school, you want to go with things that nobody has so you could look nice and fresh," she says. "At the time my Neighborhood Youth Corps paycheck was like forty-five dollars a week—ha!—and they would pay you every two weeks. So how am I gonna turn over my money? I mean, this is not enough money!"

Cindy calculated it would cost a little more than half her paycheck to rent the rec room in their apartment building at 1520 Sedgwick Avenue. Her brother, whom she knew as Clive but everyone else knew as Kool Herc, was an aspiring DJ with access to a powerful sound system. All she had to do was bulk-buy some Olde English 800 and Colt 45 malt liquor, hot dogs, and buns, and advertise the party.

She, Clive, and her friends hand-wrote the announcements on index cards, scribbling the details of the time and location below a popular song title like "Get on the Good Foot" or "Fencewalk." If she filled the room, she could charge a quarter for the girls, two for the guys, and make back the overhead on the room right there. And with the profit—presto, instant wardrobe.

Clive had been DJing house parties for three years. Growing up in Kingston, Jamaica, he had seen the sound systems firsthand. The local sound was called Somerset Lane, and the selector's name was King George. Clive says, "I was too young to go in. All we could do is sneak out and see the preparation of the dance throughout the day. The guys would come with a big old handcart with the boxes in it. And then in the nighttime, I'm a little itchy headed, loving the vibrations on the zinc top 'cause them sound systems are powerful." He wanted to be at the center of that kind of excitement, to be exactly like King George.

Cindy and Clive's father, Keith Campbell, was a devoted record collector, buying not only reggae, but American jazz, gospel, and country. They heard Nina Simone and Louis Armstrong and Nat King Cole, even Nashville country crooner Jim Reeves. "I remember listening to Jim Reeves all the time," Clive says. "I was singing these songs and emulating them to the fullest. That really helped me out, changing my accent, is singing to the records."

In the Bronx, his mother, Nettie, would take him to house parties, which had the same ambrosial effect on him that the sound systems had. "I see the different guys dancing, guys rapping to girls, I'm wondering what the guy is whisperin' in the girl's ears about. I'm green, but I'm checking out the scene," he recalls. "And I noticed a lot of the girls was complaining, 'Why they not playing that record?' 'How come they don't have that record?' 'Why did they take it off right there?'" He began buying his own 45s, waiting for the day he could have his own sound system.

As luck would have it, Keith Campbell became a sponsor for a local rhythm and blues band, investing in a brand-new Shure P.A. system for the group. Clive's father was now their soundman, and the band wanted somebody to play records during intermission. Keith told them he could get his son. But Clive had started up his own house party business, and somehow his gigs always happened to fall at the same times as the band's, leaving Keith so angry he refused to let Clive touch the system. "So here go these big columns in my room, and my father says, 'Don't touch it. Go and borrow Mr. Dolphy's stuff,'" he says. "Mr. Dolphy said, 'Don't worry Clive, I'll let you borrow some of these.' In the back of my mind, Jesus Christ, I got these big Shure columns up in the room!"

At the same time, his father was no technician. They all knew the system was powerful, but no one could seem to make it peak. Another family in the same building had the same system and seemed to be getting more juice out of it, but they wouldn't let Keith or Clive see how they did it. "They used to put a lot of wires to distract me from chasing the wires," he says.

One afternoon, fiddling around on the system behind his father's back, Clive figured it out, even the echo function. "My father came home and it was so loud he snuck up behind me," he remembers.

Clive's guilt was written all over his face. But his father couldn't believe it.

Keith yelled, "Where the noise come from?"

"This is the system!"

Keith said, "What! Weh you did?"

"'This is what I did,'" Clive recalls telling his father, revealing the hookup. "And he said, '*Raas claat,* man! We have sound!!!'

"So now the tables turned. Now these other guys was trying to copy what I was doing, because our sound is coming out monster, monster!" Clive says. "Me and my father came to a mutual understanding that I would go with them and play between breaks and when I do my parties, I could use the set. I didn't have to borrow his friend's sound system anymore. I start making up business cards saying 'Father and Son.' And that's how it started, man! That's when Cindy asked me to do a back-to-school party. Now people would come to this party and see these big-ass boxes they never seen before."

It was a Saturday, the 11th of August, 1973. Cindy, Clive, and their friends brought the equipment down from their second-floor apartment and set up in the room adjacent to the rec room. "My system was on the dance floor, and I was in a little room watching, peeking out the door seeing how the party was going," he says.

It didn't start so well. Clive played some Jamaican reggae tunes, ones guaranteed to rock any yard dance. Like any proud DJ, he wanted to stamp his personality onto his playlist. But this was the Bronx. They wanted the breaks. So, like any good DJ, he gave the people what they wanted, and dropped some soul and funk bombs. Now they were packing the room. There was a new energy. DJ Kool Herc took the mic and carried the crowd higher.

"All people would hear is his voice coming out from the speakers," Cindy says. "And we didn't have no money for a strobe light. So what we had was this guy named Mike. When Herc would say, 'Okay, Mike! Mike with the lights!' Mike flicked the light switch. He got paid for that."

By this point in the night, they probably didn't need the atmospherics. The party people were moving to the shouts of James Brown, turning the place into a sweatbox. They were busy shaking off history, having the best night of their generation's lives.

Later, as Clive and Cindy counted their money—they had made

three hundred dollars!—they were giddy. This party could be the start of something big, they surmised. They just couldn't know how big.

Making a Name

Clive Campbell was born to Keith and Nettie Campbell, the first of six children. He lived on Second Street in the Trenchtown section of Kingston, Jamaica, the same yard from which Bob Marley and his friends Peter Tosh and Bunny Wailer emerged. As the family's fortunes grew, they moved to Franklyn Town on the eastern side of the city. "We had like seven different fruits growing in our yard. We had different types of peppers, flowers, you know, it was tight!" Clive recalls. "Every Sunday we'd look forward to go out to the beach after church."

But political violence in Kingston was rising, and his mother convinced his father they should immigrate to America. Her firstborn would join her, then the rest of the family would follow.

Clive Campbell came to New York City on a cold November night in 1967. A fresh snowfall lay on the ground, something the twelve-year-old had never seen before. He took a bus from Kennedy Airport into the gray, unwelcoming city. This wasn't the America he had seen on his neighbor's television, or imagined from his father's records. He had no idea how to begin again, he says, "All I could do was just look out the window."

He recalls, "Now I'm living in a tenement building. There's no yard. This is all boxed and closed in." Clive looked and spoke and felt like a country boy. "Here I am all hicked out, got a corduroy coat on, with the snow hat with the flip-up-and-come-over-your-ears. I had that on with these cowboy boots," Herc says. "And this girl at school started teasing the hell out of me. She was calling my shoes 'roach killers.' She had the whole hall laughing, 'Ah roach killers, roach killers!'"

At Junior High School 118, Clive began running cross-country and track and winning medals. For a time, he even rolled with the Cofon Cats, the same gang that Benjy Melendez had once joined. "The gang members started asking us to be division leaders because they see we have respect," Herc says. "And I had a few other things to worry about besides the gangs, like getting my ass whipped by my father."

Instead Clive tuned into rock and soul radio disc jockeys like

Cousin Brucie and Wolfman Jack, listening to these smooth men rap their silver-tongued rap. He began going to "First Fridays" youth dances at a local Catholic school and at Murphy Projects. His mother took him to house parties, where the Temptations, Aretha Franklin, Smokey Robinson, and, most important, James Brown became his tutors. They were teaching Clive how to lose his accent. By the time Clive began attending Alfred E. Smith High School, some of his Jamaican friends didn't even know he was Jamaican. He was in the process of reinventing himself.

He wasn't alone. All across the city youths were customizing their names or giving themselves new ones and scrawling them in marker and spraypaint across the naked city surfaces. Graffiti writers were the vanguard of a new culture. Crossing gang turfs to leave their names, slipping through the long arms and high fences of authority, violating notions of property and propriety, they said "I'm here" and "I don't care what you think." Gang members, who had trapped themselves in their own neighborhoods, had to give them respect.

"I was in the Savage Nomads," one famous Bronx writer said. "But if I was [tagging] C.A.T. 87 and the guys from other neighborhoods saw my name, instead of trying to beat me up they would ask for autographs."[1]

The modern-day graffiti movement began in Los Angeles's Mexican American and in Philadelphia's Black neighborhoods.[2] One Philly teenager, CORNBREAD, started tagging subways to attract the attention of a beauty named Cynthia.[3] So many kids copied him that by 1968, the movement had spread to New York City. CORNBREAD's protégé, TOP CAT, moved to Harlem and brought with him the "gangster" style of lettering and taught it to a Puerto Rican teen who tagged JULIO 204 and a Greek American who wrote TAKI 183. By the summer of 1970, their tags were everywhere in the city. After the *New York Times* featured a big picture of a TAKI tag, thousands of New York teens—young women like BARBARA 62, EVA 62, and CHARMIN 65, and young men like JOE 182, JULIO 204, and LEE 163d—sought their own fame, writing their names on buildings, bus stops, and subway station walls.[4]

Clive and his friend Richard picked up markers and spraycans, too. Rich became UNCLE RICH and Clive became CLYDE AS KOOL.[5] "They couldn't recall my name Clive," he says. "So the closest you could come was Clyde, from the Knicks basketball player. They'd be like, 'You mean like 'Clyde' Frazier?' 'Yeah. Clyde. Let's leave it like that.' So I started to write that. And where I picked 'Kool' from was this TV cigarette commercial."

"Wherever you see 'UNCLE RICH,' you see 'CLYDE AS KOOL,'" he says. "I put a little smiling face in it, the eyes, the nose, and mouth and a little cigarette hanging out, and a little tam on it, like a little Apple Jacks hat."

He joined the EX-VANDALS, the legendary supercrew from Brooklyn that revolutionized the name game when its members SUPER KOOL 223 and EL MARKO began painting top-to-bottom masterpieces on subway cars in late 1971 and early 1972.

But Clive would finally make his name elsewhere. He was running track, pushing weights, playing rough schoolyard basketball. His classmates kidded him, dubbing him "Hercules" for his bullish power drives to the hoop. "I went back to the block and I said, 'Yo fellas, this guy at school, man, he's calling me Hercules. I know he means well, but I don't like it.' So I said, 'What's the shortening for Hercules?' They said 'Herc.' Aaaaaah—sounds unique! So I said, 'Yo man, just call me Herc, leave off the 'lees,' just call me Herc.' Between high school and the block, I put the two names together and I dropped the CLYDE. I started calling myself Kool Herc, and that was it."

The Man with the Master Plan

Buzz spread about Cindy and Herc's back-to-school party quickly, and they found themselves throwing parties almost on a monthly basis at the rec room at 1520 Sedgwick in the West Bronx. The crowds were mostly high school students too young or too clean to fall under the waning influence of the gangs. Herc would tell the weed-smokers to head around the block, and, at Cindy's suggestion, he'd also play slow jams.

Cindy says, "My father was always there. People knew him in the neighborhood and they respected him so we never had violence or anything like that. We didn't have to hire security guards. We never searched people. When people came, they came out of respect. It was a recreation thing for them to meet people. A lot of people met their boyfriends or girlfriends there."

Herc's rep traveled along the Bronx high school circuit as well, after Cindy, through her role in student body government at Dodge High School, secured a successful boat cruise dance. By the summer of 1974, when Herc was playing regular parties to a loyal following, he decided to play a free party on the block. "And after the block party," he says, "we couldn't come back to the rec room."

Outdoors, he knew he was putting the sound system at risk, and that fights could potentially break out. "So when I come out there, I said, 'Listen. The first discrepancy, I'm pulling the plug. Let's get that straight right now. There's kids out here, there's grown folks out here and we're gonna have a good time. So anybody start anything any disturbance or any discrepancy, any beef, I'm pulling the plug because I'm not gonna be here for the repercussions. Alright?' So they said, 'Alright, Herc, no problem,'" he says. "We broke daylight. I played to the next morning."

Along with his immigrant friend Coke La Rock, Herc distinguished their crew by bringing the vibe of Jamaican sound system DJs. Herc hooked up his mics to a Space Echo box just like they did in Kingston. With their technical knowledge, Coke and DJ Clark Kent helped make sure Herc had the best sounding system in the area.

They set off their dances by giving shout-outs and dropping little rhymes. They developed their own slang. At an after-hours spot Herc spun at, a drunken regular greeted his friends with the call: "To my mellow! My mellow is in the house!" With lines like these, the two created larger-than-life personas.

Herc carefully studied the dancers. They loved songs like James Brown's "Give It Up or Turnit a Loose" and Rare Earth's "Get Ready," which allowed them to showcase their dance moves, often elaborations of moves people had seen James Brown doing on TV. Zulu Nation DJ Jazzy Jay, who began as a b-boy, says, "You could be dancing with your girl and spin away from her, hit the ground, come back up. It was all about 'smooth.' Like how James used to slide across the floor and the fancy footwork and all of that." They even called it "burning."

Herc realized that these songs were popular for a specific reason. "I was smoking cigarettes and I was waiting for the records to finish. And I noticed people was waiting for certain parts of the record," he says. The moment when the dancers really got wild was in a song's instrumental break, when the band would drop out and the rhythm section would get elemental. Forget melody, chorus, songs—it was all about the groove, building it, keeping it going. Herc zeroed in on the heart of the record—the break.

He started searching for songs by the sound of their break, songs that he would make into his signature tunes: James Brown's indelible classics from 1970 to 1972 that bridged Africa and the Americas, the nonstop conga epics from The Incredible Bongo Band called "Apache" and "Bongo Rock," Johnny Pate's theme to *Shaft in Africa,* Dennis Coffey's "Scorpio"—Black soul and white rock records with an uptempo, often Afro-Latinized backbeat.[6]

Pioneer b-boy and Zulu King Anthony "Cholly Rock" Horne remembered he and his crew came to rock at Herc's parties to Cameroonian Afro-funk band leader Manu Dibango's song "Senga," which they called "the Kool Herc serioso jointski." But their favorite was another Dibango song called "Soul Makossa," which had them chanting as if they had found a connection to their deep African roots: "Mama ko mama sa mako makossa!"

Then Herc took his records to the bathtub where he soaked off the labels. "My father said, 'Hide the name of your records because that's how you get your rep. That's how you get your clientele.' You don't want the same people to have your same record down the block," Herc says.

In a technique he called "the Merry-Go-Round," Herc began to work two copies of the same record, back-cueing a record to the beginning of the break as the other reached the end, extending a five-second breakdown into a five-minute cipher. "So what I did here was go right to the yoke," he recalls. "I cut off all anticipation and played the beats. I'd find out where the break in the record was at and prolong it."

Before long he had tossed most of the songs, focusing on building excitement through the breaks alone. His sets drove the dancers from climax to climax on waves of churning drums. "And once they heard that, that was it, wasn't no turning back," Herc says. "They always wanted to hear breaks after breaks after breaks after breaks."

To accommodate larger crowds, Herc moved his parties from the block into Cedar Park. He had seen construction workers hooking up power by tapping the light posts. He found a tool shed in the park, and sent a boy to climb through the window to plug into enough juice for the sound system. The results shocked the borough, and brought in new audiences who would follow him wherever he played.

Sharon Green, who would soon transform herself into one of the youngest, most formidable MCs as Sha-Rock of the Funky Four + 1 More, remembered begging her mom to let her go to a park jam. When she got there, she was overwhelmed. Coke La Rock and Timmy Tim were on the mic with the echo box, rapping, "The sounds that you hear is def to your ear . . . have no fear 'cause Herc is here." When Herc dropped Baby Huey's record "Listen To Me," she wrote in her autobiography, "I almost lost my mind. I just stood behind the ropes, shocked and amazed as if something came over me. I can't explain it. All I knew was I was going to come back to another Herc jam."[7]

A teen from Fox Street in the South Bronx named Joseph Saddler, who called himself Flash, also heard about Herc's exploits and went up to Cedar Park to see it for himself. He recalls, "I seen this big six-foot-plus guy with this incredible sound system, heavily guarded. People just enjoying themselves from like four years to forty. I'm like, wow! He looked sort of like this superhero on this podium playing this music that wasn't being played on the radio. I liked what he was doing and what he was playing, and I wanted to do that, too."

Herc assembled his own clique of DJs, dancers, and rappers, and dubbed them the Herculords: Coke La Rock, DJ Timmy Tim with Little Tiny Feet, DJ Clark Kent the Rock Machine, the Imperial JC, Blackjack, LeBrew, Sweet and Sour, Prince, Whiz Kid, and two female MCs, Smiley and Pebblee Poo. He called the booming sound system, which had become famous in its own right, the Herculoids.

Gangs were changing into crews. Jazzy Jay says, "In every area, there would be a DJ crew or a breakdance crew. They would be like, 'Okay, we all about our music and we love our music, but you come in this area wrong and we all about kicking your ass.' Competition fueled the whole thing." Herc's parties drew in the crews, gave them a chance to strut their stuff and make their names. He and Coke La Rock kept the peace by taking a live-and-let-live policy and skillfully working the mic, exhorting them with a "You rock and you don't stop!" and shouting out folks in his audience.

Their shout-outs especially kept the peace and the vibe chill. They spotlighted people whom society otherwise ignored. Herc shouted out the local shot callers, gang leaders, neighborhoods, high schools, housing projects, guys trying to impress girls, girls trying to impress guys, crews that might otherwise be causing trouble, kids whose parents were trying to get them to come home. As Sha-Rock wrote in her autobiography, "When Herc gave you a shout out, you best believe everybody in the park knew you were somebody. Everybody always wanted that status."[8]

The action was in the dance ciphers, with the kids who had come for Herc's "Merry-Go-Round," and were becoming personalities in their own right. They had too much flavor to conform to the precision group steps of dances like the Hustle. They would simply jump in one after another to go off, take each other out, just "break" wild on each other. Herc called them break boys, b-boys for short.[9]

"It was a place for every b-boy and b-girl to be," Sha-Rock says. When Herc announced it was time to rock, the cipher opened for the dancers and the excitement crested. "You knew it was about to go down."[10]

In 1975, Herc was doing all-ages dances at the Webster Avenue P.A.L. But he was turning twenty, and didn't only want to serve the teen crowd anymore. He found a club called the Twilight Zone, and began hosting parties there. At a hot spot called the Hevalo, he passed out flyers for his Twilight Zone shows until he was chased out. One day, he vowed, I'll play this spot. On a stormy night, Herc emptied the Hevalo by playing a party at the Zone. "Rain," he says, "was a good sign for me." The Hevalo's owner quickly called him up to make a deal. Soon Herc was playing the Hevalo and another club called the Executive Playhouse for an adult crowd.

Whether in the clubs or the park, they all came to hear Herc's breaks and his rap: "You never heard it like this before, and you're back for more and more and more of this here rock-ness. 'Cause you see, we rock with the rockers, we jam with the jammers, we party with the partyers. Young lady don't hurt nobody. It ain't no fun till we all get some. Don't hurt nobody, young lady!"

By 1976, he was the number one draw in the Bronx. No more roach killers. DJ Kool Herc dressed the role, sporting fabulous Lee or AJ Lester suits. All the high rollers, bank robbers, and hustlers from Harlem were coming up to see him. Coke La Rock and Dickey were turning up the echo on the mic and kicking rhymes like, "There's no story can't be told, there's no horse can't be rode, no bull can't be stopped and ain't a disco we can't rock. Herc! Herc! Who's the man with a master plan from the land of Gracie Grace? Herc Herc!"

Herc says, "The reputation was, 'Who is making money up in the Bronx? Kool Herc and the guy Coke La Rock with the music.'"

1977

By 1977, Herc and his competitors had divided the Bronx into a new kind of map, one based not on gang turfs, but where the parties were. It wasn't about what block to avoid, it was about which block the party was at.

In the South Bronx from 138th to 163rd Streets, where the Savage Skulls and the Ghetto Brothers had once run, Grandmaster Flash, with his sound system called Gladiator, backed by the local Casanova Crew, was emerging as the area celebrity. In the Southeast, where the First Division of the Black Spades hailed from, was Disco King Mario and his Chuck Chuck City Crew, and Afrika Bambaataa and Zulu Nation. In the north, there was DJ Breakout and DJ Baron of Brother's Disco, with their system called the Mighty Sasquatch, backed by the Nine Crew. The West Bronx neighborhood and the East Bronx nightclubs were still Herc's. Herc remained the undisputed king of the borough by virtue of his records, his loyal crowd, and his sound system.

"It was ridiculous. He was god," says Zulu Nation DJ Jazzy Jay. At a legendary Webster P.A.L. contest, Herc drowned out Bambaataa's system with little effort. Every time Grandmaster Flash came to a Herc party, Flash chuckles, "Herc always used to embarrass me."

But the increased competition had an effect on Herc. By the end of the spring, Herc noticed his audiences were declining. "People are getting older now, it wasn't all about me. All of a sudden now you're not eighteen no more, you're twenty-four and twenty-five. You can drink now. You ain't coming to no little seventeen, eighteen-year-old party," he recalls. "And other people was coming up."

Under Mayor Abraham Beame, mighty New York City was heading toward massive financial ruin. Journalists mourned Gotham's fallen glory, complaining about graffiti, the broken subway system, and the prostitution in Times Square.

Then, after dark on July 13, as if an invisible hand was snuffing them, the city's street lights blew out. New York had plunged into a blackout. Looters took to the streets in the ghettos of Crown Heights, Bedford-Stuyvesant, East New York, Harlem, and the Bronx. At Ace Pontiac on Jerome Avenue, fifty brand-new cars were driven out of the showroom. On the Grand Concourse shopkeepers armed themselves with guns and rifles, but for the next thirty-six hours most would be helpless against the rushing tide of retribution and redistribution.

"That particular night, one thing I noticed," a resident would later say, "they were not hurting each other. They weren't fighting with each other. They weren't killing each other."[11]

"It was an opportunity for us to rid our community of all the people who were exploiting us," graffiti writer James TOP told historian Ivor Miller. "The things that were done that day and a half were telling the government that you have a real problem with the people in the inner cities."[12]

A thousand fires were set. Prisoners at the Bronx House of Detention blazed up three dormitories. Hundreds of stores were cleaned out, including not a few DJ stores. After the blackout and the looting, there were plenty of new crews in the streets with brand-new sound systems.

Herc's main rivals were luring away his crowd. Grandmaster Flash had precision, sophistication, and an entertainer's flair. Afrika Bambaataa had his rare records and the power of the Bronx River Houses behind him. Many of the Bronx DJs followed the money and audiences to Harlem. DJ Hollywood was rocking well-dressed crowds with his high-powered disco rhymes. Other DJs like Lovebug Starski and DJ Lonnie Green were spinning at a new club called Harlem World.

Cholly Rock attended the opening night of Harlem World and saw Andre Harrell, who used to rap in the park with Disco King Mario, now up onstage with Alonzo Brown in a suit-and-tie as a rap duo called Dr. Jeckyll and Mr. Hyde. They were projecting a new kind of money-making sophistication at Harlem World. Cholly Rock saw the new divide as "shoe culture versus sneaker culture." The sneaker culture kids had defined the canon of b-boy dances at Herc's jams. Now the shoe culture folks were going to the discos. They saw themselves as more mature and didn't welcome the b-boys in to the disco jams. But the momentum shifted to the shoe culture.

Herc says, "I stayed behind, I didn't move with them to downtown. I stayed up in the Bronx."

A few months later, as Herc was preparing for another night at the Playhouse, now renamed the Sparkle, he heard a scuffle by the door. "Mike-With-The-Lights had a discrepancy with somebody at the door," Herc recalls. Mike was refusing to allow three men into the club and they were becoming increasingly agitated. When Herc got to the door, one of the men drew a knife. Herc felt it pierce him three times in the side. As he put his bloodied hand up to block his face, the attacker stabbed him once more in the palm before disappearing with the others back up the stairs and into the night. "It made me draw back into a little shell," Herc says, exhaling for a long moment.

His time was passing. But the new culture that had arisen around him had captured the imagination of a new breed of youths in the Bronx. Herc had stripped down and let go of everything, save the most powerful basic elements—the rhythm, the motion, the voice, the name. Hip-hop was on its way.

3
Getting It Together

He called himself Afrika Bambaataa, and he was a teenager with a big rep. He came up on the other side of the Bronx from Herc and Cindy, in the Southeast Bronx, where the landscape was dominated by the large towers and sprawl of the housing projects called the Bronx River, Soundview, and Bronxdale Houses. Not far to the east were some of the last white neighborhoods in the Bronx, and these would become desegregation's bloody frontline.

In 1971, the year of the Bronx gang truce, a young Bambaataa was bused to Stevenson High School at the eastern, white edge of Soundview as part of a court-ordered desegregation mandate. The appearance of Black students, some of whom were Black Spades, caused white gang members to organize and a racial war broke out. School grounds became stomping grounds, with the gangs as the shock troops.

But by 1981 Bambaataa was in the middle of a very different kind of desegregation, a wholly voluntary one. He was taking the music and culture of the Black and brown Bronx into the white art-crowd and punk-rock clubs of lower Manhattan. The iron doors of segregation that the previous generation had started to unlock were battered down by the pioneers of the hip-hop generation. Soon hip-hop was not merely all-city, it was global—a Planet Rock.

Many old school Bronx hip-hoppers look back on those heady days—the '70s turning into the '80s—with a sense of wonder that something they had been involved in as wide-eyed youths could have become so big, so powerful. Never Bambaataa. To him, it was always supposed to be this way.

"Each step was a stepping stone, the gang era and all that, that helped to bring about this formation," he says, as if he had already been to the mountaintop long ago.

At Bronxdale in the months following the peace treaty, two First Division Black Spades were becoming popular DJs—Kool DJ Dee and Disco King Mario. As the Spades faded, Mario's Chuck Chuck City Crew kept the neighborhood protected and oversaw the outdoor parties they threw. Bambaataa studied what they were doing, and began throwing his own parties at the Bronx River Community Center just steps from his apartment's front door.

As a member of the Spades' Tenth Division centered at Bronx River, Bambaataa had been appointed warlord, because he was unafraid to cross turfs to forge relationships with other gangs. He says, "I was a person who was always in other areas. So if I was a Spade, I still was with the Nomads. If I was with the Nomads, I was hanging with the Javelins. When I came into any group, I had the power, the backing of the other group I was with. Although I was a Spade, I still had power and control of some of the Nomads, some of the Javelins." Soon, Bambaataa's ability to move between gangs did not look like a weakness, but a strength. "I was the person that if you had problems, I could rally up three to four hundred at one time and move on you," he says.

Now that the Bronx was changing, he was determined to found a group of his own. The group he called the Bronx River Organization was meant to replace the Spades. In some ways, the move resembled the Ghetto Brothers' transformation.[1] Bambaataa says, "We had a motto: 'This is an organization. We are not a gang. We are a family. Do not start trouble. Let trouble come to you, then fight like hell.'"

Jayson "DJ Jazzy Jay" Byas had moved into the Bronx River Houses in 1971 after his family's Harlem tenement was consumed by a fire. Jay says, "Bam used to put his speakers out the window and play music all day. He used to live right outside what you'd call the Center. The center of Bronx River was like a big oval. The community center was right in the middle and Bam used to live to the left of it. He used to play his music, and I would ride my bike around all day popping wheelies, you know?"

"When he walked through the projects," he recalls, "he was like The Godfather walking through Little Italy." Jay first DJed for the Chuck Chuck City Crew, but he recognized Bambaataa's musical genius. He went to Disco King Mario to tell him he was joining

Bambaataa's crew and wanted his records back. Mario said he couldn't go without a fight. He was known to be formidable in the streets and extra nice with his hands. But he respected Jay for standing up to him and allowed Jay to walk out with his pride and all his records, except for one—Kraftwerk's "The Robots," a German dance record Bambaataa had helped introduce to the Bronx.

Each weekend in Bronx River, Bambaataa would preside over a ritual of motion and fun. Jazzy Jay says, "Block parties was a way to do your thing, plugging into the lamppost. Sometimes we used to play till two in the morning. And we had the support of the whole community. It's like, we'd rather see them doing that, doing something constructive than to be down the block beating each other upside the head like they used to do in the gang days."

Kool DJ Dee, Disco King Mario, and other Bronx DJs like DJ Tex played funk and disco music songs in full. In Brooklyn, Pete DJ Jones and Grandmaster Flowers were mixing dance records together. But Bambaataa was taken more by DJ Kool Herc's break-centered—as opposed to song-centered—style. Bam's sound became a rhythmic analogue to his peacemaking philosophy. His set-lists had the same kind of inclusiveness and broad-mindedness he was aspiring to build through The Organization.

He mixed up breaks from Grand Funk Railroad and the Monkees with Sly and James and Malcolm X speeches. He played salsa, rock, and soca with the same enthusiasm as soul and funk. He eclipsed the other DJs as the most renowned programmer in the borough. He became known as the Master of Records, a sound shaman who had hundreds of hard-rocks dancing to his global musical mash-up of Kraftwerk, Fela Anikulapo-Kuti, the Pink Panther theme, the Rolling Stones, and the Magic Disco Machine. The party was a place to move the body, the mind, and the soul.

Bambaataa realized that to grow The Organization he needed to drop "Bronx River" from the title. He wanted people from other neighborhoods to join. But he had even bigger ambitions.

Peace, Unity, Love & Having Fun

As a youth Bambaataa was fascinated with the 1964 movie *Zulu*, which recounted the 1879 siege of Rorke's Drift in Natal, South Africa.

When the young Bambaataa saw it in the early '60s, he was captivated by powerful images of Black solidarity. Before the attack on Rorke's Drift, hundreds of Zulu warriors appear atop the ridge, leaving the imperial soldiers awestruck and fearful. They bang their spears on their shields, give a resounding war cry, and storm the garrison. Although many of them fall before the British muskets, they just don't quit. Into the night, the Zulus continue their assaults and succeed in setting the outpost on fire.

"That just blew my mind," Bambaataa says. "Because at that time we was coons, coloreds, negroes, everything degrading. We was busy watching Heckle and Jeckle, Tarzan—a white guy who is 'king of the jungle.' Then I see this movie come out showing Africans fighting for a land that was theirs against the British imperialists. To see these Black people fight for their freedom and their land just stuck in my mind. I said when I get older I'm gonna have me a group called the Zulu Nation."

But on January 6, 1975, police killed his cousin Soulski on Pelham Parkway in a bloody shootout. A month after Soulski's killing, Bronx cops shot dead a fourteen-year-old who had been joyriding in a stolen car. A police spokesperson claimed the officers fired after the boy had lunged at them with a knife, but autopsies showed he had been shot through the back. Both these incidents precipitated a different kind of crisis than Cornell Benjamin's had for the Ghetto Brothers. This time, the gangs' rage was focusing outward toward the authorities. The cops were acquitted and the Bronx gangs were ready to roll. But community leaders urged the youths not to retaliate, to let the justice system do its work. Bambaataa had finally reached his turning point. He and his followers decided not to attack the police. He had committed to an alternative.

Months before Soulski's passing, Bambaataa won a Housing Authority essay contest. The prize was a trip to India. "You had to write an essay on why you would want to go to India. So I won, but when it was time for me to meet up with the people that send you off to go, I was outside giving out flyers for the next party I was giving and forgot all about it. So I lost the trip, which was great, because the following year I won the trip to go to Africa and Europe," he says.

For a youth who had known nothing but the streets of the Bronx, the trip was life-changing. "I saw all the Black people waking up in the early morning, opening their stores, doing the agriculture, doing whatever they have to do to keep the country happening," he says. "Compared to what you hear in America about, 'Black people can't do this and that,' that really just changed my mind."

His head bursting with ideas, Bambaataa came back to the Bronx ready to transform The Organization. "My vision was to try to organize as many as I could to stop the violence. So I went around different areas, telling them to join us and stop your fighting," Bambaataa says.

As the summer of 1975 drew closer, the word began getting out. Jazzy Jay says, "I remember my friend came up and said, 'Yeah, you heard that cat Bambaataa? He's calling himself Afrika Bambaataa and the Zulu Nation now. He got some movement called the Zulu Nation.'"

Zulu Nation was returning the Bronx to an era of style, celebration, and optimism. "It was no more where you had the Hell's Angels looking type jackets or you rolling around in dirt-stank shit just to show you were an outlaw and you could be the most dirtiest bastard out there," Bambaataa says. "It almost flipped back to the '50s gangs where they was wearing the nice satin jackets and the nice names. As you got into the graffiti artists, then you had the aerosol paintings on the jackets. People was getting more cool. It just started switching the whole culture around into this whole 'party and get down' atmosphere."

Movement was literally at the heart of the organization, in the form of the Zulu Kings and Zulu Queens dancers. "The Zulu Kings started with five main guys: Zambu Lanier, Kusa Stokes, Ahmad Henderson, Shaka Reed, Aziz Jackson. Then came the Shaka Kings and Queens. And it was just as many women that could tear guys up on the dancefloor as there was men," Bambaataa says. Then the rappers came in. "We had Queen Lisa Lee and Sha-Rock, who was the first two females that was blowing it up, then Pebblee Poo."

But if Bambaataa was to continue to expand his vision beyond his sphere of influence, he would now need to convince the Latinx youths on the other side of the Bronx River that the peace was for real.

During the early '70s, while white gangs had pressed the Black Spades from the east, the Puerto Rican gangs—especially the Savage Skulls and the Savage Nomads—were a buffer on the west. The Bronx River remained a dividing line between African American youths and Puerto Ricans.

Ray Abrahante—who would later become an original member of the Rock Steady Crew and gain fame as the graffiti writer named BOM 5—was then an eleven-year-old Baby Skull. He had followed his older cousin, a shot-caller, into the gang. Soon after he joined, two young Skulls ended up dead, and the fingers pointed to the Black Spades.

A few blocks away, the 174th Street Bridge connected East Tremont with the Bronx River Houses, but this was no-man's land, a no-crossing zone. Abrahante was a reckless kid. One day he wandered onto the bridge on his bike. A burly Black tagger was spray-painting BAM 117, WRITERS INC. Abrahante, who was the Baby Skulls' tagger, took the spraycan, and wrote his own tag SPIDER. He wasn't wearing his colors, and by the size of this guy, he knew not to write SKULLS next to his name. He handed the spraycan back to the tagger, and they gave each other an unspoken recognition. Then they went back their separate ways.

A few days later, when Abrahante went across the bridge again, he had it in his head to try to tag the Skulls name deep in Spades territory. He headed across the bridge in full colors, and cruised into the Bronx River Houses. A group of Spades came out from the basketball courts, hurled bottles at him, and chased him back across the bridge. He noticed that the tagger he had met on the bridge was with them, simply watching.

In September, Abrahante received a flyer for a party in the Bronx River Houses. The promoters had been going through the neighborhoods, shouting, "Free jam! Come one come all, leave your colors at home! Come in peace and unity." His cousin didn't believe it. "Don't go," he said, "it's a setup. The Spades will pound you."

It was a warm afternoon when he and some Skulls and Nomads walked across the bridge. They joined the crowd heading toward the Community Center. Abrahante noticed a lot of gang members, maybe even the ones who had bottled him, but he was surprised to see a lot of Puerto Ricans as well. At the door, they lined up to be searched by a pair of big bouncers. But the mood was one of anticipation, not tension as he had expected.

The music was blasting. Onstage, a DJ worked two turntables. Abrahante recognized the music and the dances from the gang parties and the park jams, but it was like he was experiencing it again for the first time. When the room filled, the DJ stopped the music. Then that guy from the bridge got on the microphone.

"Bambaataa talked," Abrahante recalls. "He was saying how happy he was that people came out. That this gang thing, the cops put us up to this stuff. Society put us all in here to fight against each other and kill us off, and we're not getting nowhere."

Abrahante was impressed. "A week later, I was meeting more and more kids, and he was trying to open Bronx River to everybody. I mean it was inspiring." With the Universal Zulu Nation, hip-hop had its first institution, and its enduring message: peace, unity, love, and having fun.

Black Girl Magic

Hip-hop's young scene was hardly just a boy thing. Long before DJ Kool Herc and Afrika Bambaataa were throwing parties, Black girls had rhyming games that showed up in the form of elaborate jump-rope routines called "the double dutch." They had hand-clapping games that required team effort, sharp hand-eye coordination, and keen wit—since there were clean PG versions that you did in front of your parents and raunchy ones you did outside. They might recite variations of popular rhymes like this:

Miss Mary Mack, Mack, Mack
All dressed in black, black, black,
With long long hair, hair, hair
All down her back, back, back.
With silver buttons, buttons, buttons
All down her back, back, back

She asked her mother, mother, mother
For fifty cents, cents, cents
To see the elephants, elephants, elephants
Jump over the fence, fence, fence

Or another rhyme like:

Eenie meanie sassaleeny,
Oops ah tumbalini,
Achi cachi Liberace, I love you,
Take a peach, take a plum,
Take a stick of bubble gum,
No peach, No plum
No stick of bubble gum
Saw you with your boyfriend last night
(How'd you know?)
I was peeking through the keyhole

It wasn't unusual to see these girls execute those rhymes while simultaneously doing complicated, competitive dances. In time, quite a few male MCs would bite, rearrange, or repurpose the rhymes they heard their sisters and girl cousins say and incorporate them into their own routines.

Women and girls were always present at the early park jams and block parties. During the hot summer months in the Bronx, such gatherings were commonplace. They were where socializing, flirting, and courting took place. But the women and girls who were at these block parties hardly sat on the sidelines as spectators, waiting to be whisked off their feet. They set style and fashion in the cipher as dancers, rappers, and DJs.

Queen Kenya, Cholly Rock recalled, was one of the first women to MC for Afrika Bambaataa. Then Zulu Queen Lisa Lee showcased her top-notch rhyme skills for Disco King Mario and Bambaataa's rap crews, the Soul Sonic Force and the Cosmic Force. Sometimes Lisa Lee performed with DJ Pambaataa of the Casanova Fly Girls. Pebblee Poo and Smiley were with the Herculords, before Pebblee Poo joined up with her brother Master Don and The Death Committee out of Harlem to record the early rap hit "Funk Box Party." They called themselves "fresh to death," shortened in street slang to simply "fresh to def."

MC Debbie D started off with a crew called DJ Patty Duke and the Jazzy 5. She made a name for herself and, on party flyers, came to be known as "Grand Mistress of the Ceremony" or "Queen MC Debbie D." She linked up to perform with DJ Wanda Dee, and the two became famous as a duo that was down with both DJ Kool

Herc and Zulu Nation. Later they merged with Queen Lisa Lee and Sha-Rock to form the all-woman supergroup called Us Girls, which was prominently featured in the landmark movie *Beat Street*.

The first all-female crew was the Mercedes Ladies. In the Bronx, people heard their name before they actually saw them perform. Even though hip-hop had brought greater peace to the borough, it was still raw, rough-and-tumble. People still needed to roll with a crew for backup—that was what it meant to be "down by law," that you were connected and protected. So the Mercedes Ladies developed a powerful mystique.

Their name was immortalized on party flyers. At parties, when their name rang out, shouts went up and the energy got higher. Rumors circulated that the Mercedes Ladies was an all-girl crew that had so many members, they were like an all-female Zulu Nation. Others said they were the girl division of the notorious Casanova Crew, and that they would rob and smash on you if you stepped to them wrong. Other stories had them as the ones who were responsible for Grandmaster Flash's success.

According to group member Sherri Sher, Mercedes Ladies were a crew of twenty-one women who initially started out wanting to be party promoters. Some of the crew began performing as MCs and DJs. Aside from Sheri Sher, the crew included: DJ Baby D, RD Smiley, Zina Zee, Eve-A-Def, Sweet P, Sty-Sty, and DJ La Spank. At the parties they rocked, dozens more women showed up in shirts sporting their name. Everywhere they rolled, they were squad deep.

The women were determined not to be seen as a gimmick. Nor did they want to waste anyone's time, least of all their own. They wanted to be seen as dope MCs and DJs. No special treatment was afforded them. They carried and set up their own equipment. Everyone had to pull their weight. They started performing on bills with the L Brothers, Grand Wizzard Theodore, and the Fantastic Romantic 5.

Long before she became Queen Lisa Lee, Lisa Counts grew up the daughter of John Counts, a professional football player who was forced into retirement after breaking his collarbone. John raised her and her brother as a single parent. Because her father was working such long hours, they grew up mostly on their own. She told interviewer Kevin Kosanovich, "You either had to be in a gang to survive or be friends with them or part of them some kind of a way or you would be picked on." She had many friends in Bronx River, and she was drawn to people who had been affiliated with the Black Spades. But Bambaataa was organizing Spades into what would become The Organization, and then the Mighty Zulu Nation.

"I had a lot of anger as a young child," Lisa said, "and when I got into the Zulu Nation, I was embraced with nothing but love. That became my family. And Bambaataa—when he speaks, you want to listen. He has a lot to say that is of substance."[2]

She says he would tell her and her peers, "Where you are right now, this is not it. There are bigger things out there for you."[3]

As she started seeing youths around her changing their style from being in gangs to rocking, she asked her father for a mixer and two turntables and a microphone. He thought that it might keep the kids out of trouble, so he bought it for them. At home, they practiced playing music, breaking, and writing rhymes.

One night she went to a high school dance that Disco King Mario and Afrika Bambaataa were playing at Junior High School 123. She asked to rock the mic, and so impressed Bambaataa and their crew with her rhymes that he put her name on the flyer for the following week.

Bambaataa did not tolerate women being called names. "He made everyone address all the women that were with the Nation as a Queen. So we were treated with a lot of respect," she says. "They became my family because they made me learn to respect myself and not accept anything less than that."[4] That is how she took the name Queen Lisa Lee.

When she stepped onstage at Bronx parties, her electric performances became legendary. Sometimes she told stories or sang rhymes to the theme of *Gilligan's Island.* Sometimes she didn't even need music. She would rap:

> Sophisticated queen MC—yes of course that's me, mistress of ceremony
> The one that's gonna take you to the top of the key
> Introducing myself MC Lisa Lee
> The blast from the past, the perv in every word
> Super female rapper yes the best you heard
> Lisa Lee is known to be the people's choice
> I get the parties rocking with my sexy voice[5]

Like Sha-Rock and, later on, Roxanne Shanté, Queen Lisa Lee and the other women pioneers knew they had to rap better than most of the guys just to break in the door. "And if a woman was to step on the mic and she was to hold her own? She was actually doing double what a dude can do," said rapper Chuck D in Ava DuVernay's documentary *My Mic Sounds Nice*.

The crowds recognized what was really happening—and responded by celebrating them with lots of love. In the beginning, long before it seemed as if hip-hop was only for the guys, it was for everyone.

4
Wild Styles

It may be hard to imagine now, but during the mid-seventies, most of the youthful energy that became known as hip-hop could be contained in a tiny, seven-mile circle.

Take a map of New York City and shift your gaze up from Manhattan to the Bronx. Place the point of your compass in the heart of Crotona Park and trace the circumference. Beginning in the east, there was the Zulu Nation empire; along the northern rim, Edenwald projects and the Valley, where the Brothers Disco and the Funky 4 + 1 More rocked the parties, and the 2 and 5 train yard, where thousands of masterpieces by BLADE and TRACY 168 and THE FABULOUS 5 began and ended their subversive circuits; to the west, past Kool Herc's Sedgwick Avenue and Cedar Park cipher, the Ghost Yard, the misty, violent backdrop of graffiti lore, and Inwood and Washington Heights, where TAKI 183 first picked up his pen; farther down through the southern curve, Harlem, where disco DJs rapped on demand, and Spanish Harlem, where the Baby Kings chapter of the Spanish Kings gang did the outlaw dance on the hard concrete. There were eruptions happening in Brooklyn, Queens, Long Island's Black Belt, and the Lower East Side. But in 1977 this circle felt like a hothouse of style, the tropic zone of a new culture.

Richie "Crazy Legs" Colón, the leader of the Rock Steady Crew, tells this story: One night in 1976, when he was a wide-eyed ten-year-old, his cousin Lenny Len and a neighborhood buddy, Afrika Islam, began practicing moves to a new dance in his living room. He had been learning to box, was picking up some martial arts, but this dance, he wanted to know everything there was to know about it. He had to wait until the following summer when Lenny took him to his first jam in a schoolyard on Crotona Avenue and 180th Street, near the heart of the seven-mile circle.

"Ah, I was just blown away," Crazy Legs recalls. "I just saw all these kids having fun, comparing the graf on the wall to their books, checking out the whole scene, and it was my first time watching the dance with the music being played, so it made more sense. I just immediately became a part of it. My cousin started teaching me how to get down, a few moves here and there, and I guess it just kept on going."

He had just been initiated into a kind of secret Bronx kids' society. Later he would say that jam had made him a witness to the rise of hip-hop's "four elements"—b-boying, DJing, MCing, and graffiti. These kids never grew up expecting the whole world to be watching. This was just for them. What TV camera would ever capture their struggles and dreams? They were invisible.

But invisibility was its own kind of reward; it meant you had to answer to no one except the others who were down. It meant you became obsessed with showing and proving, distinguishing yourself and your originality above the crowd. It put you on a relentless quest to prove to them that you were bigger, wilder, and bolder than the circumstances dictated you should ever be, to try to generate something from nothing, something no one else had, until everyone around you had to admit that you had something they might never have, something that might even make other people—big, important people—stand up and take notice themselves, offer you money, give you power, or try to crush your very soul. That was the key to having style.

Graffiti

After TAKI 183 got his name in the *New York Times* in 1971, graffiti took off. "Every new school year was a new graffiti season," says IZ THE WIZ.

To Hugo Martinez, the sociology student and youth gang member who in 1972 organized the first graffiti association, United Graffiti Artists, "Graffiti writing is a way of gaining status in a society where to own property is to have identity." Your name was your currency, and you created value by making your mark. "You started on your street, then you went to the buses. You take over your neighborhood, then you take over your home line, then you take over your division, then you take over 'all city,'" says Luke "SPAR ONE" Felisberto.

You wanted fame. You tagged everywhere you went. You and

the other writers staked space as if it were a turf to claim with your names. The train riders treated your tags as invasions of their daily anonymity. But then maybe you hung yourself off the side of a building or climbed the steel beams supporting an elevated subway station to rock a tag that would make cleaners scream in frustration and other writers shake in jealousy. Or maybe you were outrageous enough to hit the biggest, riskiest target you could find, as the pioneering female writer STONEY did in 1972 when she tagged the Statue of Liberty.[1]

The "pieces," on the other hand, were personal pageants of light, line, and color, rolling billboards for the self. And when writers added style to these, it was like they had begun printing million-dollar bills. Soon hundreds of kids were scaling barbed wire fences, leaping over the instant death of electrified third rails, and running from police just to piece cars in the train yards and layups in ever bolder detail and wilder style.

There were centers of power outside of the Bronx and uptown. The Brooklyn crew the EX-VANDALS, for instance, had spread back along the train lines to the Bronx. The graffiti movement was surprisingly desegregated. First practiced largely by inner-city youths of color, by the mid-seventies the second generation of writers saw Upper East Side whites apprenticing themselves to Bronx-based Blacks, Brooklyn Puerto Ricans learning from white working-class kings from Queens. They met up in the back cars of off-hour trains or in the afternoon at the Writer's Benches at 149th Street or Atlantic Avenue. Together they went on spray paint–stealing raids—they said they were "inventing" paint—and midnight bombing runs. They created an alternative world—in itself, quite an invention.

There were rebel codes to follow, and as one of a small number of girl writers among the ten thousand boys getting up, LADY PINK had to break through all of them. In 1979, she had begun tagging her boyfriend's name, KOKE, after he was sent back to Puerto Rico by his parents, she chuckles, "for being naughty." After being accepted into the High School of Art and Design soon afterward, she found a core group of ambitious teens intent on making an impact on the graffiti scene. They were all well aware that famous writers like TRACY 168, DAZE, and Lee Quiñones had already come through the very same halls.

"We specifically had a Writer's Table," she says. "So for years and years whoever was the best of the best automatically got the best table. Anyone who was worthy would sit, anyone else who wasn't worthy would just stand around. And that would go on for at least four periods of lunch!"

She wanted badly to be down, she says, but "I was getting sexism from ten-, twelve-year-olds saying that you can't do that, you're a girl. It took me months to convince my old homeboys from high school to take me to a train yard. They were not having it. They were not taking some silly little girl into danger like that. So I had to harp on them and convince them and finally they said, 'Fine. Okay. Meet us inside the Ghost Yard.' They left it to me to find my way in there and meet them inside."

The Ghost Yard was a vast train depot perched on the northern tip of Manhattan on the Harlem River at 207th Street, a servicing shop for cars from many different lines. It had been built on a graveyard, and at night a howling wind often rose from the river. Because of its wealth of cars, a number of graffiti crews turned the Ghost Yard into violently contested ground.

PINK recalls, "I walked around the entire yard, couldn't find my way in. So I just climbed the nearest ten-foot fence. They tell me it was in sight of the guard tower, but no one stopped me. So I was inside the train yard and I waited for them. I see my friends coming through the bushes, and then they just come up to the fence and they just peel back a whole section of it like a big doorway."

She was down, but the trials would not end. "I had to prove that I painted my own pieces. Because whenever a female enters the boy's club, the world of graffiti, immediately it's thought that she's just somebody's girlfriend and the guy is putting it up. But they're not gonna believe that some girl is strong enough and brave enough to stand there for that period of time and do something big and massive and colorful. They just think that she's on her knees and bending over for the guys. And that's the kind of word that went out about me and goes out about every single girl that starts to write," she says. "So you have to stand strong against that kind of adversity and that kind of prejudice or you're just a little b---h slut."

But separate from the movement's sexism, PINK knew, all the toy writers had to prove themselves. Graffiti was not for the weakhearted. "You've gotta be strong, carry your own point, have a lot of endurance, a lot of nerve. You can't go hysterical and run screaming.

You also have to be strong in character that if you get grabbed [by the cops] and they put the squeeze on you and they're beating you silly and they have you upside down and they're painting your balls purple, will you stay shut or will you sing and tell them all your friends and phone numbers and everything that they want?" she says. "'Cause this is a serious game."

Graffiti is, PINK says, "an outlaw art. When we train other graffiti writers, we're not training fine artists to exhibit in a museum. We're training criminals. We're training kids how to take life in their own hands and go out there and hopelessly paint on some wall or some train that will do nothing for you except get you fame with other vandals and criminals."

New York's spraycan writers presented their own stunning defense. "If Art like this is a crime," they wrote, "may God forgive me."[2] Every time politicians and bureaucrats tried to eliminate graffiti, whether covering over street tags or repainting the entire 6,800-car subway fleet, it came back harder. It just gave the teens a clean canvas—and encouraged even more kids to try it as well. Every "buff" launched a new explosion of style: more quantity, but more quality, too.

Homely letters grew outlines, colors, patterns, highlights, depth, shadows, arrows. Names were bubblized, gangsterized, mechanized. Letters dissected, bisected, cross-sected, fused, bulged, curved, dipped, clipped, chipped, and disintegrated. They filled with shooting stars, blood drips, energy fields, polygons. They floated on clouds, zipped with motion lines, shot forward on flames. And they got bigger and bigger. Expanding from window-downs to top-to-bottom to end-to-ends, the pieces began appearing as dazzling thematic murals by 1974, covering entire sides of twelve-foot-high, sixty-foot-long cars.

Innovators like PHASE 2, RIFF, TRACY 168, and BLADE inspired another generation of stylists including DONDI, KASE 2, and SEEN. These writers dreamed and painted big, and this was the era of some of the most legendary cars. The biggest were two ten-car, whole-train productions—CAINE 1, MAD 103, and FLAME ONE's "Freedom Train" bicentennial tribute and the FABULOUS FIVE's 1977 "Christmas Train." BLADE's 1980 nuclear blast whole-car sampled the expressionist ghost of Edvard Munch's "The Scream." FAB 5 FREDDY painted a 1979 whole-car tribute to

Warhol's famous ode to Campbell's soup cans that shelved his influences alongside himself, offering a "Pop Soup," "Da-Da Soup," and "Futurist Soup," next to a "Fred Soup." His writing partner, Lee Quiñones, seared feverish statements about war and violence into unsuspecting subway riders' heads. He called the 5 line, where they bombed, "a rolling MoMA."[3]

Style would make you friends, inspire loyalty and devotion, spawn a hundred imitators. It would make you enemies, unleash jealousy and fear, bring down the brute force of authority. The one thing style would never leave you was neutral. As King KASE 2 would say in the movie *Style Wars,* "When they see you got a vicious style, they wanna get loose about it. And that's what keeps it going."[4]

B-Boys and B-Girls

By 1975, the b-boy dance had been picked up by kids too young to get into the clubs. It used to be a private thing for them, something they taught each other in living rooms or building hallways, something to do at house parties, but the outdoor jams brought the dance out in the open. Now that the gangs no longer controlled the streets, the bedroom b-boys could travel across the borough to find other kids to battle.

As in the ciphers at Herc's parties, there were rarely group routines, instead the spotlight was on each dancer's style. "Each individual cat got up and did his thing," Jazzy Jay says. "Plus it wasn't like today where they come down and put down some nice linoleum so you don't get burnt up. I mean, we used to b-boy right in the middle of the park with broken glass everywhere! And you'd get up and you'd be all scratched and bruised and bleeding and you would be ready to go right back in the circle. You'd just wipe the glass off your elbows and go right back in."

Jorge "Fabel" Pabon, a b-boy historian, first encountered the dance in his projects during the mid-seventies, at the Jackie Robinson Houses in Spanish Harlem, watching a Puerto Rican gang called the Baby Kings. He says, "The style of a b-boy, I never saw nothing like it. I'd never seen a dance approached like that original b-boy flavor, that straightforward, aggressive sort of I'ma-tear-up-this-floor feeling. A lot of times in my neighborhood I didn't see smiles on their faces. They were on a mission to terrorize the dance floor and to make a reputation, ghetto celebrity status."

The dance looked different from the floor-spinning form that would become popularized a decade later, Fabel says. "It was all strictly top-rocking, interesting drops to get down to the floor, incredible blitz-speed footwork. It was actually really unpredictable. Bouncing around, pivoting, turning, twists, front-sweeps, you know? And very aggressive, really aggressive, to the point that I thought it was a gang dance at first."

In fact, the line between dance and martial art was thin. Street-dance legend Rennie Harris says, "If you really look at hip-hop dance, it's really a rites-of-passage thing. You never see the arms release down. They're always up in fighting position. It's *going to war.* What do we say? We say you're going to *battle.*"

Many specific b-boy styles had their roots in the gangs, practiced from the Bronx and uptown Manhattan to the Brooklyn ghettos of Bushwick and Bedford-Stuyvesant, as a prelude to a rumble. According to Luis Angel "Trac 2" Matteo, "They would have a get-together between the rival gangs for specific turf and the two warlords would go at it, and the winner to that dance actually decides where the rumble's going to be held."[5] One of the war dances became known as "the up-rock," which gave a new meaning to the old Apache line. Rivals lined up across from each other, and went head to head—making as if they were jigging, stabbing, battering each other.

In the 1930s, Zora Neale Hurston had written that African American dance was "dynamic suggestion. No matter how violent it may appear to the beholder, every posture gives the impression that the dancer will do much more."[6] In the 1970s, Trac 2 says, b-boying was "a lot of motion and a lot of gestures, what one person was going to do to another, what one gang was going to do to another gang."[7] Sometimes a dance was enough to settle the beef, sometimes the dance set off more beef. This was style as aggression, a competitive bid for dominance.

The b-boys tapped into the same spirit that had given rise to New Orleans's Mardi Gras Indian gangs—segregated Blacks who, from the early 1900s, came out on special "masked Indian" days in boldly colored, hand-sewn costumes to meet and confront other gangs, dancing rank by rank to the second-line street rhythms, climaxing in a great showdown between the two Big Chiefs—or Harlem's original Lindy Hoppers, the pioneering African American jitterbuggers who emerged from pool-hall gangs like the Jolly Fellows in the late 1920s to galvanize uptown's integrated nightclubs and then, a decade later, the entirety of American popular dance with their floor steps and air steps and breakaways.

It is impossible to see b-boying now and not be impressed by its similarities to forms of Angolan and Brazilian *capoeira*, Cuban *rumba,* or Chinese *kung fu*—all of which by now have been incorporated into the dance. But, Crazy Legs emphasizes, the dance evolved in a very specific time and place. "We didn't know what the fuck no *capoeira* was, man. We were in the ghetto! There were no dance schools, nothing. If there was a dance school it was tap and jazz and ballet. I only saw one dance school in my life in the ghetto during that time, and it was on Van Nest Avenue in the Bronx and it was a ballet school," he says. "Our immediate influence in b-boying was James Brown, point blank."

By the mid-seventies, Puerto Ricans had begun adopting the b-boy dance. Between 1975 and 1979, crews proliferated, including mixed or dominantly Puerto Rican crews. Coming from Bronx River, Beaver and Robbie Rob led the Zulu Kings crew. Near Crotona Park, a number of mainly Puerto Rican crews were making their name—Salsoul with Vinnie and Off, Starchild La Rock with Trac-2, Rockwell Association with Willie Will and Lil Carlos, the Bronx Boys (also called The Disco Kings) with Batch. To the west on Burnside Avenue, there was the Crazy Commanders, with the infamous "man of a thousand moves," Spy. The dancers often formed new alliances under new names in the struggle to stay on top.

From top-rocking and up-rocking, the dance descended to the floor. "It got into elaborate footwork, into a freeze, and then you mixed up the top-rocking, then the floor-rocking, the spin into a freeze," says Rock Steady member "DOZE" Green. Crazy Legs says, "Ours was just a natural progression from standing up to going down. It's funny because a natural progression would be from down to up, but for b-boys, it's up to down."

Styles evolved quickly, Legs says, because, "it was like, what you gonna have next week? What you gonna have when you go to Mom and Pop's Disco or the Crotona Avenue basement party? 'Cause all the dope b-boys are gonna be there. And that's what you strive for—you strive to take your move to the next level. It's about shock value, always shock value, but keeping it flavor and stylized and making it yours."

Richie "Crazy Legs" Colón wanted to recapture the spirit of that block party he had attended in 1976. But by the time he was ready to battle the older b-boys, many of them weren't even doing the dance anymore. He and his cousin Lenny sought out and battled two leaders of the original Rock Steady Crew from Echo Park, Jimmy Dee and Jimmy Lee, and lost. Still they had shown so much heart that the leaders made them members. But it wasn't like it was. The legends had drifted away from the dance and the crews had dissipated. Crazy Legs says, "There weren't too many crews out there when I moved into Manhattan. Very few people were doing the dance." He was being cheated of his chance to prove himself. He was all of thirteen years old, and he ached for the past.

So Crazy Legs embarked on a mission. Like a character in one of the Times Square *kung fu* flicks they watched every weekend, he traveled through the city to find and challenge every remaining b-boy. After they battled, he would ask them to join the crew. Soon, he says, the older leaders decided to give him the Rock Steady Crew name and make him the leader. The new Rock Steady Crew became a magnet for isolated Bronx-styling youths across the city, a second-generation supergroup, the last b-boys standing.

When they practiced their moves in the park at 84th and Amsterdam, they may have made an odd sight. But they were adding new moves. Frosty Freeze came up with new freezes, like the Suicide—where he did a flip and landed on his back. Crazy Legs and Ken Swift did the same for spins, injecting into the dance stunning new body mechanics, physics, and speed. Soon Rock Steady members had gone beyond the backspin and headspin into windmills and handspins. Crazy Legs says, "All these moves that we came about doing were by accident. I didn't set out to evolve the backspin. I was practicing a chair freeze and I over-rotated and I spun fast. And then I over-rotated again on another time, and went into a continuous backspin and kept on doing it."

Rock Steady Crew began rolling into skating rinks and parks and dances to shock teens with their style. They won audiences over, and their ranks swelled. Crazy Legs says, "Rock Steady back then was at least five hundred deep." Then one by one, members headed off to form their own crews. The Rock Steady members who remained derisively called them "expansion teams." But some of them, like the New York City Breakers and the Dynamic Rockers, would become Rock Steady's fiercest competitors.

By then Rock Steady had already done its job. They didn't know it then, but their vision of the Bronx old school would indelibly shape the hip-hop generation. They had revived the dance, canonized old moves and invented bold new ones. Throbbing with uptempo post-*bugalú* Afro-Latin rhythms and good vibes, songs like Booker T & The MG's "Melting Pot," Herman Kelly and Life's "Let's Dance to the Drummer's Beat," and Lonnie Liston Smith's "Expansions" captured their optimism. One of their theme songs, a classic by the Jimmy Castor Bunch, said it all: "It's Just Begun."

DJs and MCs

When Kool Herc first came on the scene, he stayed ahead of the other DJs with the power of his sound system. Bambaataa changed the game with his programming genius. Both men were titans in the streets, backed up by major crew. But in the beginning, Joseph Saddler didn't have expensive equipment, a deep record collection, or a posse of hardrocks. All he had was his style.

He was the fourth of five children of Barbadian immigrants, a boy in a house of girls, living on Fox and 163rd Streets among Skulls and Spades and Ghetto Brothers. He was less attracted to the street life than he was to the broken radios lying in the street. "I was a scientist looking for something. Going inside hair dryers, and going inside washing machines and stereos and radios, whatever you plugged into the wall," he recalls. As strung out junkies plundered arson-devastated abandoned buildings for copper pipes to support their smack habit, Saddler scoured abandoned cars for their radios and speakers. He took them back to his bedroom to see if he could make them sing again.

"I wanted to know what's a resistor? What's a capacitor? What's a transformer? What's AC? What's DC? Why do these things do what they do?" he says. "Although there was crazy violent things happening around me on Fox Street, I was in my own world, in my own room."

Saddler went to a Kool Herc or a Pete DJ Jones jam to hang back in the cut and take it all in—the DJ, the crowd, the equipment, the music. Back in his room with his screwdriver, soldering iron, and insatiable curiosity, the kid who would become Grandmaster Flash was theorizing the turntable, pondering the presentation of the party, trying to figure out how to turn crowd-rocking into a science.

The thing that both Herc and Jones did was release the break on the record from the song. But Herc, Flash felt, was sloppy. The break went around, but it never came back on beat because Herc was dropping the needle all over the place. Flash saw Pete DJ Jones seamlessly extending disco records by mixing two copies of the same record, and realized he could apply the same technique to the music he really loved—the breaks Herc was spinning.

Apprenticing himself to Jones, he began to work toward the idea at weekend parties in an abandoned apartment in his building. Weekdays, he studied the mixer and the turntable. He considered Jones's simple circuit—begin break on record 1, recue record 2 on the headphone, end break 1, begin break 2, recue break 1. Then he understood that each record's rhythm had its own circumference to trace, that the break could be measured from point to point, and he developed a theory based on sectioning off the record like a clock. This was his breakthrough, he says. "I came up with the Quick Mix theory, which was like cutting, the backspin, and the double-back."

After months of study and refinement, Flash finally felt he had perfected the mix. In the summer of '75, it was time to take it to the waiting world. But the reaction was not what he had expected. "The first time I did it, the crowd just stood there, just watched me. I was hoping to get, 'Whoa yes, I love it!' But it was like, no reaction, no movement. Just hundreds of people standing there. They were just trying to understand.

"And I cried for like a week," Flash says. "Why did things go wrong?"

It was a lesson. You could be smart, you could be good, you could be scientific, but being smart and good and scientific wasn't going to rock a party all by itself. And Flash figured he'd got off easy that day—if a party wasn't being rocked, violence was always lurking right behind. He was going to have to win his crowds over to his new style. So Flash set his mind to theorizing the rest of his show. "I realized I needed vocal accompaniment to help spark this concept," he says.

Robert Keith "Cowboy" Wiggins was a former Bronx River Black Spade who had moved down to the South Bronx, and was already a street legend known for his fists. When he started hanging out with Flash, he became known for his party-starting raps. He linked up with two more regulars at Flash's jams, the Glover brothers, Melvin "Melle Mel" and Nathaniel "Kidd Creole."

In 1976, they moved into a club called the Black Door, run by gang peacemaker turned promoter Ray Chandler, who enlisted as security a group called the Casanova Crew—tough dudes who were former Black Spades, who some said rolled as much as five hundred strong and sometimes made their presence known by chanting "Casanova all over!" Later, they moved on to the Dixie. They also continued to play the parks—St. Ann's, Mitchell, 23 Park, 63 Park. Flash and his MCs were changing the game. Crowds cared less about speaker size than showmanship and style. Aaron Bryant, who would later become DJ AJ and spin for Kurtis Blow, had been a devoted follower of DJ Kool Herc. But he says "Kool Herc couldn't draw a crowd after people saw Flash."

Here's where the MCs began to play an increasingly important role. As Flash looked around, he saw more competition from up-and-coming crews, so he kept adding more MCs. Grandmaster Flash and the Three MCs became the Furious Four and finally the Furious Five, as they added Mr. Ness (later called Scorpio) and Rahiem.

Rapping evolved quickly. It could be practiced any place at any time. It was portable with endless possibilities. It was the perfect art form for a generation of youths who had found traditional societal avenues for self-expression all but cut off.

Cowboy, Flash's first rapper, had led the art of MCing. He would get on the mic, praise his DJ, Flash, and get the crowd to "Say ho!" and "Throw your hands in the air and wave 'em like you just don't care!" He shouted out the single moms, told all the sexy ladies to say "Owwwwwww!" As Scorpio told hip-hop historian Jay Quan, "He could rock any crowd with no script, nothing written down . . . It was different hearing it back then because no one had said it before." MCing was about keeping audiences hyped with call-and-response. It was a difficult art that, for years to come, many rappers would not choose to master. It required the special skills of understanding how to move a crowd, improvise, and keep them involved.

But all the earliest MCs did it—rappers like Cowboy, Lovebug Starski, and DJ Hollywood considered themselves entertainers first.

Flash's MCs—Cowboy, Melle Mel, and Kidd Creole—were expected to rap for the entire duration of a party. Here's where they started developing their own styles and personalities, and connected to Black oral cultural traditions, drawing on signifying and toasting rhymes that had been around for generations. Kidd Creole might kick a rhyme like:

A lime to a lemon, a lemon to a lime
I rock the rhymes right on time
I'm too cold to burn, too hot to freeze
I'm aiming to please the young ladies

Here he had simply updated age-old rhymes in lines one and three, adding his own flavor in lines two and four. He might follow that by starting with an old toasting line again and then adding in his style:

I'm too hot to handle, too cold to hold
I'm always in control, I play the role
They call me the Kidd Creole!
Kidd Creole is solid gold
Kidd Creole is the Prince of Soul!

If Cowboy rocked the call-and-response and Kidd Creole entertained, Melle Mel commanded audiences like a preacher with his deep baritone, which he would later use to powerful effect on songs like "The Message."

They developed routines. Each MC would rap his bars and then pass the microphone off to his partner after introducing him or her with some transitional lines. Then the crews began to rewrite playground songs, double-dutch rhymes, the dozens, Black Panther chants, and famous rapped lyrics from songs by Shirley Ellis and the Last Poets. They devised ever more intricate lines, finishing each other's rhymes. They started throwing in unexpected melodies and harmonies, leading the crowd higher and higher.

By the time they had become the Furious Five, they had blended MC styles with rehearsed rapped and sung lines. They had mastered the flow—getting in the groove with the DJ and the break, flowing with each other, and mastering the flow of energy between themselves and the crowd. It was not an easy thing to do but they made it look easy.

One night, Mr. Ness got off beat, but he stayed in rhyme until he got back on it, and finished triumphantly with a couple of classic hip-hop lines, instructions on how to party properly, and disses of a French imperialist, a Confederate general, and the most famous casualty of the Indian Wars:

Ya dip, ya dive, you will agree
Flash has got the security
Walk through the door and do me a favor
Be sure to be on your best behavior
Rock rock y'all ya don't stop
Napoleon lost at Waterloo, Custer lost and Lee did too
Flash is the man that can't be beat
And he never ever, never ever, never ever ever
Heard of the word "Defeat"!

While the MCs kept the energy high, Flash unveiled eye-catching tricks—cutting while flipping around, scratching with his elbows, cross-fading with his backbone. Sometimes he would bring out thirteen-year-old Theodore, soon to be named Grand Wizzard Theodore, who had applied Flash's theories to invent the scratch, and who could drop a needle right onto the breakbeat. With a complete show, Flash's DJ innovations—the scratch-and-mix techniques and the high-performance dazzle—finally took hold. "I got ridiculed for a couple of years. 'You're the guy that ruins records!'" laughs Flash. "But all the DJs had to change their style."

By the late 1970s, DJs who weren't already rapping, like Lovebug Starski, DJ Hollywood, and Eddie Cheeba, were looking to line up rap crews as raw as the Furious. And one by one they did: the L Brothers, the Mighty Force and DJ Disco Wiz, the Cold Crush Brothers with Charlie Chase, Grand Wizzard Theodore and the Fantastic Romantic 5, the Crash Crew, the Cosmic Force, the Jazzy 5, and the Funky 4 + 1 More.

At this point, none of the crews could imagine hearing themselves on a record or rocking on television. Instead crews hoped to have cassette tapes of their live performances played, traded, copied, and passed around. If their tapes could be heard from boom boxes at high volume, in the streets, at a spirited basketball game at a crowded court, from the open window of an apartment on a hot summer day, blaring on someone's bus or subway ride home, or on the tape deck in an OJ cab, they knew they had made it. The proof came on the weekend—in the size of the crowd of people at the block party or rec center where they were performing.

The Sure Shot

The Funky 4 + 1 More came from the North Bronx, formed around a crew led by two DJs, Baron and Breakout, called Brother's Disco. The rap crew was formidable—featuring high-powered rappers with reps like KK Rockwell, Lil' Rodney Cee, Keith Keith, and Jazzy Jeff. Their star was Sharon Green, known as Sha-Rock, hip-hop's first female MC and the group's star attraction, their "sure shot."

Originally from North Carolina, she was the second oldest of four. Her mom and stepfather were politically active in the Civil Rights Movement. But the family's time in North Carolina was turbulent. When Sharon was eight years old, the police and a next-door neighbor who was a member of the Black Panther Party were involved in a shooting incident. Her family moved to the Bronx.

Sharon grew up in a house that exposed her to classic soul music in the form of artists like Isaac Hayes, The Delfonics, Betty Wright, James Brown, Millie Jackson, and the Stylistics. Her entry into hip-hop came around 1976 when she tried her hand as a b-girl. She described herself as the Nine Crew's secret weapon.

Later, after she heard Kool Herc and his MCs Coke La Rock and Timmy Tim perform, she thought about doing more than just dancing. By the time she was attending Evander High School, she heard the Brother's Disco was holding auditions for MCs. Hers was so amazing the four guys made her the "+1" of the group. As Sha-Rock, she became one of the most influential MCs, known as the "Mother of the Mic."

At the shows, she writes, "The men would wear all white shirts with the lettering that read *Brother's Disco*. The females would wear shirts that had *Sister's Disco* written on them. And of course, I would wear the famous green shirt with yellow letters that read, *I'm Sha-Rock and I Can't Be Stopped.*"[8]

People crowded the ropes separating the crew from the audience. The girls, the guys—even the stickup kids with their guns tucked into the pockets of their sheepskin coats—watched the MCs exchanging rhymes, going back and forth. But when Sha-Rock got on the mic, time stood still. She was tall and fly. She dressed as if she were going to the high school dance, in a long-sleeved silk blouse with a bow and her hair tied back in a tight ponytail.

She had the demeanor of a hardrock, someone who could not be moved and held her square. No one was acting brand new with her. People paid attention because Sha-Rock was a dope MC who would hurt your feelings if you stepped to her wrong on the mic. They called her "A-1." She'd let the crowd know, "Well, I'm Sha-Rock and I can't be stopped. To all the fly guys, gonna hit the top." Then she'd step back from the mic and fold her arms in a b-girl stance as the crowd went wild.

Sha-Rock's influence would be enduring. At the time, DMC of Run-DMC was just Darryl McDaniels, a student at a Catholic school in Harlem and a hip-hop fan. He saved up his allowance so he could buy rap crew tapes from his friends—Grandmaster Flash and the Furious Five, Bambaataa with Jazzy Jay and the Jazzy Five live at Bronx River, the legendary battle between the Cold Crush Brothers and the Fantastic Romantic 5 MCs, or the battle between Busy Bee and Kool Moe Dee. But then he heard a tape of Sha-Rock in a battle, with the echo machine cranked up to the max. It was, he says, "life changing."

"It was a tape of her rhyming over [The Whole Darn Family's] 'Seven Minutes of Funk.' And she said some crazy dope rhymes," DMC recalls. She said,

To all of you my name is Sha (Sha)
I'm not a millionaire I don't have a car (car)
But here's one thing I want you all to know
I'm a good loving person from long time ago (go)
One of a kind (kind)
Rock Your Mind (mind)!

DMC was amazed with her. He says, "I stood there in my house and rewounded that tape over for three days straight!"

Soon, many of the biggest rap crews would be making records, and when, at the request of Blondie's Debbie Harry, they rocked on *Saturday Night Live* in 1981, Sha-Rock and the Funky 4 + 1 More became the first rap crew to appear on a national television show. They had been offered a tour slot opening for Blondie, but after losing a fight with Sugar Hill Records owner Sylvia Robinson over unpaid royalties, the group broke up. A few years later, Run-DMC would put big echo machines on their own records in tribute to Sha-Rock and take rap music to even larger audiences.

It was clear to the youths that their cultural uprising—which still did not have a name—was going to amount to more than just a seasonal fad.

5
Hip-Hop Is Dead

By 1979, rapping, DJing, breaking, and graffiti had spread far outside the seven-mile cipher. Tapes of the rap shows were being passed hand-to-hand in the Black and Latinx neighborhoods of Brooklyn, the Lower East Side, Queens, and Long Island's Black Belt. Kids in the boroughs were building sound systems and holding rap battles with the same fervor the Bronx once possessed all to itself. Rap had even slid into an award-winning Broadway musical called *Runaways,* whether or not the middle-aged theatergoers had any idea what they were listening to.

But in the Bronx, it seemed to the kids who had come up in the early '70s that the youth arts of rapping, DJing, breaking, and graffiti were actually fading. "I called it the Great Hip-Hop Drought," says Jazzy Jay. "Everybody started fleeing away from hip-hop."

The kids raised on Herc and Bam and Flash and Lovebug Starski and DJ AJ had graduated from high school and were looking for the next thing. Block parties happened less often. Hip-hop had moved to the clubs like the T-Connection and Disco Fever. "People started growing up and calling that 'kiddie music,'" says Jay. "You ain't gonna go into no high school gymnasium to party no more."

He longed for the old days of battling at the Webster Avenue P.A.L. "It was a terrible time," Jay says. "I done got all my techniques down pat, I done got my belts, I done whipped Flash's ass, I done whipped Theodore's ass, I'm looking for whose ass can I whip next! I'm like, you mean I done went through all of these stepping stones just to *not* be the man? Hip-hop is gonna die like this?"

The audiences had moved on from Bronx sound-system battles and outdoor jams to the drinking-age uptown nightclubs, depriving b-boys and DJs of their competitive setting. The word on the street was that Grandmaster Flash was now rocking fancy spots like the Renaissance Ballroom, where he was doing less cutting and scratching than mixing and blending. MCs were doing less party-starting and more routine-writing, trying to perfect their stage acts. And disco nightclub DJs in Harlem were finding success by adapting the Bronx rap styles and mixing techniques into their gigs, offering a more sophisticated version of the Bronx beat for a maturing crowd.

Even Flash was worried about where it was all headed. "I was wondering where my core audience was going," says Grandmaster Flash. "They were going to see people like DJ Hollywood, who would get a party going from twenty-three and older. When they moved on, they wanted to wear a dress or they wanted to wear a suit. They were just getting older and their taste changed in music."

He continues, "When I went to go see DJ Hollywood, I would say, 'Oh Regina, what are you doing here? I haven't seen you in a long time!' 'Yeah this is where I come now.' And there was this guy who was saying these incredible rhymes on the mic, he was about three, four hundred pounds and he had the crowd in an uproar the same way my Furious Five would have them. DJ Hollywood was quite incredible, he had the people singing his rhymes. So a lot of our audience was going to parties like that now, Eddie Cheeba parties, Hollywood parties, Pete DJ Jones parties. The bottom sort of dropped out. It was either you survive and you go with the changes or you get left back."

The DJs themselves wanted more. It was no longer about playing out for free to establish a rep. They wanted to make a living. But the economics of the music had changed. "If Friday was the 25th you would see DJ Hollywood in five places on five different flyers. How was this possible? How could he be in Manhattan, the Bronx, and Queens all in one night?" Flash says he asked himself. "Only to discover that he didn't carry a sound system. All he did was carry his records. He had a crew and a car. And he would do an hour here, get in the car, do an hour there, an hour there, and an hour there. After a while, people that had the huge sound systems became a dinosaur. Because now you could go and do five parties. And if you had a little record out, you could *really* make some money."

Flash learned this last point the hard way. By 1979, independent Black record producers like Harlem's Bobby Robinson and Paul Winley, and Englewood, New Jersey's Sylvia Robinson (no relation to Bobby) had all heard about the rap phenomenon and were scouring the clubs in the Bronx and Harlem and doing their math, trying to figure out if rap could be financially viable. Flash and the Furious Five were at the top of everyone's signing wish list.

In 1979, a couple of records came out that tried to package the hip-hop sound for a commercial audience. Both came from older, seasoned musicians who knew something great when they heard it. But while the funk group The Fatback Band's "King Tim III (Personality Jock)" and Afro-Filipino salsa star Joe Bataan's "Rap-O Clap-O" were not bad, young hip-hop heads thought the styles were dated and couldn't stand up to the real stuff from groups like Flash and the Furious Five.

But Flash refused to meet with any record label heads. To him, the idea was absurd. Who would want to buy a record of Bronx kids rapping over a record that already existed? He and the Furious Five were still a big draw in the clubs, and making a record wasn't like getting onstage was—guaranteed money in the bank.

"I kinda kicked these guys to the side. I kinda like had my security keep them people away from me. I didn't want to talk deals. As bad as they wanted to talk to me, no is no. That was that," he says. As long as he had gigs to do all week, that was a sure bet, and he was content to play that game.

Then in October of 1979, the game changed forever.

Death and Rebirth

In retrospect, it makes perfect sense that a no-name group using partly stolen rhymes—the very definition of a crew with *no* style—would have been the first to tap hip-hop's platinum potential. When three anonymous rappers stepped into Black indie label owner Sylvia Robinson's studios to cut "Rapper's Delight," they had no local expectations to fulfill, no street reputations to keep, no regular audience to please, and absolutely no consequences if they failed.

Sylvia Robinson and her son Joey had been trying to sign a rap group but had been met with skepticism from Bronx luminaries like Flash and Lovebug Starski. Undoubtedly, the appearance of "King Tim III (Personality Jock)" on a B-side of a single by Brooklyn funkateers the Fatback Band in the summer of 1979 raised the pressure on the Robinsons to make a deal.

Henry "Big Bank Hank" Jackson was a Herc follower and a Bronx nightclub bouncer who somehow became a manager for Grandmaster Caz and the Cold Crush Brothers. He was making pizzas in New Jersey to pay for Caz's sound system. Jackson was rapping along to a Caz tape one afternoon at the parlor when Sylvia and Joey Robinson—introduced to him by a friend—asked him to come for an audition. On the way back, two other rhymers jumped into Joey's car, Guy "Master Gee" O'Brien and Michael "Wonder Mike" Wright, and the three rapped together that evening. Sylvia Robinson immediately signed them to be the first group on her new imprint, Sugar Hill Records. Nobody knew who they were.

The record was an astonishing fifteen minutes long. In the Black neighborhoods of Long Island, Chuck D, then a nineteen-year-old MC, remembers the impact of "Rapper's Delight." "I did not think it was conceivable that there would be such thing as a hip-hop record," he says. "I could not see it." The famous DJ Eddie Cheeba had been out to Long Island and broken "Good Times" to Black audiences in May, promising as he played it that his own rap record would be out soon.

"I'm like, record? How you gon' put hip-hop onto a record? 'Cause it was a whole gig, you know? How you gon' put *three hours* on a record?" Chuck says. "Bam! They made 'Rapper's Delight.' I'm thinking, 'Man, they cut that shit down to *fifteen minutes*?' It was a miracle."

Chuck first heard "Rapper's Delight" while he was on the mic. "Good Times" had been the record of the summer of '79. One night in October, Chuck was rocking his Cheeba-styled party rhymes over "Good Times." "All of a sudden, the DJ I'm hearing he's cutting in this shit behind me. Right? And I'm rhyming over *words*," he laughs. "The crowd don't know. They're just thinking that I'm rhyming and I'm changing my voice or whatever. I held the mic in my hand, I heard words and I lip-synched that motherfucker. Folks thought that shit was me. I was a bad motherfucker after that, believe! The next day, Frankie Crocker broke that shit on BLS. By the next party, folks were looking at me like, 'Pshhhh. You a bad motherfucker, but you ain't *that* nice!'"

Three unknowns beating superstar Eddie Cheeba at his boast. A rap on a vinyl record rocking a crowd harder than a live rap. In fifteen minutes, clearly, the whole world had changed.

"Rapper's Delight" crossed over from New York's insular hip-hop scene to Black radio, then charged up the American Top 40 and swept around the globe. Imitations popped up from Brazil to Germany to Jamaica. It quickly became the bestselling twelve-inch single ever pressed. At one point, 75,000 copies were selling a week and the indie upstart from across the Hudson was straining to keep up with the demand.

But to the Bronx heads, the whole record was a sham. Assembled in a New Jersey afternoon, the rap amateurs of the Sugarhill Gang were a studio creation that had never stepped on a stage until after their single became a radio hit. They hadn't paid their dues. And Bronx crews like the Furious Five and Caz's own Cold Crush Brothers had long perfected intricate routines that made the Sugarhill Gang sound basic and played out.

But "Rapper's Delight" had all the stuff that sounded good on the live bootleg cassettes playing in the OJ Cabs and on the boom boxes—the funny stories, the hookish slang, the same kind of stuff that would strike listeners around the world as both universal and new. "Rapper's Delight" was perfectly accessible to folks who had never heard of rap or hip-hop or the Bronx.

The success of the Sugarhill Gang transformed the scene overnight. Artists and labels scrambled to cash in. The Funky 4 + 1 More and the Treacherous Three signed with Bobby Robinson's Enjoy Records. The Sequence signed with Sylvia Robinson. Afrika Bambaataa agreed to record for Paul Winley. Two Bronx-based reggae labels, Wackies and Joe Gibbs Music, put out rap singles. Kurtis Blow, managed by a young Queens native named Russell Simmons, became the first major-label rap artist when he signed to Mercury for the likable platinum-selling hits "Christmas Rappin'" and "The Breaks." And even Flash finally relented when he and the Furious Five struck a deal with Bobby Robinson. "Superappin'" was released a month after "Rapper's Delight." In Flash's mind, having a record out might increase their club bookings.

But if "Rapper's Delight" turned rap into pop music, "Superappin'" shows how pop changed the entire culture. In unison, the Furious Five raps, "And it won't be long 'til everyone is knowing that Flash is on the beatbox going, that Flash is on the beatbox going . . . and . . . and . . . and . . . sha na na!"[1] In the original routine, the Furious Five would pause and point to Grandmaster Flash as he banged out a drum solo on the electronic drum machine he called his "beatbox." But on the record, Flash is nowhere. The Five shout out Flash as "the king of the Quickmix," but he never gets to demonstrate why. Instead the house band plays one of Flash's favorite songs, the Whole Darn Family's "Five Minutes of Funk." When the Five shout, "Can't won't don't stop rockin' to the rhythm, 'cause I get down when Flash is on the beatbox," the whole culture shifts. It is the moment rap pushes the DJ aside as the center of the culture.

The Sugarhill Gang helped revive the dying Bronx club scene. But club-going turned into a more passive experience than ever. The b-boys disappeared and, Charlie Ahearn says, "Nobody was dancing. Period! Rap became the focal point. MCs were onstage and people were looking at them." The new indie rap industry had no place for them, other than to advise the house bands on how to emulate the spirit of their turntable routines. "This is 1980," Ahearn says. "In other words, hip-hop is dead by 1980. It's true."

How Hip-Hop Got Its Name

Folks in hip-hop love to say hip-hop is dead. That's because hip-hop is youth culture, and youth is a passing condition.

The cycle of style in hip-hop is about three to five years. That's the length of time it takes for, say, a sixteen- or seventeen-year-old, who looks up to their older friends or cousins, wanting to imitate their style, their dances, their slang, their everything, to become as old as their older friends or cousins once were and start dictating to the next set of sixteen- or seventeen-year-olds their own style, dances, slang, *their everything.* By that time, the older friends or cousins are snorting in disgust at the young kids who are changing hip-hop again. They don't recognize hip-hop anymore as the thing that they made. That's when they start saying stuff like, "Hip-hop is dead."

So in 1979, the kids who had invented it in the early '70s were saying hip-hop was dead. And yet hip-hop had just begun.

In fact, even though "hip-hop" were the first words in the Sugarhill Gang's "Rapper's Delight," at that time *no one*—not even the young Bronx kids who had invented it—was calling it that. Hip-hop wasn't *hip-hop* yet.

Lots of great rap records quickly came out, as the scene's top crews finally got their own shot at putting their rhymes on wax, groups like the Treacherous Three, the Funky Four + 1 More, Grandmaster Flash and the Furious Five, and solo Harlem rapper Kurtis Blow.

But people did not broadly start calling all of this—not to mention the DJ music, the dances, and the visual art that were often associated with rap—"hip-hop" until after September 1982, when a downtown reporter named Steven Hager published an article in the *Village Voice.* "Who knows?" Hager wrote. "In another five years, hip-hop could be considered the most significant artistic achievement of the decade."[2]

The story was called "Afrika Bambaataa's Hip-Hop" and the heroic protagonist of it was the young former Black Spades gang warlord with an awesome 'frohawk and a face like stone. When white outsiders asked him if there was a name for all the things that they were seeing he and his seemingly vast nation of homies do, Bambaataa told them, "hip-hop." He began talking about the movement's "four elements"—DJing, rapping, breaking, and graffiti writing. (He later added a fifth, knowledge.)

By then it had been nearly a decade since Cindy Campbell and DJ Kool Herc's party. By the beginning of 1983 the scene that Herc created had scaled to Bambaataa's ambitious prophecy—it was a movement with a name, a past, and a future. Just as Chuck Berry, Little Richard, and Fats Domino had been pioneers of rock and roll even though the music wasn't called that when they first made it, Herc, Bambaataa, and Flash were now pioneers of this thing called hip-hop. The kids who came after them were the ones who made the name stick.

But if this story tells us why the term "hip-hop" spread, it still doesn't tell us where it came from.

Certainly the word "hop" had long been linked to Black musical genius—at least since the late 1920s when dancers like "Shorty" George Snowden, Herbert "Whitey" White, Norma Miller, and Edith Matthews had popularized the spectacular and physically demanding Lindy Hop in Harlem.

In African American youth culture the words "hip" and "hop" together have a long history. Father Amde Hamilton of the influential Los Angeles rap precursors the Watts Prophets says that when he was growing up along Central Avenue in 1950s Los Angeles, the older folks used to call teen house parties "them old hippity hops."

Chuck Brown, the godfather of D.C.'s go-go scene, said that the weekend youth dances they played at the area churches were sometimes called "hip hops." The term wasn't always used in a positive way. Zulu King Cholly Rock said that sometimes older DJs like DJ Hollywood would separate themselves from the younger folks by telling the b-boys at their uptown clubs to "take that hippity-hop stuff outside!"

As for "hip," the scholar Clarence Major has linked the word to the Wolof verb *hepi* ("to see"). "So from the linguistic start," John Leland wrote in *Hip: A History*, "hip is a term of enlightenment, cultivated by slaves from the West African nations of Senegal and Gambia."[3] Hip-hops, we might imagine, could literally be places of vision, and where the masses could feel free to move.

In old school legend the origin of "hip-hop" goes back to the days when rapping was really about MCing, the lost art of moving the crowd. In the days before "Rapper's Delight," the primary job of an MC was to keep the crowd engaged, whether through his call-and-response chants or unique rhymes by which they might remember him.

The story involves two of the most important party-rockers of all time: Grandmaster Flash and the Furious Five's Keith Cowboy and the rapping DJ Lovebug Starski. As it's been told, a good friend of Cowboy and Starski named Billy was about to ship out to join the army. So at Billy's last party, Cowboy reminded him that his days of freedom were over by marching across the stage like a drill sergeant on the beat, chanting, "Hip-hop-hip-hop-hip-hop." The crowd loved it.[4]

By the end of the evening, Cowboy and Starski were still backstage, playing with the two words. Starski told the journalist Peter Scholtes, "I'd say the 'hip,' he'd say the 'hop.' And then he stopped doing it, and I kept doing it."[5]

Soon Starski had a new line to try out at parties: "Hip, hop, hippy to the hippy hop-bop." Cowboy did, too: "I said a hip-hop, a hibbit, hibby-dibby, hip-hip-hop and you don't stop." Perhaps it was Sylvia Robinson, who had once tried and failed to sign Lovebug Starski, who prompted Wonder Mike to start the record the way he did, using Starski's trademark party lines. What is certain is that these lines were part of the MC canon by the time the Sugarhill Gang's

Wonder Mike stepped to the mic to record the intro to "Rapper's Delight."

In November 2012, during a lecture at Cornell University, Afrika Bambaataa was asked how, of all the words he could have chosen to describe the youth movement that he, Herc, and Flash had helped to create, he had come to settle on "hip-hop."

"Well, I chose the name 'hip-hop' because of the clichés brothers was using in their rhymes—Love Bug Starski and Keith Cowboy from Grandmaster Flash and the Furious Five," he said. "And I liked the sound of what they were saying. And when the media come to speak to me—'cause we could have called it 'the go-off,' 'the boyoyoing,' the 'scat rap,' and all that type—but I liked that sound."

"I said, 'This is *hip* and when you feel that music you gotta *hop* to it, so that's when we called it 'hip-hop.'"

6

Zulus Meet the Punk Rockers Downtown

It was morning in President Ronald Reagan's bright, white America. In 1980, when Reagan's campaign took him through the dead land of Fort Apache to Charlotte Street, he followed almost exactly the same route that Jimmy Carter had taken in 1977. Then, Carter had given his sound bite: "I'm impressed by the spirit of hope and determination by the people to save what they have."

Three years later, on the same empty block, the only things new were John Fekner's graffiti stencils on the blasted brick walls, which read: FALSAS PROMESAS and BROKEN PROMISES. Reagan stopped in front of one of these stencilled walls and said to the media: "I'm impressed with the spirit of hope and determination by the people to save what they have."[1] He hadn't even bothered to make up a new sound bite.

Reagan's policies were wreaking havoc on Black and brown communities, but hip-hop was providing an alternative. Under Reagan, the nation was racially and culturally resegregating, but hip-hop was a force for desegregation. In 1982, as the economy tanked and unemployment skyrocketed, especially among youths of color in urban neighborhoods, Crazy Legs, a true believer in the power of hip-hop, saw what many others saw—a bit of magic happening. "It was the beginning of the breaking down of racial barriers," he says, "'82 was the beginning of worldwide understanding."

Older white photographers like Henry Chalfant and Martha Cooper were capturing pictures of the subway graffiti art in its high period of style, while opening doors for hip-hop among journalists, academics, and arts-world leaders. Young "downtown" promoters and scene makers like FAB 5 FREDDY, Ruza "Kool Lady" Blue, and Michael Holman were throwing parties, doing exhibitions, and starting cable TV shows in white Manhattan neighborhoods that showcased "uptown" b-boys, b-girls, graffiti artists, and DJs—mostly young kids of color from neighborhoods in the Bronx, Brooklyn, Manhattan, and Queens.

When spring bloomed in 1981, the giddy affair between uptown and downtown topped the charts. Deborah Harry—who, by the number of spraypainted canvases dedicated to her, seemed to be the object of every graffiti artist's desire—was sweetly sighing out of every radio in the country in her group Blondie's hit "Rapture": "Wall to wall, people hypnotized, and they're stepping lightly, hang each night in rapture."

One of the people she name-checked was FAB 5 FREDDY, born Frederick Brathwaite. He was a tall, slim African American raised in the "Do-or-Die" Bedford-Stuyvesant neighborhood of Brooklyn. He looked out at the world from behind his ever-present black cat-eye Ray-Ban shades. FAB was a graffiti artist, a rapper, and a connector of such charisma, charm, and grace that he seemed more than anyone else to have brought together the uptown Black and Puerto Rican hip-hop scene with the downtown white art scene. He bridged the graffiti artists, DJs, and MCs with downtown art gallery owners, club promoters, and alternative press journalists.

Soon, Afrika Bambaataa, Rock Steady Crew, and the Zulu Nation DJs and MCs were playing the downtown clubs, mixing with the movers and shakers of the art world. Graffiti artists were moving their art from the subways to canvases and selling them out of Chelsea and Soho galleries. Jorge "Popmaster Fabel" Pabon, a Rock Steady Crew member from Spanish Harlem, recalls, "Here we are looking at punk rockers and different types of bugged out people, you know, those Village type people. It was a whole new experience."

Fabel recalls, "We fed off of the crowd a lot; to get them hyped was half of the reason we did it. Well, at least a quarter. Three-fourths were for more selfish reasons," he chuckles. "Like, there's some fine girls around here, yo!"

In the Clubs

The main club was called the Roxy and it opened in 1982, the year hip-hop made its global impact. To its ecstatic followers, the Roxy would become "a club that changed the world."[2]

Run by Kool Lady Blue, the Roxy was in a huge, nearly block-long roller rink in Chelsea on West 18th Street and Tenth Avenue.

She opened the club with all of the scene's leading lights, at the beginning of a hot summer when graffiti and b-boying and hip-hop music were on everyone's minds. After clearing the bouncers, nightclubbers stepped up into a long hallway that featured neon-colored graf murals and felt the tricky beats set their hearts to racing. They were stepping into another world.

"The regulars were Bam and Afrika Islam, and then Grandmixer D.ST, Jazzy Jay, Grand Wizzard Theodore, Grandmaster Flash, and I'd rotate them," Blue says. "We had no booth. The DJ would be in the center of the floor on a podium. Everyone could see what he was doing, and he was kind of elevated to rock star status." On both sides of the DJ, large projection screens displayed Charlie Ahearn's slides of Bronx b-boys, rappers, and scenemakers. Nearby, the Rock Steady Crew convened all-night ciphers on the beautiful blonde wood floors. PHASE 2 designed the club's flyers and he, FUTURA, DOZE, and others often did graf pieces live onstage. In the crowd were people like Andy Warhol, Keith Haring, Jean-Michel Basquiat, Madonna. It was the place to be.

FAB 5 FREDDY recalls the turning point as the July night Blue decided to book a screening of a punk rock movie, *The Great Rock 'N' Roll Swindle,* before the regular opening of the club. "[The film] attracted all of these cool punks, white new-wave heads, whatever," he says. "And then the crowd for the hip-hop night started to come and I was wondering like, 'Yo what's gonna happen?' And everybody kinda bugged out looking at each other. You had these ill b-boys with the poses and shit, checking out these kids with the crazy haircuts and that whole vibe. And everybody kinda got into each other, so to speak. That's when it really kinda took off as the first really major downtown club that had like a legitimately mixed scene."

Crazy Legs, now all of sixteen, was amazed at how far he and his crew had come in three short years. "We were the stars," he says. "When we had started performing, we were the people that were at the jams in the Bronx outside the ropes. Now we had become the people that were inside the ropes. Now we had the opportunity to perform with Cold Crush Brothers, Fantastic Five, Grandmaster Flash, Grandmixer D.ST, Funky 4 + 1 More, we became part of that elite clique in hip-hop. We thought about that a lot. We were just appreciating the fact that we were at a place where we could be recognized for our skills by all these people we wanted to be."

"We were just innocently having fun," he says, "not realizing that we were setting a foundation for what is a multibillion-dollar-a-year industry."

Planet Rock

In April of 1982, Afrika Bambaataa unleashed a grand statement for hip-hop. It was called "Planet Rock." Bambaataa realized, "I could use my albums to send messages. And the record companies played their role of sending these messages to all these places." The song "Planet Rock" was an electronic mashup of two Kraftwerk songs, "Numbers" and "Trans-Europe Express," and Babe Ruth's "The Mexican," all huge breakbeat records. But when he and his Zulu rap crew the Soulsonic Force recorded it with producer Arthur Baker and keyboardist John Robie using the latest technology, it sounded like the future.

"Planet Rock" sucked the listener into another world—where dramatic melodies drifted across a big bass soundscape, "where the nights are hot, where nature's children dance inside a trance," where everyone could rock it, don't stop it. "Planet Rock" was hip-hop's universal invitation, a hypnotic vision of one world under a groove. The Soulsonic Force shouted, "No work or play, our world is free. Be what you be, just be!"

Bambaataa says, "I really made it for the Blacks, Latinos, and the punk rockers, but I didn't know the next day that everybody was all into it and dancing. I said, 'Whoa! This is interesting.'" It became a smash at the Roxy and in clubs all around the world. It went on to sell 650,000 copies. But its importance would be felt far beyond the number of copies it sold. It would shape the sound of electronic music, techno, and Southern rap for decades to come. And more than that, it signaled to everyone that the hip-hop movement was here to stay.

"'Planet Rock' had more impact than any record I've ever been involved in," Silverman says. "The only record I can think of in the hip-hop movement that maybe had more of an impact was 'Rapper's Delight' because that's the first one that opened the door. But 'Planet Rock' took it in a whole 'nother way. That was the record that initiated that it wasn't just an urban thing, it was inclusive. It was okay for rockers, new wavers, uptown coming downtown. That's when they started pouring in from France and England to cover hip-hop. That's when hip-hop became global."

Outside the floating world of the Roxy, Reagan's recession had bloated unemployment levels to the highest levels since the Great Depression—thirty million searching for work.[3] The official Black unemployment rate hit 22 percent.[4] Poverty rates were soaring, too. Black poverty hit a twenty-five-year peak in 1983, with 36 percent of the population counted as living below the poverty level. It was much worse for young people. One estimate was that only one in five New York City teens had a job, only one in ten African Americans, the lowest ratios of youth employment in the country.[5]

"The Message," released just weeks after the Roxy opened, was a downtempo track that seemed like the morning—a Reagan morning—after a great party, when you had to return to the punishing day-to-day grind.

"Don't push me, 'cause I'm close to the edge," rapped Melle Mel. "I'm trying not to lose my head. Uh-huh-huh huh-huh. It's like a jungle sometimes, it makes me wonder how I keep from going under."

It was credited to Grandmaster Flash and the Furious Five, but there is a story behind that as well. The song was a home-studio concoction of Sugar Hill songwriter and house band percussionist Ed "Duke Bootee" Fletcher. Bootee and Sugar Hill mogul Sylvia Robinson could not interest Flash in recording it. He and the other four rappers in the group felt the song had no energy, that the lyrics would get them booed offstage by their fans. Folks went to a party to forget about depressing things like this.

But Robinson and Bootee recorded the track anyway, with Furious Five rapper Melle Mel adding a memorable last verse from an early version of "Superappin'." Robinson decided "The Message" had to be released as a single. Flash saw where this was going, and he pushed the rest of the Five into the studio to try to rap Bootee's lines. It didn't work. The ensuing tug-of-wars between the group and the label and between Mel and Flash resulted in Flash leaving Sugar Hill the following year. The video appeared, with Flash and the crew lip-synching along to a rap they had not written. After that, the crew slowly fell apart.

But Robinson's instincts had been exactly right: the record became the fifth rap single to reach gold-selling status, and an enduring classic. The single certainly did not represent the first time rappers had chosen to touch on themes of racial justice—Kurtis Blow's "The Breaks," "Hard Times," and "Tough," Brother D and the Collective Effort's "How We Gonna Make the Black Nation Rise," and Tanya "Sweet Tee" Winley's "Vicious Rap" were just some of the examples. But because it was set to a beat too slow to rock a crowd, "The Message" focused the listener on Bootee and Mel's vivid lyrics and their delivery—neither frenetic nor flamboyant, but instead, by turns, resigned and enraged. Flash's instincts had been correct, too: it was the grimmest, most downbeat rap ever heard.

And that vibe matched a rising disgust with Reaganomics, the culmination of fifteen years of benign neglect, and a sense of hopelessness that only seemed to be deepening. It's among hip-hop history's greatest ironies that "The Message," so artificial and marginal by the standards of the culture at the time, would prove to be a song so truthful about the generation's present and its future.

The Wild Style

1982 was a big year for hip-hop for another reason: the movie that Charlie Ahearn and FAB 5 FREDDY made called *Wild Style*. There would be other movies about hip-hop soon enough. But more than any other, *Wild Style* presented these New York City youth cultures as part of a vibrant, cohesive, unstoppable whole called hip-hop. As Grandmaster Caz of the Cold Crush Brothers rapped in the movie's theme song: "We won't bore you with an explanation. Just sit back and let us give you a demonstration."

FAB 5 FREDDY says, "I once read somewhere that for a culture to really be a complete culture, it should have a music, a dance, and a visual art. And then I realized, wow, all these things are going on. You got the graffiti happening over here, you got the breakdancing, and you got the DJ and MCing thing. In my head, they were all one thing." FAB understood the history of artistic movements, and he realized that he was right in the middle of and at the start of a big one.

Charlie Ahearn, an East Village filmmaker who had just filmed a *kung fu* documentary short called "The Deadly Art of Survival" in the Smith housing projects on the Lower East Side, saw the same thing FAB did. "It was a high school youth culture," he says. "And to me, it was a radical avant-garde culture." Days after meeting at a radical art exhibition in Times Square in 1980, the two were plotting out how to make the movie that would change both their lives, and the lives of generations to come.

The movie had a plot, at first. Ahearn was out, he says, to make a "Bruce Lee movie. A simple hero, a simple story. Lee Quiñones was gonna be the hero. What is his problem? He's in love with this girl, but she doesn't know he's the famous graffiti artist. That's it. That's all the movie is."

They had developed a script, in which the main protagonist was a graffiti writer, ZORO, who struggles with deciding whether to quit the scene and enlist in the army after a friend is injured while they paint a train. As he moves toward his decision, he moves through the nascent hip-hop scene—through clubs and art galleries and the train yards—to find himself painting the amphitheater for a huge outdoor jam. LADY PINK says, "There was a script that we all chuckled about. Picture that, a white guy just introduced to the scene and he's trying to write slang. That was funny!"

There were no professional actors. Instead, the mysterious graffiti artist Lee Quiñones played ZORO, and it seemed as if almost everyone who was anyone in the Bronx hip-hop scene had roles playing themselves or close imitations. They gave the movie its authenticity. FAB had now taken on a key lead role as Phade, the promoter who brings the graffiti artists downtown. As Ahearn and FAB shot the film, they threw out the script and focused on the set pieces. What resulted was a movie that was light on plot and heavy on capturing brilliant live rap performances, realistic depictions of dangers graffiti writers faced, and an intimate look at the young people shaping a hip-hop movement on the verge of blowing up worldwide.

Graffiti writer ZEPHYR, who designed and executed the eye-popping opening animation sequence and logo with REVOLT, says, "the whole thing of the whole sensibilities of the downtown and the uptown, and the woman Neva who wants to seduce Lee—'Oh can I buy your painting? Oh sit down!' All that shit seems like it's laughable when you watch the movie, and yet it all happened.

All those things were so real. Charlie didn't say, 'I'm gonna parody the scene.'"

Charlie and FAB shot for about two years at hip-hop's turning point, and captured memorable scenes. They caught the Bronx rappers on the stoop and in the limo, at the Dixie and the Amphitheatre, even on the basketball court. They walked into a marquee rivalry between Charlie Chase's Cold Crush Brothers and Grand Wizzard Theodore's Fantastic Five (also known as the Fantastic Freaks) and their battles became a major theme for the movie. They captured three of the most electrifying, influential ensemble routines ever committed to tape.

The movie's climax was a feverish reimagining of a Bronx park jam, yet another downtown presentation of the four elements, but with one crucial difference. Instead of taking hip-hop upmarket, *Wild Style* went back to the people hip-hop came from. Ahearn had always been concerned about *where* he screened the work as much as *what* was being shown. His greatest ambition for *Wild Style* had been to screen it in Times Square where the b-boys and b-girls, the street rappers, the Five Percenters, all the folks from around the way, hung out and watched *kung fu* flicks. So the show was staged at an abandoned amphitheater near the Williamsburg Bridge in East River Park.

The cast and crew cleaned it and fixed it up and Lee and others painted it into full hip-hop glory. Then they invited all the neighborhoods to the party. In a sense, it really was a park jam. No permits, no city fees. The night of the shoot, thousands had gathered and the show was getting into full swing when the law finally showed up. As the police car pulled near the gate, Ahearn ran over, clipboard in hand, and said, "Oh man, I'm so glad you guys showed up. We thought you would never get here. We just need you to stand right here and help us keep this thing together." The cops took one look at the scene, got back in their car, and drove off quickly, never to return.

In the end, Charlie and FAB got their wish. *Wild Style* opened in Times Square in November 1983. On opening night the line ran all the way down the block. The b-boys and b-girls watched it, laughed, cheered, tagged the bathroom, and one night, they broke windows there to try to steal the movie posters. But they watched it over and over. This was their lives on screen—finally. It became the second most popular movie in New York City that month, outgrossing even the Baby Boomer film *The Big Chill*.

It was morning in Reagan's America, but as hip-hop spread around the world, it would become the way that millions of young people would express themselves.

LOOP 2

1983-

1990

7
The Big Crossover

City by city, country by country, Bambaataa's Planet Rock was being born. Charlie Ahearn and FAB 5 FREDDY took a huge entourage to Japan to premiere *Wild Style.* Kool Lady Blue sent the stars of the Roxy to tour England and France—Afrika Bambaataa and the Soulsonic Force, the Rock Steady Crew, the World Champion Fantastic Four Double Dutch girls, FUTURA, DONDI, Grandmixer D.ST and the Infinity Rappers, RAMMELLZEE, and FAB 5 FREDDY.

Meanwhile hip-hop was hitting the big screen and the small screen, reaching audiences around the world. But the results were mixed. After the unexpected success of 1983's *Flashdance*—which featured Rock Steady Crew members b-boying to "It's Just Begun" and body-doubling in Jennifer Beals's climactic audition—Hollywood decided to cash in, and 1984 and 1985 saw a wave of big hip-hop flicks. The two biggest movies—*Breakin'* and *Beat Street*—were the first out of the box in the summer of 1984. *Body Rock, Fast Forward, Krush Groove, Delivery Boys, Turk 182, Rappin',* even *Breakin' 2: Electric Boogaloo* followed—and failed—in short order.

The movies kicked the "breakdance" fad into high gear. The New York City Breakers, now managed by Michael Holman, donned bodysuits to spin at the Summer Olympics in Los Angeles, peddled how-to-break books, high-fived Gene Kelly at Lincoln Center, and earned an ovation from Ronald and Nancy Reagan at his second inauguration. Rock Steady Crew, now managed by Kool Lady Blue, signed a recording contract with Malcolm McLaren's British label, Charisma, and started taking singing lessons. The Dynamic Breakers commanded performance fees that started at $10,000 and lent their name to a line of "Breakdance Fever" toys, including branded plastic jewelry, wristbands and headbands, and sunglass/visor sets. Toy stores sold thousands of "breakdancing" linoleum mats. Thom McAn ordered 17,000 shell-toed "Wild Style" brand shoes that, despite their name, were not related to the movie at all. McDonald's, Burger King, Fruity Pebbles—all did hip-hop-themed commercials. Hip-hop was everywhere, but now it was being treated like a fad. And the kids who had come up from the underground would find themselves and their culture chewed up and spit out like bubble gum.

Graffiti was no longer the cool thing in the downtown art galleries. Many of the Rock Steady Crew members came home to find the doors to Hollywood and the big time closing. After *Beat Street,* every kid across the country wanted to breakdance and every city council and shopping mall official wanted to ban it. But the only thing that put a stop to it all was too much marketing.

In a few more years, rap would eclipse all the other movements.

Graffiti would be pushed off the subways, as the MTA completed the buff of all of its subway cars and brought the subway art era to an end. Graffiti would pour out onto the streets and highways and freight trains, initiating a new wave of police crackdowns and internecine fights. Style wars dispersed to thousands of distant cities, where fervent new movements opened new frontlines with local authorities.

B-boying, a dance style that had already died once in New York, would be replaced by a succession of fad dances. Steps like the Whop, the Reebok, the Cabbage Patch, and countless others got everyone back on the dance floor. But each one disappeared faster than b-boying had. Third-generation breakers continued the art form as Rock Steady's disciples popped up in cities around the globe. "I remember when we were filming *Krush Groove* with Run-DMC and LL Cool J," the b-boy Richie "Fast Break" Williams told journalist Cristina Verán. "Jam Master Jay said to me, 'You're still doing that shit? That's played out!'"[1]

The DJ was replaced by the rap producer, who took the sound of back-to-back cutting and scratching and programmed it into a drum machine. The old-school all-night MC routines of the Bronx and Harlem were dying off—*Wild Style* seemed to have been the lasting and almost final tribute to the old school. Instead, rappers and producers were writing short pop songs with hooks. The music was now being built for the record and the radio, no longer for the club.

Rap was the ideal form to spread hip-hop culture. It was endlessly novel, reproducible, malleable, perfectible. Now the only thing standing in the way of hip-hop conquering America and the world was cultural segregation. In the United States, radio was divided: Pop and rock stations played mostly white acts for majority white audiences, R&B stations played mostly Black acts for Black audiences.

But a group of young artists, producers, and promoters from outside the Bronx and uptown scene were ready to take all of this on.

The New Kings

In 1984, the biggest rap crew was a trio from Queens—Joseph "Run" Simmons, Darryl "DMC" McDaniels, and Jason "Jam Master Jay" Mizell. Queens was the borough where Black families had moved to get away from the congestion and the troubles of the city. When their families came to Queens, they moved into suburban homes and for a short time, the neighborhood was integrated. But quickly, many of the white families moved away and when they left, Queens was resegregated.

"It was as if we were the Black Plague," Run's father, Daniel Simmons Sr., told Run-DMC's biographer, Bill Adler. "They still cared about their children and did not despair when the bakers closed and the meat merchants fled."[2] But families like theirs continued on, trying to keep their kids on the straight and narrow, setting up their college funds.

What were once white-only areas quickly became largely Black areas by the 1970s. The kids found themselves caught between middle class suburban life and the tougher conditions of the city. Run's brother, Russell Simmons, recalled to Adler, "We could either stay on the block, which was nice, or we could go to the corner, which was like any corner in any other neighborhood in the city. On the corner two blocks from us was a heroin house." He, his brother, and his friends DMC and Jay learned to navigate both worlds. His was a comfortable household but he still joined the Seven Immortals gang for a short while, before he quit to promote hip-hop parties and manage Kurtis Blow, Whodini, and Run-DMC as Russell "Rush."

When Run-DMC were getting started, they had to take long trips to perform in the Bronx and Manhattan. At first they dressed like Busy Bee and rapped like the Furious Five. But as they became more confident, they changed their look and sound. Their plaid suits gave way to a black-on-black presentation—black fedoras, black tees, black jeans, black Black Panther Party–style leather jackets, black glasses for DMC, and fat gold chains, finished off with white Adidas shelltoes with black stripes.

Using booming drum machines, their echoing raps contrasted sharply with the house-band disco rhythms that had fueled most of the early records and the crisp electro polyrhythms that replaced it. They had taken it back to the big booming drum breaks. Everything about them was stripped down, as if all the color of the old school was reduced back to its basic elements.

Run-DMC had signed to a single deal with the small indie label Profile Records for two thousand dollars. That single, "It's Like That"/"Sucker MCs," sold 250,000 copies. It sounded less like they wanted to please the crowd, and more like they wanted to shock them—not just in the old-school party-rocking, party-shocking way, but into waking up to the problems of the world. "It's Like That" started where "The Message" left off, recognizing all the trouble in the world:

Unemployment at a record high
People coming, people going, people born to die
Don't ask me because I don't know why

By the end of the song, Run and DMC are trading line for line, and preaching to the listener: "The next time someone's teaching, why don't you get taught." Other songs on their first album, named after the group, like "Wake Up" and "Hard Times," would offer similar themes.

Set to producer Larry Smith's powerful big beat attack, which replicated a DJ's back-to-back break-cutting on a drum machine drenched in heavy reverb, "Sucker MCs" is the crew's origin story. Russell had told Run and DMC, "Just mention [Larry's musical group] Orange Krush and tell 'em where you go to school." So DMC raps, "I'm DMC in the place to be / I go to St. John's University."

The crew's publicist and biographer, Bill Adler, would call the record "half creation myth and half devastating diss." It was a loud and proud song rappers would quote, DJs would scratch, and producers would sample for decades to come.

"Rock Box" was the biggest musical risk, the first rap song with a loud, blazing rock guitar solo. Music critics and rock fans embraced it, while rap fans scratched their heads. But behind the song was a strategy—Run-DMC had their mind set on crossing over to the white audiences beyond the city, living in the suburbs.

Rock ruled the radio airwaves. The people who made decisions about what got played believed rock was for everyone, but rap was just for Black audiences. In 1981 MTV went on the air, promising to revolutionize the industry by showcasing music videos twenty-four hours a day. But it would not play artists who made what it deemed "Black music."

Radio and MTV were segregated. MTV had burst onto the scene by championing rock and new wave, and all but excluded Black artists. Only after Columbia reportedly threatened to boycott the young network in 1983 did MTV begin airing Michael Jackson videos. By the summer of 1984, the video for "Rock Box" had become the first rap video on MTV, a breakthrough.

It was hard to imagine the audacity necessary for a rapper to call himself the "King of Rock." But that's exactly what DMC and Run did with their next album. And they would continue to play rock jams—just like Herc, Bambaataa, and Flash had, and Jimi Hendrix and Chuck Berry before them, because after all rock had come from Black music—until they collaborated with the rock band Aerosmith on their third album with a cover of "Walk This Way" and took hip-hop to another level.

Another rapper on the other side of the country named Ice-T said, "Until Run-DMC, I thought hip-hop was something that was only going to be done in basements and in clubs. I went to a Run-DMC concert and they actually made me believe that hip-hop could be big. Rap was never at that level. We'd never seen it like that."[3]

Desegregating America

At Def Jam Recordings and Rush Artists Management, Russell Simmons and Rick Rubin's crew had big crossover dreams. They signed a cocky teen idol from Queens named LL Cool J and a trio of young white private school punk-rock skateboarders who had been transformed by the downtown hip-hop clubs and called themselves the Beastie Boys, and had hits with each of them—LL Cool J's "I Need a Beat" and the Beastie Boys' "Rock Hard." Not long after they met and began working together, they signed a million-dollar deal with a major label, Columbia.

Bill Adler was one of Russell's first hires. Adler immediately understood what set Simmons apart from the Black-owned indie pioneers like Enjoy and Sugar Hill. "He was never gonna just be a guy who operated within the confines of Black cultural institutions," Adler says. "He was gonna take this Black culture and promote it everywhere."

When Russell met Rick Rubin, a twenty-one-year-old, gnomic Jewish longhair with a broad taste in music and a talent for fomenting white teen cultural rebellion, he found the perfect partner. Rubin had grown up on Long Island playing metal and punk, and became a rap devotee listening to the underground radio shows. When he moved to Manhattan to attend New York University, regular trips to the Roxy sealed his love for hip-hop. He started making records in his dorm room—like T La Rock's "It's Yours," with its intricate rhymes and wall-rattling drums—that conquered the streets.

Rubin had a hardcore aesthetic. "I think Rick helped radicalize Russell's rhetoric," says Adler. "He used to say, 'We're gonna pull the mainstream in our direction simply on basis of the integrity of the records themselves. We are going to win with no compromise.'"

Winning meant they had to desegregate radio and music video. They hired a staff that thought like them—white men and women who loved rap, Black men and women who loved rock—and the team set out to pull off a racial crossover of historic proportions. Beastie Boy Mike D recalled that on a typical day in the tiny Def Jam office, Russell "charmed us, yelled at some people on the phone, yelled something we couldn't decipher to [staffer] Heidi [Smith] in the front room, talked about how Run-DMC would be the first rap group on the cover of *Rolling Stone* and how we would follow them and be even bigger."[4]

"Walk This Way" was released on July 4, 1986. Run-DMC and Aerosmith cut a video together, in which they literally knocked down the walls separating rap and rock, Black and white, and performed together triumphantly before a mixed audience of b-girls, b-boys, and rock fans. MTV's programmers took a look at it, added it to their rotation the next day, and it became the hit of the summer. By the end of 1986, Def Jam's strategy had been perfectly executed. They had broken through rock radio with Run-DMC's "Walk This Way" and on rap radio with the Beastie Boys' "Hold It Now, Hit It." The Black group crossed over to white audiences with *Raising Hell,* then the white group crossed over to Black audiences with *Licensed to Ill.*

"Going out anywhere with Run-DMC in 1986 was bizarre," Mike D would write of their subsequent tour. "They were so large that by the time their Raising Hell tour got to Miami, the promoters upgraded their venue from basketball arena to baseball stadium."[5]

Two months after its release, *Raising Hell* became the first rap album to be certified platinum for a million copies sold. In its first year alone, it sold three million copies. The Beasties' album hit platinum three months after its release, and in time went on to sell over ten million copies. But more important was its social impact. To Bill Adler, "Rap reintegrated American culture."

Def Jam's epochal feat of pop desegregation unleashed an eight-year rap signing blitz. Majors realized that rap music was not a fad, and not just beloved by Black audiences, and that they were far behind the curve. By the end of 1986, majors were moving in the other direction, trying to sign every rap act they could.

Hard Times

Run-DMC's pop success was double-edged. They had ushered in a major social breakthrough by desegregating American culture. But even as the *Raising Hell* album bolted to platinum and they headed out of New York City with the Beastie Boys, LL Cool J, and Whodini on a sixty-four-date tour, they were moving into a new America that felt less innocent, and more plagued by rising problems in the cities. President Reagan's policies were creating homelessness and unemployment, and coming down especially hard on urban neighborhoods and African Americans.

"Hard times are coming to your town," Run-DMC warned. "So stay alert, don't let them get you down."

In the cities, especially, things were taking a raw turn. The story of a young New Yorker named Michael Stewart illustrated many of the reasons why. Michael was slim, Black, about six feet and 140 pounds, a handsome twenty-five-year-old with ambitions as an artist and model. He wrote graffiti. His name would capture more fame in death than in life.

In the early morning of September 15, 1983, he left the Pyramid Club in the East Village and headed into the subway station to catch the train back home to Brooklyn. He was alone but feeling good. He'd had a six-pack's worth of beers. It was warm out. No one else seemed to be on the platform. Perfect time to tag. He pulled out a marker and scrawled "ROS," and a white Transit Authority policeman walked up to arrest him. At this point, it was about ten minutes to three in the morning.

At twenty minutes after three, Michael Stewart was facedown on a gurney in the Bellevue Hospital emergency room. He had bruises all over his body. His face and hands were turning blue. His neck was scarred below his Adam's apple. There was swelling around his eyes, back to his temples and behind his ears. He was hog-tied—the cops had handcuffed him, secured his ankles with tape, and then tied his wrists to his ankles with cord. He had no heartbeat, no pulse, no blood pressure. He was not breathing.

The medics could not remove Stewart's clothes because he was still handcuffed and bound. The head nurse tried to turn him sideways to help him breathe. She would later testify that the transit police had fumbled around for nearly five minutes trying to find the key to the cuffs. Finally, the medics were able to get Stewart breathing again. But he lay comatose. Through all of this, the police charged the unconscious Stewart with criminal possession of cocaine and marijuana, and resisting arrest. Thirteen days later, Stewart died in his hospital bed.

In the two trials that followed, the public would learn that eleven transit cops had been involved with Stewart's arrest. Hospital tests on Stewart revealed no trace of drugs in his body. The MTA quietly dropped the cocaine charge.

It was still a mystery why so many had been needed to subdue a 140-pound man. They said he had become violent, and they denied that they had beaten him. But the swelling around Michael's eyes and the mark on his neck were evidence that he had been choked viciously with a nightstick. Other bruises indicated he had suffered serious blows to the head, but the city's Chief Medical Examiner, Dr. Elliot Gross, ruled Stewart had died of a heart attack.

The family did not believe him. The Stewarts' lawyer, Louis Clayton Jones, accused Gross of working in "some sort of collusion" with the transit police. Gross's actions in the coming weeks only made the family more suspicious. Before the Stewart case was over, Gross changed his opinion of the cause of Stewart's death three more times.

In 1982, police misconduct complaints in New York City hit a new high. The gap between police and communities of color was growing. In response to a congressional inquiry, the police department found that an overwhelming number of cases of police brutality involved white officers and citizens of color. More worrisome was the fact that nearly half of those cases had resulted in death.[6]

As the case proceeded, eyewitnesses described a story completely different from the Medical Examiner's. Officer John Kostick had arrested and cuffed Stewart for tagging the subway station wall. Stewart suddenly made a dash for the stairs leading to the street and Kostick tackled him. Four other officers hastened to help Kostick pin Stewart facedown on the ground. One of the cops pulled Stewart's head up and punched him. Then they put him in their van and drove him to the precinct headquarters at the Union Square station.

Stewart again tried to escape. But he was caught by the officers and thrown to the ground. They descended on him, beat him, and choked him with nightsticks. Witnesses said they saw Stewart facedown on the ground, screaming. They said the cops kicked him until he became silent. He was then hog-tied, picked up, tossed into the back of the van, and driven to Bellevue Hospital for "psychiatric examination." In the van, he apparently struggled again, and one of the officers beat him further until he stopped. His body was dangled partly over the back seat when the van pulled up to Bellevue's emergency entrance. Only after Stewart was on the gurney did the officers realize he was not breathing.

But two years after Stewart had been killed, and two trials later, all of the officers were acquitted of all charges.

"What we have witnessed has been a farce," Jones, the Stewarts' family lawyer, said. "And all the players happened to be white. The six defendants, the six defense lawyers, the two prosecutors, the twelve jurors, the judge, and even every court officer in the well of the courtroom was white. The only Black person there was the victim, and he was unable to testify."[7]

Raising Hell

In June of 1986, on the Raising Hell tour, Run-DMC stepped onstage in Philadelphia's Spectrum Arena, and during their performance of "My Adidas" asked the sold-out crowd to thrust their shelltoes in the air. They did it again at their hometown Madison Square Garden show. This time, an Adidas executive was in the house, and offered them an endorsement deal on the spot. Now it was clear that the rap star could be a pop superstar, with the power to move people and markets. Hip-hop had entered a new era.

But so had the hip-hop generation. For youth of color, especially Black and brown youth in the cities, the mid-eighties were a time of growing unrest. And the weight of intensified policing, the crack cocaine trade, and gun violence was also beginning to show up in hip-hop music all across the country.

Local politicians across the country were becoming increasingly worried about rowdy youths, and some cities began to pass noise ordinances to ban boom boxes, and to debate whether to establish curfews and laws that would prevent young people from gathering or cruising on town boulevards on weekends. When scuffles broke out among small groups of teens after Run-DMC's summer concerts in Pittsburgh, Cincinnati, and New York City, politicians blamed rap music for bringing "dangerous mobs" of young people of color.

"All of us rappers get a raw deal by newspapers, man," Run responded. "Rap music and rappers are about making people, especially young people, feel good about themselves. Because most older people and almost all white people don't understand it, they got to down it. I just wish they'd chill out and stop hassling us."[8]

But at the end of the summer of "Six in the Morning" and "P.S.K.," as the Raising Hell tour was heading into its final stretch, Run-DMC's limo pulled up to the Long Beach Arena in Southern California. They anticipated fourteen thousand fans anxiously awaiting them inside. Instead they found a full-scale melee in progress. Gangbangers were throwing up signs. Chairs were being thrown. The soundman was being beaten. Someone let off some gunshots and the crowd rushed for the exits.

Local radio personality Greg Mack from 1580 KDAY, the nation's first all-rap format station, was MCing the show. He told Brian Cross:

> This guy threw this other guy right over the balcony onto the stage while Whodini was performing, so they got up on the stage trying to talk to the guy, next thing you know a whole section was running, gangs were hittin' people, grabbing gold chains, beating people . . . I got the girls, ran to the car, there was a Crip standing next to me getting his shotgun, getting ready to do God knows what.[9]

The following year, when fans came to see Run-DMC and the Beastie Boys, they had to run a gauntlet. As *New York Times* writer Jon Pareles noted, "Airport-style metal detectors on the way into Madison Square Garden, and helmeted, club-wielding police officers on the way out, lent Monday's sold-out rap show by Run-DMC and the Beastie Boys the air of a concert in a prison."[10]

It was an ominous sign of things to come—not just for rap fans, but for young people all across the country.

8
Coast to Coast

In the mid-1980s, hip-hop's future no longer belonged solely to New York's Black and brown kids. Thanks to hip-hop's crossover, youths were breaking in Tokyo, getting up on the Berlin Wall, rapping in Rio de Janeiro. Just as it had been in the Bronx, hip-hop was a way for invisible youths around the world to say, I AM HERE.

But it also represented a way for young people of color in the United States to express themselves in the changing conditions they were experiencing. The sound and the style of the Bronx struck a nerve with them because what was happening there was also happening in North Philadelphia, West and East Oakland, the Southside of Houston—everywhere there were Black and brown youths.

Youths like Brad Jordan, who was coming up in the South Acres neighborhood of Houston. He had been surrounded by music in his family—his cousin was the singer Johnny Nash, who had a number one global hit with the reggae-inflected song "I Can See Clearly Now"—and he started playing electric guitar at a young age. He had wanted to become a rock star like his heroes, Kiss. But then he and his friends heard Run-DMC.

"It was *hip-hop,* and we were all about the four elements—breakdancing, graffiti, DJing, and rapping. That's all we talked about. That's damn near all we did," he wrote in his autobiography, *Diary of a Madman.* "I remember being so into it that we'd take little plastic action figures and stick coins in their backs so we could make them do backspins on the lunch tables or in class. We were that down.

"And then records like 'Rock Box,' and, later, Beastie Boys' 'Fight for Your Right' and 'No Sleep Till Brooklyn' made all of the rock shit I'd been doing and my whole background cool," he added.[1] Hip-hop seemed to absorb everything he'd been about. His musical destiny now seemed clear.

He started beatboxing, then DJing and making mixtapes. "Once I started DJing, I was determined to be the best. I'm talking everything—the best blends, the best mixes, the best cuts, the best records, all of it. Shit, I even started rapping just so I could be a better DJ."[2] But in time, he would become more known as a rapper than a beatboxer or a DJ. He became Scarface of the Geto Boys, and hip-hop was making him aware that there was a nation of young people out there just like him, in Oakland, Atlanta, Seattle, Philadelphia, and Detroit, all going through the same difficulties, facing the same problems, and getting creative about it.

Each city had its own pioneering figures—folks like Too Short and Freddie B. in Oakland; Hugh E MC, Rapping 4Tay, Frisco Kid, and DJ Big Bob in San Francisco; Shy D and Kilo in Atlanta, Sir Mix-A-Lot and Nasty Nes in Seattle; Lady B, Cosmic Kev, Cash Money, and Jazzy Jeff in Philadelphia; Awesome Dre, Prince Vince, and The Wizard in Detroit. And every city had its own hip-hop creation myth, including its own neighborhood stories that reflected what Dug Infinite, a pioneering Chicago b-boy, once called "the complexities, the politics, and the struggles folks were facing every day." In New York City, the boroughs outside the Bronx had their trailblazers, too: Cipher Sounds, Infinity Machine, Woody Wood, Davy DMX, and Hurricane of Solo Sounds in Queens; Grandmaster Flowers, Master D, Fantasia, and Maboya in Brooklyn. Every region, every city, every block had a tale to tell.

As Scarface wrote in his autobiography, "It's powerful and empowering to know that you're not alone even when your back is against the wall and the shit is just straight horrific, knowing that it ain't just you or your crew or your block or your town or your police department or whatever it is—that's some powerful shit."[3]

The South Gets Hot

At the end of the 1970s, Miami was undergoing major changes. Immigration from the Caribbean that brought Cubans, Haitians, Jamaicans, Brazilians, and many others transformed the city into what would soon be called "the capital of Latin America." The city became a central hub for the cocaine trade. It was one of the primary points through which drugs came into the United States, and money flowed back to the cartels.

Then a series of disturbing incidents of police brutality came to light. An eleven-year-old Black girl was assaulted by a white policeman. A Black teacher was beaten by police officers in his home. And then in December of 1979, a Black motorcyclist was beaten to death by a group of six white Dade County police officers. When they were acquitted, riots began in the Black Miami neighborhoods of Liberty City and Overtown that went on for four days and left eighteen people dead.[4]

At the same time, Black youths were creating a music-centered culture. Perhaps no other city outside of New York and Los Angeles had as big a sound system/mobile DJ culture as Miami in the 1970s. DJ groups competed to throw parties in the parks, on corners, and later on radio and in all-ages clubs. The music was uptempo, rooted in lively Afro-Caribbean street parade percussion-oriented music like junkanoo, samba, and calypso, in the way salsa and mambo had influenced the Bronx. In 1978, Miami even had its own pioneering rapper—an underground R&B star, Clarence Reid, who had cut funky, freaky comedy records under the name Blowfly.

When "Planet Rock" hit, Miami audiences went wild. They loved the chants and the fast pace and deep-bottomed bass and the fluttering hi-hats that recalled the sounds of shakers or tambourines. Hip-hop had renewed the sounds of the African diaspora.

Luther Campbell grew up in Liberty City around the sound system culture, inspired by local DJ crews like International DJs, South Miami DJs, SS Express, and the Jammers. When he was seventeen, he joined the Ghetto Style DJs. With his entrepreneurial mind and big ambitions, he got the crew lots of gigs in the lucrative market of high school dances. He became the crew's main MC and hype man, and built the Ghetto Style DJs into major promoters, hosting Run-DMC, the Fat Boys, and others. Soon they were throwing parties under the name Pac Jam.

His Pac Jam club nights in Homestead and North Miami, along with clubs like Bass Station, were all-ages and defined the Miami sound. The crowds loved anything that had deep bass—reggae, freestyle, "Planet Rock," and Def Jam Recordings—music for dancing and for driving. People began to put large subwoofer cabinets in the trunks of their cars to bump their jams as they rolled down the Miami highways, and cruised slow through the neighborhoods.

At the Pac Jam parties, youths seemed to be inventing new dances every week. One day a producer made a song based on a new dance, "Ghetto Jump." Campbell, who had begun calling himself "Luke Skyywalker," realized he wasn't getting a penny from this record. So he decided to figure out how to make one himself.

One day he heard a record called "2 Live" by a crew from Northern California in which a rapper who called himself Fresh Kid Ice rhymed, "Like Luke Skywalker, I got the force / Whenever I rhyme I am the boss." Campbell invited the crew—Chris "Fresh Kid Ice" Wongwon and Chris "Mr. Mixx" Hobbs—to perform in Miami and then asked them if they would record a record based on a new dance jumping off at Pac Jam, "Trow the D," which would later be called twerking. In early 1986, 2 Live Crew released the single, based around the Miami breakbeat classic "Listen to the Drummer's Beat" by Herman Kelly and Life. The record caught fire from Miami to Texas to California to Philadelphia and back to New York City.

Suddenly, with the sound of Miami Bass, Southern rap was on the map.

A Queen from Queens

Up in New York City, the next generation of crews was coming of age. They were knit together by the rise of late-night hip-hop radio shows. On WHBI, John "Mr. Magic" Rivas started the first rap show, followed by the World Famous Supreme Team. Magic moved to the larger commercial station WBLS in 1982 and began the popular *The Rap Attack*, co-produced by Tyrone "Fly Ty" Williams and featuring a young DJ named Marlon "Marley Marl" Williams.

Williams lived in the Queensbridge Projects, the largest housing projects in the United States, and had a fourteen-year-old friend named Lolita Shanté Gooden, who had developed a rep for being the most feared battle rhymer in the area. Marley had built a makeshift studio in his sister's apartment, and one day looked out the window to see Shanté taking her laundry downstairs. Together Marley and Shanté would put Queensbridge on the map, paving the way for MC Shan, Tragedy the Intelligent Hoodlum, Mobb Deep, and Nas.

Shanté had first picked up the mic in a summer park jam at the age of ten and honed her skills in the Hegemen Group Home for Girls, where she had been sent at the age of twelve. It was, she would say, the last stop in her preteen run-ins with authority. In the streets, teens dissed the girls sent to Hegemen as "Hegemonsters."

To avoid public ridicule and embarrassment, Shanté told no one that she had spent time at the group home.

But, she recalls, "Hip-hop was actually our way of being able to cope with what our circumstances were and our situation was. Hip-hop was an alternative to fighting each other. So we would battle from floor to floor, from dorm to dorm, from room to room."

At the group home, she says, "Every time you go somewhere, there's always somebody who will hit a beat up on a wall. Like, *boom boom bap ba boom ba boom bap,* and they wait to see who's going to MC or who's going to rhyme."[5] She battled the other girls, and when the guys came around, she battled the guys. She never lost.

Years later, she was performing on a bill with the popular crew called the Fat Boys. One of them, Prince Markie Dee, looked at her and said, "I know you, you the group home girl. They don't know you from the group home." Then he joked, "I should tell 'em."

"Go 'head, tell. Go 'head," she said, deadly serious.

Markie reassured her that he would keep her secret safe. But inside, she was scared that he might blurt it out sometime. So when Shanté got onstage she turned defiant. She boldly freestyled, "I'm up here on the mic and I do it all alone, and I don't give a fuck 'cause I'm from the group home." The crowd cheered. That type of fearlessness made Shanté the kind of rapper who would strike terror in the hearts of her opponents. At fourteen years old, only the boldest and the dumbest would attempt to test her.

In spring of 1984, four young men out of Brooklyn—Kangol Kid (Shiller Shaun Fequiere), Educated Rapper (Jeffery Campbell), Doctor Ice (Fred Reeves), and Mixmaster Ice (Maurice Bailey)—formed a group called UTFO. They recorded a single with the group Full Force called "Hanging Out" that didn't exactly set the world on fire. But DJ Red Alert, whose KISS-FM radio show was competing with Mr. Magic's, loved the b-side, a track called "Roxanne Roxanne." Over a loud drum machine programmed to Billy Squier's "Big Beat" break, the crew rapped hilariously about trying to get with a stuck-up woman named Roxanne who rebuffed all their romantic advances.

Mr. Magic and Marley Marl loved the track as well, and booked UTFO for a holiday charity show. The group was supposed to perform as a favor to the two for all the airtime they had garnered. But UTFO didn't show up as promised. Marley Marl decided he would get some musical revenge.

One weekend Marley saw Shanté heading down from the next building to do her laundry. He called down to her from the window, told her he knew she was one of the best and that he wanted to cut a record with her. Shanté was not in the mood—her mom had given her a twenty-minute time limit to get the laundry done, and was keeping her on a short leash since she had gotten back from the group home. But she knew Marley worked at the Sergio Valente jeans factory, so she bargained with him right there. Get me some fresh new Valente jeans, and I'll do it, she told him. Bet, he said. She loaded the clothes and went up to Marley's apartment.

Marley explained that the concept was for her to become the character Roxanne and talk shit about each of the rappers. Marley cued up UTFO's instrumental, and Shanté stepped to the mic and rapped:

> Well my name is Roxanne, don't you know
> I just cold rock a party and I do the show
> Said I met these three guys and you know it's true
> Now let me tell ya and explain them all to you . . .

Then she proceeded to destroy all of UTFO's rappers one by one. Kangol was reduced to the dude she met "with the name of a hat" whose "Pig Latin didn't make no sense." She lectured the Educated Rapper on how to be a fly MC. She said the Doctor "ain't really cute and he ain't really great. He don't even know how to operate." She dropped some complex lyrical styles and some funny braggadocio just to show she could. Then she asked the devastating question, "Why'd you have to make a record 'bout me? The R-O-X-A-N-N-E?" For any girl weary of egotistical men and street harassment, the song felt like a fist-pumping, knee-slapping manifesto. The legend of Shanté—now that she would be known as *Roxanne* Shanté—is that she did the entire recording in one take. It is said she took just seven minutes to record it all—seven, the number of perfection.[6] Then she went down to put her clothes in the dryer.

Mr. Magic and Marley Marl played the song she recorded that day, "Roxanne's Revenge," on their show, and the phones lit up with people wanting to know how to get it. Marley Marl linked up with a Philadelphia-based indie label called Pop Art that pressed up a couple of hundred copies. In turn, UTFO's label, Select, sued for copyright infringement. As part of a settlement, Shanté rerecorded her song and cleaned up some of the language that existed in the original release and the new version was an even bigger hit. That was just the beginning.

UTFO's producers Full Force recorded a song called "The Real Roxanne," featuring a young artist named Joanne Martinez rapping lyrics that UTFO had written. Now there were two Roxanne "answer records"—the wildly popular revenge record from Shanté, and the other by UTFO and Full Force cashing in on the popularity of the first.

In the resulting "Roxanne Wars," over thirty more answer records were released, including "The Parents of Roxanne" by Gigolo Tony and Lace Lacy, "Yo My Little Sister (Roxanne's Brothers)" by Crush Groove, and "Roxy (Roxanne's Sister)" by D.W. and the Party Crew. There was even a Roxanne Dance—"Do the Roxanne (Dance)" by Dr. Rocx & Co. Shanté had literally opened the door for dozens of female rappers.

But none of these records were tough enough to challenge her dominance until Doreen "Sparky D" Broadnax-Piggott took aim on "Sparky's Turn (Roxanne You're Through)." Sparky called herself the champ, telling Shanté, "I think it would be better if you just broke camp." Produced by Spyder D and backed by Russell Simmons and Rush Productions, her record attracted the attention of DJ Red Alert and the KISS-FM crew, who pumped up the record to challenge Mr. Magic, Marley Marl, and the WBLS crew.

But this beef was all onstage and on wax. Shanté and Sparky went out on tour together, with Marley Marl and DJ Red Alert as their respective DJs. The two took the boxing metaphor all the way with an album called *Round 1,* in which the two teens traded brutal disses and posed for the cover in gloves. "We took this thing very seriously," Sparky says, "pulling no punches."[7] But at the end of the day, they went home friends.

As the Roxanne Wars waged on, Shanté recorded a classic, scathing record called "Bite This." Her opening line, over Marley Marl's booming Art of Noise–style beat, was unforgettable: "The rhymes you're about to hear me recite are dedicated to all of those that bite." Shanté took on all those she deemed the fake Roxannes, including the Real Roxanne and Sparky D. Then she went after the Rush Artists roster, including LL Cool J, Kurtis Blow, and Run-DMC, saying they made her feel disgraced to be part of the "MC Race."

Lyric for lyric, Shanté easily bested all of them, and she was still only fifteen years old.

Follow the Leader

Hip-hop in the 1980s brought a powerful diversity of voices to the fore, all across the country. And by 1986, the styles were about to switch up once again. Marley Marl, Roxanne's DJ and producer, would play a central role.

In 1983, Marley had launched his producing career with a classic single, "Sucker DJs (I Will Survive)," featuring his smooth-rapping then-girlfriend, Dimples D. On his early dance records, like Aleem's 1984 club hit, "Release Yourself," he used a sampler to repeat and pitch up and down vocal snippets: "Release yourself! Re-re-rererere-rererere-release yourself! Yo-yo-yo-yourself!"

While trying to sample a voice from an Art of Noise record for another song on his affordable new E-mu Emulator, he accidentally caught a snare snap. Punching it a few times, he suddenly realized the machine's potential percussive capabilities. The sampler had been meant for melodies, but Marley understood that it could also work like a drum machine, and imitate what DJs had been doing from Herc through Flash and beyond—running the breakbeats back-to-back.

On the 1986 hit "The Bridge" by MC Shan from the Juice Crew, he revealed the fruits of his discovery, with a stunning loop of the Honeydrippers' "Impeach the President" drum break. No more tinny, programmed, DMX or Linn drums, which stiffened the beat and reduced most rappers to sing-songy rhyming. On top, Marl kept his vocalists bathed in billowing echoes, but on the bottom, the groove suddenly felt slippery. Inevitably, the rappers he worked with responded with more intricate rhymes.

Marley Marl's roommate was a DJ from Queens named Eric Barrier, and his rapper was a Five Percenter from Wyandanch, Long Island, named William Griffin Jr., who called himself Rakim Allah. Rakim was about to graduate from high school, where he was the star quarterback, when a mutual friend introduced him to Barrier. The two hit it off, and Barrier asked Marl about recording something in their studio. They headed into Marl's studio and cut the demo for Eric B. & Rakim's "Check Out My Melody." MC Shan sat in.

Rakim obviously had lyrics, battle rhymes funneled through Five

Percenter poetics. He didn't just slay MCs, he took them out in three sets of seven. "My unusual style will confuse you a while," he rhymed. "If I was water, I'd flow in the Nile."

Shan and Marl weren't sure they understood this guy. At the time Shan ruled New York City with an excited, high-pitched delivery. But Rakim refused to raise his voice. "Me and Marley would look at each other like, 'What kind of rap style is that? That shit is wack,'" Shan recalled.[8]

"More energy, man!" he yelled at Rakim.[9]

Figuring "My Melody" was too sluggish, they gave Rakim another beat that was almost ten beats per minute faster. Based on Fonda Rae's "Over Like a Fat Rat" and James Brown's "Funky President" and alluding to Marl's by-now famous jacking of "Impeach the President," the concept became "Eric B. Is President."

Marl and Shan listened to Rakim's intro in amazement: "I came in the door I said it before. I never let the mic magnetize me no more." In the lyric, Rakim described the act of rhyming as if it were a pitbull on a long leash, an undertow pulling into a deep ocean of words, and, above all, a dangerous habit from which there was no return:

But it's biting me, fighting me, inviting me to rhyme
I can't hold it back
I'm looking for the line

It made them believers.

Rakim's mother was a jazz and opera singer. His aunt was rhythm and blues legend Ruth Brown. His brothers were session musicians who had worked on early rap records. He was a gifted saxophonist and had participated in statewide student competitions. He brought that sensibility to his rhymes. He says, "I kind of got my rhythms from sax players like John Coltrane, Charlie Parker. I learned how to drop my words in certain spots in a saxophone style, like sporadic and crazy."

He also approached his rhymes in a spiritual kind of way, as if he was channeling words and cadences from somewhere above. "I get the track. I listen to the track," he says. "It's saying, 'Tell me what's wrong.' Then I start telling them what's wrong."

The neighborhood he grew up in was like the one Run and DMC grew up in—once a refuge for Black middle-class families, whites had fled, government services and businesses had fled, and its corners were now plagued by hustlers doing dirt. William was a smart student with a lean athleticism and a nose for trouble that kept him close to the streets. By his teens, he was a graffiti writer turned stick-up kid, getting high, staying paid, holding down corners in Wyandanch and spinning drunkenly out of the projects in Fort Greene, before he became Muslim and took the name Rakim Islam Master Allah.

He covered the graf burners he had painted on his bedroom wall with primer. Photos of Elijah Muhammad, Malcolm X, and Minister Louis Farrakhan went up. He met Eric, Marl, and Shan, cut the record, abandoned a football scholarship to the State University of New York at Stony Brook, signed with Rush Management, and became a rap legend.

Rakim never smiled. Draped in African gold, inside Dapper Dan customized faux Gucci suits, he stood tall in a way that assured he was in supreme control of his body. He was, as he put it, "serious as cancer." He rapped in riddles, like, "Who can keep the average dancer hyper as a heart attack?"

To him, hip-hop represented a personal journey to freedom, and anyone could choose to take that freedom wherever they wanted. As Rakim told a journalist, "You're dealing with heaven while you're walking through hell. When I say heaven, I don't mean up in the clouds, because heaven is no higher than your head, and hell is no lower than your feet."[10]

The Crack Era

And yet out on the streets, things were starting to get ill. Drugs were ravaging the communities. Cocaine was coming up to the United States along illegal routes from South America into big cities like Miami and Los Angeles. At first cocaine was a drug for rich people. In a 1981 cover story featuring a martini glass filled with cocaine, *Time* magazine toasted the "all-American drug," the powder that made you "alert, witty, and with it." But by the end of the 1980s, cocaine would be much more widely available to people of all economic backgrounds, and more devastating to entire communities.

In Los Angeles, an illiterate former tennis champ named Ricky "Freeway Rick" Ross began making crack cocaine. He started first by selling powder cocaine to wealthy Black clients. But then he learned how to make cocaine cheaper by cutting it with baking soda and cooking it into rocks that would come to be known as crack cocaine. Crack was intensely addictive, and proved extremely profitable for pushers and gang members. By the mid-1980s, in many Black and brown neighborhoods across the country, it seemed like it was suddenly everywhere.

Aqeela Sherrills, then a teenage Grape Street Crip, watched his Watts neighborhood change. "Once an individual got hooked on it that was their only pursuit. They was robbing, stealing, jacking, everything. Then you think about some of the neighborhood killers. When they was strung out on the shit, they was robbing a dice game, getting into it with some cats, shootouts would happen. Cats who was like big-time drug dealers in the neighborhood, all of a sudden they were strung out, with nothing."

"The whole quality of life in the neighborhood just changed," he says. "The neighborhood was already tough, but people literally lost their families to drugs and the violence that came out of people utilizing drugs and making money off drugs. Folks went to jail for the rest of their life. People got murdered. It just totally devastated the neighborhood."

Illadelph Lives

Ninety-five miles to the south of New York City, Philadelphia was always in a slightly different kind of orbit. A small city in comparison to its sister to the north, Philly nonetheless always had as much of an impact on New York as New York did on it. The modern graffiti movement began in Philly and went up the I-95, while hip-hop went in the other direction.

In the 1970s, Black neighborhoods all across the country had their own dances and their own mix of favorite bands or musical acts. While the kids in the Bronx were b-boying/b-girling, in Philadelphia they were doing what they called "stepping" or "iking" (pronounced "Ike-ing") or "GQ." Rennie Harris was a teenager who learned the dance from one of the original steppers' younger brothers. Stepping groups had names like the Mighty Boomshakers, the

Flamingos, the Franchise, the Stepping Masters, Disco Kings and Queens, and the Great Gatsbys. They were throwbacks to the days of the tapdance social clubs. "If it was a Saturday, and there was nothing going on and you walked around in a goddamned suit," Harris recalls, "the community of the street knew you were a stepper."

Young Rennie topped off his suit with a derby. He wore monogrammed designer socks and spats, and carried a cane. His pants had nickels sewn into the pocket that jingled to the beat when he moved. At a party, he and his fellow steppers leaned against the wall, feet split at right angles, one hand on their waists, the other on their canes, staring down their rivals. Then the DJ would put on a song like Kool and the Gang's "Love the Life You Live" or the Blackbyrds' "Rock Creek Park" and the crowd would clear the floor for the steppers.

They would sidle in and out, one hand behind their back, the other tapping the cane, stomping their feet down on the one and four, syncopating around the three. As they came to the center of the floor, they accented their footfalls with crisp turns and slides inherited from tap and the Temptations. There, one by one, they went off, light on their feet like the Nicholas Brothers, quickening and complicating the rhythms. Rennie might end his performance by sidling up to his rivals and kicking his foot up as if to toss dirt on them. He'd slide back and smoothly pull up his pant leg to reveal his spat and sock. Then he'd dust his shoe and shoulder in two swift motions, and fall back into his position with his cane, looking mean and impressive.

By 1979, however, stepping as a dance was fading away. And hip-hop was about to come in. Rennie would eventually make his name and become a legend doing popping, or, as they called it in New York, "electric boogaloo."

In West Philly, Wendy "Lady B" Clark was hearing hip-hop for the first time through her basketball-playing friends who were going back and forth to New York. She grew fond of listening to their Kool Herc tapes, and when she went with them to Brooklyn and the Bronx and saw some of the pioneers and her friends rock the mic, she decided to as well. A radio host brought her to T.E.C. Records, an independent label, and they signed her to do a single.

"I took all the rhymes I knew," she told journalist Cristina Verán, "put them on three-by-five cards, and stuck those on this big board, arranging and rearranging them all night to decide which rhyme flowed better after the other."[11]

She stepped in the booth and in a single take rapped lines like:

I got a little red book with a thousand pages
With a listing of men that are ranked from all ages
To the beat y'all, check it out y'all, don't stop

"To the Beat Y'all," the first solo rap record by a woman, was released not long after "Rapper's Delight," and she soon found herself rocking shows in the tristate area, including the Harlem World.[12] When she returned home, she got a job on WHAT-FM, and with her *Street Beat* show, became one of the most important radio DJs in hip-hop history, helping to break every imaginable rap artist over the next three decades, including Philadelphia acts like Three Times Dope, The Roots, and Jazzy Jeff and the Fresh Prince, who would become better known as Will Smith.

"What hip-hop did for me at that point and what I think it did for the Black community is we put down our guns and we put down our knives," she told a class of students years later. "It was a better way for our children then to express their feelings, to let out their rage."

As crack came into the cities, and job opportunities shriveled during the Reagan era, a rapper named Jesse Weaver, who called himself Schoolly D, gave his record "Gangster Boogie" to Lady B to play on her show. Schoolly had flipped Run's braggadocio on "Sucker MCs" to another level. He wasn't standing in a b-boy stance, he was shocking ladies with his "gangsta lean," selling weed, and pulling guns. But his other records felt even more intense. Schoolly used a cheap drum machine, his partner DJ Code Money's scratch, and billowing doses of reverb to create menacing tracks like "Gucci Time" and "P.S.K."—the initials for his crew, the Park Side Killers. Lady B told him no record company would touch it. It was too much. But she could also see that times were changing. Schoolly D released his records independently and began finding both a huge audience for them and a lot of people who hated their violent edge.

"To us, it was art. To you [outsiders], it was just like, 'We've got to stop these voices,'" Schoolly D told the hip-hop journalist Soren Baker. "I was making records for my peers, to uplift my situation, and it was workin'. I wanted to tell my stories the way I wanted to tell my stories."[13]

These were going to be different stories for a new era.

9
What We Got to Say

A generation after the Civil Rights Movement had pushed Americans to directly address racial segregation and poverty, President Ronald Reagan was reversing their victories. Young people coming of age during the 1980s faced the consequences of the return of segregation and inequality.

Reagan's policies reduced basic social services for the poor and redistributed wealth to the rich. The racial wealth gap grew. In 1983, the median white family owned eleven times the amount of wealth as the median family of color. By 1989, the gap had nearly doubled.[1] Homelessness spread like a plague. Many people of color felt less secure than they had a generation before. Hip-hop gave voice to these angry and dispossessed young people.

The crew that would become Boogie Down Productions began in a homeless shelter in the heart of the South Bronx. The two young men who formed the crew, Scott Sterling and Lawrence Parker, were in many ways opposites, and their first meeting turned into a confrontation.

Parker was a street kid fascinated by the Hare Krishnas who would come to feed the homeless. The other kids around him started calling him "Krishna," and he adopted the nickname "Kris." He had left home at the age of thirteen. By day he studied philosophy in public libraries, tagged KRS-ONE on walls and subways, and wrote rhymes about police brutality and nuclear war and devastating wack rappers. At night he slept on subway grates, in the park, or at homeless shelters.

He was staying at the Franklin Street Shelter in the heart of the South Bronx when Scott Sterling walked in, a college graduate in a suit and tie holding a briefcase. As the new social worker, one of Sterling's jobs was to distribute subway tokens to those staying at the shelter to go to job interviews. But Kris often sold the tokens to buy food, alcohol, or weed. Inevitably, the two started arguing over the way Kris was flouting the rules. One day, Kris yelled at Scott, "You're one of those handkerchief-head house negroes, tap-dancing for the white establishment. You ain't got nothing to do with us, you're a sellout!"

"You don't know who I am!" Scott yelled back. "All you homeless Blacks who want to sit on your ass, you're lazy and you're wasting your life." Then security pulled Kris out to the street.

But as it turned out, the two had a lot in common. Despite the buttoned-up way he dressed at the shelter, Scott was a huge hip-hop head. He rocked a local club known as the Broadway RT under the name DJ Scott La Rock, and was learning to make beats from a soon-to-be-famous Bronx producer named Ced Gee. As young kids, both Scott and Kris had enjoyed the outdoor parties thrown by Cindy Campbell and DJ Kool Herc or Afrika Bambaataa, and had probably been at the same jams. But where Scott's household was without drama, Kris's mother suffered through an abusive relationship and struggled to keep it together. To get control over his life, Kris left home and lived on the streets. Scott's mother sent him to a Christian school where he excelled in basketball and went on to college. The two arrived at the shelter from different places, but they would leave together.

Not long after their fight, Kris happened to be at Ced Gee's house, working on raps with some friends, when again, Scott walked in. Each couldn't believe that the other was there. Scott warmed up enough to invite Kris to his club gig.

As Kris told hip-hop journalist Brian Coleman, "It was like another world. And I look to see the source of the music, and it's Scott Sterling. I was blown away. I was humbled and embarrassed."[2] The two became the closest of friends. When some MCs at the club dissed Scott, Kris got angry. "So I jumped onstage and smashed all five of these MCs," he recalls.[3] That night they became MC KRS-One and DJ Scott La Rock of Boogie Down Productions (BDP).

They cut a demo, and landed a record deal with a tiny Bronx label called B-Boy Records. But when they took the record to Mr. Magic, Magic dissed it. Kris listened to a record Magic was pushing, a record by MC Shan of the Juice Crew and Marley Marl called "The Bridge," in which Shan paid tribute to Queensbridge rappers. Kris got the idea to write an answer rap to it, and started the next big battle in hip-hop.

Shan had led off "The Bridge" with these lines:

You love to hear the story again and again
Of how it all got started way back when
The monument is right in your face
Sit and listen a while to the name of the place—the Bridge,
  Queensbridge

KRS would later say that he was offended. To him, Shan was claiming that Queensbridge was the birthplace of hip-hop, and by extension dissing the Bronx. For years afterward, Shan argued he had never meant to suggest that. But KRS's response would become a classic record. It was entitled, simply, "South Bronx."

Ced Gee and Scott built a track from James Brown samples, big drums, and horn stabs, and KRS gave a lesson on the history of hip-hop—starting with Herc and Coke La Rock, namechecking Bambaataa, Grandmaster Flash, and Rock Steady Crew. He rapped, "As odd as it looked, as wild as it seems, I didn't hear a peep from a place called Queens."

MC Shan responded with "Kill That Noise" and BDP came back with "The Bridge Is Over." The Bridge Wars were on. Fans across the boroughs tuned in each week to hear Mr. Magic and Red Alert playing each new battle and answer record on the radio. It was like the old-school battles that used to take place in the parks had now been elevated over the airwaves to a cipher of millions. By the end, Boogie Down Productions had made their name on the backs of the Juice Crew.

It was a new day. Run-DMC had crossed over to massive success, and now hip-hop's next generation seemed more interested in returning to the stories of the 'hood. "In a way, around 1986 and '87, Run-DMC, LL Cool J, Fat Boys, and others had gotten so big that there was a whole other audience that was being alienated," KRS-One said. "We appealed more to that alienated audience, the audience that felt that rap was getting too commercial."[4]

KRS didn't want to be known only as a battle rhymer. He rapped that he came "not as a king or queen," but as a teacher. He and Scott put together songs with bloody stories of the rawness of the streets in Reagan's America, plagued by crack cocaine and gun violence. When a reporter asked Scott La Rock why they titled the album *Criminal Minded,* he answered, "People think we're all stickup kids in the Bronx, but the government are bigger gangsters and hoodlums than we will ever be."

He added, "We're just portraying how things are. That's how this country is. The strong will survive, the weak will perish. That's it. If you want it, you take it."[5]

The scale of *Criminal Minded* was intimate, made for the headphones. Scott and Ced Gee's music was slower, sparer, and more spacious than Marley Marl's and Run-DMC's. KRS-One delivered menacing lines as if he was standing right next to you, wearing a knowing, confident smirk. If violence was the reality they faced, KRS proposed hip-hop as the release. "Poetry is the language of imagination," he rapped. "Poetry is a form of positive creation."

He said, "The purpose of the album was to attract a thug-type audience, so we could teach them later on."[6]

But then the unthinkable happened. On August 27, 1987, as the group was working on its second album and negotiating to move to a major label, Scott had gone to try to squash a beef between his sixteen-year-old friend Derrick "D-Nice" Jones and members of another crew at Highbridge Projects.[7] Like Black Benjie sixteen years before him, Scott went to make peace. He ended up being the only one in the crew to be hit in a hail of bullets from a nearby roof. He died of his gunshot wounds.

Tragedy pushed twenty-two-year-old KRS-One into a starring role. He responded by posing like Malcolm X on the cover for the next album, *By All Means Necessary,* toting an Uzi in a self-defense stance. 1987 had begun with massive protests over the racist murder of a young Black teen in the Howard Beach neighborhood of Brooklyn, ample reason for self-defense against racist violence. But Scott's death pointed to the fact that Black-on-Black violence was also a reality. KRS cut a tribute to his fallen comrade called "Stop the Violence."

"Some people look at me and see negativity, some people look at me and see positivity," he rhymed on the record. "But when I see myself, I see creativity."

Violence was death. Creativity was life. Regardless of what the outsiders thought they saw when they looked at Black youth—and to an extent, many of those in the generation for whom hip-hop spoke—hip-hop was about choosing life in the struggle against oppression and death.

The mainstream media had taken notice of hip-hop, but sometimes for the wrong reasons. In 1987, gang fights broke out during a UTFO show in Los Angeles, a boy was stabbed to death at a Dana Dane show in New Haven, Connecticut, and two teenage girls were trampled in an after-concert stampede at a show in Nashville, Tennessee, featuring Eric B. & Rakim, Public Enemy, and NWA. Violence was also on the rise in rock concerts, but the media had a new reason to fix blame on youths of color, and calls for rap show bans spread.

On September 10, 1988, one youth was killed and dozens others were hurt at a Saturday-night homecoming show for Eric B. & Rakim, Kool Moe Dee, and Doug E. Fresh at the Nassau Veterans Memorial Coliseum in Uniondale. "It was time," one of the organizers, the journalist Nelson George, wrote, "for rappers to define the problem and defend themselves."[8]

D-Nice and KRS produced a record, "Self Destruction," that featured an all-star group of rappers called the Stop the Violence Movement. Their lineup included MC Lyte, Heavy D, Doug E. Fresh, and others. They put together a book, shot a video, and staged a march through Harlem. The song became a hit and raised $250,000 for the National Urban League's anti-violence programs. When *By All Means Necessary* dropped, it was received as one of the most important message albums in hip-hop history.

"It's not all about bragging anymore," KRS-One told a reporter. "The fad is intelligence as opposed to how much gold you have."[9]

Fighting Apartheid

If there was a single moral struggle that gripped the '80s in the same way that desegregation had the '60s, it was the global fight against apartheid, the racist system in South Africa that allowed a white minority, outnumbered five to one, to maintain political and economic power over the native Black majority.

Pedro Noguera, a student leader at UC Berkeley during the mid-eighties, says, "apartheid was such a stark situation. It was so clear. How repressive the regime was, how unjust apartheid was—in some ways it was easier to see the issues there than it was to see the issues here."

President Ronald Reagan bent over backward to support the South African white-minority apartheid regime. In 1985, he stirred global uproar by saying, "They have eliminated the segregation that we once had in our own country—the type of thing where hotels and restaurants and places of entertainment and so forth were segregated. That has all been eliminated."[10] But while Reagan was prematurely hailing the end of South African segregation, the apartheid regime had declared a state of emergency in an attempt to crush the rising Black movement. Between 1984 and 1986, the regime detained 30,000 protestors and killed 2,500 more.[11]

At the same time, students in the United States pressed states and universities to take their financial investments out of South Africa. During the springs of 1985 and 1986, hundreds of campuses exploded in demonstrations. Hip-hop artists released records, joined the cultural boycott against South Africa, and proudly supported the protests. In 1989, a collective of artists formed called Hip-Hop Against Apartheid, releasing a song called "Ndodemnyama (Free South Africa)." Stetsasonic and Queen Latifah joined Jesse Jackson to do an anti-apartheid song called "A.F.R.I.C.A." The Fat Boys, Kurtis Blow, Run-DMC, Melle Mel, and Afrika Bambaataa participated in the cultural boycott against South Africa, and joined a project called Artists United Against Apartheid that released a record called "Sun City" that raised more than a million dollars for anti-apartheid organizations.

The tide of protests had an effect. On July 18, 1986, the University of California divested $3.1 billion from South Africa.[12] In August, the state of California voted to divest $11 billion of stock. Emboldened, Congress passed the Comprehensive Anti-Apartheid Act of 1986, which banned any new investment in South Africa, except in Black-owned firms, and ended arms sales and military aid. When Reagan vetoed the bill, Congress overrode his veto.

In 1990, after nearly three decades behind bars, Nelson Mandela, the man that the Reagan supporters and right-wingers had once called a racial terrorist, was released from jail. Four years later, he stood as the first elected Black president of the country, and he paid tribute to American anti-apartheid activists by consciously evoking the memory of Dr. King: "Free at last! Free at last!"

Apartheid gave the young students of color a way to understand racism and the power of whiteness—not only in South Africa, but in the United States. As Rakim rapped on "The Ghetto," "Not only there but right here's an apartheid."

Let's Organize

Young people—especially Black youths—had grown up in a dog-eat-dog world in which governments slashed funding for education and social services. In cities such as Detroit, Chicago, Cleveland, and New York, many youths of color lived under increasing racial and economic isolation.[13] A generation after the landmark Brown v. Board of Education decision had begun racially desegregating public education, schools were again resegregating. More than 60 percent of Black and Latinx students attended predominantly minority schools.[14] Young whites remained the most segregated group of all. The average white student attended schools that were over 80 percent white.[15]

Sociologists now spoke of an "underclass," a segment of communities of color permanently locked into poverty and joblessness. In this context, Chuck D of Public Enemy described crack cocaine as a "white tornado" that decimated communities of color.

With social problems mounting, artists got organized. Some were inspired by the 1984 and 1988 presidential campaigns of Reverend Jesse Jackson, who was the first viable African American candidate to run for the highest office in the land since the historic run of Shirley Chisholm in 1972. Some were studying Afrocentricity, a term and concept defined by scholar Molefi Asante and historian John Henrik Clarke to center a Black perspective of the world. Many were weary of the violence.

In Los Angeles, gang peacemaker Michael Concepcion organized the West Coast Rap All-Stars, including NWA, MC Hammer, Digital Underground, and Ice-T, to do a record called "We're All in the Same Gang" calling for an end to gang and gun violence. In New York, the Stop the Violence Movement grew out of meetings at the Latin Quarter nightclub organized by an elder, Paradise Gray, with Afrika Bambaataa, Professor X of the X-Clan, Boogie Down Productions, Stetsasonic, and many others.

Paradise says, "We called the meetings to discuss the problem of young folks having their chains snatched." They educated each other about how the jewelry was made—via the blood diamond trade and exploitative gold mining in Africa. The artists began wearing red, black, and green African medallions instead of gold chains. "A more conscious style of dressing and lyricism spread across the world," Paradise says.[16]

"I know we changed the culture of the community to allow people to be open to revolutionary ideas . . . It changed the entire rap industry's message," he adds. "The best political scene is a party-oriented one."[17]

Still, the attacks on Black youths continued.

A City Divided

On a cold December day in 1984, a white subway rider named Bernhard Goetz shot four Black boys—two in their backs—in a crowded car, after one asked him for five dollars. Then he disappeared into the downtown station, a face in the crowd. When he emerged two weeks later whites welcomed him as the city's hero. Thousands of dollars poured in for his bail and defense. This "subway vigilante," Goetz's supporters said, was the silent majority's fed-up avenger.

Not long after the 1986 Congressional anti-apartheid victory, a twenty-three-year-old Trinidadian American named Michael Griffith was run over by a car and killed in Queens after being beaten and chased by a white mob shouting, "N----r, you're in the wrong neighborhood!"

The incident began the Friday afternoon before Christmas. Griffith; his friend, Timothy Grimes; his stepfather, Cedric Sandiford; and his cousin, Curtis Sylvester, had gone to Far Rockaway to collect a paycheck for some construction work Griffith had done. When they were returning back across Jamaica Bay on a lonely stretch of Cross Bay Boulevard after dark, Sylvester's 1976 Buick overheated. Griffith, Sandiford, and Grimes left Sylvester with his car and hiked three miles into the nearest neighborhood, Howard Beach, in the gathering darkness.

Nestled in the inner Jamaica Bay amid soft salt marshes, Howard Beach was a whites-only enclave in a city that was almost half people of color. Griffith, Sandiford, and Grimes were walking up the road into Howard Beach when a group of white youths drove by screaming racial epithets at them. The three continued on, then stopped at the New Park Pizzeria and asked for directions to the nearest subway station.[18] They sat to rest and eat. But by the time they had gotten up to leave, the white boys in the car had returned. They had a dozen others with them.

This crowd was drunk. Some had baseball bats, others had tree switches. The whites yelled at them, "N----rs, you don't belong here." When they stepped forward to leave, the mob surged forward and began beating them. Sandiford covered himself and yelled, "God, don't kill us!" Grimes suffered a blow but ran north into the cold night. Griffith and Sandiford ran west, with the mob in pursuit in a car and on foot.

Eight blocks away, the mob caught up with them. In a field next to the Belt Parkway, they beat the young Black men mercilessly. Sandiford played dead as Griffith slipped through a hole in the fence onto the six-lane parkway. When Griffith tried to cross the parkway—perhaps confused, certainly in pain and terror—he was struck by a car. His body crushed the hood and he bounced off the windshield out toward the dividing barriers. Police later found Sandiford, badly injured and dazed, stumbling blindly through the streets. They harassed Sandiford, treating him as a suspect.

To New York City's Black community, the message of Michael Griffith's death, coming on top of the Michael Stewart killing and Bernhard Goetz's shootings, was clear. It was time for some action. Thirty-one-year-old Reverend Al Sharpton led a series of marches into Howard Beach. Separated by thin blue police lines, the marchers faced off with angry white residents. Young anti-apartheid activists called for a "Day of Mourning and Outrage" and a boycott of white businesses. On January 21, ten thousand marchers led police all over the city before they stopped at Mayor Ed Koch's residence.

"Mayor Koch, have you heard? Howard Beach is Johannesburg," they chanted below his window. "Black power! African power!"[19]

Three years later, another murder of a young Black man, this time in a primarily Italian neighborhood of Brooklyn called Bensonhurst, drew eerie parallels to the Howard Beach incident.

On the evening of August 23, 1989, sixteen-year-old Bed-Stuy resident Yusuf Hawkins and three friends went to see a used car for sale. They stepped into a store to ask directions and get some drinks and candy bars. They walked a few blocks up the street past a schoolyard where a mob of more than twenty young white males was gathering. A neighborhood girl had taunted the white mob that day, telling them that Black and Latinx guys were coming around to party with her. Armed with bats and golf clubs, the mob was preparing to chase the outsiders out of their 'hood.

When Hawkins and his friends passed, the mob left the yard and followed them up the street. As Hawkins neared the address of the car owner, the mob stopped them. "What are you n----rs doing here?" one yelled. Then Joey Fama stepped out of the mob and said, "To hell with beating them up. I'm gonna shoot the n----r!"[20] Fama shot Hawkins four times in the chest, and he died shortly thereafter.

In the following weeks, the Reverend Al Sharpton marched into Bensonhurst chanting, "No justice, no peace!" He was met by angry young whites holding up watermelons and screaming "N----rs go home!"[21] On September 1, in another Day of Outrage protest, Sonny Carson and his son's hip-hop crew, X-Clan and the Blackwatch Movement, led ten thousand demonstrators through downtown Brooklyn toward the Brooklyn Bridge, where they engaged in a bottle-throwing, baton-swinging standoff with the police that left forty-four cops injured.

At the same time, a real estate developer named Donald Trump was calling for the execution of five Black and Latinx teenagers who were suspects in the rape and brutal beating of a white woman who had been jogging in Central Park on a spring night in April. This case of the Central Park Five and the Central Park Jogger further polarized the city. Newspapers rushed to call the arrested teens "savage" and "a wolf pack," implying that these boys of color had chased a white woman into the woods to violate her.[22]

It was a narrative straight out of a Ku Klux Klan fantasy, and Trump cast himself as the hero. "I want to hate these murderers and I always will," he wrote in full-page ads he took out in New York newspapers. "I want them to understand our anger. I want them to be afraid."

Civil rights leaders immediately cast doubt on the story. But the teens and their families received death threats.[23] Trump's pressure, one of the lawyers for the defense said, "contributed to an atmosphere that deprived these men of a fair trial."[24] One of the accused, Yusuf Salaam, asked, "If we were white, would Donald Trump have written this in the paper?"[25]

The teens who had been accused of the crime were thirteen- to sixteen-year-old schoolboys, and there was no evidence that any of them had been near the scene of the crime. But police forced fake confessions from them. Many years later, the actual rapist confessed, DNA evidence verified his guilt, and Justice Charles Tejada of the New York Supreme Court concluded that all the teens had been wrongfully convicted and set them free. The Central Park Five would become known to history as The Exonerated Five. But by then, each of them had been forced to spend seven to thirteen years in prison.

The profound anti-Blackness inherent in all of these events could not be ignored, and they set the backdrop for the rise of a group called Public Enemy.

Public Enemy #1

Adelphi University in Long Island, with its redbrick buildings and its tree-lined walks, might have seemed an unusual place for a cultural revolution to begin. But that's where the huge posse, the "force so strong that you can't resist," came together.

They included rappers Carlton "Chuck D" Ridenhour, William "Flavor Flav" Drayton, Richard "Professor Griff" Griffin, business mind and advisor Bill Stephney, music producer Hank "Shocklee" Boxley, and journalist Harry "Allen" McGregor. "We were the rebels," says Bill Stephney, "and hip-hop was everything to us."

In 1982 they turned the college's radio station WBAU into Long Island's rap outpost on Saturday nights, hosting Run-DMC's first radio interview, and bringing in guests like Grandmaster Flash. They realized they shared a point of view about the way they wanted to use music to change their world. Crack had ushered in an era of conspicuous wealth and raw violence, and even the slang reflected the change. It was all about "getting ill," "cold getting dumb." Chuck complained, "It's like being content with being stupid."[26] The times required a harder kind of intellect.

Bill Stephney challenged Chuck, "Why don't you be the one?" Chuck wasn't so sure. But then he was writing as if he had the freedom to say what folks couldn't before: "I'm a MC protector, US defector, South African government wrecker. Panther power—you can feel it in my arm. Look out y'all, cause I'm a timebomb tickin'!"

Hank built a studio at 510 South Franklin in Hempstead where the crew made promos for their radio shows and worked on their demo. Bill got a job at Def Jam and Rick Rubin told him he was interested in signing his friends. They brought in a four-song demo that included "Public Enemy #1," "The Return of Public Enemy" (which would become "Miuzi Weighs a Ton"), "Sophisticated B---h," and "You're Gonna Get Yours." Rubin immediately offered Chuck an album deal. "I was like, well, I'm not going to go in there by myself," Chuck says. After he negotiated to include Flavor Flav and Hank, the deal was done.

Chuck created alter egos for the crew. Hank became Hank Shocklee, a clever retort to the legacy of the racist scientist William Shockley, who believed Blacks were genetically inferior to whites. Richard Griffin, a friend from Roosevelt who directed a martial arts school and rolled with the Nation of Islam, took the name "Professor Griff" and the title that Eldridge Cleaver had held in the Black Panthers, "Minister of Information." Unity Force, the Spectrum City's security team run by Griffin, were renamed the Security of the First World (S1Ws).

Hank assembled the musical team. Hank's brother Keith, also known as "Wizard K-Jee," came aboard. Army fatigue–wearing Eric "Vietnam" Sadler—like Stephney and Flavor Flav—was a veteran of the Long Island funk cover-band scene and was learning to program drums and synthesizers. Spectrum City DJ Norman Rogers became "Terminator X." Paul Shabazz and the DJ for the Kings of Pressure, Johnny "Juice" Rosado, also made key contributions. Hank's team became known as the Bomb Squad.

Chuck was the authority, the bass. Then there was the crazy DJ MC Flavor, whom Hank had renamed Flavor Flav. He would be the treble. Bill didn't like the idea at first. "I wanted the group to be so serious, I didn't want Flavor in the group. Flavor was like a comic cut-up, so my thing was, 'Here we are trying to do some serious shit, how are we gonna fit this guy in?'" he says. "They were completely right. With Chuck being serious, with the stentorian tones, you needed a break, you needed someone to balance that or else it would have been too much."

Chuck, Hank, and Bill had to come up with a new name for the crew. Hank says, "We had to create our own myth for ourselves." One night while they were recording their first album, Bill returned from Def Jam to 510 South Franklin. On a bulletin board, Hank had written the crew's new name: "Public Enemy." Chuck drew up a striking logo—a silhouette of a young Black man in a gunsight.

Stephney loved it: "We're all public enemies. Howard Beach. Bernhard Goetz. Michael Stewart. The Black man is definitely the public enemy."

Old school rappers—and most of the new schoolers, for that matter—invited comparison with earlier Black entertainers like Cab Calloway, Pigmeat Markham, Oscar Brown Jr., Shirley Ellis, Rufus Thomas, Slim Gaillard. But Public Enemy and Boogie Down Productions pointed back to the voices of Black radicalism, as heard on the albums of the Watts Prophets, the Last Poets, H. Rap Brown, and Gil Scott-Heron. Boogie Down Productions and Public Enemy were the musical counterpart to the activists out in the streets and on the campuses fighting apartheid and racism. Public Enemy even called themselves "the Black Panthers of rap."

Chuck and Harry Allen, who had begun writing for local newspapers, regarded mass media as hostile to Black people. Allen called himself the "media assassin" and coined the term "hip-hop activism" to describe how they could use the media to get across their message. The crew wanted to attack stereotypes and take over the media. Chuck says, "We were all gonna bumrush the business from a bunch of different angles, be it radio, journalism, records."

So Public Enemy called their first album *Yo! Bum Rush the Show.* Chuck said, "Where's the news about our lives in this country? Whether or not radio plays us, millions of people listen to rap because rap is America's TV station. Rap gives you the news on all phases of life, good and bad, pretty and ugly: drugs, sex, education, love, money, war, peace—you name it."[27]

In time, he would refine this idea. Rap was Black America's CNN, he said, an alternative media network that allowed young Black people to speak directly to each other. "You've got to understand, Public Enemy and rap music are dispatchers of information," Chuck D said. "We're almost like headline news, the invisible TV station that black America never had."[28]

The record did decently in the South and the Midwest, but New York City wasn't feeling Public Enemy. Melle Mel heckled the crew at their first show at the Latin Quarter. Mr. Magic played "Public Enemy #1" only once, making a point of saying that he hated it.

Then Eric B. & Rakim's "I Know You Got Soul" came out, just weeks after *Yo! Bum Rush the Show.* When Chuck and Hank heard it, they realized that hip-hop's development had suddenly accelerated. Envious and yet confident that the game had somehow shifted decidedly in their direction, they retreated to their studio. They had to top it. So they began working on a song they called "Rebel Without a Pause," flipping the title of the 1955 James Dean movie with a can't-stop-won't-stop attitude.

"We knew we had to make something that was aggressive," Hank says. So they went to work, making an irresistible beat that sounded like a tea kettle ready to explode. Rakim had rapped, "It ain't where you're from, it's where you're at." Chuck flipped that into a call for Black solidarity: "No matter what the name, we're all the same—pieces in one big chess game." He rapped,

Impeach the president / Pulling out the raygun (Reagan)
Zap the next one / I could be ya shogun! (Show gun)

"Man, you got to slow down," Flavor yelled over the break. "Man, you're losing 'em!"

Stephney took the record to club DJs at the Latin Quarter and the Rooftop, clubs that had dissed PE, and watched from the booths as the fader slid over to "Rebel" and the room instantly hit the boiling point. "Just to see kids go crazy," Stephney remembers. "In many instances, fights started."

"Rebel" and its followup, "Bring the Noise"—in which Chuck ripped crack-pushing, Black incarceration, and the death penalty, all in just the first verse—stormed the airwaves, boom boxes, and car stereos that summer and fall. They became unavoidable. There would be no dead air on Public Enemy's second album, *It Takes a Nation of Millions to Hold Us Back,* not a second wasted. "Armageddon has been in effect," Professor Griff boomed on the live clip opening the album. "Go get a late pass!"

Public Enemy positioned themselves as heirs to James Brown's loud, Black, and proud tradition. *Nation of Millions* was the sound of Black youths in a national emergency. Chuck and Flav described coming of age in a state of unending war. The songs represented their organized resistance. "I never live alone, I never walk alone," Chuck rapped on "Louder Than a Bomb." "My posse's always ready and they're waitin' in my zone." On the album's centerpiece, "Black Steel in the Hour of Chaos," he described a prison uprising—an allegory for the Black freedom struggle from slavery to the present—with the words: "They could not understand that I'm a Black man, and I could never be a veteran."

Within two months of its release, *It Takes a Nation of Millions to Hold Us Back* had already sold a million copies. But Chuck had a different number he was concerned about. "We want to build five thousand new Black leaders," he told his audiences.

When Public Enemy came to Philadelphia, the city declared it "Public Enemy Day" and gave them a parade. "We're in open cars, coming down on Market Street, waving at folks and stuff," says Stephney. "But what struck me, we saw these guys who were at that point in their mid-forties. They had all run back, it seemed, into their apartments and homes and two-story brick houses in Philly and gotten all their old Panther shit out. Got the berets, got the black leather jackets, got their camouflages out and everything. You're seeing these graying forty-something Black men, tears in their eyes, throwing the Black Power salute like the revolution has come back."

Spike Lee had a new movie coming out, *Do the Right Thing,* about a Brooklyn block that explodes in racial tensions on the hottest day of the year. It was to be his statement on the strangling of Michael Stewart, the killing of Michael Griffiths in Howard Beach, and how to find a way to live together. He commissioned Public Enemy to do the title track. Chuck, Keith, and Eric came up with a song they called "Fight the Power." In turn, it would become an anthem for the summer, a chant and a soundtrack for the protests around the murder of Yusuf Hawkins in Bensonhurst.

Lee's idea for the video was to stage a "Young People's March to End Racial Violence." On the day of the march, "Fight the Power" T-shirts were handed out to the youths, as well as placards for them to carry featuring images of Angela Davis, Jesse Jackson, Paul Robeson, Frederick Douglass, Medgar Evers, Thurgood Marshall, Marcus Garvey, Muhammad Ali, and the Public Enemy logo.

Hundreds marched up from Eastern Parkway to the block where the movie had been shot. There the group performed the song on a red, black, and green stage framed by a large photo of Malcolm X, as the crowd danced and mugged for the cameras. Then it began, with Chuck proclaiming, "1989! The number, another summer," marking the moment for history.

When their next album came out, it would be titled *Fear of a Black Planet.* For better or for worse, it was going to be a hip-hop world now.

10

All About Reality

If there was one city that might challenge New York to be the center of hip-hop, it would be Los Angeles. The sprawling metropolis was just as culturally diverse, and facing massive change of a magnitude most other cities could not yet fathom. As in New York, young people of color were navigating the divide between creativity and violence. But Los Angeles had its own unique history, sound, and destiny. To begin with, LA moved in a different way. New York had developed a love for the breakbeats. But in California, dancers reacted to the sound of the bass—in particular, the slapping bass styles popularized by Larry Graham of Sly and the Family Stone, and later, the 808 drum kick of songs like "Planet Rock" and Egyptian Lover's "Egypt Egypt."

In New York and other cities with mass transit, boom boxes were banned by the late 1980s, so the sound changed as people listened on portable personal music players like the Sony Walkman. But everywhere else, especially where people spent a lot of their time in automobiles, car-speaker technology favored a heavy ribcage-rattling bottom.

Los Angeles, with its extensive freeways, and Black Los Angeles, in particular, with its history of extensive migration from the South, had always been a city of funk. Groups like the Bar-Kays, Kool and the Gang, Parliament/Funkadelic, and Zapp and Roger found some of their greatest successes there. Bay Area rap pioneer Todd Shaw, better known as Too Short, grew up in Los Angeles before moving to the Bay Area for his teenage years. "In New York, they said if it wasn't the drums of James Brown, then it wasn't gonna work. Where does the beat of West Coast hip-hop come from? It comes from the funk bands," he says. "If it wasn't funk groove, it wasn't West Coast."

The influential *Soul Train* TV show moved to Los Angeles in 1971, and it immediately began broadcasting the dance styles, slang, and culture of Black Los Angeles to the rest of the country every week. At the heart of this scene was a dancer named Don Campbell, the key member of the *Soul Train* dancers, and one of the most influential dancers of the funk and hip-hop era. Campbell formed a group with choreographer Toni Basil that they called the Lockers. They were known for doing a dance that Campbell had started in 1970 called "locking," which he created by adding joint locks on his arms and body to a dance called "The Funky Chicken." The Lockers evolved the dance with aerial moves popularized decades before by jazz dancers like the Nicholas Brothers, including splits, half-splits, knee drops, and angled pointing freezes.

In 1972, the Stax record company staged one of the largest concerts of the decade, a community benefit at the Los Angeles Memorial Coliseum called Wattstax. When Rufus Thomas began playing "The Funky Chicken," the mostly Black crowd of 112,000 broke through the barriers and stormed the field to dance. In defiance of the Stax execs and the stadium authorities, thousands joyously did the Campbellock dance before returning to their seats. It was filmed for national movie release, so the moment was captured for eternity.

If breaking was New York's contribution to hip-hop dance, then California brought what would become known as the funk styles. West Coast hip-hop pioneer and community activist Jeff "General Jeff" Page argues that the birth of Los Angeles hip-hop goes back to Campbell's original introduction of locking, which he dates to Campbell's nineteenth birthday, January 8, 1970.

By the early 1980s, the LA hip-hop scene had a club called Radio, modeled in part on the Roxy's "Wheels of Steel" night, presided over by local rap kingpin Tracey "Ice-T" Marrow and Zulu Nation DJ Afrika Islam. New York–style b-boying went off there, but West Coast funk styles dominated the dance floor. Aside from locking, there was popping, a surging, stuttering elaboration of the Robot and Shields and Yarnell's mime, pioneered by Fresno dancer Boogaloo Sam of the Electric Boogaloo Lockers; and strutting, a set of styles that had come down from San Francisco, Oakland, Sacramento, and East Palo Alto's Black, Chicano, and Asian and Pacific Islander 'hoods to take hold with LA's Samoan gangs.[1]

Radio—and its successor, Radiotron—made the Roxy's diversity look like an upscale fashion ad. Arturo "Kid Frost" Molina Jr. and his *cholos* rolled down to the club in their low-riders, sporting their Pendletons and khakis. There were slumming Hollywood whites and South Central Korean American immigrants escaping long hours at the family business. Everyone but the hardest brothers left alone the menacing Blue City Strutters—a Samoan Blood set from Carson that would become the Boo-Yaa Tribe. Radio faded eventually, but not before inspiring a Hollywood movie called *Breakin'* that featured a lot less breaking than California funk style dances and similarly inspired kids around the world to copy legendary Locker Adolfo "Shabba-Doo" Quiñones and his protégé, Michael "Boogaloo Shrimp" Chambers' popping and locking routines.

Los Angeles also had a deep history of mobile DJ sound systems, dating back to the early 1970s. They started as disco-oriented parties—the pioneering LA DJ Alonzo Williams called himself "Disco Lonzo" and his sound system was called Disco Construction. Uncle Jamm's Army was led by Rodger "Uncle Jam" Clayton, who began throwing house parties in 1973 in South Central. A decade later, the Army was regularly filling the Los Angeles Convention Center and the Sports Arena. One of the Army's DJs called himself Egyptian Lover and had a huge hit—everywhere except New York City—with an uptempo dance rap single inspired by "Planet Rock" and named after himself. At their wild dances, the Army showed out in army fatigues and bright Egyptian costumes. They stacked thirty-two booming Cerwin-Vega speakers in the shape of pyramids.

Then things turned real bad real quick.

Dance crews like the Carson Freakateers, Group Sex, and the Hot Coochie Mamaz gave way to the Rolling 60s Crips and the Grape Street Boys. Playlists featuring frenetic sensual funk like Prince's "Head" and the Army's own "Yes Yes Yes" slowed down for a new audience that wanted Roger's "So Ruff So Tuff" and George Clinton's "Atomic Dog." The Freak was replaced by the Crip Walk. American-made .22s were replaced by Israeli-made Uzis. Chains got snatched, folks got robbed. One night a woman pulled a gun out of her purse and shot a guy in the jaw.

In the summer of 1985, the hottest mixtape in Los Angeles was a homemade cassette made by nineteen-year-old Compton rapper and DJ Toddy Tee in his home studio. On the tape, Toddy Tee rapped over instrumentals of East Coast hits about the new world that crack cocaine had made. Whodini's "Freaks Come Out at Night" became "The Clucks Come Out at Night"; UTFO's "Roxanne Roxanne" became "Rockman, Rockman." Most famously, Rappin Duke's "Rappin' Duke" became "Batterram," a tale about the V-100 armored military vehicle equipped with a massive battering ram that LA Police Chief Daryl Gates used to bust down the doors of crack houses. To his surprise, the song became a local sensation.

Ice-T and his Chicano friend Kid Frost had cut a handful of tracks in the early '80s to no great consequence. Instead, Ice-T had parlayed his street rep into a starring role in *Breaking and Entering,* a 1982 cult movie about the LA dance scene that inspired a much more PG-oriented 1984 hip-hop musical movie, *Breakin',* and led to his casting in a role for that movie. He had started rapping as a teenage Crip with lines inspired by the Crips' poetry books and Iceberg Slim pulps, like:

> Strollin' through the city in the middle of the night
> N---as on my left and n---as on my right
> Yo I Cr-Cr-Cr-Cripped every n---a I see
> If you bad enough come fuck with me.[2]

Toddy Tee's "Batterram" and Schoolly D's "P.S.K." gave Ice-T the juice to revisit his old gang rhymes. In 1986, he dropped "Six in the Morning" on the b-side of his single, "Dog N' the Wax." "That song," he told journalist and photographer Brian Cross, "turned out to be my identity."[3]

The tale of a "self-made monster of the city streets, remotely controlled by hard hip-hop beats," "Six in the Morning" was a revisionist rap history told from the hard streets of Los Angeles. The tale begins in 1979, the same year as "Rapper's Delight," with an early morning escape from the cops. "Didn't know what the cops wanted, didn't have time to ask," he sneers.

As he runs, he stops on the corner to roll some dice, ends an argument with a woman by beating her down, and finally gets arrested and thrown in jail, where he causes a riot. When he emerges from prison seven years later, it's 1986, the old school is over, the action has moved west, and the whole world has changed. "The

Batterram's rolling, rocks are the thing," he raps. "Life has no meaning and money is king."

By then, Lonzo had moved from sound system parties to running a nightclub called Eve's After Dark in Compton and promoting his parties at Skateland U.S.A. and another club called Dooto's. He was also running his own label, Kru-Cut Records, and had secured a major label contract from CBS Records for his group, the World Class Wreckin Cru, which featured two talented young DJs named Antoine "DJ Yella" Carraby and Andre "Dr. Dre" Young. Lonzo used the advance money to build a studio at his house.

Even though they were underage, Yella and Dre spun at Eve's, started up a mixtape side-hustle, and learned how to make beats in Lonzo's studio. They became two of the first mix DJs on LA's KDAY, an AM radio station led by programmer Greg Mack, who had made the visionary decision to change the station's playlists to predominantly rap. New tracks that Yella and Dre put in the mixes on the weekends often became Monday's hottest sellers. In 1984, Dre helped produce the Cru's dance-style raps, which were modeled on Egyptian Lover, Kraftwerk, and Run-DMC records, and when it came time to take pictures or perform, he and Yella got dressed up in expensive-looking clothes and grimaced as Lonzo's manager fussed over their hair and makeup.

They were a generation younger than Lonzo, and they knew things were changing around them.

Boyz-N-the-Hood

When nineteen-year-old O'Shea Jackson returned to South Central Los Angeles in the summer of 1988, he was hopeful. All he had ever wanted to do in life was rap, and now it looked like he might be able to make something of it. Arizona had been hell—hot, dry, and boring. Still, his architectural drafting degree from the Phoenix Institute of Technology might get Moms and Pops off his back for a few months, and within that time perhaps he could write some rhymes, make some records, cash some checks, and soon move out of his folks' house.

Just two years before, he had been a junior at Taft High School, bused from his home in South Central to the suburbs of San Fernando Valley, slipping out on the weekend to grab the microphone at Eve's After Dark nightclub in Compton as the rapper named Ice Cube. He and his partners Tony "Sir Jinx" Wheatob and Darrell "K-Dee" Johnson had a group named CIA (Criminals In Action). They dropped sex rhymes to delighted crowds over the hits of the day.

Eric "Eazy-E" Wright was in the crowd every weekend, prowling for talent. Wright had seen the South Central hip-hop scene quickly mature around him in the early '80s. Now the diminutive twenty-three-year-old drug dealer hoped to make some quick cash on rap, a way to go legit after years of hustling. At Eve's, Wright would catch Yella and Dre spinning records.

Dre, his cousin Tony, and O'Shea had been neighbors in the South Los Angeles neighborhood near Washington High School, and Dre had taken a liking to the CIA boys, especially O'Shea "Ice Cube" Jackson. He got them a gig at Skateland where he was DJing for Lonzo. He told them how and what to rap—filthy X-rated rhymes. After they stole the show and got invited back, he helped them make mixtapes to get their name out, got them a shot at Eve's. He introduced them to Lonzo, who got them a single deal for CBS, and produced their CIA record for Lonzo's Kru-Cut label. But now they were all indebted to Lonzo, who gave them all weekly stipends against their royalty checks.[4]

Wright had begun talking to Dre, Yella, and Jackson individually. Wright told Jackson he would put them all together and form a South Central supergroup. Why not? Jackson figured. "Eazy had a partner named Ron-De-Vu, Dre was in the World Class Wreckin Cru, I was in CIA," recalls Ice Cube. "We all kinda was committed to these groups so we figured we'd make an all-star group and just do dirty records on the side."

So one night early in 1987, Young and Wright were in Lonzo's studio with a stack of rhymes that Jackson had penned. Wright had bought some time for an East Coast duo called HBO that Dre had found. The idea was that the duo's slower New York–styled cadences and accents would be more marketable than the uptempo techno-pop rhymes that sold everywhere else. New York, after all, was supposed to represent the best of the best. They didn't know it yet, but they would soon make this notion obsolete.

Although they had come up in 111 Neighborhood Crip territory, Cube and Dre were not active gang members. Perhaps it was because Cube was being bused out of his neighborhood or maybe it was because he was a jock. As far as Dre was concerned, banging didn't pay.[5]

But it wasn't hard for them to notice that the streets were changing. Crack cocaine was making 'hood millionaires, and increasing the body count. Since 1982, the number of gang homicides had doubled.[6]

Yet the music on the West Coast was still about Prince-style purple leather suits. The World Class Wreckin Cru was a perfect example. Even though he had played a central role in creating their slick uptempo dance sound, Dre had begun thinking his gig with the Wreckin Cru was corny. But he owed Lonzo lots of money. Lonzo not only owned the studio Dre used, he had given loans to Dre, sometimes bailed him out of jail for not paying his parking tickets, and even let Dre take his old car.

While Lonzo was still paying off the note, the car got stolen and ended up impounded. At the same time, Dre landed himself in jail once again, just as Lonzo was coming up broke and ready to cut him off anyway. Wright saw his chance, and offered the nine hundred dollars to bail him out.[7] But Dre had to agree to produce tracks for Wright's new record label, Ruthless. What the hell, Dre figured. That's why he was now in Lonzo's studio on Wright's dime. He was working off the bond and the fees for getting the car back.

So there they were in Lonzo's home studio—Dre, Eazy, Ice Cube, and these New York rappers. Dre working with a New York group seemed like an admission of defeat. Cube was tired of being a follower. He had done sex rhymes, he'd done East Coast. Maybe he wanted to show these no-name New Yorkers what Los Angeles was really about. The rap he penned for them was packed with local detail, violent in the extreme.

The reaction was immediately polarizing. On hearing the lyrics, HBO refused to do it, saying the track was "some West Coast shit," and walked out. Dre, co-producer Laylaw, and Wright looked at each other—now what? Dre suggested that Wright take a turn with the track. Wright was reluctant. He was supposed to be a manager, not a rapper. Dre pressed, half joking and half not wanting to see a great beat and precious studio time going to waste. When Wright reluctantly agreed and they began recording "The Boyz-N-the Hood," one painstaking line at a time. Eazy-E would launch a new era in hip-hop.

A few hours later, Dre stepped back into Lonzo's living room where everyone was hanging out and, laughing, popped in the cassette. While the rest of the crew cracked up at Wright's transformation, Lonzo knew it was a hit. "Don't laugh," he told them. "Stranger things have happened!"[8]

The record hit the streets in September of 1987, but Cube had already left for Phoenix. The single he cut for Lonzo had not done anything. Who knew what this Eazy-E single would do? "The rap game wasn't looking too solid at that time, so I decided to go ahead and go to school," he says. "I went to a technical school just to make sure that I did what I wanted to do for a living, no matter what."

But while Jackson was working with T-squares, the record had taken off. By the end of 1987, it was the most requested record on KDAY. Wright went from selling the record out of his trunk to swap-meet vendors and retailers to a distribution deal with indie label Macola. He had even paid Lonzo $750 to introduce him to his white Jewish manager, a music biz veteran named Jerry Heller.[9]

A year after they had cut "Boyz," the single was taking hold on the streets, selling thousands of copies every week.

Cube was proud of his rhyme. It was raw and vivid—and it represented the suppressed story of Black Los Angeles, in which generations of migrants from the South had been condemned to segregated neighborhoods, being harassed by police, and having their creativity met with violence. Dre added a pounding set of bass drum kicks to help drive home Eazy-E's singsong chorus:

Now the boys in the hood are always hard
You come talking that trash we'll pull your card
Knowing nothing in life but to be legit
Don't quote me boy, 'cause I ain't said shit

The kids knew Eazy's mask instantly. They might have quoted his lines in their own adrenalin-infused, heart-poundingly defiant stances against their parents, teachers, the principal, the police, the probation officer.

So Eazy-E's mask stayed. The mercenary b-boys were suddenly a group, perhaps even the "supergroup" Wright had talked about. They named it NWA, which stood for N---az With Attitude, a ridiculous tag that set impossibly high stakes. Now they had an image to uphold.

So Ruff So Tuff

A generation before, on the night of August 11, 1965, a routine drunk driving arrest on Avalon Boulevard and 116th Street escalated into a night of rioting. White police had stopped a pair of young Black brothers, Marquette and Ronald Frye, returning from a party only a few blocks from their home, for driving erratically. As a crowd formed in the summer dusk and their mother, Rena Frye, came out to check on her car and scold the boys, dozens of police units rumbled onto Avalon. In an instant, the scene began to deteriorate.

Soon the cops were beating Marquette with a baton. Seeing this, Frye's brother and mother tussled with other cops and were arrested as well. Another woman, a hairdresser from down the street who had come to see what was going on, was beaten and arrested after spitting on a cop's shirt. Chanting "Burn, baby, burn!" the crowd erupted.

For decades, housing discrimination and violent, white supremacist cross burning–style racism had prevented Black residents from being able to move outside of the neighborhoods of downtown, Watts, and South Los Angeles. They were forced to live in overcrowded conditions, while police prevented them from crossing the imaginary boundaries where the white neighborhoods began. In those hot summer nights, people's years of frustration poured out into the streets.

Over the next two nights, the police were ambushed by rock-throwing youths. They were attacked by women who seized their guns. Their helicopters came under sniper fire. Systematic looting and burning began. Among the first things to go up in smoke were the files of credit records in the department stores.[10] Groceries, furniture stores, and gun and surplus outlets were hit next. After these places were ransacked, they were set ablaze. One expert attributed the riot's blueprint to the local gangs—the Slausons, the

Gladiators, and the mainly Chicano set, Watts Gang V—which had temporarily dropped their rivalries.[11] Rioting lasted five days and resulted in $40 million in damages and thirty-four dead. Until 1992, they were the worst urban riots ever recorded.

After the riots, more than a million whites fled the city for the suburbs on the Westside, north in the San Fernando Valley, east in the Inland Empire, and south in Orange County. But Watts became a hotbed of political and cultural activity. As author Odie Hawkins wrote, "Watts, post outrage, was in a heavy state of fermentation. Everybody was a poet, a philosopher, an artist or simply something exotic."[12]

The gangs, as Mike Davis wrote, "joined the Revolution."[13] Maulana Ron Karenga put together the United Slaves (US) Organization by recruiting the Gladiators and the Businessmen.[14] The powerful Slauson leader Alprentice "Bunchy" Carter led many other gang members to reject Karenga and affiliate with the revolutionary nationalist Black Panthers.[15] The poets who gathered at the Watts Writers Workshop became some of the most influential artistic voices. With two albums, *The Black Voices: On the Streets in Watts* (1969) and *Rapping Black in a White World* (1971), the four young poets who called themselves the Watts Prophets set the blueprint for all of Los Angeles rap two decades later. In a bulldog voice—one that Eazy-E would later evoke, and that would be sampled by dozens of gangsta rap producers—Anthony "Father Amde" Hamilton growled, "The meek ain't gon' inherit *shit,* 'cause I'll take it!"

But the FBI immediately went after the movement. Their Counterintelligence Program—also known as COINTELPRO—was designed to undermine the Black Power movement by fostering bloody tensions between the young Black radicals and revolutionaries. They succeeded all too well. On the morning of January 17, 1969, at UCLA, a Black Student Union meeting ended with Maulana Karenga's US Organization and Bunchy Carter's Black Panthers shooting at each other. Carter and John Huggins were killed.

When it was all over, everyone realized that the organizations had been provoked by the FBI into this bloody conflict. But the authorities continued to destroy the movement leaders. LA police arrested Geronimo Pratt, a new Panther leader, on false charges and had him sent away for life. Even the Watts Writers Workshop was destroyed through the efforts of an FBI double agent. As in the Bronx with Tupac Shakur's mother, "uncles," and "aunties," the radicals and revolutionaries were literally removed from the scene by incarceration or bullets.

Filling the void of leadership was Raymond Washington, a charismatic teen at Watts's Fremont High School who had been a follower of Bunchy Carter. In 1969, he formed the Baby Avenues, carrying on the legacy of a fading local gang, the Avenues.[16] Over the next two years, he walked across the Eastside with a gangsta limp and an intimidating walking cane, kicked his rap to impressed youths, and built the gang.

The Baby Avenues wore black leather jackets in a display of solidarity with the Panthers' style and credo of self-defense. But somewhere along the line, the goal changed to simply beating down other Black youths for their jackets.[17] Godfather Jimel Barnes, who had joined in the early days when Washington came to the Avalon Gardens projects, says Washington had summed up his vision in this way: "Chitty chitty bang bang, nothing but a Crip thang, Eastside Cuz. This is going to be the most notorious gang in the world. It's going to go from generation to generation."[18]

The origins of the name are now shrouded in legend. It may have been a corruption of "Cribs" or "Crypts." It may have stood for "C-RIP," all words that represented the gang's emerging "cradle to grave" gang-banging credo. Or it may have come from an Asian American victim's description of her attacker, a "'crip' with a stick."[19] In any case, as OG Crip Danifu told LA gang historian Alejandro Alonso, "'Crippin' meant robbing and stealing, and then it developed into a way of life."[20]

For years, Mexican *pachuco* gangs had been the most organized and most feared in town. Now the Crips would transform young Black Los Angeles. They spread south to Compton and west to South Central. When Washington was kicked out of Fremont and sent to Washington High on the Westside, he recruited Stanley "Tookie" Williams, and Crip sets expanded into South Central Los Angeles. By 1972, where there had recently been none, there were eighteen new Black gangs.[21]

Youths on Compton's Piru Street organized themselves into groups they called Pirus or Bloods. Other Crip rivals also emerged. In 1973, the beefs turned bloody. Through the efforts of Bobby Lavender, Sylvester "Puddin'" Scott, and others, Brims, Bloods, and Pirus formed a Bloods confederation.[22] Gang fashion had shifted from Black Power dress to an appropriation of Mexican American *cholo* style—Pendletons, white tees, khakis—and when Crips began flagging blue, Bloods flagged red. Like a national map on the night of a presidential election, the Los Angeles grid was now being tallied into columns of red and blue. Soon there were so many Crip sets they even went to war with each other.

"During the late '70s it slowed down," Athens Park Bloods member Cle "Bone" Sloan says, "because n---as started working in the factories. When they took the jobs away, shit started back up. Then cocaine hit the streets and n---as were in it for real."[23] As the 1980s dawned, Raymond Washington was dead in prison, killed by a rival, and 155 gangs claimed thirty thousand members across the city.[24]

Factory closures left 124,000 out of work. OG Blood turned peacemaker Bobby Lavender saw the effects: "Thousands of parents lost their jobs. Homes and cars were repossessed. People who had just started to become middle-class were losing everything and sinking down."[25]

During the Reagan recession of 1983, Los Angeles's official unemployment rate hit 11 percent.[26] But in South Los Angeles it was much higher, at least 50 percent for youths.[27] Almost half of children in South Los Angeles lived below the poverty level.[28] Infant mortality in Watts was triple the rate in Santa Monica, only twenty miles away.[29] By any index, conditions had deteriorated for the children who had come of age after the Watts Uprising.

As one resident of the Nickerson Gardens housing projects in Watts put it, "In the '60s, General Motors in neighboring South Gate was the future. In the '70s, King Hospital was the future. Now the future in Watts and South Central is jail. You see that new 77th Street LAPD station? It's beautiful. You see anything else in the community that looks better than that jail?"[30]

What the South Bronx had been to the 1970s, South Los Angeles would be for the 1980s. One song popular on the street, that

Uncle Jamm's party anthem by the artist Roger, summed it all up: "So rough, so tough out here."

The Sound of the Police

Meanwhile, downtown, security fences and security forces sprung up in commercial buildings and around gated communities. Police Chief Daryl Gates's army locked down the interior. Gates had been trained by Chief William Parker, whose heavy-handed policing of Black residents had helped instigate the Watts riots.

In 1988, after a shootout between Crip gangs near UCLA left an Asian American woman dead, City Hall leaders voted to add 650 officers to LAPD, bringing the department to its largest size in history. Chief Gates pushed for millions in emergency funds for a new military-style operation against the gangs and received it.

LAPD freely profiled and brutalized youths of color. Twilight Bey, a former Cirkle City Piru, described a typically harrowing day in the life of a young Black male in South Central.

> **TWILIGHT**: One of the things that would always happen is [the police] would stop you and ask you "What gang are you from?" . . . In some cases, if you had a snappy answer and by that I mean, if you were quick and to the point and had one word answers they would get up in your face and grab your collar, push you up against the police car and choke you. Or they would call us over and tell us to put our hands up and place them on the hood of the police car. Now, usually the car had been running all day, which meant that the engine was hot. So the car is burning our hands which meant that we would have to remove our hands from the car. When that happened, the police would accuse of us of not cooperating. Next thing you know you would get pushed in the back or knocked over . . .
>
> You have to remember most of us at that time were between the ages of twelve and sixteen. Just a year ago we were ten, eleven, and playing in the sheriff's basketball league where they would treat us like little kids. A year later

when we are close to being teenagers we are suddenly being treated with all this abuse.

In a lot of cases you had kids who had chosen never to be a gang member . . . If you told them you weren't in a gang, they would look at whatever graffiti was written on the wall and put you on record as being part of that gang.

DAVEY D: . . . It seems like it was some sort of sick rite of passage so that by the time you became a grown man you knew to never cross that line with the police.

TWILIGHT: Yes, that's exactly what it was. It was some sort of social conditioning. Instilling fear is the strongest motivation that this world has to use. It's also the most negative . . . What I mean by that is, if you are constantly being pushed into a corner where you are afraid, you're going to get to a point where you one day won't be. Eventually one day you will fight back. Eventually one day you will push back. When you push back what is going to be the end result? How far will this go?

Straight Outta Compton

NWA's new album, *Straight Outta Compton*, captured the increasingly tense mood in Los Angeles, and all across the country. Years later, the Houston rapper Scarface would write, "As badly as the country wanted to make everything a *Cosby Show* moment, the reality for the majority of Black America was really more 'Boyz N the Hood.'"

NWA had quickly sold over 300,000 copies of "The Boyz-N-the Hood." So when O'Shea "Ice Cube" Jackson returned from Phoenix, he joined up with Wright's neighbor from Compton, Lorenzo Patterson, who called himself MC Ren, and an associate of Dre and Wright, Tracy "The D.O.C." Curry. They penned the lyrics for Eazy-E's solo debut, *Eazy Duz It.* When it came out in 1988, it quickly went gold.

Then they turned their attention to the NWA album. If other artists like Public Enemy and De La Soul were going to be positive, Afrocentric, and pro–Black women, Dr. Dre said, "I wanted to go all the way left. Everybody trying to do this Black power and shit, so I was like, let's give 'em an alternative."[31] They decided to go as far out as they could, to be as extreme and offensive and shocking as they could be. In "Straight Outta Compton," "Fuck Tha Police," "Gangsta Gangsta," and "I Ain't Tha 1," Ice Cube portrayed himself as an untouchable rebel without a cause. Police, girls, rivals—none of them could get in Cube's game.

Reaganism had eliminated youth programs while bombarding them with messages to "Just Say No" to sex and drugs; it was all about tough love and denial and getting used to having nothing. But excess was the essence of NWA's appeal. "Gangsta Gangsta" was the first single released from these sessions. On it, Ice Cube hollered,

> And then you realize we don't care
> We don't "Just say no"
> We're too busy saying, "Yeah!"

After the album was officially released on January 25, 1989, it went gold in six weeks. Because the sound was so powerful that it had to be named, someone called NWA's music "gangsta rap" after Cube's anthem. Cube would have preferred they had paid more attention to the next line of the chorus—a sample of Boogie Down Productions' KRS-One rapping: "It's not about a salary, it's all about reality." To him, this was "reality rap." But the "gangsta rap" label stuck.

Police, law enforcement, and right-wing conservatives weren't pleased with NWA's success. Police departments across the South and Midwest faxed each other the song's lyrics. Tour dates were abruptly cancelled. Cops refused to provide security for NWA shows in Toledo and Milwaukee. In Cincinnati, federal agents subjected the crew to drug searches, asking if they were LA gang members using their tour as a front to expand their crack-selling operations. Nothing was ever found.[32]

In August, FBI assistant director Milt Ahlerich fired off a letter bluntly warning Priority Records about "Fuck Tha Police":

> Advocating violence and assault is wrong, and we in the law enforcement community take exception to such action . . . Law enforcement officers dedicate their lives to the protection of our citizens, and recordings such as the one from NWA are both discouraging and degrading to these brave, dedicated officers.

> Music plays a significant role in society, and I wanted you to be aware of the FBI's position relative to this song and its message. I believe my views reflect the opinion of the entire law enforcement community.[33]

The letter came as NWA was touring, and had the effect of further mobilizing police along the tour. NWA's tour promoters tried to secure an agreement from the band not to perform the song. The national 200,000-member Fraternal Order of Police voted to boycott groups that advocated assaults on officers of the law. But in Detroit, where local police showed up in riot-control numbers, the crowd chanted "Fuck the Police" all night, and the crew decided to try anyway. As Cube began the song, the cops rushed the stage. The group fled.

But young people were increasingly uninterested in the kind of white bread entertainment that conservative groups were promoting. The surprising success of Ted Demme and FAB 5 FREDDY's MTV all-rap video show, *Yo! MTV Raps,* in 1988 made African American, Chicano, and Latinx urban style instantly accessible to millions of youths. Even though MTV banned NWA's "Straight Outta Compton" video two months after the record's release, the album became an undeniable cultural phenomenon. FAB 5 FREDDY bucked upper management and brought his *Yo! MTV Raps* crew to tour with NWA through the streets of Compton.

"That's how we sold two million," Bryan Turner, the head of NWA's record label, says. "The white kids in the Valley picked it up and they decided they wanted to live vicariously through this music. Kids were just waiting for it."

Like a hurricane that had gathered energy over hot open waters before heading inland, *Straight Outta Compton* hit American popular culture with the same force with which the Sex Pistols' punk album *Never Mind the Bollocks* had hit the UK eleven years earlier. Hip-hop critic Billy Jam says, "Like the Sex Pistols, NWA made it look easy, inspiring a Do-It-Yourself movement for anyone from the streets to crank out gangsta rap tapes." All one had to have was a pen and a pad of paper, a mic, a mixer, and a sampler. Thousands of kids labored over their raps in their dark bedrooms, then stepped onto the streets to learn firsthand the vagaries of hustling and distribution—all just so that people could hear their stories.

"We're born and raised in Compton!" NWA bellowed. After *Straight Outta Compton,* it really was all about where you were from. The gangsta rappers were more right than they ever knew. Where you were from was exactly the story.

LOOP 3

1991–

1997

11
City on Fire

In 1991, two videos changed the course of a generation. Rap songs had long been exposing untold stories of violence against Black people, but these two videos suddenly made the horror of it inescapable for all.

After midnight on Sunday, March 3, Rodney King was beaten by five police officers at the entrance to Hansen Dam Park in Lakeview Terrace. He had led police on a chase in his battered old Hyundai before stopping there.

After a hard week of work, he had been unwinding on a Sunday, drinking malt liquor and watching a basketball game with friends. By midnight, he was drunk and behind the wheel, being chased down the highway by a police car, pushing the limits of what his Hyundai could take, terrified of being sent back to prison. His carmates were yelling at him to pull over.

In the video, King is a shadow in the middle of a uniformed cipher of policemen. He is lit by sirens, headlamps, and a helicopter searchlight. He is a dark mass being tossed and rolled by flashing batons for a minute and a half. By the time he had whimpered, "Please stop," and was hog-tied, he had suffered fifty-six baton blows and shoe stomps and kicks to the head and body. Within twenty-four hours, the video was being broadcast nationwide.

Two weekends later, on the morning of March 16, Latasha Harlins was shot dead by Korean American storekeeper Soon Ja Du at the Empire Liquor Market Deli at 9127 South Figueroa in South Los Angeles. Harlins had been orphaned when her mother was shot to death when she was nine. When her mother's killer got off with a light sentence, she decided she wanted to become a lawyer. She had sprouted to a slender five foot five, and though she was now having difficulties fighting with other girls in her ninth-grade year, her aunt and grandmother doted on her.

Harlins had spent the evening at a friend's place, and as she walked back home, she decided to purchase a bottle of orange juice for breakfast. She put it in her backpack and went to the counter to pay for it. Du grabbed Harlins's sweater and screamed, "You b---h, you are trying to steal my orange juice! That's my orange juice!" Harlins yelled back, "B---h, let me go! I'm trying to pay for it."

In the video, the two are pulling on the bottle of orange juice. Harlins swings at Du a few times and then backs away. The bottle falls to the floor. Du picks up a stool and throws it over the counter at Harlins. The girl ducks and reaches down to pick up the bottle. She places the bottle on the counter. Du swipes it away. She has unholstered the gun. Harlins pivots to step away. Du has raised the gun. Harlins shudders and falls out of the frame. All of this happens in under a minute.

This video, too, became a media sensation. Black and Korean American civil rights leaders pleaded for their communities not to overreact. But before too long, events had slipped far beyond their grasp.

Protests at the liquor store began. Danny Bakewell, leader of South Los Angeles civil rights organization the Brotherhood Crusade, told the press that Blacks were tired of Koreans who would not hire community members, and who took money out of the community. Liquor stores were poor substitutes for real grocery stores. Since the 1965 Watts rebellion, very few supermarkets had reopened, and even fewer were built in the area. Vons had three hundred stores in the region, but only two in South Los Angeles.[1] Worse, study after study found that supermarkets in South Los Angeles were the most expensive in the county, with grocery prices up to 30 percent higher than those in the suburbs.[2] Politicians would not do anything about it, as if they figured liquor was more important to inner-city residents than food. Immigrant liquor-store entrepreneurs did not provide what people really needed, but they filled a void that no one else was willing to.

To K.W. Lee, the pioneering Asian American journalist and the publisher of the *Korea Times*, the mainstream media—which by now was broadcasting the Harlins videotape as often as the King videotape—was manufacturing a "race war in which Korean American newcomers were singled out for destruction as a convenient scapegoat for the structural and racial injustices that had long afflicted the inner city of Los Angeles."

The Bush recession hit Los Angeles hard in 1991. Over 300,000 jobs were lost. And now years of efforts to improve African American and Korean American relations had been crushed under a news cycle that Lee said found a "win-win-win formula of race, crime, and violence."[3]

Amid these tensions, Ice Cube was finishing his second solo album, *Death Certificate*.

Death Side/Life Side

Ice Cube had left NWA two years before, believing Eazy-E's manager Jerry Heller was shorting them hundreds of thousands of dollars from the group's album sales and concert revenues. He had gone to New York City, linked up with Public Enemy, and made an album with the Bomb Squad, *Amerikkka's Most Wanted*. He had begun studying with members of the Nation of Islam. He had started an acting career with a star turn in John Singleton's powerful movie, *Boyz N the Hood*. His music seemed more political than ever. Cube was becoming one of those five thousand leaders Chuck D had wanted to create.

Death Certificate would come out in the tense months leading up to the Los Angeles riots. On the cover of the album, Ice Cube stood next to a white body on a coroner's gurney, covered with a flag, with a tag reading "Uncle Sam" hanging from its toe. The album's "Death Side" would be "a mirror image of where we are today." The "Life Side" would be "a vision of where we need to go."

On the Death Side, he tried to speak to where he thought young Blacks stood in a racist America. On "A Bird in the Hand," Cube played a young man surveying the lack of job opportunities in his community: "Do I gotta sell me a whole lotta crack for decent shelter and clothes on my back? Or should I just wait for help from Bush or Jesse Jackson and Operation PUSH?"

On "Alive on Arrival," the low-level pusher of "A Bird in the Hand" is shot on a street corner while trying to make a sale. At King-Drew Hospital, the emergency ward is as crowded as the county jail dayroom, and although he is bleeding buckets, he attracts more attention from LAPD than the MDs. "I don't bang, I rock the good rhymes," he protests once again, before adding ironically, "and I'm a victim of neighborhood crime." The character dies while waiting in vain for treatment.

On the Life Side, Cube revisited the same themes with more political critiques. "I Wanna Kill Sam," written in the context of the

Persian Gulf War, ripped into military recruiting by comparing the United States to a slavemaster. "Us" chastises the Black community for its disunity, materialism, violence, indolence, and indulgence. On "No Vaseline," he unleashed a vicious diss of NWA, insulting them for allowing themselves to be exploited by Jerry Heller. Cube rapped, "It's a case of divide and conquer / Cause you let a Jew break up my crew." In the next verse, he upped the ante: "Get rid of that devil real simple / Put a bullet in his temple."

In "Black Korea," Cube revisits the scene from Spike Lee's *Do the Right Thing* where Korean American shopkeeper Sonny saves his store from being burned by arguing he, too, is Black. Cube's "Black Korea" focuses instead on the confrontation. As the music bursts forth, he addresses two prejudiced, "Oriental, one penny counting," proprietors who hawk him as he walks through their store. At the song's bridge, the shop erupts into argument as his friends raise their voices in his support.

By now, the original scene has been stripped of its humor, leaving only the raw racial conflict. Then the bass surges back and the song rushes to its conclusion. Cube issues a threat: "Don't follow me up and down your crazy little market, or your little chop-suey ass will be the target of a nationwide boycott." In a final defiant gesture, he raises the prospect of a racially vengeful conflagration: "Pay respect to the Black fist," he yells, "or we'll burn your store right down to a crisp! And then we'll see ya, 'cause you can't turn the ghetto into Black Korea." The storeowner, Sonny, has the last word: "Mother fuck *you*!" Like the Harlins video, all this happens in under a minute.

For "Colorblind," a song about gang-banging, Cube brought in a crew of rappers—WC, Coolio, Kam, Threat, and King Tee—who had lived the life. "Killa Cali, the state where they kill over colors, 'cause brothers don't know the deal," Threat rapped. "But every n---a on my block *can't* stop and he *won't* stop and he *don't* stop." The lyric was taken directly from the Crips motto: *can't stop won't stop*.

Cube assumed that one had to be tougher than tough to survive, that life itself was a front. But for all of the problems with his view—its dismissal of history, its victimization of women, Korean Americans, and gays, its me-against-the-world enemy-making—perhaps in that moment, Cube just could not imagine a world truer than that slice of Crip wisdom.

The Real Stakes

From the moment it was released on October 31, 1991, eight months after the release of the King video and Harlins video, no hip-hop album had ever been as controversial as *Death Certificate.* Hip-hop heads loved it. Mainstream critics hated it. Then *Billboard,* the music industry's bible, called for record store chains to boycott the record. Editor Timothy White wrote, "His unabashed espousal of violence against Koreans, Jews, and other whites crosses the line that divides art from the advocacy of crime."[4] *Death Certificate* remains the only album ever singled out for such condemnation in *Billboard* history.

James Bernard, senior editor of *The Source,* defended the rapper: "Yes, Ice Cube is very angry, and he expresses that anger in harsh, blunt, and unmistakable terms. But the source of his rage is very real. Many in the Black community, particularly Los Angeles, Cube's home, feel as if it's open season on Blacks with the Rodney King assault and the recent murder of a young Black girl by a Korean merchant."[5] Bernard and other African American fans understood the battle rhymes of "No Vaseline" and the fiery conclusion of "Black Korea" as just words, not literal calls to violence.

Ice Cube remarked that the song was:

> inspired by everyday life in the Black community with the Koreans. Blacks don't like them and it's vice versa. The Koreans have a lot of businesses in the Black community. The [Harlins] shooting is just proof of the problem, just another example of their disrespect for Black people. You go in their stores and they think you're going to steal something. They follow you around the store like you're a criminal. They say, "Buy something or get out." If it hasn't happened to you, you can't know how bad it feels for somebody to make you feel like a criminal when you're in their store and you haven't done anything.[6]

Dong Suh, a hip-hop generation son of a Korean American storeowner, penned an editorial for *Asian Week* hoping, he said, to "move away from the issue of censorship and the stereotyping of rap as violent and move toward addressing the core problem." He wrote:

> Several years ago, a prominent radio personality in Philadelphia, where my family operates a small corner store in a predominantly African-American neighborhood, expressed a similar sentiment. I clearly remember his warning that if Koreans did not respect Blacks, firebombings were likely . . . When compared to Korean Americans, African Americans are a numerical and political majority. Ice Cube does not realize that as a member of the majority, he wields real power against Koreans.[7]

The Target of a Nationwide Boycott

Upon its release, *Death Certificate* had advance orders of over a million copies, making it an instant hit. But it was greeted with boycotts from the Simon Wiesenthal Center and a group of civil rights organizations that included the Korean American Coalition, the Japanese American Citizens League, the Los Angeles Urban League, the NAACP, the Mexican American Legal Defense and Educational Fund, and the Southern Christian Leadership Conference. Guardian Angels began pickets in New York and Los Angeles at record stores. Korean swap-meet vendors and the Camelot Music chain also joined the boycott.[8]

The Korean American Grocers Organization (KAGRO) forced a boycott as well—refusing to sell bottles of the St. Ides malt liquor that Ice Cube had endorsed. At its peak, over five thousand stores across the country honored the boycott.[9] Ice Cube met with the KAGRO leaders. He apologized to the merchants and pledged to discourage violence against store owners and to continue "working to bring our communities closer together." In a follow-up letter to them, he wrote of the meeting:

> I explained some of the feelings and attitudes of Black people today, and the problems and frustrations that we confront. And I clarified the intent of my album *Death Certificate.* It was not intended to offend anyone or to incite violence of any kind. It was not directed at all Korean Americans or at all Korean American store owners. I respect Korean Americans. It was directed at a few stores where

> my friends and I have had actual problems. Working together we can help solve these problems and build a bridge between our communities.[10]

After their meeting, KAGRO leaders conceded that Ice Cube's critique was legitimate and expressed hope that Blacks and Koreans would "help each other and learn to understand each other's cultures."[11]

In the meantime, Soon Ja Du had been convicted of voluntary manslaughter in the killing of Latasha Harlins. On November 15, Judge Joyce Karlin sentenced Soon Ja Du to a mere five years of probation. As she read her judgment, she went out of her way to lecture the African American community. "This is not a time for revenge, she said, "and it is not my job as a sentencing court to seek revenge for those who demand it."[12] The African American community reacted with horror. Nobody had been asking for revenge, only justice for Latasha.

In South Los Angeles—where there were already three times the number of liquor stores as in the entire state of Rhode Island—community activists began to talk about a campaign to close liquor stores. African American, Latinx, and Asian American community leaders met behind closed doors to find common ground. But the trial of the four police officers who had beaten Rodney King was about to get underway in the 80 percent white community of Simi Valley, more than sixty miles to the north. There was a sense that some kind of disaster lay ahead.

The Truce

But before the verdict came down, peacemakers in Los Angeles were working on a historic effort. In 1990, gang wars had left 690 dead, setting yet another tragic record. The new year brought a new sense of urgency with the King and Harlins videos. For decades, peacemakers had struggled to establish agreements between gangs and had been hobbled by the enormity of the problem. But with hip-hop's cultural ferment, the efforts of social workers, the Nation of Islam, and elders like former football star Jim Brown, and the leadership of an extraordinary group of young gang members, peacemaking efforts were finally moving forward.

The center of the peacemaking efforts was the same place

where, twenty-five years before, a cultural renaissance had been launched—the city of Watts.

Edwin Markham Intermediate School was located in the dead center of the city. The kids in the neighborhood called it "Gladiator School." At Markham, youths underwent their rites of passage into ganghood. Their friends, neighbors, and relatives came from all the city's feuding sets—Bloods in the housing projects to the west, Crips in the projects to the east—and some rivalries went back a generation.

"All of the factions went to that school," says Aqeela Sherrills, who grew up with his older brother, Daude, in the Jordan Downs projects. "In '78, one of the brothers from my neighborhood got killed up there by a brother from Nickerson Gardens. And that started the war. So when I got there in '81, it was scary."

In 1984, when Aqeela was in the ninth grade, he and his homies got into a fight with kids from Nickerson Gardens. Later that afternoon, as they sat on the track and field bleachers, their rivals came back with guns and shot his best friend in the head. Boys who had played with each other in athletic leagues just a few years before were now deadly enemies, handed a cold destiny by history and geography.

But by 1990, the Sherrills had noticed that Nation of Islam Minister Louis Farrakhan had launched a "Stop the Killing" campaign. They joined the gang peace movement. At the gym in Nickerson Gardens, the peacemakers put up a new mural, entitled "Crossfire (The First Word on Peace)," a memorial to the dozens of residents who had been killed in gang warfare. The words on the wall read, "Keep the future alive," and "Nobody can stop this war but us."[13]

In the projects, fascination slowly replaced fear. By March 1992, a year after the Rodney King beating, the peace meetings had reached critical mass. "Instead of eight brothers in there, it was damn near fifty brothers, then a hundred brothers in there," Daude Sherrills says.

"Young men expressed their anger and pain but also expressed that they would try to communicate," Twilight Bey, a Blood organizer of the meetings, said. "We were asked questions that weren't ever asked before: What are we going to do to change our situation? Do we have the power? . . . Do we have any say on what happens in the political arena? What does it take to change things?"[14]

By April, Daude says, "It was time."

They found a template for a peace treaty in the library of USC's Von Kleinsmid Center for International and Public Affairs—the 1949 United Nations cease-fire agreement that had temporarily ended hostilities between Egypt and Israel. They called it the "Multi-Peace Treaty," the document called for "the return to permanent peace in Watts, California" and "the return of Black businesses, economic development and advancement of educational programs.

"The establishment of a cease-fire between the community representatives of all parties is accepted as a necessary step toward the renewal of peace in Watts, California," it read. "The right of each party to its security and freedom from fear of attack by each other shall be fully respected."[15]

Daude Sherrills added a United Black Community Code, a code of conduct for gang members. It began, "I accept the duty to honor, uphold and defend the spirit of the red, blue and purple, to teach the Black family its legacy and protracted struggle for freedom and justice."[16] It warned against alcohol and drug abuse and use of the "N-word and B-word," and even laid down rules of etiquette for flagging and sign-throwing.[17] It called for literacy, school attendance, and voter registration programs, and for community investment.

The truce leaders agreed to endorse it and to take a message back to their respective neighborhoods. On April 26, 1992, three days before the Rodney King verdict, the truce was officially in effect. Joyous celebrations broke out. Two days later, the party moved to Nickerson Gardens. Blue, red, and purple rags were tied together. Generations celebrated. It was like a family reunion. The war was over.

Sets came from all over town to the parties, often expressing disbelief that a peace was actually on. "All the neighborhoods started saying, man, if Watts can do it, we can do it," says Daude. "You had brothers from Compton, brothers from South Central. We had rivals coming in, we was negotiating cease-fires with *their* rivals, right inside the housing project developments."

But for the peace to last, it would take more than talk. There would need to be jobs, services, and support. So on April 28, as the party went down at Nickerson Gardens, the peacemakers marched with two hundred fifty Crips and Bloods from seven different neighborhoods to City Hall to announce the truce at a Los Angeles City Council meeting.

"We made a presentation to the City Council, telling them that we was coming together to bring an end to all the violence in the 'hood," says Aqeela. "We told them we would like to have access to funding."

But Council members didn't exactly jump out of their chairs. One suggested applying for a five-hundred-dollar grant. Aqeela recalls, "And they were like, 'Thank you very much,' and ushered us out of there as quickly as they possibly could."

The next afternoon, the peace party came back to the Sherills' home place, Jordan Downs. The courtyard was full and the music was bumping when the verdicts were announced.

Show Them How We Feel

At 3:15 P.M. on Wednesday, April 29, 1992, ten "not guilty" verdicts were read at the Simi Valley Courthouse. Three of the four policemen who had beaten Rodney King had been completely acquitted. The fourth, Lawrence Powell, was freed as well when the jury deadlocked on a charge of excessive force. In the case of Rodney King, as in so many other cases of police brutality against African Americans, there would be no justice.

Thirty miles to the southeast, near the intersection of Florence and Normandie in South Central, the young men debated what to do. At 4 P.M., five youths hit Pay-Less Liquor and Deli on Florence and Dalton, and grabbed bottles of 8-Ball. When the Korean American owner's son, David Lee, blocked the entrance, one of the kids smashed him on the head with a bottle. "This is for Rodney King!" they shouted, and ran into the street.

Down the block on Florence and Normandie, some started taking baseball bats to passing car windows. As cop cruisers screeched into the intersection, their cars were pelted with rocks. Two policemen chased a sixteen-year-old rock-thrower down an alley, pulled him down off a chain-link fence, and hog-tied him as he screamed "I can't breathe!" More than two dozen cops arrived, and they made two more arrests.

But the mass at Florence and Normandie Streets had lost its fear.

In the 1970s the chant had been, "It's Nation time!" Now the streets filled with the cry: "It's Uzi time! Cops gonna die tonight!"[18] At a quarter to six, on orders of Lieutenant Mike Moulin, the police unit retreated with the three arrestees to a command post farther north, at 54th and Arlington. They were abandoning the city.

Despite the growing reports of unrest, Police Chief Daryl Gates left his command post and headed out to the posh Westside. A mayor's commission had already found a pattern of racism in the police department and proposed he be replaced. Instead of reacting to the growing unrest, Gates was going to a political fundraiser that he hoped would secure his legacy. His motorcade sped down the Santa Monica Highway past the First African Methodist Episcopal Church.

Thousands were jammed into the church. On the dais, Mayor Tom Bradley, City Council members, church and community leaders, and Rodney King's mother exhorted people to keep calm and express their anger through the political system. "Operation Cool Response" was underway. But outside, angry young men and women weren't having it.

"We ain't gon' turn another cheek so they can come and kick us in the ass," one man told filmmaker Matthew McDaniels, whose footage Dr. Dre would end up using on *The Chronic*. "We gotta *do shit*!"[19]

Soon the streets were jammed: boys slow-rolling in their rides blasting "Fuck Tha Police," flash mobs of young girls shouting, "No more Simi Valley!" In West Hollywood, lesbian and gay activists marched toward Sunset Boulevard. Near UCLA, student demonstrators poured down Westwood Boulevard. And from the site of the Rodney King beating, hundreds marched to the LAPD Foothill Division headquarters, all echoing the same cry across the city: "No justice, no peace!"

Downtown, at the police headquarters called Parker Center, political protestors gathered to denounce the verdicts. Michael Zinzun, one of the city's leading activists against police brutality, told a reporter, "This community has got to realize that an unstable Black community means an unstable LA."[20]

When night fell, the activists were replaced by young men who set American flags and a parking kiosk afire and tried to storm the glass entrance before being repelled by the police. They moved into downtown, overturning police cars and setting them on fire. They threw rocks at the *Los Angeles Times* building.

At 10 P.M., nearly fifty fires burned.[21] Rioting had spread to Long Beach, Baldwin Hills, Inglewood, Pasadena, and Hollywood. Gates returned from the fundraiser, but rather than take control, he demanded a helicopter tour of the city. "He took something like an hour-and-a-half ride and never issued any instructions as far as I could determine," said William Webster, a former FBI director who would be appointed to lead an investigation into LAPD's response to the riots. "So he is just up there watching Rome burn."[22]

By midnight on April 29, the riots had taken fourteen lives. Three new fires were being reported every minute. Governor Pete Wilson had declared a state of emergency and Mayor Tom Bradley established a dusk-to-dawn curfew.

Eighteen hundred officers had reached the command post. But most were standing around awaiting instructions. The few deployments in the field were mostly placed at the edge of the inner city.[23] The neighborhoods where people of color lived had been abandoned.

Paying the Price

At dawn on Thursday, April 30, the writing on the wall read: "MEXICANS & CRIPS & BLOODS TOGETHER TONITE 4-30-92."

Looters hit the streets. Many were getting essentials—diapers, canned goods, milk, butter, and guns. "I felt some shame," said one Salvadoran refugee. "But I thought, if we don't take the food now, what will we give our children to eat? When will we be able to buy food again?"[24] Some got a lot more—shoes, clothes, toys, tires, videos, stereos, and beds.

When they were done, the arsonists moved in. They burned ice cream shops and fast food franchises, glassmakers and camera vendors, flea markets and hair salons, one-hour photos and next-day dry cleaners, check cashers, churches, and cultural centers; businesses that sold sheepskins, pagers, and lingerie; the offices of dentists, chiropractors, and acupuncturists. They torched Mobil, Union, Arco, Bank of America, The Boys' Supermarkets, and the Slauson Swap Meet.

All night, Korean Americans tuned in to Radio Korea, whose announcers were broadcasting street-by-street reports of Korean-owned businesses that were being looted or burned. They called out over the air: *Bring all your guns. The looters and arsonists are coming to Koreatown.*

Eighteen-year-old Edward Song Lee, James Kang, and two other close friends had gone to Koreatown to save their families' businesses. All day, they had fired warning shots at looters who drove into the neighborhood to scope the pickings. After dark, they heard a call on Radio Korea about looters on the roof of a restaurant on Third Street. They got into their cars and headed over.

As it turned out, the call was false. Radio Korea was being flooded with calls by stay-at-home storeowners who hoped the young men would protect their businesses. As they reached the restaurant, Lee's friend in the lead car fired a warning shot in the air. The men on the roof loosed a barrage of bullets. They were, in fact, also Korean Americans who had come to protect the businesses.

When the shooting ended, Kang was wounded. Another friend, Sam Lee, came and pulled Kang and two of his fellow passengers out of the car. Eddie Lee lay on the pavement, his white shirt stained red shoulder-to-shoulder, neck-to-stomach, and died. "I still can't forgive for this," Kang said later. "It didn't need to happen this way."[25]

Federal agents rode shotgun with police as they swept through the 'hoods looking for stolen merchandise. When stupefied residents could not produce receipts for anything in their apartment that looked new, the object—a bed, a television, a bicycle—was confiscated. One activist called it "reverse looting."[26]

The media had portrayed the riots as a Black thing. But the uprising was multiracial. Between April 29 and May 4, 37 percent of the nearly ten thousand arrestees, more than any other racial group, were Latinx.[27]

On the streets, white reporter Linda Mour from KABC-TV's Channel 7 had tried vainly to find looters who would agree to be interviewed. When she returned to the studio, she was asked by the studio anchor Harold Greene, "Did you get the impression that a lot of those people were illegal aliens?" Mour answered, "Yes."[28]

She had given police and politicians a new target: "illegal aliens." By May 2, images of burning buildings had been replaced by images of Latinx people facedown on the pavement in mass arrests—including pregnant women and mothers with their confused toddlers at their sides. A thousand Immigration and Border Patrol agents set up command posts in Pico-Union and MacArthur Park.[29]

The LAPD and the Sheriff's office turned over 1,500 immigrants to the feds for deportation proceedings. At least seven hundred were deported. One desperate mother was certain her developmentally disabled fourteen-year-old girl had been picked up by the INS and bused to Mexico.[30] Later, President George H.W. Bush took credit for the deportations, claiming that a third of the first six thousand arrested were "illegal aliens," a number that has never been substantiated.

One rap group from the Eastside had predicted this chaos. A trio of rappers from the Southgate neighborhood near Watts—Italian American Lawrence "DJ Muggs" Muggerud, Cuban American rapper Senen "Sen Dog" Reyes, and Cuban/Mexican American rapper Louis "B-Real" Freese—named themselves after an imaginary piece of real estate they called Cypress Hill. Their 1991 self-titled debut album had opened on Pico Boulevard west of downtown, in the heart of the Central American and Mexican neighborhoods of Westlake and Pico-Union, with a seething anti-police rap over a steamy blues beat.

Their sonic world was meant to stand in for the real Los Angeles: an inner city from which whites had fled, where English was broken, jobs were endangered, paranoia was palpable, and the most advanced technology was in the killing hands of the cops. But Los Angeles's real hills would never be taken, as the rioters would learn. In "How I Could Just Kill a Man," B-Real rapped,

> When you're up on your hill in your big home
> I'm out here risking my dome
> Just for a bucket or a fast ducat just to stay alive

It was as if he were staring up and waving his fist at the 'hoods that the riots would never scar.

Two Speeches

By Friday, May 1, the National Guard had posted tanks at the entrances to Westwood Village, a wealthy neighborhood near UCLA.

Dozens of Black businesses and all but two supermarkets in Compton had been burned to the ground. Korean American–owned businesses had suffered nearly $400 million of the estimated $1 billion in total property damages.[31] When it was all over, 2,383 would be wounded and 53 would be dead, most by gunfire.

Rodney King believed he should make some public statement. After the verdicts were read on April 29, Rodney King had returned home, and as the images of fires and the smiling faces of acquitted cops repeated in an endless loop, King had locked himself in his bedroom and raged at his television. "Why? Why? Why? Why?" he screamed. "Why are they beating me again?"[32]

On May 1, his lawyer finally agreed to let King speak. King was still badly bruised, and looked bewildered, broken, and unbearably sad, once again a tragic symbol of a broken city. King's voice was shaky and unstable, as if he could not close all the thoughts chasing around in his head. Poignantly, he stammered out a statement that felt more like a question, "Please, we can—we can all get along. We, we all can get along."

Later that evening, in a national address, President Bush told LA residents what they already knew, that American firepower was on the ground in their city—including FBI SWAT teams, US Marshal riot control units, and the Border Patrol. He said, "What we saw last night and the night before in Los Angeles is not about civil rights. It's not about the great cause of equality that all Americans must uphold. It's not a message of protest. It's been the brutality of a mob, pure and simple. And let me assure you, I will use whatever force is necessary to restore order."

Some had called it an uprising, others a rebellion. The official term was "civil disturbance." Korean Americans simply called it by the date it had begun: 4-2-9, *Sa-I-Gu*. Whatever the name, these days of outrage marked the hip-hop generation's passage through fire.

After this, there would be a national backlash.

12
New Wars

But first there were the parties. With calm restored to the streets, spontaneous celebrations broke out from Lynwood to Watts, South Central to Compton, Willowbrook to Inglewood, as rival gang sets tied their colors together, fired up the barbecues, and broke bread. Parks that had once been exclusive turf were thrown open. Public spaces were public once again. The rapper Kam summed up the vibe in his epochal single, "Peace Treaty," its hydraulic "Atomic Dog" bassline pumping a giddy joy:

I'ma always remember this
Because my n---as made the history books
And now the mystery looks a lot clearer
The man in the mirror's got power
It's now or never
More than ever
Black people got to stick together

For Los Angeles's war-weary youths, the gang truce and the uprising unleashed a burst of creative energy. Rappers like DJ Quik, Compton's Most Wanted, and Above The Law were making noise on the national charts. From the fiercely competitive freestyle ciphers at the Good Life Café on the Westside to the intergenerational ferment of spoken word, free jazz, and hip-hop in Leimert Park to the free-floating parties at the Pharcyde Manor in Hancock Park, an underground was taking shape. At the Hip-Hop Shop on Melrose, b-boys and b-girls gathered to advance the elements. Graffiti writers were engaged in a golden age of style wars. Street fashion labels like Fuct and Con Art were exploding. Grassroots zines like *URB* and *Rap Sheet* articulated a new West Coast aesthetic.

In the streets, gang members turned their attention to creating a future for themselves and their city. But they found resistance from the power brokers and the police.

In May, local leaders vowed to get corporations to invest more than $1 billion in the city through an organization called Rebuild LA.[1] But by any measure, the organization was a complete failure. Only half of the thirty-two supermarkets that the organization had been promised were actually built.

At the same time Rebuild LA was announced, an alternative proposal to rebuild Los Angeles, purported to come from the Bloods and Crips, was circulating. Among other things, the $3.7 billion plan called for three new hospitals and forty additional health care centers to be built and the replacement of welfare programs with manufacturing plants. It demanded increased lighting of city streets, $20 million in business loans and community job creation, new books and accelerated learning programs for inner-city schools, and community policing that incorporated former gang members. "Give us the hammer and the nails," the document read, "and we will rebuild the city."

Gang members met with the Korean American Grocers Organization, who got the point, but could only promise a handful of jobs. That was a path Ice-T had already known to be useless. "They aimed at Korean people because they felt Koreans were one step above them, so that's the closest step to the system," he wrote of the looters and arsonists in *The Ice Opinion.* "They didn't know the Koreans are just as broke as them."[2]

At the corner of Florence and Normandie, three of the four corners remained burned down. Tom's Liquors was the only building that remained. Behind it, one billboard advertised the television talent show *Star Search.* The other read: "Looking for a new career? Join your LAPD. Earn $34,000 to $43,000."[3]

"Economics plays a major role in maintaining the peace," one former gang leader told a reporter. "If we had industry and venture capital, we wouldn't have all the drug selling and robbing that's going on. Economics is the key to everything."[4]

So against all odds, the gang truce held in Watts and spread. In the weeks after the uprising, gang homicide tallies plunged, and stayed there. Deputy Chief Matthew Hunt, the police commander of the South Los Angeles area, told the Police Commission, "There's no question the amount of violent crime has decreased. People in the community say they haven't heard a shot fired in weeks. They are elated."[5]

But other police were skeptical. "I'm concerned as to the true motives of the gang members as to why they would make peace," one policeman said. "Is it so they can better fight with us, so they can better deal dope or so they can better be constructive in their neighborhoods? That would be the last item I would choose because gang members have a thug mentality."[6]

Outgoing Chief Daryl Gates said on CNN, "You know, I'd love to see peace in the city, peace among gangs," he said. "But I just don't think it's going to happen. These people simply don't have it in them, I don't believe, to create peace among the gangs or in any other way."[7]

It had become clear to peacemakers that LAPD was out to disrupt and harass peacemakers. In Compton, Congresswoman Maxine Waters and City Councilman Mark Ridley-Thomas intervened to stop police who were harassing gang members leaving a peace meeting. At Imperial Courts, police helicopters and riot squadrons swooped in to break up truce barbecues. When they did the same thing at Jordan Downs, residents and gang members sent thirty police officers to the hospital.

With this clash as a pretext, LAPD created a special "crime suppression task force," transferring forty police officers from the San Fernando Valley and the Westside to the South Bureau.[8] The FBI beefed up its Los Angeles office with twenty-six additional agents.

Author Luis Rodriguez and peacemakers Cle "Bone" Sloan, from the Athens Park Bloods, and Kershaun "Lil Monster" Scott, from the Eight-Tray Gangster Crips, wrote in the *Los Angeles Times* that "The Los Angeles Police Department told the media that the gangs were going to turn on police officers, even ambush them. Yet no police officer in South Central has been killed or severely hurt since April 29, the day the King-beating verdict came down."[9]

"Now that we're chilling, they want to attack us," Scott said in an interview. "Isn't that ironic?"

The War on Youth

The War on Gangs was a prelude for a larger crackdown on youth in general.

From the beginnings of the juvenile justice system in America, a central doctrine had been that young people were capable of redemption, and the juvenile justice system was there to rehabilitate troubled youths. But by the late 1980s a reversal had begun. The attitude that young people were no longer worth redeeming began to spread. After the riots, the trend to clamp down on young people accelerated.

Forty-eight states made their juvenile crime statutes more punitive. Forty-one states made it easier for prosecutors to try juveniles as young as twelve as adults. Some states began to consider the death penalty for juveniles as young as thirteen. Across the country, cities passed sweep laws—anti-loitering laws, anti-cruising laws, and curfews—meant to strictly regulate when, where, and how young people could gather. Now teens were too young to hang out, but too old to save.

There was one reason why. Sociologist Mike Males explained:

> The Census Bureau reports that 80 percent of America's adults over age 40 are whites of European origin (Euro-white). Thirty-five percent of children and youths under age 18 are nonwhite or of Hispanic (Latino) origin, a proportion that has doubled since 1970. In most of America's big cities, white elders govern nonwhite kids. In California, two-thirds of the elders are Euro-white; three-fifths of the youths are nonwhite or Latino.[10]

The Los Angeles Uprising had clarified the gap in a dramatic, unavoidable way, fanning fears among some older whites of a browning nation and unleashing a huge backlash. The War on Gangs quickly expanded into what young activists came to call "the War on Youth."

Gang-related offenses received enhanced punishments, and new categories of gang crimes were created. Gang databases grew. But these databases often identified "suspects" before any crime had been committed. Many youths were added by virtue of an arrest, whether or not they had been charged. Others merely fit a "gang profile." By 1999, wearing baggy jeans and being related to a gang suspect was enough to meet the definition of being a "gang member" in at least five states.

In Orange County, California, where less than half of young people were of color, 92 percent of those listed in the gang database were of color, primarily Latinx and Asian. In suburban Aurora, Colorado, any two of the following could still constitute gang membership to the local police: "slang," "clothing of a particular color," "pagers," "hairstyles," or "jewelry." Nearly 80 percent of Aurora's list was African American. One activist said, "They might as well call it a Black list."

The databases coincided with the rise of sweep laws. Cruising bans had come after a decade of street scenes—boulevards and neighborhoods where young people's cruising and partying overtook local traffic on Friday and Saturday nights. In Los Angeles, cruising bans ended street scenes in East Los Angeles, Westwood, and Crenshaw Boulevard. In Atlanta, outcry from white homeowners over the city's annual Freaknik event in 1996 resulted in a cruising ban that shut down one of the nation's biggest Black collegiate gatherings.

Between 1988 and 1997, curfew arrests doubled nationwide. In California, they quadrupled. Curfew enforcement was not colorblind. In Ventura County, California, Latinx and Black youths were arrested at more than seven times the rate of whites. In New Orleans, Blacks were arrested at nineteen times the rate of whites.

What united these new sweep laws was the idea of erasing youths—particularly youths of color—from public space. Not only were there to be no more boom boxes, sagging jeans, street dancing, or public displays of affection, there were to be *no more young people.*

The racial effects of all these sweep laws were clear. While white youths made up 79 percent of national juvenile arrests, 62 percent of youths in juvenile detention facilities were of color. Even when charged with the same offense, Latinx people and Native Americans were 2.5 times more likely to end up in custody than whites. Black youths were five times more likely to be detained.[11] Critics compared them to Jim Crow laws.

The racial and generational backlash moved next to the ballot box. In 1993, the state of Washington passed the first "three strikes" initiative in the country, establishing life without parole for convicts with three violent felony offenses. The following year, California voters passed Proposition 184, a much harsher three-strikes law.[12] The effect was to imprison thousands in life sentences for nonviolent crimes.[13]

They also passed Proposition 187, an initiative to ban all government services to undocumented immigrants, like health care, social services, and education. Playing up the image of young Latinx looters, they claimed the "Save Our State" initiative would end incentives for "illegal aliens" to immigrate. Instead, the initiative would have denied basic human services to thousands and bounced many children from the public schools. Although the measure passed, it was never implemented, and was finally ruled unconstitutional.

In 1996, California voters passed an initiative that overturned affirmative action. When the ban took effect, the number of Blacks and Latinx people admitted to the University of California dropped by 10 percent. By the end of the decade, the Justice Policy Institute estimated that nearly fifty thousand Black males were in California prisons, while sixty thousand were in California universities. Across the country, eight hundred thousand Black men were in prison, while six hundred thousand were in college.[14]

On *Amerikkka's Most Wanted,* Ice Cube had asked, "Why more n---as in the pen than in college?" Harvard criminologist James Q. Wilson offered a crackpot story that fanned the fears that motivated older white voters:

> Meanwhile, just beyond the horizon, there lurks a cloud that the winds will soon bring over us. The population will start getting younger again. By the end of this decade there will be a million more people between the ages of fourteen and seventeen than there are now . . . This extra million will be half male. Six percent of them will become high rate, repeat offenders—30,000 more young muggers, killers and thieves than we have now. Get ready.[15]

The answer to Cube's question was that voters seemed to want policing and prisons for youths of color more than educational opportunities.

Sister Souljah's declaration hardly seemed an exaggeration: "We are at war!"

The Culture War

In rap music, all the fears around race, generation, and pop culture came together.

In 1985, Tipper Gore—the wife of Tennessee Democratic Senator and future vice president Al Gore—and three other Washington wives launched the Parents Music Resource Center to censor what they thought were explicit lyrics. Gore's cause was born when she heard her daughter, Karenna, enjoying Prince's "Darling Nikki" in her bedroom. The PMRC successfully pressured the record industry to begin placing "Parental Advisory" stickers on potentially explicit records.

At first, "satanic" heavy metal artists drew most of the cultural conservatives' ire. But after NWA's brush with the FBI, Gore and the cultural conservatives turned their attention to rap music. In 1990, she wrote an editorial in the *Washington Post* ripping Ice-T for a rap from an album ironically subtitled *Freedom of Speech . . . Just Watch What You Say*: "Do we want [our kids] describing themselves or each other as 'n----rs'? Do we want our daughters to think of themselves as "b---hes" to be abused? Do we want our sons to measure success in gold guns hanging from thick neck chains?"[16]

A network of Christian fundamentalist groups sprung up to fight rap, pressing the Bush Administration and state and local politicians to ban rap groups like Miami's 2 Live Crew, Houston's Geto Boys, and Oakland's Too Short. Luther "Luke Skyywalker" Campbell, leader of the 2 Live Crew, wrote that "In the early days my music didn't stir anyone up because the audience was almost completely Black and urbanized. They heard my music for what it is. Humor."[17]

But now that hip-hop had crossed over to white audiences, Campbell wrote, "'Morality policemen' demand the right to direct what the rest of us should be allowed to see and hear. They are generally people with tiny, frightened minds who look out at the world through a combination of religious fervor, self-delusion, hypocrisy, suspicion, paranoia, and sheer ignorance. Unable to moralize their own lives, they only have time to moralize ours."[18]

Campbell's explicit music ran afoul of local Southern authorities, who arrested record store clerks and owners for selling 2 Live Crew records.[19] The campaign was led by Florida lawyer and failed political candidate Jack Thompson, who sent letters to dozens of sheriff's departments and politicians urging them to join the fight to ban rap records. "I think there is a cultural civil war going on," Thompson said.[20]

By 1990, Thompson's campaign against 2 Live Crew's *As Nasty as They Wanna Be* got the album banned in jurisdictions from

Broward County, Florida, to Ontario, Canada. After a performance in a Broward County nightclub, Luther Campbell and rapper Chris "Fresh Kid Ice" Wongwon were arrested on obscenity charges. The rock musician Frank Zappa, an early opponent of the PMRC, told *The Source* that "The whole racist aroma swinging from the metal aspect to the rap aspect is a bit suspicious. The devil stuff didn't work. The devil business only played in certain parts of the country."[21]

US Circuit Court judge Jose Gonzalez ruled 2 Live Crew's album obscene, a first in American pop music history, effectively banning sales of the record in some counties. Luther "Luke Skyywalker" Campbell, the leader of the crew, predicted that major label hip-hop acts would be the next target: "The censors will come after them when they finish with us."

Clinton vs. Souljah

His words proved prophetic. In the heat of the 1992 presidential campaign, hip-hop suddenly became a major campaign issue for both political parties. It gave a way for conservatives and Democratic candidate Bill Clinton to exploit racial and generational fears. He targeted Public Enemy member and Black youth activist Lisa "Sister Souljah" Williamson.

David Mills, a reporter who had been covering hip-hop, had asked her about Black violence against whites in the Los Angeles riots. He covered her answer word-for-word in his article:

> "I mean, if Black people kill Black people every day, why not have a week and kill white people? You understand what I'm saying? In other words, white people, this government, and that mayor were well aware of the fact that Black people were dying every day in Los Angeles under gang violence. So if you're a gang member and you would normally be killing somebody, why not kill a white person? Do you think that somebody thinks that white people are better, or above dying, when they would kill their own kind?"
>
> . . . "Unfortunately for white people, they think it's all right for our children to die, for our men to be in prison, and not theirs."[22]

Bill Clinton went to speak as a guest of Jesse Jackson at the Rainbow Coalition's political convention. The night before his talk,

Souljah had participated in the convention's youth panel. Clinton now read a selectively edited Souljah quote:

> Just listen to this, what she said: She told the *Washington Post* about a month ago, and I quote, 'If Black people kill Black people every day, why not have a week and kill white people? So if you're a gang member and you would normally be killing somebody, why not kill a white person?'
>
> I know she is a young person, but she has a big influence on a lot of people, and when people say that—if you took the words white and Black and you reversed them, you might think David Duke was giving that speech.[23]

Souljah blasted Clinton for taking her statements out of context. She had never advocated violence against whites, she said. Instead she was trying to describe the mindset of those who had committed those actions. Clinton, she said, was trying to make her "a campaign issue, a Black monster that would scare the white population."[24] Jackson and other Black leaders seethed at Clinton. "She represents the feelings and hopes of a whole generation of people," Jackson said. "She should receive an apology."[25]

But as *New York Times* writer Gwen Ifill wrote, "There is no question that the Clinton campaign is quite satisfied with the outcome of the Sister Souljah episode, and that it may become a blueprint for future risky missions to rescue the campaign's flagging fortunes."[26]

Hip-Hop vs. the World

The same week, the National Rifle Association and police organizations—which included many of the same people who had attacked NWA for "Fuck Tha Police"—called for a boycott of Time-Warner businesses over a song by Ice-T's Black heavy metal band, Body Count, called "Cop Killer."

"People who ride around all night and use crack cocaine and listen to rap music that talks about killing cops—it's bound to pump them up," the president of the Fraternal Order of Police said. "No matter what anybody tells you, this kind of music is dangerous."[27] However, they had no passion to protest Republican Arnold Schwarzenegger's cop-killing movie *The Terminator*.

Lost in the noise was a statement from the National Black Police

Association, which represented 35,000 Black cops, condemning the ban and the Time-Warner boycott. "This song is not a call for murder. It's a rap of protest. Ice-T isn't just making this stuff up," said Ronald Hampton, the Association's director. "There are no statistics to support the argument that a song can incite someone to violence."[28]

Why were white police organizations pushing so hard to attack "Cop Killer"? Across the country, calls for police reform had reached a deafening pitch since the March 1991 beating of Rodney King. Los Angeles had become a global symbol of American law enforcement's brutality against youths of color. Embattled police associations, it seemed, saw "Cop Killer" as an opportunity to change the narrative.

Just a few months after the Los Angeles riots, Charlton Heston stepped into the Time-Warner shareholders meeting and condemned Time-Warner executives. Outside, police carried picket signs that read, "Time Warner Puts Profits Over Police Lives" and "Media Moguls of Murder." They chanted, "Ban rap! It's all crap!"

Thousands of record stores pulled Body Count's album. The city of Philadelphia's pension fund voted to divest millions of dollars in Time-Warner stock. When Body Count played a show in Hollywood, one fan mused, "There are more cops out here than at Florence and Normandie."[29]

Ice-T called a press conference for July 28. Before he spoke, he showed a half-hour clip about the Black Panther Party. "One of the main problems with the press is that they don't have the slightest idea of what I'm talking about," he said. Then he announced he was pulling the song off the album so that he could offer it for free at his concerts. It was never about money, he said, "This song is about anger and the community and how people get that way. It is not a call to murder police.[30]

"The police are sending out a message to all the other record companies," he added, admitting that he and Time-Warner execs had received death threats. "I predict they will try to shut down rap music in the next three years."[31]

In fact, major labels immediately began re-evaluating their investments in hip-hop, scrutinizing their rosters for artists whose works might prove politically provocative. Kool G Rap and DJ Polo's *Live and Let Die* album was withheld. Tragedy the Intelligent Hoodlum was forced to drop a song called "Bullet," about a revenge hit on a killer cop. The centerpiece of a Boo-Yaa Tribe EP, a song called "Shoot 'Em Down" that condemned the acquittal of a Compton policeman who had killed two Samoan brothers with nineteen shots, was shelved.

Bay Area rapper Paris was signed to Tom Silverman's Tommy Boy Records, which had a distribution deal with Time-Warner. The political rapper had recorded two songs for his new album *Sleeping with the Enemy*—"Coffee, Donuts and Death" and "Bush Killa"—which had lyrics about assassinating corrupt cops and President Bush, and he had turned in cover artwork that depicted him lying in wait with a gun near the White House. "In the real world, particularly Black and Latino communities, the problem isn't cop killers, much less records about cop killers," Paris said. "The problem is killer cops."

Paris spent the next few months fighting Time-Warner to release the record before the elections. They finally gave Paris $100,000 as a settlement. With the money, Paris finally released the album on his own Scarface label three weeks after Bill Clinton and Tipper's then-husband, Al Gore, had defeated George H. W. Bush and Dan Quayle.

Ice-T spent the last months of 1992 in bitter negotiations with Time-Warner over the release of his next album, *Home Invasion*. He came to the realization, he later wrote, "that Warner Brothers cannot afford to be in the business of Black rage. They can be in the business of white rage, but Black rage is much more sensitive. The angry Black person is liable to say anything."[32] He left Time-Warner and signed a deal with Priority Records, the label that had released NWA's and Ice Cube's albums.

In just a decade, major labels had gone from playing catch-up in a musical genre they had once pegged as a passing novelty to signing every rap act they could. Now they were shaking out large numbers of rappers because of their political beliefs. The aim of the conservative culture warriors was to pressure politicians and corporations to silence Black dissent. The truth was at stake. Rappers who wanted to make statements about racism and police violence realized that they faced a difficult choice: make money for the big corporations in ways that wouldn't provoke powerful enemies or fight to protect their freedom of speech.

Banned in the U.S.A.

The unlikely defenders of free speech were the 2 Live Crew, the group that emerged from the sound systems and teen clubs of Miami to popularize twerking and the sound of nasty, raunchy sex rhymes set to booming uptempo bass music.

In response to his critics, Luther Campbell had been the first rapper to make "clean" and "explicit" versions of his records. But by 1990, conservatives had record store owners arrested for selling them, and him and the crew running from police after shows. The obscenity arrests meant the crew was dealing now with two cases—one that had banned their album sales, and one that would threaten their ability to perform their songs.

The significance of the latter case, *Washington Post* writer Hunter Schwarz wrote, was huge. "We were on a crash course with a future in which CeeLo's 'F--k You' was outlawed (the clean 'Forget You' version only, please), Eminem could never have even been a thing, and Nicki Minaj and Miley could be jailed for twerking. But that never happened—because the judicial system and public opinion pushed back."[33]

At the trial, Harvard scholar Dr. Henry Louis Gates put 2 Live Crew's music in the context of Black art and culture. He explained that they were "signifying": "It involves great teasing, cajoling, renaming people. Often it involves the use of lewd language or off-color language. Often it involves graphic descriptions of sexuality, but it is such a highly refined practice that it is taught now in university courses." He noted that "Chaucer, Shakespeare, Greek literature, Western literature" all had included "lewdity, a lot of verbal puns, sexual puns, curse words."[34]

At the same time, he argued, 2 Live Crew were making fun of stereotypes of Black sexuality. "You realize how ridiculous this all is," Gates said. "There is no cult or violence here. You can't hear any danger at all in the background. What you hear is great humor, great joy, boisterousness."

He continued, "Everybody understands what is going on. Even if they don't understand it as a literary critic, they understand it on a subliminal level. Their response is to burst out laughing, to view it as a joke, a parody. Parody is one of the most venerable aspects of any literary tradition."[35] The jury acquitted them. When the case reached the Supreme Court—the first of two times that 2 Live Crew would face that august body—they let the decision stand.

The morality police had won some battles, but not the war. All the controversy had pushed album sales to double platinum—more than two million copies. Their next album would be called *Banned in the U.S.A.* 2 Live Crew's victories for freedom of speech meant that hip-hop would not be stopped, and that the debates about their music's content—especially as it pertained to women—would continue.

The Next Episode

Ex-NWA producer Andre "Dr. Dre" Young had always been a bit mercenary. When he started with Lonzo Williams and the World Class Wreckin Cru, he rocked Prince-style gear. Then he got with Eazy-E and rocked all black. On the NWA track he made for himself, "Express Yourself," he had rapped, "I don't smoke weed or sess 'cause it's known to give a brother brain damage." In December of 1992, as the ashes from the Los Angeles riots still cooled, he dropped *The Chronic,* named after a potent strain of marijuana, with a cover that imitated Zig-Zag rolling papers.

In the middle of the culture wars, with angry youths on one side and politicians, cultural conservatives, and the police on the other, *The Chronic* seemed a sure way to get everyone focused on making green again.

Dre and his new protégé Snoop Dogg's videos for "Nuthin' but a 'G' Thang" and "Let Me Ride" drove the album beyond triple platinum. In a strange way, the duo had become reassuring. And anyway, Dre was finally moving on up—out of Compton and into the Valley—closer to his growing fanbase in the suburbs. "You've got the feeling," went the scratched-in chorus to "'G' Thang," as if it were an invitation to white middle-class boys to identify with them. "Rock the other side."

The riots had changed hip-hop forever. Before the riots, the music was often loud and noisy, the lyrics were tense, rough-edged, and confrontational. *The Chronic* was the sound of the transition. From this point onward, hip-hop would become much more refined and finished, slick pop ready for the world's ears. After a divisive presidential election between Clinton and Bush, Dre's songcraft became the focus. Critics hailed Dre as a pop music master. "'G' Thang" and "Let Me Ride" were celebrated as all-American music, compared to the California endless-summer vibes of the Beach Boys and the Mamas and The Papas.

There was a context for these songs on the streets, of course. The album spoke to the ecstatic outbreak of gang peace and the truce parties, the sense of freedom of being able to simply roll down the street without worrying about cops or enemies. Just as the gang peace movement wanted to mainstream former gang members into society, *The Chronic* wanted to push hard-core rap into the mainstream. But in Dre's music, there were no Peace Treaties, rebuilding demands, or calls for reparations, just the partying.

The Chronic marked the dividing line between hip-hop's first era and the period in which it rose to world dominance. In 1993, the popularity of *Yo! MTV Raps* was fading, and majors were clearing their rosters of potential political liabilities. On *Doggy Style,* Dre and Snoop largely ditched the inner-city blues for more smoothed-out roughness and gangsta parties, and sold even more records. As sales of *The Chronic* rose past three million, hip-hop was preparing for its biggest power moves yet.

Before the riots, cultural conservatives—whether Democrats like Bill Clinton and Tipper Gore or Republicans like Charlton Heston and Jack Thompson—had conjured fears of the corrupting influences of Black artists on white children. But afterward, it seemed corporations had decided that all these demographic and cultural changes were not so bad after all. Hip-hop offered a way for older folks to connect with and make money from this diverse, hip-hop hungry new generation.

Some weren't buying it. C. Delores Tucker, the leader of the National Political Congress of Black Women and a civil rights veteran, said, "What do you think Dr. King would have to say about rappers calling Black women bitches and whores? About rappers glorifying thugs and drug dealers and rapists? What kind of role models are those for young children living in the ghetto?"

But the Peace Treaty had given way to the new dream of making money. As the chorus to Snoop and Dre's new hit went:

> Rollin down the street smokin indo
> Sippin on gin and juice—laaaid back
> With my mind on my money and my money on my mind

13
Ladies First

In the beginning there had been Sha-Rock, Queen Lisa Lee, Pebblee Poo, MC Smiley, Sweet and Sour, and many more. The Mercedes Ladies, hip-hop's first all-female crew, worked day and night in the Bronx practicing their routines with four MCs and three DJs. "Our minds was set on accomplishing something and getting a rep for ourselves," Sheri Sher, the Mercedes Ladies' lead MC, recalls. "We didn't want to get known for shaking our butts or sporting our bodies."

Audiences went wild when they rocked routines like:

M-E-R-the-C-E-Des Girls you know with the most finesse
Calm cool and collected, to the fly guys what you want to do
One for the money, two for the show, Come on Baby D, let's rock it!

They walked off with just as much love as the guys received—maybe even more, because it was clear to the crowd that every time the women were up against the men, they were the underdogs. But the women had to work twice as hard as the guys to be allowed on stage in the first place. "Men back then," Baby D, the Mercedes Ladies' DJ, told hip-hop historian Kathy Iandoli, "they would not acknowledge the females."[1] Baby D says Grandmaster Flash was most scared of the Mercedes Ladies because their rappers were just as good as the Furious Five, and she was just as good a DJ as him. "You are me," he told her. "But you're a female."[2]

When rap moved onto records, the game changed. After a group of unknown rappers called the Sugarhill Gang shocked the hip-hop game with "Rapper's Delight" on Sylvia Robinson's New Jersey Sugar Hill Records, the record labels came calling for the male crews. The guys didn't tell them about the women rappers.

"I don't think Sylvia Robinson even knew the Mercedes Ladies," Baby D told Iandoli. One of the most important crews in rap history would never make their own record. Instead a group from the South called the Sequence became the first all-female crew to score a rap hit, when "Funk You Up" became Sugar Hill Records' second record after "Rapper's Delight," and the third rap record to break the Billboard Top 50 behind "Rapper's Delight" and Kurtis Blow's "Christmas Rappin'."

Just as the Sugarhill Gang had no rep in the Bronx or Harlem scenes, the Sequence was a group of three high school friends from South Carolina—Cheryl "Cheryl The Pearl" Cook, Gwendolyn "Blondy" Chisolm, and Angie "Angie B" Brown (who later became a neo-soul star as Angie Stone). But "Funk You Up" was an important record in rap's march toward pop music. "They had the first hook I ever heard [on a rap song]," Kurtis Blow told Kathy Iandoli.[3] The song would be so influential it inspired future hits from Dr. Dre ("Keep Their Heads Ringin'"), Erykah Badu ("Love of My Life Worldwide"), and Bruno Mars ("Uptown Funk").

From the beginning, women did as much to build the hip-hop movement as the men. They opened doors and changed the game. But all too often, they wouldn't get the love and props they truly deserved.

The Birth of "The Female Rapper"

Hip-hop has always been rooted in the battle aesthetic, and the African American game of "The Dozens," where two do combat with words, insults, and rhymes. By the time Roxanne Shanté was fifteen, she was already the people's champ in battling, having launched the Roxanne Wars and paved the way for dozens of other young women to join in. She told DJ Vlad,

> What's so crazy is that everyone felt that if you make a record about Roxanne Shanté she's going to respond. So it was actually an open door for a lot of people to get into the industry. Like if I heard there was this Roxanne in Baltimore and says she wants to battle. I'm like, "Cool. Let's go to Baltimore." And then you go to Baltimore, you battle her, you get rid of her. And then you go to North Carolina, you battle her, you get rid of her. And then you go to South Carolina, you battle them, you get rid of them.[4]

In 1985, the prestigious New Music Seminar Battle for World Supremacy was the Olympics of hip-hop. All the best DJs and MCs at the time competed at the New Music Seminar for the title of best DJ and best rapper. Judging the rap battle were hip-hop legends Afrika Bambaataa, DJ Whiz Kid, DJ Red Alert, the Fat Boys, and Kurtis Blow.

"There was rules to hip-hop," Shanté said, "and one of the rules was that in order to be the greatest, you had to have already eliminated all of the greats."[5] So of course, she entered the Battle. She was a female, fifteen years old, and she still wore braces.

Instead of different opponents facing off to eliminate each other, Shanté had to face them all and take them all down. It was a task she masterfully executed, which led her up to the semifinals against her toughest opponent of the day: Fruitkwan, a respected, socially conscious rapper from the Brooklyn crew Stetsasonic.

In the early parts of the battle, he had refrained from making sexist or obscene remarks about Shanté. But where many MCs wrote their rhymes, memorized them, and then came to battle, Shanté was blazing a trail by freestyling. She started attacking Fruitkwan for his dark skin:

My rhymes are devastating and every word that I speak,
And you see this guy here, his raps is weak
He can't go with me and that's a fact
He can't go with me because he's too damn Black.

As the clock wound down, Fruitkwan grew frustrated with his clean rhymes, and responded to Shanté with sexist, X-rated taunts. That was up Shanté's alley, and she returned his fire. By the end, the crowd was booing Fruitkwan and Shanté advanced to the finals.

Roxanne Shanté's next opponent was Chief Rocker Busy Bee, who had an infectious personality and was known for being able to get a crowd hyped. But his party-rocking rhymes fell flat with the crowd. Shanté insulted his shoes, his hat, even his name. Busy Bee was reduced to babbling rhymes that made no sense at all. Most in the crowd were sure that Shanté was taking home the title. But what happened next is still a source of controversy to this day.

When the judges scores came back, Afrika Bambaataa, Whiz Kid, and Buffy of the Fat Boys judged her performance a perfect 10. But DJ Red Alert gave her an 8, and Kurtis Blow gave her the lowest score of the day—4 points. Roxanne Shanté received 42 points to Busy Bee's 47.

There was a backstory: Shanté had dissed Run-DMC and Kurtis Blow on the devastating record "Bite This," which had been released months earlier. Both Run-DMC and Kurtis Blow were managed by Russell Simmons, who also managed Sparky Dee, one of Roxanne's opponents at the time. And they all seemed aligned against Mr. Magic, for whom Shanté had written and rapped the lyrics.

Shanté told DJ Vlad, "I think that day I lost some of my love and some of my respect for hip-hop because I always thought that it went by how talented you were and how great you were." She said that she and Kurtis Blow spoke privately years after the infamous battle and he gave her another reason for the low score:

> He [Kurtis Blow] said, "Listen, at that time hip-hop was brand new. Hip-hop was just starting to be accepted in as far as a true genre of music. Hip-hop is finally starting to go mainstream. Major labels are starting to finally give us deals and they are finally starting to take us serious. And there is just no way that they were going to continue to take hip-hop serious if the best in the world was a fifteen-year-old girl. They were not going to do that, Shanté. I'm sorry that I did that that day, but I did that for hip-hop."

One can only wonder what hip-hop history might have been like—especially for women—if Shanté had won that fateful day at the New Music Seminar in 1985.

Her male friends attempted to console her. They told her, "You're still the best female. There ain't no girl better than you."

"That is," Shanté says, "when the title 'female rapper' came out.'"[6]

Prior to the day Shanté lost, everybody was an MC and was judged against who was the best—male or female. Now, *men* were rappers. Women were *female* rappers. It was a false distinction, but it stuck.

The Godmothers

Once the term "female rapper" was a thing, expectations plunged.

Hurby "Luv Bug" Azor was a supervisor at a Sears Roebuck telemarketing office in Queens, taking sound engineering classes on the side. He was also an aspiring rap producer, whose crew included the rising star comedian Martin Lawrence and rappers Kid-N-Play, and two best friends named Cheryl "Salt" James and Sandra "Pepa" Denton. Inspired by the Roxanne Wars, Hurby convinced the two women to make a record with him that would answer Doug E. Fresh's hit "The Show." The song would be a final project for his class, but it was destined for a lot more.

Hurby wrote the lyrics, and Salt and Pepa went up to his attic and ripped their performances. When they got the tape aired on Mr. Magic and Marley Marl's show, "The Show Stoppa" became a sensation. Hurby landed a record deal with Pop Art, the same label that had signed Roxanne Shanté. Hurby put together more funky tracks, wrote more lyrics for them, and together they made Salt-N-Pepa's 1986 debut album, *Hot, Cool, and Vicious.* Salt and Pepa's big personalities simply leapt out of the grooves and worked perfectly with Hurby's optimistic, go-go influenced beats.

Suddenly they were doing shows everywhere they could. Salt says, "We'd be in Hurby's beat-up orange Datsun driving to Philly in the snow." "Tramp," "My Mic Sounds Nice," and "I'll Take Your Man" became underground hits on the East Coast. Then a San Francisco DJ named Cameron Paul remixed one of their b-sides, "Push It," and the group crossed over to pop radio, nationally, then worldwide. The record label rushed Salt, Pepa, and Deidra "DJ Spinderella" Roper into a club to shoot a video. Freshly dipped in Dapper Dan customized 8-Ball jackets and black spandex tights, they tore up the stage with their choreographed moves. Visually, it was the women's answer to Run-DMC's "Walk This Way" video, and it blew people away. Now the four of them had a platinum-selling hit on their hands.

But Hurby's expectations remained low. "I didn't give them bullshit tracks, then hope that a pretty face would get them over. 'My Mic Sounds Nice' could have been a man saying it," he told Harry Allen. "I had a theory: if a girl does something half as good as a man, she's better. Like the women's basketball team. They couldn't fuck with the men's basketball team. But, because they can do that well, they almost seem better than a men's basketball team."[7]

Salt-N-Pepa paid little attention to Hurby's questionable theory. Once the door was open, they attacked the game like they had something to prove. Salt recalls, "Russell Simmons at Def Jam gave us the thumbs down and said we'd never last, but then later tried to sign us. I was always the little kid putting on the Broadway shows for my aunties at home, but I was told that show business was not a realistic career option. So when I got the opportunity to get on the mic, it was do or die. This was going to save my life."[8]

Hurby continued to write and produce the records, but Salt and Pepa were finding their voices. They got into an argument with him about doing Beatles covers like "Twist and Shout," which was corny to them. By their third album, *Blacks' Magic,* Salt—whose personal relationship with Hurby was ending—began writing her own songs, "Expression" and "Independent," songs about women proudly taking charge of their lives that would influence artists like Beyoncé.

Then they released "Let's Talk About Sex," a groundbreaking song about safe sex. They expected controversy. But the song broke through and climbed to number thirteen on the Billboard charts. One day, ABC News anchor Peter Jennings heard his teenage daughter singing the chorus to the song. He reached out to Salt-N-Pepa to be a part of the news special and to do a PSA for AIDS. They reworked their hit into "Let's Talk About AIDS." The group would continue its activism in its music and work with Life Beat and the Gay Men's Health Crisis.

After she recorded a number of songs on *Blacks' Magic* that seemed directed at him, Salt's relationship with Hurby was officially over. Salt, Pepa, and Spinderella had also become mothers. It was time for a new start. "Hurby did kind of go, 'OK, you guys think you can write and produce Salt-N-Pepa music without me?'" Salt says. "And it was like we were kinda breaking up with Hurby. We were just tired of feeling like we were under his thumb, and that he was in control of so much."[9]

They came back with 1993's *Very Necessary.* Hurby received

producer credits, but they had written most of the record. "Shoop" and "Whatta Man" became Top 5 singles.

"[W]hether it was a track like 'Tramp,' that we didn't write, or later on, 'Shoop,' which we did write, everything that we did was what we wanted to do and what we wanted to say. That went through everything we did. From what we said, how we looked and what we wore. We always said we brought fun, fashion and femininity to hip-hop," Salt says. "We were regular chicks who liked to have fun, who made great music, who said what we wanted."[10]

Before Salt-N-Pepa paused their recording career in the late 1990s, they would sell fifteen million records worldwide, including seven million for their fourth album, *Very Necessary,* alone. With their around-the-way-girl vibe and their insistence on expressing their flair, their desires, and their power, they became one of the biggest rap groups of all time. Just as important, Salt and Pepa would inspire millions of girls and women with their message of independence, empowerment, and consciousness.

"I want to reach everyone but I have a dedication to women," Pepa said. "And women are my biggest audience: The guys love us, they think we're sexy, but the girls take us seriously."[11]

The Storyteller

One of the young women Salt-N-Pepa influenced was a Brooklyn girl, the only daughter of a single mother, named Lana Michelle Moorer. She said, "I'd already heard Run-DMC. I'd already heard Sha-Rock, but to hear Salt-N-Pepa made me say, 'This is what I want to do.'"[12]

As a young girl she had gone to an Afrocentric elementary school where she learned Swahili and Langston Hughes poems. By the time she was twelve, she was studying Salt-N-Pepa's songs, and writing rhymes and rapping with her stepbrothers, Kirk "Milk Dee" Robinson and Nat "Gizmo" Robinson, who were known as the Audio Two. Their father wanted to build a record label around the three of them. But Lana's mother was strict. "Growing up in a single-parented home, I tried her," she recalls, "and it was times where she was just not going to be tried."[13]

But Lana's mother began to see how committed she was to the

rap game. One night, Lana asked her mother if she could go to the Latin Quarter with her friend Jill. Her mother looked at her and told her, "Write me something that tells me why I need to let you go to a club at this hour."[14] Lana did, penning something that so impressed her mother that she let Lana start going to the club on the regular.

Lana was probably the youngest person hanging in the Latin Quarter, watching celebrities like Slick Rick, Rakim, and Chris Rock go by as she stood against the wall in her Mickey Mouse sneakers and Coca-Cola T-shirt. But through connections she made there, she started recording demos. She took the name Lyte, and when her first record came back it read, "MC Lyte," so that's who she became.

By the time she was seventeen, Audio Two were plunged into a battle with Hurby "Luv Bug" Azor, who allegedly took a beat of theirs for a rapper named Antoinette. Milk and Giz didn't want to diss a female, so they enlisted Lyte. Thus began the next major female rap battle, as Antoinette and Lyte went at it over successive albums. Her first record, "10% Dis"—she told Brian Coleman "that's only ten percent of what I could have said"—would stand as one of the best battle records of all time.[15]

Years later, Lyte reflected on the fact that women rappers only seemed to be recognized when they were battling other women. As she told Ebro and Laura Stylez in a Hot 97 radio interview, "It's actually fueled by men, really. The fight that exists between women is because men say that it can't be more than one [accepted female rapper]."[16]

She dressed like a tomboy because, she told hip-hop journalist Michael Gonzales, "I wanted the male rappers to listen to my rhymes as opposed to looking at my body . . . just listen to what I'm saying."[17] MC Lyte would prove to be a master of all styles, including a crossover radio track "Ruffneck," which became the first gold single by a solo female rapper. But one area where she really changed the game was in her storytelling.

"I think the seasoned MC understands that it's not just about the single that bumps in the club," she says, "but it's about that story that gets to the 'hood—when folks are in apartments that don't have AC, that, matter of fact, they don't even want to stay in the apartment because it's eight of them in a two bedroom and they're sitting out on the stoop or out in the park in the projects on the bench. This is (when) they appreciate the stories. I know I always did."

When she began recording, she took along the rhyme book she had written in from the age of twelve. The first one she recorded was about a boy she had developed a crush on, but who turned out to love smoking crack instead. When male gangsta rappers told tales about women who had fallen prey to cocaine, they talked about them as hos, mocking them mercilessly and bragging about how badly they treated the women. But when Lyte told the story of Sam, she had a sense of sadness and empathy. "Just like a test, I cram to understand you," went the chorus to her first release, "I Cram To Understand U (Sam)." MC Lyte turned Sam's addiction into a complicated subject.

On records like "Cappuccino," "Eyes Are The Soul," and "Poor Georgie," she told more stories of caution, of people living on the edge. Gangsta rappers called their music "reality rap." MC Lyte presented a different side to it. She says, "I can only be the living example of life faced in a positive manner. At the end of the day I can look myself in the mirror and say, 'You know what? I'm alright.'"

The Queen

Three years after Roxanne Shanté faced down Busy Bee, a young Newark born-and-raised eighteen-year-old named Dana Owens, rocking a pair of overalls and two braids, stood before powerful radio and record label executives at the New Music Seminar conference in the downtown New York Marriott hotel and fearlessly confronted them.

The corporate executives were talking about why they couldn't play hip-hop. They cited polling data and research. But the young woman wasn't having it. She commanded the room's attention, shocked the executives, and received rousing applause. Then she introduced herself as Latifah, a name she had given herself at the age of eight, meaning "gentle and kind." A year later, the world would come to know her as Queen Latifah with the release of her album *All Hail the Queen.*

It would be the beginning of a long career, in which she would become an award-winning musician, actress, and film and television producer. She would invest in affordable housing in her hometown and open the Queen Collective to advance gender and racial equity in filmmaking. But back then, Kierna Mayo wrote, "The very act of being a female MC, particularly in 1989, was a rule-breaker of sorts."[18]

Latifah was the daughter of a high school art teacher. She grew up in public housing in Newark. To make ends, she worked jobs at the Wiz record store and Burger King. Inspired by MC Lyte and the artists at the Latin Quarter club, she learned to make records with her crew, the Flavor Unit. As a child, she had suffered sexual abuse at the hands of a teenage babysitter, an incident that hurt her relationships with people and her image of herself. Although she would struggle with the burden of this trauma for many more years, she said, "When I was around eighteen, I looked in the mirror and said, 'You're either going to love yourself or hate yourself.' And I decided to love myself. That changed a lot of things."[19]

At about the same time she got a deal with the label that had signed Afrika Bambaataa, Tommy Boy, and began to hang out with likeminded artists at the Latin Quarter nightclub, where Paradise Gray was hosting the closed-door Meeting of the Minds sessions. Out of those gatherings came a more politically minded body of hip-hop artists, like the Jungle Brothers, De La Soul, and A Tribe Called Quest. They formed a massive crew called the Native Tongues.

"Public Enemy and Boogie Down Productions and groups like that were my inspiration," she says. "Because they took a chance and talked about social issues and things that were just going on around us, whether it was divesting in South Africa or whatever, they gave me the courage to make records like 'The Evil That Men Do.'"

In interviews she described her style as being "real" and "down to earth," and said, "I think by us bringing knowledge to our people we're bringing knowledge to every other people and let them know how we live."[20]

At the heart of her debut album was a song called "Ladies First," a collaboration with Monie Love. The song unapologetically centered women in the man's world that commercial hip-hop had become. She challenged male fans directly, rhyming,

A woman can bear you, break you, take you
Now it's time to rhyme
Can you relate to
A sister dope enough
to make you holler and scream?

Wild Style producer and *Yo! MTV Raps* host FAB 5 FREDDY directed a video that honored women and protested the horrors of the racist white apartheid government that ruled South Africa. The video showed images of people resisting white violence being inflicted on Black people. Queen Latifah is shown as a regal figure, a general of sorts overlooking a giant map of South Africa and sweeping opposition pieces off the board and onto the floor. Los Angeles rapper Medusa says, "She took her space, she made her place."[21]

But tragedy struck when her brother Lance died in a motorcycle accident. She was stunned and guilt-ridden—she had given him the bike he died on. "People come and go, records come and go, but your family is the thing that's supposed to be there always," she told *Vibe* writer Lucy Kaylin. "Death gives you a real fuck-it attitude: fuck it, fuck you, fuck everybody."[22]

She was dropped from Tommy Boy, and tried to focus on her next album. When she emerged a year later, she was more direct than ever on *Black Reign*. On the 1993 single 'U.N.I.T.Y." she challenged sexism and misogyny. It became her biggest hit and won her a Grammy. "Who you calling a b---h?" she yelled. "You gotta let them know, you're not a b---h or a ho."

She went on to some of her greatest successes after this—starring in *Living Single,* hosting her own talk show, winning Grammy and Emmy Awards, and becoming one of the hip-hop generation's biggest multimedia stars, all while representing the regal qualities befitting her name. In her autobiography, she wrote, "A queen is a queen when riding high, and when clouded in disgrace, shame, or sorrow, she has dignity. Being a queen has very little to do with exterior things. It is a state of mind."[23]

"We thought of hip-hop as ours," says the pioneering hip-hop feminist Joan Morgan. "There was no 'This is a male field and we [women] are trying to break in'—because there was as heavy an industry presence. And I think that that's why you were able to see the level of diversity."[24]

By the early 1990s, hip-hop had introduced a rich diversity of voices that the mainstream had never heard before.

14
Keeping It Real

In 1981 MTV went on the air, promising to revolutionize the industry by showcasing music videos twenty-four hours a day. Its launch was disruptive, making stars of a new generation of videogenic musicians like Madonna, Duran Duran, and U2, and doubling music sales from $3.9 to $7.8 billion dollars in a decade.[1] But in one important way, it was hardly revolutionary and more of the same old thing: it did not play Black artists.

Much of the history of the United States in the twentieth century was one of legally sanctioned racial segregation, where whites and people of color lived separately and unequally. Even after the rise of the Civil Rights Movement in the 1950s, popular culture still mirrored society. The R&B charts—which had once been explicitly called "race records"—were for Black artists. The pop charts—where the biggest-selling records were tracked—remained overwhelmingly white.

In 1983, Michael Jackson broke MTV's color line with the "Billie Jean" video, and a year later, Run-DMC's "Rock Box" led hip-hop onto the network. That was what "crossing over" meant. A Black musician had to cross over from the R&B chart to the pop chart. Michael Jackson and Run-DMC had to cross over from Black audiences to white audiences. White artists rarely had to cross over to Black audiences. But then hip-hop began to change all of that.

In 1988, a white production assistant at MTV named Ted Demme brought a concept for a rap video show to MTV's heads. The *Yo! MTV Raps* pilot debuted on August 6, 1988, with FAB 5 FREDDY as host. Within months it was the network's most watched show.

MTV quickly added former WBAU DJ and Original Concept leader Andre "Doctor Dre" Brown and radio host Ed "Ed Lover" Roberts as additional hosts, and gave *Yo! MTV Raps* daily airings. Within a year, MTV had gone from almost no rap videos to twelve hours of rap programming per week.[2] Lots of white suburban kids were tuning in. FAB 5 FREDDY understood why. "People identify with rap," he told a *Time* reporter. "You feel that you can look like that, that you can be a part of it immediately."[3]

At Tommy Boy Records, pioneering record exec Monica Lynch and her boss, Tom Silverman, realized that they were not in the record business anymore, they were in the "lifestyle" business. They diversified into clothing, designing brand-name gear and partnering with brands like Carhartt and Stussy that hip-hoppers had already made popular on the street. Hip-hop was not only selling $400 million of records a year, but hundreds of millions in other products—shoes, jeans, soda, beer, liquor, video games, movies, high-fashion clothing, Swatch watches, even Honda automobiles.

In 1986, Run-DMC had turned Adidas into a hip-hop brand with a song. Two years later, Spike Lee and Michael Jordan took it to the next level with a set of ads for a shoe company called Nike, which at the time was number two in sales, far behind its competitor, Reebok. But their "Spike and Mike" ads left Reebok in the dust, and Nike never looked back. Nike's success confirmed that American pop culture was shifting from focusing on the middle-aged to youth, from suburban to urban, from whiteness to Blackness. Hip-hop artists defined the new cool.

Blowing Up and Going Pop

As hip-hop entered the last decade of the twentieth century, it was poised to blow up. Rap was achieving bigger and bigger mainstream success. But a fault line was opening up. Hip-hop artists wanted bigger audiences and to be able to make a living, but success raised a lot of difficult new questions. Were white-owned record companies exploiting Black artists as they had done for generations? Were they supporting the artists the community loved or only promoting artists who fit racial stereotypes? How were these new white audiences really seeing Black artists? Were artists representing themselves and their communities authentically and positively? Would they be able to be faithful to their artistic visions or would they be forced to sell out—to give up their ideals, their truths, their very integrity—in order to cross over?

Stanley Kirk Burrell grew up in East Oakland in a tiny apartment with six siblings. He seemed born to entertain. He would walk down the road with his brother to the Coliseum on days that the Oakland Athletics were playing so he could dance for money. The team owner, Charles Finley, hired them as on-field batboys for $7.50 a game, and once even had Stanley take over radio game-calling duties. Reggie Jackson called him "Hammer" because he looked like a little Hank Aaron, and the name stuck.

By the time Hammer was in his early twenties, he joined Jon Gibson to record the first Contemporary Christian rap hit, "The Wall." As part of a group called the Holy Ghost Boy and the Posse, he cut a single called "The Word." His first single as a solo artist, called "Ring 'Em," became a local smash hit in the Bay Area. The record cover featured him in different dance poses. Those dance moves would go on to be central to his electrifying stage show.

But in the beginning, he rapped in an outdated Run-DMC style. His music was danceable but basic—leaning hard on the bells and 808 bass, and obvious samples from R&B hits. But he had lots of hustle, and better than just about anyone else, he knew how to please a crowd.

He assembled a huge dance, DJ, and MC crew to back him up and gained a rep in the local clubs as a stellar entertainer. With investment money from two Oakland Athletics, he pressed his own records and promoted them relentlessly, selling them out of the back of his car trunk to record stores and passers-by. Soon it seemed like everyone in the Bay Area knew his name.

In 1990, his album, *Please Hammer Don't Hurt 'Em,* climbed to number one on the pop charts and stayed there for twenty-one weeks. Vanilla Ice's album *To the Extreme* followed with a sixteen-week reign. Each of the records went "diamond"—Vanilla Ice's sold eleven million, and Hammer's over fourteen million, the two biggest-selling rap albums to that point. Change was happening. The biggest new show on television was called *The Fresh Prince of Bel-Air* and it starred a rapper from Philadelphia named Will Smith.

But as rap reached bigger mainstream success, some hip-hop heads were questioning the cost. To them, the music industry was only interested in what made money, and the history of American entertainment business had been about peddling some of the worst stereotypes of Black people for white amusement. It was dirty money. Hip-hop was meant to be a true expression of their lives and their culture. As an art form, they felt that it needed to be defended from those who would exploit it.

So they dismissed Vanilla Ice as a white faker. And they harshly criticized Hammer, whom they accused of selling out to white audiences. On "Check the Rhime," Q-Tip from A Tribe Called Quest dissed Hammer: "Rap is not pop, if you call it that then stop."[4] And when Tip rapped about "Industry Rule No. 4080"—"Record company people are shady"—it perfectly captured how conflicted many were about hip-hop becoming big business.

A Tribe Called Quest was part of a loose federation of artists who called themselves the Native Tongues, which included groundbreaking artists like De La Soul, the Jungle Brothers, Queen Latifah, Monie Love, and Black Sheep. They met in 1988, bonding over a shared understanding of Black music and culture. They drew direct inspiration from Afrika Bambaataa and the Zulu Nation—one of the Jungle Brothers even called himself "Baby Bambaataa." With their goal of advancing hip-hop as an art form that represented Black collectivity, creativity, and intelligence, they inspired a progressive, global, multiracial hip-hop underground.

Between 1989 and 1991, they released several albums that would be considered classics, including The Jungle Brothers' *Done by the Forces of Nature,* A Tribe Called Quest's *People's Instinctive Travels and the Paths of Rhythm* and *The Low-End Theory,* Black Sheep's *A Wolf in Sheep's Clothing,* and De La Soul's *3 Feet High and Rising* and *De La Soul Is Dead.* All of them were inviting, well-crafted records that drew richly on the history of African American music, and set new standards of artistic excellence.

The Native Tongues pushed each other to be as innovative as they could be. On *3 Feet High and Rising*'s opener, "The Magic Number," De La Soul's Dave "Trugoy" Jolicoeur described how they did so:

> Souls who flaunt styles gain praises by the pounds
> Common are speakers who honor the scroll
> Scrolls written daily creates a new sound
> Listeners listen 'cause this here is wisdom

The single best introduction to the Native Tongues was the video for the remix of De La Soul's song "Buddy," on which eight rappers touch the mic in under five minutes. A funny song about the joys of hooking up set to Taana Gardner's classic "Heartbeat" breakbeat, "Buddy" showed the crew getting loose in bright, colorful Afrocentric clothes, surrounded by family and friends all clapping along and having an infectiously joyful time.

Unfortunately it wouldn't last. Success soon tore the Native Tongues apart. Label, legal, and personal pressures came down, crushing the carefree optimism that they had on their earlier albums. But by 1993, A Tribe Called Quest and De La Soul had made two more classic records. The easy, polished flow of A Tribe Called Quest's *Midnight Marauders* was an expansive counterpoint to Dr. Dre's sleek gangsta rap. On *Buhloone Mindstate,* De La Soul made one of hip-hop's grandest statements on the power of Black art and music.

On "I Am I Be," they layered a collage of their friends' brief introductions—"I am Shorty, I be 4'11"," "I am Q-Tip, I be the friction"—over moody music that included solos by James Brown's former bandmates, including saxophonist Maceo Parker ("I am Maceo and I be blowin' the soul out of this horn"). Coming in the tense year after Los Angeles had burned, when politicians were condemning hip-hop and police were cracking down on youth, the song and the album simply said, "We are here. We won't stop. We will survive."

And part of that meant that they vowed never to sell out. Comparing hip-hop's moneymaking machine to a balloon, they rapped, "We might blow up, but we won't go pop."

Strictly Underground

Throughout the twentieth century, Black artists made spaces to overcome the legacies of slavery and racial segregation through artistic excellence and cultural expression. They built artistic movements—from the ferment of Harlem Renaissance to the rise of the Southern churches and cultural centers that fueled the Civil Rights Movement to the jazz clubs of New Orleans, Kansas City, and New York City, and the Black Arts theaters, salons, and galleries of Los Angeles, St. Louis, and Chicago. By the 1990s, a new generation had many historical models to create institutions that might advance hip-hop.

By then, hip-hop had been around for two decades. It had reached what Tommy Boy record label head Tom Silverman called its "third generation." The first generation had taken rap from the parks to vinyl records. This was the Old School. The second—the New School—had taken it from records to the arenas. The third reclaimed hip-hop for themselves, reinventing traditions and busily making new revolutions. These young ones—especially those coming up in Los Angeles and the West Coast—sometimes called themselves "the True School." All across the country, hip-hop heads formed a bustling, thriving underground.

Being true—or keeping it real—meant you were staying faithful to a sense of hip-hop's history, but also to your people, experience, and voice. In the face of commercialization, you would keep it real and represent yourself and your community. You would refuse to sell out—never bow to mainstream expectations, perform racial stereotypes, or compromise your ideals or your folks. Being true was about knowledge of self, authentic expression, and artistic independence. If that meant never crossing over and staying underground, so be it. As Long Island crew EPMD, whom *Yo! MTV Raps* had helped to bring to national audiences, rapped: "Strictly underground. Keep the crossover."

In this hip-hop underground, local hip-hop scenes grew and thrived all across the country. One of these was the San Francisco Bay Area, a place that defined itself as a haven for mavericks. It was where the Black Panther Party, the Ethnic Studies movement, and the literary arts movement that would become known as multiculturalism had been born. Alongside these movements, the Bay Area's rich dance scene had produced groups like the Black Resurgents and Black Messengers, who kept the political and cultural rallies moving. Dancers here continued to evolve the funk styles of Boogalooing, Roboting, and Strutting over more than three decades into the influential styles of Turf Dance by the new millennium. Graffiti writers like Mike DREAM Francisco and REFA ONE had also learned directly from the veterans of the political movements, such as the Black Panther Party's Emory Douglas and Asian American activist Greg Morozumi. The Bay Area's visual arts scene was informed by a deep history of social justice murals and a constant flow of ideas and images between activists and artists.

Because there were so many colleges and universities in the Bay Area, it was blessed with a large number of college radio stations, where young DJs could champion hip-hop. Author and influential *Vibe* editor Danyel Smith grew up listening to these shows. They played the same role for Bay Area audiences that the block parties had in the Bronx.

"To the rest of the world they were very little radio stations that came in staticky and the show was on in the middle of the night, but you were in the know and things were really exciting," she says. "And as much as I think we all liked being part of our little secret thing, we all thought, 'Wow this music needs to be heard by everyone. Someone needs to take it and blow it up, give it the respect that it deserves.'"

These DJs became so successful that they forced the local commercial radio stations to embrace hip-hop, a trend that soon spread across the country. They made stars of diverse artists like MC Hammer, Digital Underground, Paris, Too Short, the Luniz, Mac Dre, The Coup, Dan The Automator, Hieroglyphics, DJ Shadow and Sole-Sides/Quannum, and E-40 and Tha Click. Although much smaller than New York City and Los Angeles, the Bay Area became the number two hip-hop market in the country. At the beginning of the 1990s, an up-and-coming young rapper named Tupac Shakur told an interviewer, "Right now the Bay Area is how the Bronx was in 1981. Everybody is hot. They caught the bug. Everybody is trying to be creative and make their own claim."

This second wave of hip-hop radio included influential shows like Stretch Armstrong and Bobbito Garcia's show at Columbia University's WKCR in New York City, Mike Nardone's *We Came from Beyond* at Loyola Marymount University's KXLU in Los Angeles, DJ 3rd Rail's show on Northwestern's WNUR in Chicago, Nasty Nes's *Fresh Tracks* show on Seattle's KFOX, the Awesome 2-Teddy Ted and Special K's show on New York's WHBI, and Matt Sonzala's Houston show on KPFT. By the mid-nineties, Sway and King Tech's Wakeup Show in the Bay Area, the Baka Boyz in Los Angeles, and DJ Pinkhouse in Chicago had attained national recognition.

All across the country, these shows were cornerstones for the hip-hop underground's networks of b-boy, MC, and DJ battles, poetry slams, record and clothing stores, magazines, and indie record labels.

The hip-hop underground ushered in a rebirth of all the original art forms. B-boying, which for a while had lost popularity to all the fad dances, came back in a big way. Turntablism, led by predominantly Filipino American crews like the Invisibl Skratch Piklz and the Beat Junkies on the West Coast and the mostly Black crew the X-Ecutioners from New York City, became a recognized art form. The freestyle movement brought together the lost arts of MCing and battling, emphasizing off-the-dome improvisation and punch lines, and consciously took cues from the classic bebop jazz soloists. Spoken word connected hip-hop back to the African American oral tradition, and sparked a global renaissance in poetry among a new generation. Young people even began taking hip-hop into the classrooms, using it to teach writing, history, social studies, math, science, and technology. Some collectives, like Toni Blackman's Freestyle Union in Washington, DC, became hubs where all of these activities took place.

By the mid-nineties, such networks were thriving in cities like Seattle, San Diego, Chicago, Detroit, Boston, Philadelphia, and Atlanta. At national conferences like the Gavin Convention, Jack the Rapper, or How Can I Be Down, rap artists, mixshow and college radio DJs, street promoters, and hip-hop journalists got organized. Grassroots groups like the Bay Area Hip-Hop Coalition became a model for underground radio DJs, influencing national radio playlists and press coverage, and propelling underground artists into the mainstream. Independent music distribution networks, particularly in the South, generated million-dollar grossing artists and labels.

Hip-hop magazines sprung up everywhere. They were distributed outside traditional venues, at clubs, record stores, skateboard shops, and footwear and clothing boutiques. In the beginning they offered low-cost ads that attracted local, independent start-ups, including clothing lines, record labels, and club and rave promotions. The biggest of them, *The Source,* gave the rising scene a national voice that countered the mainstream media's fear of Black culture and hip-hop.

Then, in 1993, *Vibe* magazine launched with a $1 million investment from global media corporation Time-Warner, and big advertisers like Nike, Sony, and Versace. Hip-hop journalism now ranged from zines xeroxed and stapled together at copy shops to glossy, high-fashion magazines sold on global newsstands. Most of the world saw and knew the big-name artists, but below them was a massive network of local hip-hop scenes, providing room for all kinds of new voices to be heard and seen. This movement, linked together and boosted by its homegrown and corporate media, was the foundation for hip-hop's crossover into the mainstream.

In Los Angeles, the thriving scene traced its roots back to early 1980s all-ages clubs like Radio and Radiotron. Medusa had been a regular at these spots, where she gained a big rep, first dancing as Lady Tic Tut in a crew called the Groove-A-Trons, and later for her powerful rapping. While NWA had put Los Angeles back on the map with *Straight Outta Compton,* she says, "The message that they were kickin' was only a minute new component of what Cali and LA represented."

By the early 1990s, she was going every week to watch and rock in the open-mic battles at a tiny crowded cafe in Leimert Park called The Good Life. Rap elders like LA's Watts Prophets and New York's Last Poets took the stage together. Major-label recording artists visited to get their creative batteries recharged. Regulars like The Freestyle Fellowship, the Pharcyde, and Medusa influenced a generation of global freestylers.

Founded by B. Hall with her son R. Kaine Blaze, there were two rules—be dope and don't curse. Medusa says, "You came in to see if your song made it, if it was hot or not. And it forced you to really dig in your vocabulary because you couldn't cuss." If a rapper did, the crowd booed him offstage. If a rapper was wack, the crowd ruthlessly chanted, "Please pass the mic!"

"The Good Life was kind of like a healing," says film director and producer Ava DuVernay, who back then was part of a rap crew called Figures of Speech. "If you sat there any Thursday night and you really listened to what was being said, it was really like a novel telling what young people were thinking about during that time. And if they didn't have that creative outlet, I wonder what would have happened."[5]

Cafes, community centers, and clubs just like the Good Life preserved the community spirit of hip-hop, ensuring that the underground was a world where young people could always build their art and speak their truths.

Whose World Is This?

Armed with sampling technologies and bottomless creativity, the artists of this generation made music in which you could lose yourself. The Beastie Boys and the Dust Brothers' *Paul's Boutique* was a frenzied morning skateboard ride through the city; De La Soul and Prince Paul's albums like a weekend hangout at the crib full of cartoons, old records, and jokes with the smartest guys around; each album from A Tribe Called Quest felt like stepping out into a cool night ready for adventure.

Samplers made DJs into producers and, as producers, they became world builders. They built on the breakthroughs of Marley Marl, the Bomb Squad, and Dr. Dre. On the West Coast, DJ Quik made loose melodic music for cruising, while DJ Muggs's tight loops for Cypress Hill heated up crowds and got them hyped. In the South, Organized Noise made spacey funk for Outkast, and DJ Screw slowed down Houston rap to a crawl. On the East Coast, Pete Rock made mournful tributes like "They Reminisce Over You (T.R.O.Y.)" from rare soul and jazz records. DJ Premier flipped similar records in a different way, creating futuristic vistas for Gangstarr, KRS-One, and Nas.

Of all the world-builders, Bobby "RZA" Diggs and the Wu-Tang Clan may have been the most wildly unexpected.

Inspired by *kung fu* films they had seen on weekends in Times Square and Chinatown, they named themselves after Wu-Dang Mountain, where a powerful style of Chinese *kung fu* martial arts had originated. They renamed their Staten Island home turf Shaolin, after the famed Chinese temple where *kung fu* was born.

Rolling nine deep, the Clan grew out of RZA's idea to bring together family members and friends from Staten Island and Brooklyn to record a song he called "Protect Ya Neck." "I told them that if they'd put their solo careers on hold, we could work together for something much bigger. I told them, 'If y'all give me five years of your life, I promise you in five years I'm gonna take us to the top,'" he says.[6]

Each of them had lived through a lot—the daily grind of being poor, the violence of the drug trade, the same kind of police brutality that would later kill Eric Garner (at the same spot where Hype Williams had filmed the crew for the Wu-Tang Clan's "Can It Be All So Simple" video twenty years before). Ghostface had cared for two brothers with muscular dystrophy. Old Dirty Bastard struggled with mental health issues. U-God was in and out of jail trying to make ends meet selling drugs. Some of them had even been in rival gangs, fighting each other.

RZA spent much of his childhood moving from place to place. "I lived in at least ten different projects and I got to see that the projects are a science project, in the same way that a prison is a science project," he recalls. "And in comics, when a science project goes wrong, it produces monsters. Or superheroes."[7]

Not long before, RZA had signed a record deal, but the single he released—"Ooh We Love You Rakeem"—portrayed him as a cartoonish love man and failed miserably. Broke, he and Ghostface moved to Ohio and got caught up again in the drug trade. Ghost was shot but survived.

Then RZA was arrested for shooting a man in the leg. He had a baby on the way, but now he was facing eight years in prison. In April of 1992, he was acquitted of the assault charge. "My mother looked me in my eye and said, 'This is your second chance. Don't blow it.'"[8]

For him, the Wu-Tang single "Protect Ya Neck" was an all-in, do-or-die bet. But it paid off. A year after RZA had been at his lowest, the record took the rap world by storm. He was able to deliver on his word.

He masterminded a plan to have each of the crew members signed to different major labels, an unprecedented move in the rap industry. When the Clan blew up in 1993, each of the individual rappers immediately became more valuable. RZA's move forced the major labels to competitively bid for each of the Wu-Tang members. GZA signed with Geffen, Method Man with Def Jam, Raekwon with Loud, Ghostface Killah with Epic, and Ol' Dirty Bastard with Elektra, each receiving much more than they would have otherwise. By 1996, all of them had their records out and the labels had to cooperate to increase their sales.

"Usually labels are all at each other's throats," RZA recalls. But now the Wu-Tang brand was stronger than the label brands, and doubling their sales as consumers bought multiple albums at a time. "It was a wild thing to do. It was never done again."

RZA's musical production made a world that sounded unlike anyone's at the time. Other rappers, inspired by Dr. Dre, were making music that was slicker and more polished, sounding big money like a blockbuster movie soundtrack. But RZA used the sampler to sound obscure and low-tech like the dubbed old-school *kung-fu* films that he and the crew loved. The dusty samples seemed like they were played on a turntable with a worn needle.

Each of the rappers had big personalities. RZA was the originator and strategist, GZA was the teacher and philosopher, Method Man the supreme stylist, Masta Killa the calm assassin, Inspectah Deck the frontline striker, U-God the world-weary watcher, Ghostface the word-drunk storyteller, Raekwon the street theorist, and Ol' Dirty Bastard the wild card. They all rhymed with a burning hunger—both to represent and to transcend the street violence, homelessness, and depression they confronted every day.

Listeners had to puzzle out all the crew's references. Along with the references to Chinese martial arts films, religion, and war strategy, they also mixed in huge doses of Five Percent numerology, New York street slang, comic books, and shoe and clothing references. And their songs swung hard from stark observations on the desperations of poverty to the anarchic energy of a mosh pit. They called themselves Killa Bees because everywhere they went together, they swarmed. They were there, as they put it, to bring the ruckus. Their music was as unpredictable as the world they lived in.

At about the same time, farther up the East River in the sprawling Queensbridge projects, a mysterious young rapper appeared. In 1991, a seventeen-year-old prodigy who called himself Nasty Nas seemed to show up out of nowhere on a song by an underground group called Main Source called "Live at the Barbecue." It was a posse cut, the kind of song that featured each member of a crew of rappers each taking a verse—and Nas's slayed. He rapped line after jaw-dropping, shocking line about how bad he was:

> Kidnap the president's wife without a plan
> And hanging n---as like the Ku Klux Klan
> I melt mics til the sound wave's over
> Before steppin' to me, you'd rather step to Jehovah

And then he seemed to disappear back into Queensbridge.

His parents, an accomplished trumpeter and a tireless postal service worker, had named him Nasir bin Olu Dara Jones. His father, Olu Dara, had encouraged him to use music as his way to express himself, and his mother, Ann Jones, had insisted he study hard. By the time he, his brother Jabari (aka "Jungle"), and his upstairs neighbor, Will "Ill Will" Graham, were tweens, they were writing and rapping every day. "[Will] had crazy styles off the top of his head," Nas says. "I was the one who would sit down and write, so it took me longer to come up with shit."[9]

Nas and Ill Will grew up going to the park jams. They watched as MC Shan and Marley Marl put Queensbridge on the hip-hop map. One day, Roxanne Shanté came upon them rapping in a cipher and stopped to listen to them. When they got nervous around her, she told them if they hadn't gotten their raps tighter by the next time she saw them, she would personally kick both of their asses. When both Nas and Ill Will were teens, they were ready to bring the rep that KRS-One had stolen back to the Bridge.

But a year after "Live at the Barbecue," as record labels were still trying to find Nas, Will and Jungle were shot in front of their building after an argument. Nas, who had gone up to his apartment for just a second, came out to find both of them bleeding from their wounds. Jungle survived, but Will would not. Nas was devastated.

"I had these pictures of how shit would be when he grew up. How shit would fall into place. The cipher is incomplete now, 'cuz my man is gone," Nas said in an early interview. "I'm gonna represent and keep it real."[10]

In the three years between his recording debut and his 1994 debut album, *Illmatic,* Nas had experienced the same kind of loss that KRS-One had. He had been studying hip-hop, from the old school of *Wild Style* to his Juice Crew elders. But Ill Will's death made telling the stories of his neighborhood more urgent for him.

At the age of twenty, he had recorded and released an album that seemed to contain the wisdom of the ages, the sound of a young prophet with eyes and ears wide open, seeing everything around him, listening to the stories of folks coming back from prison, and carrying the weight of his entire Queensbridge world on his shoulders. Nas and his friends lived under the shadow of death—it permeated every part of the record. Making hip-hop was his way to keep moving, like sharks who have to keep moving to avoid sinking.

"I never sleep," he rapped in "New York State of Mind," "'cause sleep is the cousin of death."

On "One Love," he wrote a letter to his homie in prison, describing how the streets had changed since he had been sent up north. His block had been taken over by rivals, and even worse, his girl was messing with them. But he worried over the innocent children—a young boy had joined the drug game, a young girl coming home from a day at the beach was killed in a crossfire. School had failed him, left him feeling invisible. He realizes that to save the young ones, he himself has to become a teacher. But have the streets made the young ones too hardened to listen?

Yet amid the pain and pessimism, he was finding reasons to keep moving—to connect, to represent, to try to be free.

"Whose world is this?" he asked. "The world is yours."

Keeping It Right

As the '90s went on and underground rappers went on to commercial success, they became less concerned with the danger that hip-hop would become pop and lose its commitment to the communities that gave it life. Instead, they became alarmed with the money that white record execs were pouring into gangsta rap. They felt "studio gangstas" were playing into age-old American stereotypes that criminalized and debased Black men and women. These same stereotypes were driving support for politicians to pass an explosion of federal, state, and local "tough on crime" laws against young people, especially young people of color, that would result in a globally historic increase in the incarceration of Black and brown men and women.

On 1994's celebrated underground hip-hop anthem "Time's Up," the artist O.C. criticized rappers who talked about guns and drugs because that was what record labels wanted, but who had never lived that life. "Everybody's either crime-related or sexual," he rapped. "I'm here to make a difference." O.C. wanted to uphold the code of the underground:

> I'd rather be broke and have a whole lot of respect
> It's the principle of it. I get a rush when I bust
> Some dope lines I wrote that maybe somebody'll quote
> That's what I consider real in this field of music

And on the song "In the Woods" from the album *Buhloone Mindstate*, De La Soul's Posdnous took on gangsterism directly: "The gangsta's outdated. Fuck being hard! Posdnous is complicated."

As hip-hop grew in popularity, the questions only seemed to multiply. Perhaps, as KRS-One had rapped in 1986—and NWA reaffirmed in "Gangsta, Gangsta"—hip-hop was not about a salary, it was all about reality. And what if that reality was about the violence of poverty? Ice Cube had said rappers weren't meant to be role models, but he seemed to agree that they did have a responsibility to represent the underside of the American Dream.

But on their 1996 album *Stakes Is High*, De La Soul asked another difficult question. What should rappers do—should they simply represent reality? Or push people to do better? On "The Bizness," Posdnous dropped another startling line, "You tried 'keepin' it real,' yet you should try keepin' it right."

Stakes Is High opened with a collage of people talking about what it meant for them to hear *Criminal Minded* for the first time, the album on which KRS-One had said the line about rap and reality. Now, ten years later, *Stakes Is High* sold relatively modestly. By the standards of 1986, when gold rap records were rare, it was an important underground hit. But by the standards of 1996, when two albums by Tupac Shakur debuted at number one on the pop charts and went gold in their first week, it was considered a sales failure.

Above the global hip-hop underground, the world was changing rapidly. MTV made the decision to take *Yo! MTV Raps* off the air. It seemed like it was no longer needed. Hip-hop's crossover was complete. MTV—once an explicitly segregated network—now prominently featured Black artists, mostly hip-hop artists, at all hours of the day.

And there were still higher heights of success ahead. Hip-hop would soon become the bestselling musical genre, and a global pop cultural force. Its rise would be led by two feuding record labels, Death Row and Bad Boy, and their stars, Tupac Shakur and Christopher "Notorious B.I.G." Wallace.

15
Tupac and Biggie

Every generation has their heroes who are gone too soon, whose deaths make no sense, leaving us to pore over their all-too-brief lives for meaning for the rest of our own lives: Bruce Lee with his brain injury, Bob Marley with cancer in his toe, Billie Holiday under the bottle, James Dean behind the wheel, Jimi Hendrix with a bottle of pills, Kurt Cobain with a gun, and Tupac Shakur and Christopher "Notorious B.I.G." Wallace, gunned down in the prime of their creative lives.

Tupac and Biggie were among the largest of personalities in a movement of many. Between them they seemed to encompass most of hip-hop's mythology. They both had risen from humble roots, born to idealistic single mothers who held strong desires for a better world. They were both natural rebels. They shared a profound work ethic and a desire to survive by any means necessary. Each had generation-defining talent, with the power to express the shared feelings of millions. "They were two Geminis, born griots, and real n---as," wrote the storyteller and activist dream hampton, who was a friend to both.[1]

In the beginning, they were fast friends who seemed destined to be old men in easy chairs, sharing tall tales and hearty laughs from daylight to sunset. They understood each other instinctively, held great admiration for each other, and partied hard together. But in the end, they seemed irreconcilable enemies, pulled apart by forces much larger than themselves. People had long wondered what might have happened if Martin Luther King, Jr. and Malcolm X had ever joined forces—this was the meaning of the fire-scarred image that haunted Spike Lee's 1989 film masterpiece, *Do the Right Thing*. Maybe some time in the future people would wonder the same about Tupac and Biggie.

Dreams

Afeni Shakur and Voletta Wallace, Tupac and Biggie's mothers, were both women who had come of age in the 1960s, a time of massive social change. The Civil Rights Movement had guided Congress toward removing racist restrictions on the immigration of people of color. Jamaica-born and raised Voletta Wallace was one of the millions who had benefited, moving to the United States in 1966 at the age of nineteen in part to escape her uncle's sexual abuse. Afeni Shakur had been born in rural North Carolina but left with her mother and sister to escape her father's violence. In New York City she became radicalized and joined the Black Panther Party for Self-Defense, the Black revolutionary organization. Both had big dreams for their sons.

Voletta fell in love with a man she didn't know was married, and by the time she gave birth to her only son, Christopher, on May 21, 1972, that man had largely abandoned both of them. She raised Christopher while working long hours and taking classes to become a schoolteacher. Though she did not make much money, she spoiled him, spending whatever extra money she had to put him in the best clothes and feed him well. "The name 'Biggie,'" she wrote in her autobiography, "he earned that."

"Christopher was not a problem child at all," she wrote. "In fact, he was a pleasure to raise. He was kind and gentle and had a wonderful, warm personality. He was headstrong, though, and very very curious. You couldn't just tell Christopher something. You had to show him. He had to see for himself."[2]

Voletta invested in Christopher her immigrant dreams of American success. She put Christopher in private schools whose tuition stretched her tight budget. But when he reached high school, his teachers noted to Voletta that Christopher was a highly intelligent kid who seemed to have lost all interest in school.

As a teenager, Afeni was enrolled in New York City's famous High School of Performing Arts, but she fell into gang life. One day she heard the message of the Black Panthers, who were calling the community to defend itself and fight for their freedom. "I was captivated by the visualness of the Black Panther Party. I was captivated by the rationality of the Black Panther Party, and I was captivated by the sense of service of the Black Panther Party. For me," she said, "the Black Panther Party was a way to legitimately express my anger."[3]

She became deeply involved in the Party, writing the newsletter and becoming the New York chapter's communications secretary, one of the chapter's main leaders. But in 1969, police arrested her and twenty other key members of the Party in an attempt to shut down the Black Panthers. To the supporters who rallied on their behalf, they became known as the Panther 21. As the trial proceedings continued over the next two years, Afeni became pregnant with Tupac. She spent long months in prison fearing that she would lose Tupac because of the poor prison health care. On May 13, 1971, all of the Panther 21 were acquitted of all charges. Just a month later, on June 16, Afeni gave birth to her son, Lesane Parish Crooks, whom she would rename after the historic Inca leader Tupac Amaru, representing her revolutionary dreams for him.

But by the 1980s, both Voletta and Afeni were struggling to raise their children in an America that had dramatically changed. The Shakurs—Afeni, Tupac, and his sister, Sekyiwa—felt it dramatically. "Poverty, it's no joke," Tupac said. "If there was no money and everything depended on your moral standards and the way you treated people, we'd be millionaires, we'd be rich. But since it's not like that, we're stone broke."[4]

Afeni had given her life to activism. The Shakur name, which meant "thankful to God," was the chosen surname of a number of Black Power activists, including Assata Shakur, Tupac's godmother, who would live her life in exile in Cuba after escaping from a New Jersey prison. Tupac later explained, "In my family every black male with the last name of Shakur that ever passed the age of fifteen has either been killed or put in jail. There are no Shakurs, black male Shakurs, out right now, free, breathing, without bullet holes in them or cuffs on his hands. None."[5]

As the Reagan era took hold, and more and more social services were eliminated, Tupac's family found themselves on welfare and sometimes had to stay in homeless shelters. When Afeni lost her job in 1984, they decided to move to Baltimore. Tupac took an audition for the Baltimore School for the Arts and was accepted. He excelled at the school, starred in a production of *A Raisin in the Sun*, and developed a lifetime friendship with a young girl named Jada Pinkett. But every day he was reminded of his economic status. His classmates were largely white and upper middle-class.

Tupac was an artistic, sensitive child seeking approval, searching for male mentors. He was shy, and studied acting and poetry with a passion. He would be asked later by his attorney if he had ever joined any gangs when he was a youth. "Shakespeare gangs. I was the mouse king in *The Nutcracker*," Tupac said. "There was no gangs. I was an artist."[6]

He kept a diary in which he wrote that he would be famous, he told *Vibe* journalist Kevin Powell, "Because I had that fucked-up childhood. The reason why I could get into acting was because it takes nothin' to get out of who I am to get into somebody else."[7]

But Afeni developed a crack habit, and the family continued to fall into bouts of homelessness. She decided to send Tupac and his younger sister to Marin City, California, a low-income Black neighborhood nestled in one of the wealthiest counties in America. They were meant to live with Afeni's former Black Panther comrade as she got herself together. But when they arrived they found that Afeni's comrade was not interested in taking care of them.

Tupac was seventeen years old. He dyed his hair green and hung out with the arts students. But while each night they went home to their expensive houses, he was trying to figure out how to feed himself and his sister.

"I went through school all the way and was ready to go to college. The only thing that stopped me was money. The time all the kids in my school was writing applications to go to college, I didn't have no lights or no electricity," he said. "So when I think back to that—I'm not thuggin' for me, I'm thuggin' for my family. I paid all the bills. I feed my whole family, wrong or right. I do. And I can't stop."[8]

Tupac dropped out of school. "Leaving that school affected me so much. Even now, I see that as the point where I got off track," he told Powell.[9] He harbored a deep anger at the world that he needed to channel.

When Christopher Wallace was ready to go to high school, he was still a latchkey kid—he was on his own most days as his mother juggled jobs and classes. He was brilliant, but bored with school. He was drawn to the action on the streets—the way the hustlers dressed, the games they played, the way they talked and moved. But it wasn't the money that was attractive.

"I made sure my son had an education, a good mattress, clean sheets, good quality clothes, and I gave him quality time," Voletta Wallace told Biggie biographer Cheo Hodari Coker.[10]

To Christopher, the street hustlers he admired were father figures, men who could show him how to be a man. He dropped out of the Catholic school Voletta had him in, and transferred to a vocational school where three of his classmates were young rappers who would become known as Jay-Z, DMX, and Busta Rhymes. He got a job bagging groceries, trying to make money to buy new Timbs and sweaters. But the money was too slow. His restlessness led him into a secret life—selling drugs for fast money.

On the corners from Park Slope to East New York, the hustlers came to know the six-foot-plus three-hundred-pounder as "Big." He was literally larger than life, a joke-cracking everyday kind of kid. They knew he could even drop a dope rhyme or two for fun. He would sometimes turn up at Brooklyn open mics and steal the show with his precise, intricate, often hilarious freestyles. He seemed like a natural.

They trusted him to push their dope, too. Big hid the fly clothes he bought with the drug proceeds on the roof so his mother wouldn't know. By the time he was eighteen, he had dropped out of school and was out in the streets slinging drugs full time.

Tupac had taken up in a Marin City neighborhood called "The Jungle." He found street authenticity and parental figures in the hustlers, pimps, and prostitutes around him. They were the only ones, he said later, who took interest in him.

He tried selling crack for a second, but quit. The junkies gave him sob stories about why they couldn't pay, and he fell for their lies. The pushers told him to give them back their weight and just concentrate on his rap thing.

He had started a crew with another teenager, Ray Luv, that they called Strictly Dope, and took poetry classes in Oakland. There he met a teacher named Leila Steinberg whom he impressed with his fiery poetry about racial injustice. Leila teamed with lawyer Atron Gregory to become the group's manager, and they linked him with rising Bay Area rap stars Digital Underground, who had a national hit with "The Humpty Dance."

"Tupac was a focused, aggressive and eager brotha who had a strong work ethic for a teenager. He was real serious about his craft. He was always observing and taking notes," wrote Sleuth Pro, Digital Underground's road manager, in his memoir. "You could see Tupac was a thinker and a visionary. Most of his actions were calculated and well thought out. He was always planning for the future."[11]

By the age of nineteen, Tupac had reached a turning point in his life. He had an offer from the New Black Panther Party in Atlanta to help lead their youth chapters. He needed to decide whether to follow in his mother's footsteps or take a risk and try to break into the rap game.

In Brooklyn, Biggie was still living at home, but clocking over a thousand dollars a day. Then one day in 1990, he and his friends were arrested. He was lucky enough not to have any drugs on him, only an unregistered gun, and so received five years probation. Cops came by to talk to Voletta. Biggie had to admit to his mother he was selling dope. He also started thinking that maybe this rap thing everyone thought he was so good at might be something to actually try harder at.

He met an older hustler named Zauqael from New York who had moved to North Carolina. Together they realized they could clear tens of thousands a week by selling their New York packages down there. They bought a three-bedroom ranch home in Raleigh, North Carolina. One night the two watched the movie *Let's Do It Again,* which featured a character named Biggie Smalls, and Christopher instantly had a new nickname. When he returned to Brooklyn he cut a demo with Mister Cee, a legendary DJ who was so taken by it he sent it to *The Source* magazine. The writers there were so sprung by it, they featured Biggie Smalls in their prestigious "Unsigned Hype" column.

Biggie was suddenly on the verge of blowing up. Two major label players, Sean "Puffy" Combs and Andre Harrell, were calling to make him a deal. It looked so good that he never told his drug partner in Raleigh. When Biggie finally got the call that the deal had been done, he left for New York the next morning. Hours later, the cops raided their house. Zauqael went to jail and Biggie's drug-pushing days were over.

Looking to his future, Tupac chose Digital Underground over the New Black Panthers. And suddenly his rap career began to take off. He started as a roadie and a dancer, but soon he was recording for the group, putting in a memorable verse on Digital Underground's "Same Song." A year later, in September 1991, he had a deal with Interscope Records and had released his debut single, "Trapped."

In some ways, the song and its video foreshadowed Tupac's next six years. The video depicts Tupac rapping most of the song from inside prison. In the first verse he raps, "They never taught peace in the Black community, all we know is violence." In the second, he talks about being harassed by cops, "searchin' me, then askin' my identity," before being thrown to the ground. By the end of the song, the cop gets "shot for his brutality." For better and for worse, nobody who heard the song would soon forget it.

"Trapped" was released on September 25. Two weeks later, while heading to the bank to deposit some money, Tupac jaywalked across a street in downtown Oakland. Two police officers immediately stopped him and asked for his ID. Tupac pulled out three pieces for them. The cops started making fun of his name. He responded, "Don't you have better things to do?" and he asked them to issue a ticket so he could be on his way. One of the cops told him they could do whatever they wanted to him. Tupac told them, "Fuck all y'all."

The officer immediately grabbed Tupac by the neck, put him in a chokehold, and flung him face first into the gutter, scarring the left side of his face. The other handcuffed him. They told Tupac he would "learn [his] place while in Oakland." He responded that they were treating him like a slave, as if they were his "masters." "I like that. I like the sound of that," one of the officers replied. Then they took Tupac to jail and charged him with resisting arrest.

Atron Gregory recalls, "I went to see him the next day and his face was all jacked up and he was pissed off. We decided we're going to sue the Oakland PD."[12]

When his first court date came, Tupac was shaken to the core. Gregory says, "He'd never been in trouble. He'd never been in jail. He'd never been in court. That was his very first time. He literally ran out of the court, jumped in a cab and went back to his apartment."[13]

A month later, Tupac filed a lawsuit for $10 million. The Oakland Police Department settled out of court for $42,000. "As my video was debuting on MTV, I was behind bars getting beat up by the

Police Department. I was still an N-I-double-G-A and they proved it," he said. "All this is scars I go to my grave with. All this is learn-to-be-a-n---a scars."[14]

He would remind interviewers for the rest of his life, "I had no police record all my life until I made a record."

Me Against the World

By his own estimation, Tupac was a lucky guy. One day he accompanied his Digital Underground partner, Money B, to an audition for a movie. The movie was called *Juice,* and it was about a crew of four friends in Harlem who come apart over the violence instigated by one of them, a murderous character named Roland Bishop. Money B and others, such as Naughty by Nature's Treach, tried out for the part. But it was Tupac's pain and intensity that won the director over. His powerful performance propelled the movie to critical and box office success.

At the beginning of 1992, Tupac had a hit movie and a hit album in his debut, *2Pacalypse Now.* But trouble seemed to follow him as much as luck. Vice President Dan Quayle was attacking him for the song "Trapped" and its depiction of shooting a policeman.

But worse followed. During a Black-organized summer celebration for Marin City's fiftieth anniversary, some neighborhood acquaintances confronted Tupac and his entourage. In the ensuing chaos, a gun was drawn, shots were fired, and soon a six-year-old who had been riding around on a bicycle lay dead from a stray bullet. The bullet was traced to Shakur's gun, and although Tupac had not fired the gun, he and his brother Maurice (who rapped under the name Moecedes and later, Mopreme) were detained but not charged. Tupac called his mother and cried for a long time, then wrote "Something 2 Die 4."

In Texas, a fan named Ronald Ray Howard shot and killed a state trooper named Bill Davidson. The widow of the slain officer filed the multimillion-dollar civil suit against Tupac, claiming *2Pacalypse Now* had influenced the young murderer. Like Ice-T and other rappers, Tupac had become a political target.

But other times Tupac's anger simply got the best of him. While visiting the set of Fox TV's *In Living Color,* he had an altercation with a limo driver whom he felt was disrespecting his friend. At Michigan State University, he was arrested for beating down a local rapper.

On the set of a video, Tupac confronted Albert and Allen Hughes, the directors of *Menace II Society*, for firing him from the movie. He and a group of Crips beat down Allen Hughes, then he went on *MTV* to brag about it and was charged with assault and battery.

His manager moved him to Atlanta, not far from where his mother was living, to try to keep him out of trouble. But not long after, he got into a shootout with two white off-duty police officers at an intersection in Atlanta. The officers were brothers who were crossing an intersection when a Black driver came to an abrupt stop. The brothers started shouting at the man. Tupac's car stopped behind them while they were arguing. He stepped out to defend the driver, whom he did not know but whom he thought the two clearly drunk white men were harassing. Witnesses said that then one of the men drew his gun and fired on Tupac and his crew. They also smashed in the window of Tupac's car. Pac drew his gun, dropped to a knee, and shot one of the men in the abdomen and the other in the buttocks.

National pro-police groups brought up Tupac's lyrics on "Soulja's Story," in which he had rapped in the voice of a street warrior: "Keep my shit cocked, cause the cops got a Glock too / What the fuck would you do? Drop them or let 'em drop you?" But the district attorney refused to prosecute the case, agreeing that Tupac had acted in self-defense.

Tupac admitted to MTV's Abby Kearse on the eve of his sentencing for assaulting Hughes that he had become known for controversy. "I'm trying to find my way in the world. I'm trying to *be* somebody instead of just making money off everybody. So I go down paths that haven't been traveled before. And I usually mess up. But I learn. I come back stronger. I have not been out of the papers since I joined Digital Underground," he said, "and that's good for me because I don't want to be forgotten."[15]

His old friend Ray Luv said, "He always kinda had this ideology that he didn't need a record label, he didn't need the movies, all he needed to do was stay real. 'Cause if he stays real and he keeps telling the kids what is authentic to him, that they will always relate. He will never be begging for bread."[16] In Houston and Los Angeles, Tupac began frequenting shops where he had tattoos done. In all, he would have more than twenty burned across his body. "All his tattoos meant something," Ray Luv said. On his back, he had a cross with "Exodus 1831" written in it. 1831 was the year of Nat Turner's slave uprising. Emblazoned across his abs was "THUG LIFE." A bullet stood in for the letter "I." He told people it stood for "The Hate U Give Little Infants Fucks Everyone." It was about how racism impacted everyone, not just people of color.

In an MTV interview, Tupac updated a parable that Malcolm X used to tell about the gap between white and Black people. "I'm not going to sit at your table and watch you eat, with nothing on my plate, and call myself a diner," Malcolm X said. Tupac insisted that, a generation later, the gap between white and Black people had not gotten any better. He said:

> If I know that in this hotel room, they have food every day and I'm knocking on the door every day to eat, and they open the door, let me see the party. Let me see like them throwing salami all over the place. I mean, just like throwing food around. But you're telling me there's no food in here?
>
> Every day I'm standing outside trying to sing my way in. You know, I'm saying (sings): "We are hungry. Please let us in. We are hungry, please let us in." After about a week, that song is gon' change to [sings]: "We hungry. We need some food." After two or three weeks, it's like: "Give me all the food or we go breaking down the door." After a year then you just like, "I'm picking the lock, coming through the door blasting!"
>
> It's like you hungry, you've reached your level. We *asked.* Ten years ago, we was asking with the Panthers. We was asking with the Civil Rights Movement . . . now that those people that were asking, they're all dead and in jail, so now what do you think we're going to do?
>
> And we shouldn't be angry? And my raps that I'm rapping to my community shouldn't be filled with rage? It shouldn't be filled with the same atrocities that they gave to me? In the media they don't talk about it. So in my raps, I have to talk about it. And it just seems foreign because there's no one else talking about it.
>
> All the society is doing is leeching off the ghetto. They use the ghetto for their pain, for their sorrow, for their culture, for their music, for their happiness, for their movies—to talk about boys in the hood . . . I don't want to be fifty years old at a BET "We Shall Overcome achievement awards." Not me. I mean, when they see

me, they know that every day when I'm breathing, it's forced to go farther. Every time I speak, I want the truth to come out.[17]

Tupac's music was exploding in popularity. His 1993 album, *Strictly 4 My N.I.G.G.A.Z. . . .* , went platinum with songs like "Holler If You Hear Me," "I Get Around," and especially "Keep Ya Head Up" (built on samples of two deeply hopeful songs, Zapp's "Be Alright" and the Five Stairsteps' "Oooh Child" and whose video was dedicated to Latasha Harlins), winning critical praise and establishing three sides of his personality: the Black Power rebel, the smooth operator, and the empathetic son and friend who aches for his mother and his friends in their daily struggle. If his life sometimes appeared to be an endless action-film performance, his music presented him as the angry, sensitive child maturing into a voice expressing a generation's joys and pains.

For his part, Tupac was always aware of how people perceived him. "They want me, when they first see me, to humble myself . . . just because they're scared of me. But I don't feel like that's my job—to humble myself to show you that I'm not a threat. I'm not a threat, unless you're a threat to me," he said to BET's Ed Gordon. "One on one, I believe honestly that I can talk. I believe that I have the ability to reason, I have logic, I have compassion, I have understanding. If we talk, there's no problems. But that's not what happens."

When he was in court, he said, there were times he couldn't defend himself. It wasn't because he didn't comprehend what they were saying or he didn't know what to say, it was the exact opposite. "It's like being exiled from society," he said. "The anger comes from—I'm tired of waiting for my pass to get into society."[18]

"Right now where I'm at, the world is harsh and I just don't got no beautiful stories," he said. "Everything I'm saying is a warning, is a plea for help. If everybody is so damn worried about me why ain't nobody came to help me?"

Party and BS

Tupac and Biggie's friendship burned hotly for only about two years. Their beef would last almost as long.

In the beginning, they were fast friends. Biggie had just cut his first single, "Party and Bulls--t," and was trying to get a toehold in the game. Tupac was a year older and already a star. In 1993, on a promotional tour, Biggie traveled to Los Angeles and Tupac showed up at their hotel in a drop-top convertible to bring him and his crew back to his house. At the house they had a freestyling session, then Tupac cooked them up some steaks and the party continued into the evening.

"Party and Bullshit" was Tupac's favorite song. On set for the new movie he was shooting with John Singleton, he played it over and over. Soon Tupac was having Biggie stay over at his house every time he was in Los Angeles. And when Tupac went to Brooklyn, he rolled up in a limo and hung with Biggie and the crew shooting cee-lo and chilling. By the end of the year, they would be sharing stages with each other across New York, sometimes rocking freestyles together to the roar of the crowd. They made plans to record together.

"I always thought it to be like a Gemini thing," Biggie later recalled to *Vibe* writer Larry "The Blackspot" Hester. "We just clicked off the top and were cool ever since."[19]

Biggie's streetwise vibe was exactly the kind of authenticity Tupac craved. Tupac had locked down a role for his next movie, *Above the Rim*, in which he was to play a street criminal. And he was hanging out with real thugs and killers from Brooklyn. Biggie took Tupac aside and warned him about some of them. But Pac paid Biggie no mind.

For his part, Biggie was trying to leave the game. After North Carolina, he had made up his mind. His ex-girlfriend was pregnant with his first child, and his mother had been diagnosed with breast cancer. He and his girlfriend had split, but he resolved to be a good father, to be present for his daughter in a way his father had never been for him. Biggie was especially devastated by Voletta's cancer. He refused to see her in the hospital because he couldn't consider the thought of his mother leaving him.

Puff Daddy had been fired from Uptown Records, throwing the future into uncertainty. Biggie had doubts both about Puffy's new label and about the pop direction that Puffy wanted him to go in. But Tupac advised Biggie that he needed to make records for the females—that was the main way he would become successful. Biggie asked Tupac to manage him. But Pac said, no, Puff will make you a star.

While Tupac was having run-ins with police and others, Biggie was recording his first album, *Ready to Die.* He often showed up without lyrics written, sat in a chair and stared at the ceiling, only to step to the mic and astonish his producers and engineers with all the rhymes, the stories, the lines that poured out of him. On songs like "Gimme the Loot" and "Warning," he was a storyteller of the first rank, building cinematic, suspenseful scenes.

Biggie's singles—"Juicy," "Big Poppa," and "One More Chance"—were the songs that Puffy wanted him to do, and though he was skeptical about Puff's crossover moves, he revealed his personality on them. Biggie was funny, intimate, and seductive, full of sweet talk, charming humblebrags, and promises of a pleasurable evening. Even if some of his claims to poverty were exaggerated, "Juicy" was his brilliantly composed, started-from-the-bottom story, one of a "born sinner, the opposite of a winner." He rapped:

Considered a fool 'cause I dropped out of high school
Stereotypes of a Black male misunderstood
And it's still all good

Biggie was a lazy-eyed giant who described himself as "heart-throb never, Black and ugly as ever," who possessed none of Tupac's whip appeal. But he became a sex symbol for his way with words. In the coming years, the press would be full of gossip about his relationships with Faith Evans, Lil' Kim, and Charli Baltimore.

On the title song, he could drop a funny lyric like, "I got techniques dripping out my buttcheeks / Sleep on my stomach so I don't fuck up my sheets." But what could make someone who seemed to enjoy life so much say that he was "ready to die"? Biggie told his producer Easy Mo Bee he was writing about all the despair he was feeling. The last song on the album was called "Suicidal Thoughts." It ended with a gunshot, the sound of a body falling to the ground, and a heartbeat slowing and stopping as Puff Daddy cried, "Ayo Big!"

The first song on the album—"Things Done Changed"—had revealed why. All the kids who used to go to each other's barbecues were now adults armed to the teeth and playing for keeps in the drug trade. By the third verse, he had revealed how stressed he was from the hustle, the constant threat of a violent death, and his mother's fight with cancer. On "Ready to Die," he rapped, "Shit is real and hungry's how I feel." He had put everything into the record because it was all he had. If this didn't work, he didn't know what else he could do.

Meanwhile, Tupac had caught yet another case, one that he would not be able to escape—a rape charge involving him and three others.

Who Shot Ya?

Biggie's album debuted in 1994 to ecstatic reviews from the hip-hop community, pleasing New York heads especially, who claimed that *Ready to Die* and Nas's *Illmatic* were signs that the crown had been returned to the East Coast. At the same time, Tupac was spiraling down. He faced cases in multiple states, including charges of sexual assault, weapons possession, and sodomy.

On a night in November 1993, he had met a young woman named Ayanna Jackson at a nightclub. They spent the evening together consensually. Two nights later, Tupac invited her to meet him at his hotel after a show. When she arrived, she found him in the room with three other men, including a Brooklyn heavy nicknamed Haitian Jack. She said that Tupac told her, "Relax, baby. These are my boys. I like you so much I decided to share you with them."[20] She told him, "No, I came here to be with you. This is not what I want." Then, she said, the other men ripped her clothes off as Tupac held her by her braids. At some point, Tupac left her in the room, she said, and went to another room to take a nap while they raped her.

Just the year before, on "Keep Ya Head Up," he had rapped, "I wonder why we take from our women, why we rape our women. Do we hate our women?"

His shows were cancelled left and right. He lost a starring role in John Singleton's next movie, *Higher Learning*. He couldn't get TV roles. His daily schedule instead became a series of court appearances. He went on BET to do a candid interview with Ed Gordon and said that anyone who believed he was a rapist should get "Brenda's Got a Baby" and "Keep Ya Head Up" and "listen to them thoroughly."

He said, "I did that from my heart. So that if they do try to put a rape charge on me, my sisters could say, 'He ain't about that.' Now if my sisters can't say that, you won't hear another 'Keep Ya Head Up' out my mouth. You understand me? 'Cause it's a struggle on Black males today."

He said he wanted to be his generation's leader. He said, "I got the whole world fearing me. At twenty-three. Weighing 160 pounds. And I ain't even started. I haven't even wrote my plan out yet and they scared."

He admitted to Ed Gordon, "I honestly did not care whether I lived or died. But now, I cannot die with people thinking I'm a rapist or a criminal. I can't leave until this shit is straight. I'm not suicidal. I can't go until y'all really know what time it is."[21]

He added, "God has cursed me to see what life should be like."

He sometimes relaxed by going to see Biggie and the crew in Brooklyn. But mostly he was frustrated. When he learned that Haitian Jack was taking a plea for a small fine and no jail time, Tupac went to the newspaper and called him a snitch.

He was also quickly running out of money. He was asked by James "Jimmy Henchman" Rosemond, a friend and associate of Haitian Jack, to record a guest verse on a song for an artist whom he managed, Little Shawn. Tupac arrived at the Quad Recording Studios in Times Square on November 30, 1994, to record the song. He was due back in court in two days to hear the verdict in his rape case.

He arrived with his friend Stretch, a rapper from a crew called Live Squad, Stretch's friend Freddie Moore, and his sister's boyfriend. As they walked up to the studio door, Lil Cease from Biggie's crew Junior M.A.F.I.A. stuck his head out a window from above and hollered. Biggie, Puffy, Andre Harrell, and him were upstairs working on a song called "Player's Anthem."

As they stepped into the lobby, Tupac felt something was amiss. There were three men in the lobby in camo fatigues, but they didn't answer when he greeted them. In an instant, two of the men pulled out 9mm guns and told them to get on the floor and give up their jewels. Tupac would later say that he refused to lie down, and when he reached for his gun, he was shot. The men pistol-whipped him and took $40,000 of jewelry. Oddly, they left a diamond-encrusted watch on his wrist.

After the men ran off, Tupac and his entourage stumbled outside, saw a police car, and decided instead to head up in the elevator.

When the elevator doors opened, Puffy, Biggie, Andre Harrell, and Jimmy Henchman stared at them. Tupac was bleeding from the head and leg, and he started pacing the floor saying he had been set up. Andre called for an ambulance. Some of the others got busy hiding the guns, including Tupac's. As he was rolled out on a stretcher, a photographer raised a camera to take a picture—and Pac threw up a middle finger at him.

At the hospital, Tupac was still conscious, a fact that stunned the doctors in the trauma unit. They told him he had been shot five times. By the next afternoon, they had done emergency surgery on his leg. By 7:00 P.M. he had checked himself out of the hospital. His mother came to take him to a safe house. All night he had been thinking about who was trying to kill him. "My life was in danger," he later said. "I knew what type of n---as I was dealing with."[22]

Biggie went to the hospital to take Tupac's gun back to him. But he was already gone.

The next day, December 1, Tupac showed up at the courthouse, his head and leg bandaged, rolled up in a wheelchair. He left in the afternoon, before the verdict was read, because his leg had begun to numb—and checked in at a local hospital under an assumed name. That afternoon the jury announced their verdict. He was acquitted of the sodomy and weapons possession charges but guilty of the sexual assault charge. He was later moved to Rikers Island and held on $3 million bail.

Kevin Powell visited him there in January, and Tupac—while he admitted he was nervous—did not hold back. He told Powell, "The excuse maker in Tupac is dead. The vengeful Tupac is dead. The Tupac that would stand by and let dishonorable things happen is dead. God let me live for me to do something extremely extraordinary, and that's what I have to do."[23]

In the interview, he implied that Haitian Jack and Jimmy Henchman were behind the hit, and insinuated that Andre Harrell, Puffy, Biggie, and even Stretch might have known about it as well. He wondered if Ayanna Jackson was part of a conspiracy against him: "I don't know if she's with these guys or if she's mad at me for not protecting her," he said. "But I know I am ashamed—because I wanted to be accepted and because I want no harm done to me—I didn't say nothing.[24]

"This Thug Life stuff, it was just ignorance. My intentions was always in the right place. I never killed anybody, I never raped anybody, I never committed no crimes that weren't honorable—that weren't to defend myself," he said. "I'm going to show people my true intentions, and my true heart. I'm going to show them the man that my mother raised. I'm going to make them all proud."

In February, he returned to court for his sentencing. Ms. Jackson told the court that she had been living in constant fear and had received death threats. She told the court, "He should not be allowed to use his so-called celebrity status to avoid the consequences of his actions."

Tupac tearfully apologized to Jackson. But he added, "I'm not apologizing for a crime. I hope in time you'll come forth and tell the truth." He then apologized to "the youth of America" for "falsely representing them." And he again cried as he admitted, "I got so involved in my career that I didn't see this coming, that I wasn't more focused."[25]

He then addressed the judge, saying, "Your honor, throughout this entire court case, you haven't looked me or my attorney in the eye once. It's obvious that you're not here in the search for justice, so therefore there's no point in me asking for a lighter sentence. I don't care what you do 'cause you're not respecting us, this is not a court of law; as far as I'm concerned, no justice is being served here, and you still can't look me in the eye. So I say, do what you want to do, give me whatever time you want, because I'm not in your hands, I'm in God's hands."

State Supreme Court Justice Daniel Fitzgerald told Shakur, "This was an act of brutal violence against a helpless woman. A woman's decision to have consensual sex with one man does not give him license to give her to other men to have sex."[26] And he chastised Shakur for crimes that have been "escalating in violence as his career has progressed." He sentenced Tupac to one and a half to four and a half years in jail, requiring him to serve eighteen months before being eligible for parole. His attorneys appealed, which would make it possible for him to be freed on bail.

Tupac's *Vibe* interview with Kevin Powell was published. Biggie couldn't believe what he read. "When I read the interview I felt like he was just shitting on everybody. I always said that he was the realest n---a in the game," he said, devastated that his friend had turned on him. "I don't know what he was trying to hide, or if he was scared. I figured that with the shit he was talking in *Vibe*, he was just confused more than anything."[27]

Later, even after Tupac was gone, Biggie was still going over it all. How could Pac have got it so wrong? "He knows that I was at the hospital with his mother when he got shot in that studio," he told Cheo Hodari Coker. "He knows after he left the hospital and went to his girl house uptown, me and Stretch went up in some weed spots to get this n---a a half ounce of weed, and bring him some weed to his girl crib. He know this.

"That shit hurt me, man. It hurt me."[28]

Who shot Tupac? In 2011, a man named Dexter Isaac, who had already been sentenced to life in prison for an unrelated murder, confessed that he had been paid $2,500 and some of the jewelry he had taken for what was meant to be just a simple robbery. And who had set it up? Isaac named Jimmy Henchman, the same person Tupac would call out, along with Haitian Jack, by name in his Makaveli track "Against All Odds."

And why had they fired on him? One theory was that they had not. Investigators and journalists poring over the evidence agreed with what they were hearing from insiders: Tupac accidentally shot himself in the leg when he reached for his gun in his waist. Then, to ensure he wouldn't fire on them, the attackers at Quad Studios beat him mercilessly. They hadn't had time to grab the Rolex before fleeing into the night.

By then, of course, all these confessions were way too late. When 1995 had rolled around—with Tupac convinced that Bad Boy wanted him dead—the die had been cast for both his and Biggie's ends.

Hit 'Em Up

If there was any chance to reconcile, that was gone by February of 1995, three months after Tupac was shot. Not long after Tupac was sentenced to serve time at Clinton Correctional Facility, Bad Boy released a new Biggie song that would leave Tupac enraged. It was called "Who Shot Ya," and although it had been recorded long before the Quad Studio incident, the timing of the release had everyone buzzing. Were Biggie and the Bad Boy camp taunting Pac? Biggie said it had nothing to do with the shooting, but as far as Tupac was concerned, Biggie and Puff were now his mortal enemies.

In August, when *The Source* was set to present its awards gala at Madison Square Garden, the hip-hop media was rife with talk of an East Coast–West Coast war. The mood was tense as Biggie was set to take top honors for Best Album, Lyricist, Video, and Performer of the Year. Suge Knight stepped onstage to accept an award for Best Soundtrack for Tupac's film *Above the Rim*. Dressed in red, the color of his Blood set, the Mob Pirus, the Death Row Records head told a stunned crowd: "Any artist out there that want to be an artist and stay a star, and don't have to worry about the executive producer trying to be all in the videos, all on the record, dancing—come to Death Row!"

The remarks were a thinly veiled diss directed at Puffy, and the audience booed. Later, when Dr. Dre was called to the stage by John Singleton for the Producer of the Year award, the New York crowd started booing again. Snoop Dogg stepped to the microphone and asked: "The East Coast don't have love for Dr. Dre and Snoop Dogg? Y'all don't love us? Well, let it be known, then."

Puff had his turn onstage when Bad Boy artist Craig Mack came up to receive the Song of the Year for "Flava in Ya Ear." He took the high road, saying, "I'm the executive producer who I feel that earlier remark was about. Contrary to what everyone may feel, I would like to say, I am very proud of Dr. Dre, Death Row, and Suge Knight for their accomplishments. I'm a positive Black man and I make music to bring us together, not to separate us, and all the East and West stuff need to stop." When Snoop won Artist of the Year, he and Puffy gave each other a hug. But by then the damage had been done. Even the mainstream media was talking about the rising tensions between Death Row and Bad Boy, Suge and Puffy, East Coast and West Coast.

In September, at an Atlanta party for Jermaine Dupri attended by both the Bad Boy and Death Row camps, one of Suge Knight's friends was killed after a confrontation outside the Platinum City nightclub. Witnesses pointed the finger at Puffy's bodyguard.

At the same time, Tupac was wallowing in jail. His album, *Me Against the World,* which he had cut during the year before he had been shot, debuted at number one. It featured some of the best music of his career, including a heartfelt tribute to Afeni called "Dear Mama," and grim portraits of desperate, suicidal young Gs on "If I Die 2Nite" and "So Many Tears."

But although he had dozens of family members and friends to support, he had no money. As his appeals stalled in court, he wasn't sure how long he would be in jail. He read books and came up with ideas for community organizations and wrote screenplays. But he worried his career was over. And he feared that no one would have his back on the streets.

Suge Knight was promising to push the courts to move on his case. He promised to bail him out if he would sign with Death Row. He promised to buy a house for Afeni. He promised to make Tupac a superstar. He promised to have Tupac's back.

Tupac's advisors and close family friends all cautioned him not to sign with Death Row. He admitted to them, "I know I'm selling my soul to the devil."[29] But then the New York Court of Appeals suddenly allowed him to post bail. Tupac signed the deal. Death Row's parent record label Interscope and Time-Warner put up the $1.4 million bail amount. Suge Knight and his attorney, David Kenner, took a private jet and a white stretch limo to pick him up, and Tupac walked into the free light on October 12, 1995.

In the coming months, Tupac was almost always seen in public wearing red, as if he had affiliated himself with the Bloods, like Suge. His public attacks on Biggie and Puffy intensified. "I was gonna quit rappin' but then Puffy and Biggie came out in *Vibe* magazine and lied and twisted the facts," he told Sway on the Wake Up Show. "I'm trying to get out the game and they wanna dirty up my memory. They wanna dirty up everything I worked for. So instead of quittin,' it made me wanna come back and be more relentless to destroy who used to be my comrades and homeboys."

He seemed more paranoid and unhinged, and, at the same time, more in control than ever. His work ethic was astonishing. In a single session, he could cut song after song after song, as if it had all been building up inside him. Just four months after walking out of jail, he released a double album, *All Eyez on Me*. He sounded more angry and more focused than ever. It went on to spawn his biggest hit, the Dr. Dre–produced "California Love," and sold five million copies.

He had become the biggest rap star in the world. And he was still using his platform to fight the power. He appeared at a Brotherhood Crusade rally in Los Angeles, and brought along Snoop Dogg, MC Hammer, and members of the Dogg Pound, 6 Feet

Deep, and The Outlawz to demonstrate against a California ballot initiative called Proposition 209, which meant to end affirmative action in the state. He also talked about opening up the borders and ending deportations. They intended to do a big concert in September featuring Death Row artists and former Uptown artists Mary J. Blige and Christopher Williams to raise enough money to fight the conservatives who were attacking affirmative action and immigration. He spoke about organizing his fans into a political party made up of those who had been oppressed by the system.

But most of his anger was directed toward the East Coast rap scene. "I feel like we never got [the respect] we deserved," he told Sway. "So now I'm doing what the East Coast would have did if the West Coast did this to them. I'm riding for my side."

"Everybody should understand what I'm doing. It's gangsta shit. It's warrior shit. And it's all by the rules of the game," he added. "I'm gathering attention for dialogue which is what you do in a struggle for power."

And he also was acting out of control, in a way his friend dream hampton described as "bizarre, baffling, and worst of all, dishonorable."[30] He cut a brutal battle rap called "Hit 'Em Up," in which he bragged about sleeping with Biggie's wife—it never happened, according to Faith Evans—and dissed a long list of East Coast rappers. At one point, when Snoop appeared to try to be cooling things out with Puffy and Biggie, Tupac got the crew to warn Snoop to stop.

With the Bad Boy and Death Row rivalry leading the way, hip-hop had become bigger business than ever. Lots of people were being fed off hip-hop. It was no wonder beefs had taken on a violent edge. Entire livelihoods were at stake. With so much money to be made, the situation kept escalating.

There were murmurs that Puffy had begun hiring Crip sets for Bad Boy security when he was on the West Coast, that Death Row had been funded by criminal money. Stories circulated of promoters, producers, and employees who said they had been beaten or tortured who had worked with Death Row. In March, when the Bad Boy entourage tried to leave the parking lot after the Soul Train Awards, they found themselves surrounded by the Death Row contingent.

Tupac was hollering, "West Side! Outlaws!" Biggie stared at him but didn't say a word. Suge told Biggie to step forward, and said to the Bad Boy crew, "Yo, I wanna talk to him." Lil' Cease later recalled that, at that moment, his boys took their guns out. Suge started yelling for police to arrest them. They backed Biggie into the limo and drove away through the Death Row crowd.

Biggie said later he recognized Tupac's wild performance. "I was like, 'That's Bishop!' Whatever he's doing right now, that's the role he's playing." It was the last time Tupac and Biggie ever saw each other.

Vibe magazine had begun publishing an annual "Juice" issue, spotlighting the growing cultural and commercial power of hip-hop. In 1996, that issue happened to come out in September. The magazine put Puffy and Biggie on the cover, and they finally spoke out about Tupac's accusations, fed up by his "Hit 'Em Up" diss.

"He knows who shot him. If you ask him, he knows, and everybody in the street knows, and he's not stepping to them, because he knows he's not gonna get away with that shit. To me that's some real sucker shit," Puffy told journalist Larry "The Blackspot" Hester. "We know that he's a nice guy from New York. All shit aside, Tupac's a nice, good-hearted guy."[31]

Biggie, who resolved to never take Tupac's battle-bait, seemed sadder still. "'This shit's just got to be talk'—that's all I'm saying to myself. I can't believe he would think that I would shit on him like that," he said. "But ain't no man gonna make me act a way I don't want to act. Or make me be something I'm not. I ain't a gangster, so why y'all gonna tell me to start acting like a gangster. I'm trying to be an intelligent Black man. I don't give a fuck if n---as think that it's corny or not."[32]

O.G.'s in the game, like Chuck D and Ice-T, understood that something deeper and more dangerous was going on. In the same September 1996 issue of *Vibe* with Biggie and Puffy on the cover, they broke it down to music editor Danyel Smith:

ICE-T: . . . that beef they got, that's real, that's not East Coast–West Coast shit.

CHUCK D: That's between those two camps right there.

DANYEL: Why is it happening? Isn't part of it about straight competition to sell records?

ICE-T: . . . Why can't *Vibe* talk positively about *The Source*? Because it's competition. Right now rap is business, millions of dollars are exchanging hands.

CHUCK D: It's business but you gotta at least tell motherfuckers, "Don't be backing up onto the Tec," you know what I'm saying? We have to remember that this is the shit that made us. We have to take care of it.

Behind the scenes, Tupac's longtime advisors were trying to get him to back off his rhetoric, and help him build his own business separate from Death Row. He seemed to agree. He wanted to quash the beef with Biggie. Then in September, he decided to go to Las Vegas with Suge to see Mike Tyson fight.

Somebody's Gotta Die

On September 7, 1996, following the Tyson fight at the MGM Grand Hotel, Tupac was shot and killed at a stoplight. He was sitting in the passenger seat of Suge's black BMW, with the window down, when a white Cadillac pulled up, a man reached out with a gun and shot him at least four times. He died six days later from his injuries. He was just twenty-five years old.

Earlier in the evening, Tupac had been caught on hotel surveillance cameras stomping down a Crip from Los Angeles, whom one of the Death Row entourage said had stolen his diamond-encrusted Death Row pendant not long before. Crip and Blood sets launched a war, leaving a trail of bloodshed across Los Angeles unseen since before the 1992 peace treaty.

But what had happened to the long-lashed, big-eyed dreamer who had written of the rose that grew from concrete? Where was the warrior who would lead us to free political prisoners and a revolution for oppressed peoples? How had hip-hop come to this? These were the questions that swirled through the hip-hop world in the wake of Tupac's death.

The writer dream hampton wrote a sad elegy for Tupac that concluded, "I want to say that for me hip-hop is dead. A chapter is undoubtedly closed, and as a generation we're poorer without Tupac, our fearless trickster. But then there's *Life After Death*. And it never stops."[33]

Across the country, Biggie was crying to Faith on the phone. He seemed heartbroken and inconsolable. All the money they had made for so many people couldn't save them. Cheo Hodari Coker recounted a private moment Biggie spent with the legendary hip-hop photographer Ernie Paniciolli a week after Shakur's death. "Let me tell you something," Biggie told Ernie. "In five years me and Duke would have been doing things together. We would have been recording together and we would be taking all the money, 'cause individually, nobody can touch us, and together you *know* nobody can touch us."[34]

As the fall stretched on, Biggie welcomed the birth of his and Faith's boy, Christopher Jr., and then got into a major car accident that had him in a wheelchair. As he rehabilitated, he began using a cane to get around. He was anxious to begin work on his second album, which would be called *Life After Death*. He worked, like Tupac, at an incredible speed and quickly wrote a double album's worth of songs, not to mention featured verses for Junior M.A.F.I.A. and other artists.

At one point he had invited Snoop, who was still on Death Row even though Suge was back in prison, to come to the studio to hear his new song, "Somebody's Gotta Die," where he gave a shout to him. Snoop later appeared on Steve Harvey's show with Puffy to call for peace.

One of the last songs Biggie recorded was "Going Back to Cali." He seemed eager to put any East Coast–West Coast tensions to rest. But to some Tupac fans, it was like "Who Shot Ya?" At best, too soon, at worst, a blatant power play. Was Biggie being brave or foolhardy? Yet with the album completed, he did head west, back to California to get some sun, make the video for "Hypnotize," and promote the album on national radio shows like Sway and Tech's Wake Up Show.

He explained to interviewers that if *Ready to Die* was about facing his despair and anger, he had put it all behind him on the new album. Now he was ready to live. He was even talking about God. His mother had survived breast cancer. He had two healthy children. He had blessings to count. He told Sway that talking about God surprised people. "They think it makes you soft," he said. "But if God is with you no one can be against you." When he and his homie D-Roc went to Los Angeles, they had Psalm 23 tattooed on their arms.

"I'm just trying to blossom more into being a father and a man," he told Cheo Hodari Coker in his last interview. "I want people to look at Big like, 'Look at Big. He grew. He's a businessman now. He's a father now. He's taking control of his destiny. He's movin' up.'"[35]

He added, "I think there are a lot more lessons I need to learn, a lot more things I need to experience, a lot more places I need to go before I can finally say, okay, I've had my days."[36]

But although he was thoughtful and jovial in most of his interviews, he left a disturbing note in his two California radio interviews with Sway. When asked whether or not he had a hand in the killing of Tupac, Biggie chuckled, grinned coyly, and said, "I ain't that powerful—yet."

It was almost as if Biggie wanted to keep some mystery about him and the incident. As he wrapped up the interview, DJ Franzen Wong came over to talk to him. During the brief exchange, Biggie said he was chillin' in LA and everything was good. Franzen nodded but told Biggie to be careful in LA. "Things aren't always as they seem," Franzen noted. Lots of others had the same advice. Shaquille O'Neal told Biggie to be careful. On the streets, Biggie and Puffy would sometimes be yelled at by Tupac and Death Row fans. Rap-A-Lot Records head James Prince told Puffy, "It's not safe here for you."[37]

And the image Biggie presented also seemed grim. Puffy had Biggie take his album cover photo in a cemetery, standing next to a hearse. The first song was "Somebody's Gotta Die" and the last song was "You're Nobody (Until Someone Kills You)." What was it all really about?

Regardless of what everyone thought, he was having a good time in California. People were talking about getting him in movies or television. He blew off a trip to London so that he could lounge in Los Angeles a little longer.

On March 9, 1997, six months after Tupac had been killed, *Vibe* magazine and Qwest Records threw an afterparty for the Soul Train Music Awards at the Petersen Automotive Museum. Aaliyah, Ginuwine, Chris Tucker, and Wesley Snipes were in the house. Puffy and Biggie, still largely immobile, held court at a VIP table. At the awards, there had been some booing when Biggie stepped onstage. But when the first guitar stabs of "Hypnotize" came on, all the memories of the confrontation with Death Row the year before, all the heckling in the events and on the streets, all of it dissipated as the capacity crowd went wild. After midnight, the fire marshals moved to shut down the party, leaving the Bad Boy entourage to figure out their next moves.

They decided to head up to Steve Stoute's afterparty, and piled into two Suburbans. Puffy got in the first and Biggie climbed in the passenger seat of the second, just as Tupac had with Suge. As "Goin' Back to Cali" boomed out the speakers, they pulled out to the intersection at Wilshire and Fairfax. Puffy's white Suburban made it through the light. Biggie's green Suburban was stuck in the left-turn lane.

A Black Impala pulled up alongside. Biggie turned to see a man pointing a 9mm gun out the Impala's window at him. He was shot four times. He was declared dead a half hour later. He was just twenty-four years old.

The Question Remains

Hip-hop has always remained close to the beating heart of the communities from which it emerged—in particular, Black communities that have been ravaged by historic and ongoing racism, but also from which so many hopeful visions of human freedom have sprung.

In hip-hop, creativity and violence have had a deep relationship. Hip-hop began when young people turned away from gang violence. Throughout its history communities have made great creative advances whenever they did so—especially after the 1971 and 1992 gang peace treaties. In 1997, after Biggie's murder, everything seemed to stop cold for a moment, as if a generation needed to retreat into some soul searching.

The Source placed a picture of Biggie on its cover just before press time, wrapping it over a cover that had already been printed featuring Scarface. The headline was stark: "Now What? The Tragic Marriage of Hip-Hop and Violence." Editor-in-chief Selwyn Seyfu Hinds concluded in the cover story, "I've cried for Big. I've cried for the part of us all that died with him. Now I'm just weary."

He added, "But know this—we can blame the government; we can blame America; we can blame our eternally hostile elders; we can blame each other. Shit, we can kill each other until there's no one fucking left; but in the end, the choice is ours. What now, my people?"[38]

Baron Davis was Los Angeles's top high school basketball player at the time. He recalled, "It was like the streets kinda died. It was like *all* the wind had been let out of LA. The whole city was depressed. *How could we be responsible?*"[39]

Vibe's editors published some of the outpouring of letters they received. One, from a Harlem writer named Garrett E. Jenkins, read: "I am writing this letter to apologize for a brutal act that I committed. I am the individual who is responsible for the death of Christopher Wallace. I am the individual responsible for the death of Tupac Shakur. I am the driving force behind the exploitation of violence in music and televised media. Who am I? I am the hip-hop consumer . . . I helped make Tupac's "Thug Life." . . . I never questioned the lyric content of Biggie's songs. All I cared about was they were bangin'."[40]

No one felt safe. West Coast rappers didn't want to go to New York. New York rappers didn't want to head to Cali. Instead, Minister Louis Farrakhan—the only authority whom both sides respected—called for rappers to come to a summit at his home in Chicago on Thursday, April 3, 1997.

From the East Coast came artists like Doug E. Fresh, Channel Live, and Chuck D. From the Midwest came Bone Thugs-N-Harmony and Common. From the South came the Goodie Mob. From the West Coast came Snoop Dogg, Ice Cube, and The Dogg Pound. Suge Knight was in jail. Diddy did not show, but sent a message to the minister of his full support for the meeting.

The Bronx rapper Fat Joe had gotten word just the night before, while he was out bowling with his crew. He wanted to know if Ice Cube was going to be there. He wanted to confront Cube, who had once been shown so much love in New York, but had now formed the Westside Connection with Mack 10 and W.C., and was making records that dissed the East Coast. After being assured Cube would be present, Fat Joe—who had a fear of flying—jumped in a car and drove from New York to Chicago. When he arrived he was still wearing his bowling shirt and bowling shoes. The meeting was that important.

Also in attendance was the Black Power icon, former SNCC leader, and Black Panther member Kwame Ture, who had once been known as Stokely Carmichael. Ture spoke at length about how outside forces—from music industry executives and media outlets to law enforcement—were fanning the flames of conflict. He detailed a history of how the US government had turned Black civil rights and human rights organizations against one another. He also imparted strategies on how folks could avoid divisions and encouraged everyone to "organize, organize, and organize." His heartfelt remarks moved some to tears.

At first Doug E. Fresh could barely speak. But then he raised his voice to talk about the roots of hip-hop and how he had come up under the tutelage of DJ Kool Herc and Afrika Bambaataa. He said he could not believe how much the industry had become corrupted.

Ice Cube had shut down his movie set early that morning and chartered a private plane to Chicago. He and his Westside Connection partners walked in after the meeting had been underway for a couple of hours, bringing a hush to the room. Cube was involved in beefs with Common, former friends Kam and Shorty from Da Lench Mob, and East Coast rappers like Fat Joe. Cube immediately went over to Common, hugged him, and apologized.

But the tension was not completely dissolved. Fat Joe told Cube, "When I heard you were gonna be here, I got in my car and drove fifteen hours just to see the whites of your eyes. I wanted to see you face to face and ask you why you did what you did?" He said that there were folks in New York who wanted to cause Cube some bodily harm.

Ice Cube seemed taken aback by Joe's remarks but explained that many hip-hop artists outside of New York keenly felt the rejection from the birthplace of hip-hop's elite. East Coasters had accused West Coast rappers of ruining hip-hop by creating "gangsta rap," Cube said. But that term was not one he or anyone he knew had ever attached to their type of music. They called their music "reality rap" and they saw themselves as street reporters. Cube said there was a double standard: New Yorkers dissed rappers like him while they honored artists like Wu-Tang—and even Fat Joe himself—who were rapping about the same subject matter, street life. If the Westside Connection had dissed East Coast artists, it was no different from East Coast artists dissing West Coast artists.

As an artist, Cube said, he saw nothing wrong with rappers battling on records. It was a tradition within hip-hop. But now things were on edge, with people taking things personally, neighborhoods turning against each other, and people getting killed. Cube suggested that maybe battling needed to be suspended until the drama died down. By the end of the day, he had made peace with Common, Fat Joe, and Kam and Shorty as well.

It was a day for reconciliation. Kurupt from the Dogg Pound and Bizzie Bone of Bones Thugs-N-Harmony squashed their beef. Snoop Dogg spoke about his commitment to take his music in a whole different direction even if it meant diminishing record sales.[41]

Minister Farrakhan returned to the concept of "divide and conquer." Beefs had broken out over "rap versus hip-hop," "old school versus new school," and "East Coast versus West Coast." These were artificial, he said. They were being manipulated for the sake of sales or reputation. When he concluded, the artists rose to exchange phone numbers and made promises to keep lines of communication open with each other. After the event, they announced at a press conference that the East Coast–West Coast feud had ended.

Hip-hop was set to embark in a different direction.

LOOP 4

1998–

-2020

DIRTY SOUTH,
NEM, BRAZIL,
TH AFRICA
DJ DRAMA
KENDRICK
HUSSLE,
S MATTER

16

New Queens & Kings

If the 1990s had begun with hip-hop blowing up all around the world, it would end with hip-hop at the center of global pop culture. And there now, in the spotlight, was a rich spectrum of voices that the mainstream once might never have made room for, representing communities that might have never been seen, telling stories that might never have been heard. While artists from New York and Los Angeles still loomed large in the hip-hop galaxy, stars seemed to emerge from everywhere. These new queens and kings expanded the boundaries of the art.

For their February 1998 issue, *Vibe* magazine highlighted some of the new royalty. There was Method Man, LL Cool J, Busta Rhymes, and Master P. Representing the queens, there was Lil' Kim, Lauryn Hill, Missy Elliott, and Foxy Brown. In bold letters, the covers read, "RAP REIGNS." Even after the deaths of Tupac and Biggie, hip-hop was more popular than ever. In 1998, rap sales totaled 81 million, making over a billion dollars.[1] Some days it felt as if hip-hop's supremacy would never end. But the feeling would not last.

The New Queens

It was a golden era for women in hip-hop. Yo-Yo, who had stomped into the decade with her Intelligent Black Women's Coalition, says, "There was such a variety of music that I think whoever you were, you had a chance to shine within your music."[2] The range of artists who rocked the mic and made waves during the 1990s included Da Brat, Nikki D, The Poetess, Oaktown 357, JJ Fad, Ladybug Mecca, Boss, Conscious Daughters, Lady of Rage, Medusa, Bahamadia, Trina, Hurricane G, Queen Pen, Charli Baltimore, Suga T, Da 5 Footaz, Body and Soul, The Anomolies, and Eve, among many others. But as *Vibe*'s cover had revealed, the artists most people were talking about were Lil' Kim, Foxy Brown, Missy Elliott, and Lauryn Hill.

Lil' Kim and Foxy Brown had come up on the streets of Brooklyn and attended the same high school across the street from Prospect Park.

Kimberly "Lil' Kim" Jones was from Bedford-Stuyvesant, was on the streets trying to stay away from an abusive father, and knew Biggie from hanging out on Fulton Street. One day, Biggie stopped her and asked her to spit a verse. Impressed with her style, he put her on with his crew, Junior M.A.F.I.A., which also included his cousin James "Lil' Cease" Lloyd, and a large crew composed of other Brooklyn rappers he had assembled.

Inga "Foxy Brown" Marchand, born Trinidadian American of African, South Asian, and Chinese descent, was a few years younger than Kim, and grew up on the other side of Atlantic Avenue, in a brownstone in the cushier neighborhood of Park Slope. She dreamed of being a criminal justice attorney.[3] But she was also intrigued by the street life and was gaining a rep on the open mics as a talented rapper. At one point, Biggie debated including her in Junior M.A.F.I.A., too.

Instead, Kim became the "Queen B" of the crew. With her raspy, deep voice, she came off as tough. Biggie set out to craft her image—a streetwise girl who talked dirty and presented herself provocatively. When Junior M.A.F.I.A.'s "Players Anthem" and "Gettin' Money" hit in 1995, Kim became a star.

At the same time, Marchand was frequenting open mics and experimenting with different identities. She rocked the mic at the Lyricist Lounge, an underground spot, as Queen Nefertiti. Then when she got a demo deal with a major label, she transformed herself into Big Shorty. But that fell apart quickly. So she entered a high school talent contest and destroyed all of her competitors. Her neighbor Samuel "Tone" Barnes of the Trackmasters production team and powerful industry mover Chris Lighty decided to slide her onto a remix for LL Cool J's "I Shot Ya," one of the biggest street hits in 1995. Her cousin DJ Clark Kent linked her with Jay-Z and she blew up with a razor-sharp cameo on his "Ain't No N---a." Soon record labels were in a bidding war for the seventeen-year-old, and she chose to sign with Def Jam.

Lil' Kim's debut album, *Hardcore,* came out on November 12, 1996, and hit number eleven on the pop charts. Foxy Brown's debut, *Ill Na Na,* followed a week later and entered at number seven. Both were lyrically blazing and wildly popular. Both set off a firestorm of controversy with their sexually explicit lyrics, and set in motion a big debate around female respectability and freedom.

The two rappers were unapologetic about their desire—whether sexual or material. They dropped brand names and spit raunchy rhymes. An MTV News report asked bluntly, "Are Foxy Brown & Lil' Kim Taking It Too Far?" But others, like the rapper Jean Grae, believed "Kim and Foxy were the sexual revolution."

Foxy Brown said it was a new era—that she was bound to be different from Queen Latifah, Yo-Yo, and MC Lyte. She and Kim called out a double standard against women. "Men have been doing it (talking dirty and materialistic) for years," Lil' Kim said, "and finally, finally there's a woman who comes out and takes up for these women. And then there's other women who are not happy with me taking up for them. Why?"

During the horrors of slavery, when white slavemasters could assault Black women with impunity, the story of Jezebel arose to provide cover for the masters' crimes. A Jezebel was a Black woman who was said to have an insatiable sex drive. Even after slavery ended, the story continued as a stereotype that justified the lack of prosecution of assaults against Black women, and men limiting women's freedoms.

At the same time Black women's clubs and organizations advanced "the Cult of the Lady"—or what would be come to be called "respectability politics"—to encourage Black women to dress modestly, downplay any sexual appeal, and deny pleasure. The Black feminist scholar Paula Giddings described this movement in her book *When and Where I Enter*:

> Now a woman had to be true to the cult's cardinal tenets of domesticity, submissiveness, piety, and purity in order to be good enough for society's inner circles. Failing to adhere to any of these tenets—which the overwhelming number of Black women could hardly live up to—made one less than a moral, "true" woman.

The debate raged: Were Kim and Foxy reinforcing vulgar, immoral Jezebel stereotypes? Or were they in control of their images and allowing other women to express themselves and their desires? Were their images making it harder for Black women? Or were they liberating them? As *The Source* asked on a joint cover featuring both of them: *Harlots or Heroines?*

In 1999, cultural critic Joan Morgan wrote the first book on hip-hop feminism, *When Chickenheads Come Home to Roost.* The answers, she said, weren't so simple. She wrote that she needed a new kind of feminism, one that was about giving Black girls and women the confidence to be able to express themselves the way they wanted, but to also recognize when they were being exploited and fight off other people's attempts to take advantage of them. She wrote that she wanted "a feminism brave enough to fuck with the grays."[4]

She added, "The keys that unlock the riches of contemporary Black female identity lie not in choosing Latifah over Lil' Kim, or even Foxy Brown over Salt-N-Pepa. They lie at the magical intersection where those contrary voices meet—the juncture where 'truth' is no longer black and white but subtle, intriguing shades of gray."[5]

Hip-hop feminism found another musical echo in R&B artists like Mary J. Blige and TLC. Mary J. Blige came out of Puff Daddy's Uptown camp and TLC from Atlanta's rich underground to personify "hip-hop soul," fighting off the criticism of male underground purists to rise to massive success. They helped lay the foundation for the success of later artists like Aaliyah, Erykah Badu, Meshell Ndegeocello, Angie Stone (who had been a rap pioneer with The Sequence), and Jill Scott, as well as male artists like D'Angelo, Maxwell, Bilal, and what would become the "neo-soul movement."

One of the most influential hip-hop artists of the decade was someone who bridged the battle-ready attitude of Kim and Foxy and the soulful vibes of Mary and Erykah, someone whom the *Vibe* writer Martine Bury called "a Jersey girl with a voice of gold"—the rapper/singer Lauryn Hill.[6]

Raised in the New Jersey suburb of South Orange, not far from where Queen Latifah came up, Hill was a prolific child performer. At thirteen, she stepped onstage at the Apollo in Harlem and shakily began singing the Jackson 5's "Who's Loving You." The crowd unforgivingly booed her and she left the stage shaken.

But by the time she was a senior in high school—where she was a cheerleader, ran track, was chosen as homecoming queen, and racked up a report card of all A's—she had acted in an Off-Broadway hip-hop musical as an understudy to MC Lyte, and picked up a supporting role in *Sister Act 2.* She had also joined Wyclef Jean and Prakazrel "Pras" Michel in a rap crew called the Fugees. She enrolled in Columbia University and joined the crew to record their debut album between classes.

Producer and engineer Gordon "Commissioner Gordon" Williams recalled how she won over the hardrocks hanging out at the studio: "She had twists in her hair, and she was quiet. But her talent was so big, it filled up the room. In the studio, she was freestyling and singing in between; she turned into the lion and they turned into mice. The more she did, the more timid these thugs in the studio would get."[7]

The Fugees' uneven first album, *Blunted on Reality,* did not make a lot of noise. But Hill's heartfelt cover of Roberta Flack's "Killing Me Softly" helped make the Fugees' second album, *The Score,* one of the biggest hip-hop albums of all time. It sold six million copies in the United States, and was named one of the best albums of the decade. Yet tensions within the group led the trio to drift apart from each other, and they would never make another album together.

Lauryn Hill began recording her solo album, *The Miseducation of Lauryn Hill,* in the summer of 1997. She was writing, she said later, "songs that lyrically move me and have the integrity of reggae and the knock of hip-hop and the instrumentation of classic soul."[8]

Circumstances were not easy. With the collapse of the Fugees came the end of her relationship with Wyclef Jean. She also worked through the birth of her son, Zion, and her pregnancy with her second child, her daughter Selah. But the album met all the advance hype. It debuted at number one and earned five Grammys, including Album of the Year. *The Miseducation of Lauryn Hill,* Morgan wrote, "remains a revered, iconic piece of work."[9]

Thembisa Mshaka, who was hired to help market *Miseducation,* remembered listening to an advance cassette of the album in the office of a Columbia exec, another young Black woman. "As we sat in the dim, soft purple light, I was grateful for the semi-darkness because we were both crying. It was like Lauryn was singing about everything young women grappled with, feared, questioned, and ultimately came to realize about themselves and the world—in one album."[10]

Its biggest hit was "Doo Wop (That Thing)," which leaned against the times, powerfully criticizing men who disrespected women, asking, "How you gon' win when you ain't right within?" Its message to girls and women was even stronger: Be you, and don't depend on men or material things for your self-respect. Hill rapped, "Don't be a hard rock when you really are a gem."

"It was the era of the gangsta b---h," hip-hop journalist Akiba Solomon told the writer Joan Morgan in *She Begat This: 20 Years of The Miseducation of Lauryn Hill*. "For [Lauryn] to talk about the fullness of the Black experience was important and brave because at the time, there was a whole swath of people in hip-hop pretending that they weren't middle class."[11]

But perhaps the heart of the album is the first song she delivered to her label, "To Zion," a dedication to her then unborn son. She sang,

Everybody told me to be smart
"Look at your career," they said
"Lauryn, baby, use your head"
But instead I chose to use my heart

Even Lauryn Hill faced her own battle with respectability politics. Joan Morgan wrote, "For many fans, Lauryn was seen as the desirable antidote to Lil' Kim and Foxy Brown's hypersexuality. A smart, articulate Ivy leaguer who came from a two-parent home, Hill was the kind of 'good' Black girl who didn't have a baby out of wedlock."[12]

But as Hill said in a radio interview, "I see a lot of women online like, 'Oh I feel sorry for you. Oh, your career is over.' And it's like, why can't I have both? As a woman, why can't I have both? Why do I gotta choose a career or a baby? I want both."[13]

The album was about how one must undo all the wrong she has learned in order to become who she wants to be, about achieving self-love and love of community. Her close friend and manager, Jayson Jackson, says, "You're hearing the hopes, dreams, and desires of a person, both in a worldly and a spiritual sense."

The Dirty South

In 1994, Nas's *Illmatic* and the Notorious B.I.G.'s *Ready to Die* made some in New York feel like the hip-hop crown had come back to the movement's birthplace. But in 1995, the rest of the hip-hop world proved that the crown would never again belong solely to the Big Apple.

New Orleans–born rapper Percy "Master P" Miller had ended up in Oakland, California, to play basketball and study for a business degree. But his rapping career also found a welcoming environment in the independent-minded Bay Area scene. By 1995, he was selling hundreds of thousands of records that featured himself and his brothers Silkk the Shocker and C-Murder. His record label, No Limit Records, signed a groundbreaking distribution deal with Priority, the same company that had distributed NWA, Ice Cube, and Eazy-E's Ruthless Records. With his sales success, he branched out into doing wildly popular direct-to-video DVD films, like *I'm Bout It,* that offered music-driven street tales. Indie rappers took note of Master P's business model: build a devoted local following, negotiate deals with bigger companies from a position of strength, and make them work for him.

One of the label's first releases after the deal was *Down South Hustlers: Bouncin' and Swingin',* which showcased some of those rappers, including 8Ball & MJG from Memphis and UGK from Port Arthur, Texas. It was like they didn't need the East Coast's approval. And it was a sign of what was to come.

That summer, at the same 1995 Source Awards ceremony where Suge Knight had insulted Puffy Combs, and Snoop Dogg had called out the New York crowd, two twenty-year-old rappers from Southwest Atlanta nervously sat in the audience awaiting the announcement of the winner of the Best New Rap Group.

Andre Benjamin, dressed in a purple dashiki, and Antwan "Big Boi" Patton, in Atlanta Braves gear, knew they had made a great debut album. Inspired by the rich lyricism of the Native Tongues and the Bay Area's Hieroglyphics, as well as the detailed street tales of the Geto Boys and LA's g-funk stylists, Outkast told the stories of their neighborhood—Southwest Atlanta, or the SWATs—over Organized Noize's easy-flowing funk. They captured the tempo and feel of life in the South in a way no other had.

Outkast's *Southernplayalisticadillacmuzik* was so good it made New York heads take notice. *The Source* made it their lead album review and gave it an extremely rare 4.5 mics. But the review also revealed just how little esteem New York held for the South. As *The Source*'s Rob Marriott wrote, "The South has always posed a problem for most hip-hoppers. No matter what they accomplish, we're hard-pressed to give the South its due."[14]

That night, when Outkast was announced as the winner, Dre and Big Boi pumped their fists. And then they heard the New York audience booing them. Big Boi kept a poker face as they walked to the stage. But Dre was so pissed he started clapping his hands in defiance. "I'm tired of . . . closed-minded folks," he said, silencing the crowd. "But it's like this: *The South got something to say.*"

New York's rejection made them even more determined to do their own thing. Their next album, *ATLiens,* featured "Elevators (Me & You)," a molasses-slow reflection on the price of fame, the appearance of success, and their struggle to be heard. On subsequent records, they explored and mastered a breathtaking array of new styles—from heavy metal–tinged bass music on "B.O.B. (Bombs Over Baghdad)" to harmonica-tinged blues ("Rosa Parks") to state-of-the-art hip-hop ("Aquemini," "So Fresh, So Clean") to old-soul-meets-space-age-rock-and-roll ("Hey Ya"). They had a whole lot to say.

And in the coming decades, rappers from the Gulf Coast beaches, across the rivers, fields, swamps, hills, and valleys all the way over to the Atlantic seaboard would remember Dre's words as the moment the Dirty South rose up from the bottom to conquer hip-hop.

Atlanta was the capital of hip-hop's new geography. The southern city had produced Arrested Development's critically acclaimed six-times-platinum-selling album, *3 Years, 5 Months and 2 Days in the Life Of . . . ,* Jermaine Dupri's hit-making teen-centric hip-pop label So So Def (featuring Da Brat and Kriss Kross), and of course, Outkast's extended family of music-makers, which included underground heroes like the Goodie Mob and crossover chart-toppers TLC. By the end of the decade, the city's radio, high school talent shows, and strip clubs had sparked so many new trends it was hard to keep up. The long list of stars Atlanta produced would stretch into the new century and include T.I., CeeLo, Ludacris, Lil Jon, Ying Yang

Twins, Wacka Flocka Flame, Gucci Mane, Jeezy, Childish Gambino, Migos, Future, Young Thug, and 21 Savage.

Cool Breeze, a rapper from the East Point suburb of Atlanta, gave the new movement its name, "the Dirty South," on a 1995 Goodie Mob track of the same name. "What you really know about the Dirty South?" he asked in the chorus. And soon, folks all over the world would have an answer to that question. As 21 Savage would put it, *a lot.*

In Texas, UGK (Underground Kingz) emerged from Port Arthur on the Gulf Coast, while artists like Mike Jones, Slim Thug, and Paul Wall kept Houston rolling. In Memphis, Three 6 Mafia started a new style called crunk, for "cranked up." In New Orleans, where so much of American music had been born, the new sound was called bounce.

A young DJ named Mannie Fresh inherited his turntables and his love for records from his father, who was a local party celebrity. As a teen, he became an area star in his own right by building the bounce sound from New Orleans street parade rhythms, forgotten rap records like the Show Boys' 1986 single "Drag Rap," and an 808 drum machine.

He recalls, "Bounce was really started just throwing 808 breaks. I'd go to a party and find two songs that had 808 breaks, just the instrumental part of it. You'd get an MC that would just hype the crowd, [while I'm cutting] them two 808 tracks back to back. And it just elevated into somebody putting it on wax."

Fresh's wildly percussive tracks for Cash Money Records made breakout hits of The Hot Boys' "We on Fire," Juvenile's "Ha" and "Back That Azz Up," and Lil' Wayne's "The Block Is Hot" and *The Carter*. B.G.'s 1999 hit, "Bling Bling," gave a name to the shiny diamond-encrusted chains, pinky rings, watches, and fronts they sported with their white tees, and to a new era of materialism in hip-hop.

The Virginia Beach area was home to producer Teddy Riley, who, after his chart-topping successes from the late '80s into the early '90s with Bobby Brown, Guy, Heavy D and the Boyz, and Michael Jackson, relocated to the seaside town from Harlem. He helped mentor young musicians like Pharrell Williams and Chad Hugo (who recorded as The Neptunes), and Tim "Timbaland" Mosley and

Missy Elliott. There in Riley's studio, they incubated the sounds that would top the pop charts well into the new millennium.

As a girl, Missy Elliott had been sexually assaulted by a cousin. Her mother suffered domestic abuse at the hands of her Marine sergeant father. At fourteen, after her father pulled a gun on her mother, the two left him and started a new life. Missy decided that she wanted to entertain, and formed an all-girl group with three of her friends. When the R&B group Jodeci came to perform in town, they did a backstage audition and impressed Devante Swing, who moved them to New York and pushed them to make hits. Missy rose to the challenge, writing for Jodeci, Raven Symoné, and her own group, Sista.

But some of the male record execs body-shamed her, refusing to believe she could ever be a star. In music videos, they substituted other women to lip-sync her lines, and they shelved Sista's album. When Devante Swing turned abusive, she left the group for good, and returned to Virginia. She resigned herself to working behind the scenes as a writer and producer. "Maybe I don't have the look," she recalled thinking. "I don't have to worry about being judged."[15]

Then Puffy gave her a break, having her rhyme on a remix for R&B artist Gina Thompson. Her turn in the video—in which she first dropped her famous "hee hee hee how" laugh—made her a sensation. She and Timbaland were introduced to rising star Aaliyah, and the three produced her groundbreaking double-platinum–selling *One in a Million* album. Elektra CEO Sylvia Rhone, the first Black woman to lead a major record company, offered Missy a deal that gave her not just an album contract, but a label. Rhone told Missy, "Just be you."

In 1997, Missy and Timbaland shocked the world with *Supa Dupa Fly* and its lead single, "The Rain," a percolating take on an old southern soul song by Ann Peebles that even featured the sound of an on-beat cricket. Timbaland's beats were minimal and futuristic, the perfect foil for Missy's expressionistic lyrics. He would go on to transform pop with his work for Justin Timberlake, Nelly Furtado, Beyoncé, and Jay-Z.

Missy then teamed with forward-thinking director Hype Williams for some of the most distinctive and eye-popping videos ever made. In the video for "The Rain," she ticked and tocked and bounced like a superheroine in a massive black balloon suit, looking like an Afronaut. She had taken the male execs' criticism of her body, flipped it, and reversed it. "We came up with this idea of being in a big plastic garbage bag," she says. "Basically, I said, I'ma show them. I'ma make a record and it's gonna be big. And I'm gonna be big, too. And I mean, literally!"[16]

She also wanted the video to illustrate the power of sisterhood. She shouted out Lauryn Hill on the track and showcased Yo-Yo, Lil' Kim, and Da Brat getting their grooves on. Even as the record industry marginalized women artists in the 2000s, Missy was unstoppable. Of her first six albums, one went gold and five went platinum. Missy had the last laugh.

Hip-Hop at the New Millennium

Each hip-hop region, down to the area codes, had its distinctive sounds and scenes. When the internet became more prominent in the new millennium, artists would begin collaborating more and experimenting with styles outside of the area in which they had come up. But for now, people were putting themselves on the map by doing their own thing exactly where they were at.

Philadelphia, which had existed in an orbit just outside of New York's power center, built up a musically rich scene led by the Roots, hip-hop's most famous and accomplished band. The amiable and ultra-versatile drummer Ahmir "Questlove" Thompson and the more reserved but ferociously original lyricist Tariq "Black Thought" Trotter got their start busking for dollars on the corners of Philly's South Street. Over the course of two decades, they came to put instrumentalists, craft, and ideas first. Their 1996 video, "What They Do," directed by Charles Stone III, clowned the materialism of Bad Boy and Death Row and other commercial rap videos. But they also built up a local scene, helping launch artists like Jill Scott, Eve, and Beanie Sigel. They became a sort of Everyband, playing with everyone and, through their music, concerts, and collaborations, exerted a profound impact on not just hip-hop, but "neo-soul," R&B, jazz, and rock.

The San Francisco Bay Area—stretching from San Jose up to San Francisco, and Oakland, Vallejo, and Sacramento—continued its own unique trip with its hyphy movement. Named by rapper Keak Da Sneak, "hyphy" was a combination of the words, "hype" and "fly," and the scene centered around the local turf dance and auto sideshow scenes in what was known as the "Yay Area." Producers like Rick Rock turned up the tempo, and found a home for their new sound on local radio and in clubs. In 2002, Vallejo rapper Mac Dre—whose colorful personality, captured on a crazily popular DVD series called *Treal*, and run-ins with the law made him a local hero—dropped "The Thizzle Dance." In the tradition of Digital Underground's "The Humpty Dance," which Tupac had helped introduce a decade before, it gave his "folkers" a hilarious way to "go stupid" and move together. Mac Dre was murdered in Kansas City in 2004, and did not get to see the movement reach its peak, when E-40 released "Tell Me When to Go" two years later.

In the mid 1990s, the midwest asserted itself as well. In Minneapolis and St. Paul, the area that produced Prince and his associates, an indie-minded underground rose up, led by the Rhymesayers collective, which included Atmosphere, Aesop Rock, Brother Ali, and others, with community-based anchors at Juxtaposition Arts, founded by veterans of the local graffiti and hip-hop scene, and Intermedia Arts, which hosted national B-Girl Be Festivals that centered women in hip-hop.

From Cleveland, Bone Thugs-N-Harmony merged the double-time rhyme styles favored in the Los Angeles freestyle underground with lyrics that verged on the gothic. As a group of friends and relatives, they had survived foster care and homelessness to chase down Eazy-E for an audition. After he signed them, they went on to multiplatinum success. In St. Louis, Nelly broke out with a song called "Country Grammar," in which he shouted out Oakland's Too Short and New York's Onyx, and positioned St. Louis rap as the stylistic midpoint between north and south.

Detroit's James "J Dilla" Yancey produced trend-setting hits for The Pharcyde ("Runnin'"), De La Soul ("Stakes Is High"), Q-Tip ("Breathe and Stop"), and Common ("The Light"). As Eminem put Detroit on the map, Dilla defined the underground sound with his work for his own group, Slum Village, and his own treasured beat tapes, and many local artists including Proof, Invincible, and Platinum Pied Pipers.

His was a profoundly Black sound—pieced together carefully from rare funk, jazz, disco, and bossa nova records—and defined by technical skill and deep soul. Producers wondered how he was able to get his machines to sound so seamless, warm, and human. His work, Questlove said, was "like solving a ten-thousand-piece puzzle in record time." Dilla was at the center of a production crew with Questlove, D'Angelo, and the Roots' James Poyser who, in a three-year period, produced some of the most important hip-hop and R&B records of all time—including The Roots' *Things Fall Apart*, D'Angelo's *Voodoo*, Common's *Like Water for Chocolate*, Erykah Badu's *Mama's Gun*, and Talib Kweli's *Quality*. In 2006, Dilla died from complications from lupus at the age of thirty-two. He was, Questlove said, "the music god that music gods and music experts and music lovers worship."[17]

But New York was still hungry. In the early 1990s, a young rapper from Brooklyn named Jay-Z heard about another hot rapper from Yonkers named DMX, and through his manager—a friend named Damon Dash with whom he had started a company called Roc-A-Fella—sent word that he wanted to battle. DMX was actually working a stash house in Baltimore, so his managers—two brothers named Joaquin "Waah" Dean and Darrin "Dee" Dean who called themselves Ruff Ryderz and had grown up in the apartment at 1520 Sedgwick Avenue one floor above DJ Kool Herc and Cindy Campbell—sent for him.

The managers settled on a neutral spot for the battle, a pool hall at 168th and Webster in the heart of the South Bronx not far from where, two decades before, the Ghetto Brothers clubhouse had been. That's how Jay-Z and DMX ended up in a packed room, on top of pool tables, surrounded by a loud crowd rooting on their hometown heroes. Rhymes were spit, guns were waved, but everyone went home safe, buzzing about the performances, and Jay and D left with newfound respect for each other. At that point, both were grinding. After Biggie's passing, both would bring the spotlight back to New York.

When the Dean brothers' nephew Bronx-born Kasseem "Swizz Beatz" Dean began producing hype tracks to fit DMX's aggressive bark, they broke through with "Ruff Ryders Anthem." Ruff Ryderz expanded to include The Lox, Eve, Chinese American rapper Jin, and producers like Dame Grease and PK. In Harlem, The Diplomats, also known as Dipset, got hits from Cam'ron and Jim Jones, Juelz Santana, and the crew, too.

In Queens, Ja Rule took the gruffness into a more pop direction and his records with singer Ashanti like "Always On Time" and "Mesmerize" made them what journalist Ethan Brown called "the Marvin Gaye and Tami Terrell of the hip-hop generation."[18] But he soon got into a rap battle with a small-time drug-pusher-turned-rapper from South Jamaica who had named himself after a murdered Brooklyn gangster.

That rapper, Curtis "50 Cent" Jackson, had linked up with Run-DMC's Jam Master Jay, who taught him how to rap, and built his rep writing rhymes dissing New York's rap elite by name. As the beef between Ja Rule and 50 Cent spiraled to include drug gangs, 50 was stabbed in the chest. He then wrote a song called "Ghetto Qu'ran" that named some of Queens's biggest drug dealers and exposed their business. Soon after, he was shot nine times at close range by an assassin, and Jam Master Jay was murdered. The word was that 50 had made too many enemies in the industry and on the streets.

Somehow he survived the shooting. Impressed with 50 Cent's story, Eminem tracked him down and, in turn, introduced him to Dr. Dre. The album they made together—*Get Rich or Die Tryin'*—was a sensation. 50 Cent became known as a canny businessman, turning himself into a powerful brand. He lent his name not just to albums, but to books, clothing, video games, alcoholic drinks, films and film companies, and all kinds of consumer goods. His deal with the Glacéau water company—makers of Vitaminwater—made him a reported $100 million alone. His success was an indicator of just how big a business hip-hop had become in the era of bling and violence.

New Kings, New Contradictions

But the King of New York was Shawn "Jay-Z" Carter. He became infatuated with hip-hop in the 1980s growing up in the Marcy housing projects in Bedford-Stuyvesant, Brooklyn, during the peak of the crack era. "My life after childhood has two main stories: the story of the hustler and the story of the rapper," he wrote in his autobiography, *Decoded*.[19] Like his friend the Notorious B.I.G., he dropped out of school to push drugs.

In hip-hop, he apprenticed himself to The Jaz and Big Daddy

Kane but continued to hustle until one day rival pushers fired at him three times at close range. He took the fact that they missed as a sign he needed to do something else with his life. With friends Damon "Dame" Dash and Kareem "Biggs" Burkes, he started Roc-A-Fella Records, selling his CDs as hard as he had pushed drugs. In 1995, after years of dead-ends in the industry, he released *Reasonable Doubt* and his career finally began to take off.

Like Biggie, Jay impressed his collaborators by recording some songs whole without writing down a single word. He too was enamored with puns and wordplay, and he was also a keen and skilled storyteller, a talent he illustrated on songs like "D'Evils" and "Regrets." He was interested in revealing the hard-knock-life psychology of a young kid in the struggle. He wrote:

> To tell the story of the kid with the gun without telling the story of why he has it is to tell a kind of a lie. To tell the story of the pain without telling the story of the rewards—the money, the girls, the excitement—is a different kind of evasion. To talk about killing n---as dead without talking about waking up in the middle of the night from a dream about the friend you watched die, or not getting to sleep in the first place because you're so paranoid from the work you're doing, is a lie so deep it's criminal.[20]

By 2000, he had recorded five albums, all platinum. He had co-founded Rocawear clothing, which he would later sell for over $200 million. And he had brought the hip-hop nation together, paying respects to the South musically and lyrically on songs like "Can I Get A . . ." and "Big Pimpin'," and erasing a bit of the memory of the regional divide.

As aware as he was of hip-hop and Black history, he also understood his singular importance. On "Izzo (H.O.V.A.)" from *The Blueprint,* he rapped about the entertainment industry with none of the worry that A Tribe Called Quest had demonstrated at the beginning of the 1990s:

I do this for my culture, to let them know
What a n---a look like when a n---a in a roaster
Show them how to move in a room full of vultures
Industry is shady, it needs to be taken over
Label owners hate me, I'm raising the status quo up
I'm overcharging n---as for what they did to the Cold Crush

But what, some asked, was he doing for the Cold Crush? If Jay-Z was claiming something like reparations, what responsibility did he have to the community now that he was successful? Not long afterward, he announced he had secured a shoe deal with Reebok, and that he was retiring from rap with his next album, *The Black Album.*

Journalist Elizabeth Méndez Berry met with Jay-Z as he was finishing the record.[21] When she met him, he was wearing a Che Guevara T-shirt—the revolutionary guerrilla who helped Fidel Castro bring socialism to Cuba—with a fat gold chain and Biggie's diamond-studded platinum Jesus piece. "I couldn't even concentrate on the music," she wrote. "All I could think of is that big chain bouncing off of Che's forehead."[22]

Jay later wrote, "[T]o have contradictions—especially when you're fighting for your life—is human, and to wear the Che shirt and the platinum and diamonds together is honest. In the end I wore it because I meant it."[23]

After the album dropped, it was announced that Jay-Z would become the next CEO of Def Jam. He soon exceeded the power and influence of all those he had once looked up to—forming his own entertainment agency, Roc Nation, starting his own music streaming service, Tidal, and marrying Beyoncé Knowles. "Success," he said, "could only mean self-sufficiency, being a boss, not a dependent."[24]

One student who took this philosophy to heart was Kanye West. The son of a scholar and a former Black Panther, Kanye grew up in a Chicago suburb as a strong student with a deep interest in music, fashion, and the arts. But he broke his college professor mother's heart when he decided to drop out of college to pursue music. But by the time he was twenty-two, he was producing underground hits for Jay-Z's Roc-A-Fella label. By the age of twenty-five he had produced five tracks for *The Blueprint,* Jay and

Beyoncé's "'03 Bonnie & Clyde," and unforgettable tracks for Scarface ("Guess Who's Back"), Talib Kweli ("Get By"), and Alicia Keys ("You Don't Know My Name").

He wanted to rap, but even Jay and Dame couldn't see how to market Kanye, who was the furthest thing from a street hustler or a thug. At his rap audition for them, Dame recalled, "Kanye wore a pink shirt with the collar sticking up and Gucci loafers."

Jay said, "I didn't see how it could work."[25]

But aware that Jay was ready to retire, Dame signed him. Then Kanye got into a car accident that broke his jaw. Concerned he wouldn't be able to finish his album, he wrote and recorded "Through the Wire" with his mouth wired shut. The album, *The College Dropout,* debuted at number two in 2004, and signaled a major shift in the rap industry.

Over the next decade, Kanye pioneered countless new hip-hop production styles. He could break down samples like a Pete Rock or DJ Premier, achieve the crispness of a Dr. Dre or DJ Quik, and construct a hit like Swizz Beatz or fellow Roc-A-Fella producer Just Blaze. He created and discarded new sounds at an astonishing rate.

But just as important, he also cleared the way for a more introspective, vulnerable kind of hip-hop star. He began his trilogy of albums—*College Dropout, Late Registration,* and *Graduation*—with "We Don't Care," a punch-line-rich song with a serious message: don't listen to what people say about you, because we're all in this struggle together. On songs like "Jesus Walks" and "Spaceships," he identified with the pushers on the corners and the nine-to-fivers working for racist managers, and wished deliverance for them. On "All Falls Down," "Diamonds from Sierra Leone," and "Can't Tell Me Nothing," he confronted the contradictions of being materialistic while understanding the violence and emptiness that accompanied it. "We shine because they hate us, floss 'cause they degrade us," he rapped. "They made us hate ourselves and love they wealth."

In September of 2007, the last of the trilogy, *Graduation,* was set to be released on the same day as 50 Cent's third album, *Curtis.* For months, hip-hop pundits billed it as if it were a heavyweight showdown like Muhammad Ali vs. Joe Frazier. It would be bougie vs. street, "conscious rap" vs. "gangsta rap," sensitive man vs. macho man. When the first week had ended, *Graduation* outsold *Curtis* by

250,000 copies, taking the number one Billboard spot with a stunning 957,000 copies sold. Hip-hop fans called it a tipping point—hardness was out, self-awareness was in.

Just two months later, Kanye's beloved mother suddenly died from complications from cosmetic surgery. He was crushed by her passing, broke up with his then-fiancée, and fell into a long depression. His music and outlook on life changed dramatically. When he resurfaced, it was with the cold, minimal, wrenching *808s & Heartbreak*. He recorded much of it with Auto-Tune technology, which allowed him to fix his musical pitch and also to mask himself. He had always represented himself nakedly, but in the depths of his despair, somehow he sounded more raw and human behind a robotic sound.

Kanye would rise to even higher heights. But at the beginning of the new decade, Kanye's mentor, Jay-Z, and Jay-Z's partner, Beyoncé Knowles, became much more controlling of their public personas, restricting media access. By contrast, Kanye and his partner, Kim Kardashian, became media personalities whose every word and act could be scrutinized in real time. Jay-Z rarely let someone behind his mask. Kanye's contradictions were on display for the whole world to see. While at the top of his success, he rapped about being suicidal: "No one man should have all that power." In a sense Kanye's life reflected the way that hip-hop's successes had only intensified and created new pressures as it neared its fifth decade.

Storms and War

By now, it seemed difficult to remember a time when youths of color had not been represented in the media, whether as consumers or producers. But there was a price to be paid.

After the 9/11 attacks, President George W. Bush ramped up two wars in Afghanistan and Iraq that would go on for over a decade. Many expected that rappers would step up with protest music. The majority of troops serving in the Middle East, not to mention many of the youths in the cities they were occupying, came from the same kind of poor, marginalized conditions that hip-hop's pioneers had come from. Surely hip-hop could produce a Curtis Mayfield or a Marvin Gaye?

But Jay-Z's album *The Blueprint,* which had actually been released on September 11, 2001, and a rap beef between Jay and Nas, were the biggest headlines in the hip-hop world. If the biggest artists were selling big brands, even so-called conscious rappers had become part of the machine, selling Levi's jeans and Gap clothing. Artists were slow to respond to the war, said M-1 of Dead Prez, because hip-hop had lost its commitment to its communities. He said, "A lot of people are not seeing what has to be and are looking at it from just a red, white, and blue angle."

But censorship attacks on politicized artists became a major issue. In September of 2001, the Bay Area rap crew the Coup was set to release an album called *Party Music,* full of engaging funk and Boots Riley's languid, witty rhymes that criticized war, violence, and exploitation. The original cover art depicted Boots and his partner, DJ Pam the Funkstress, blowing up the World Trade Center with a guitar tuner. Its record company halted the release of the record and demanded a new cover. Nas's record "Rule," which called for peace, was barely promoted by the record label. Two of the nation's largest radio networks, Clear Channel and Citadel, removed a long "blacklist" of antiwar songs from their stations' airwaves.

Then the national recession, combined with the rise of file sharing and online piracy, led to the deepest plunge in sales in record industry history. The hip-hop industry, in particular, was decimated. Local record stores and regional record distributors closed down. As major labels and radio stations came under the ownership of fewer, bigger companies—this was called 'media consolidation'—they took fewer chances with new artists. It meant that a smaller number of artists would get a chance to be heard nationally.

Hip-hop had always been a young person's game, but the biggest rap stars in the mid-2000s were aging quickly: Eminem was thirty-two when he released *Encore,* Jay-Z was pushing thirty-six when he returned from his "retirement." Unless their cities had been able to maintain independent systems of distribution—as in Atlanta, Oakland, and New Orleans—it would be a difficult decade for new young artists to come up.

Women in hip-hop lost the most. By the turn of the millennium, women artists realized that things had changed and that their Golden Age was coming to a close.

Yo-Yo saw the rise of rappers like Kim and Foxy and thought, well, maybe it's over for me. Eve realized, "Being a female in the industry you were encouraged to show a little more leg, a little more ass, a little more whatever."[26] *Vibe* put Foxy Brown on its cover under the lines: "Sex Sells, Rhyme Pays." Joan Morgan noted that the industry seemed to have found its formula. As O.C. had once rapped, all the Black male rappers were crime-related, and all the Black women rappers were sexual. Big money had a distorting effect, especially when the economy went bad. It would be another decade before hip-hop had the Crunk Feminist Collective, and another two before it had Cardi B, Megan Thee Stallion, and City Girls.

For the big artists, as Master P, 50 Cent, and Jay-Z understood, a rap record was no longer an event. It was just a way to build your brand. It was just the commodity that helped sell the other commodities. Jay-Z wrote, "Timberland and Courvoisier, Versace and Maybach. We gave those brands a narrative, which is one of the reasons anyone buys anything: to own not just a product, but to become part of a story."[27]

But even if hip-hop was a commodity, and a diminished one at that, it still continued to build culture and community. Even as many hip-hop fans grew tired of the limited kinds of rap music played on radio and television, they were using hip-hop to teach, organize, and build communities.

In 2005, thousands gathered at the University of Chicago to be a part of the first Feminism and Hip-Hop Conference. For three days, artists, scholars, activists, and even political candidates and video models debated hip-hop art and politics and discussed how to change hip-hop to better represent gender issues and women's needs. The conference helped shape a transformation in hip-hop, through the rise of new arts, education, and activism.

One panel featured "video vixen" Melyssa Ford and a group of scholars. Ford, who had been studying psychology and forensic science when she broke into the industry, talked about the difference between a "video ho"—a women who would give everything up to a male director for a shot at stardom—and a "video vixen"—who called her own shots and expressed herself. But the women hip-hop scholars rose to challenge her, asking if Ford was allowing her sisters to be treated badly and not taking responsibility for her role in supporting other women and fighting against men's exploitation.

Hip-hop continued to produce surprising moments. In 2003, New Orleans rapper Juvenile scored a number one pop song with his track with Soulja Slim, "Slow Motion." Slim had written the original song about having a dance with a stripper. But after Slim was murdered on his own front lawn, Juvenile finished the song and turned the video into a tribute to a fallen friend. The video depicted a joyous community barbecue, where families enjoyed a beautiful day together, former rivals buried the hatchet, and everyone danced together.

New Orleans had a long tradition of honoring those who had passed with a street parade. At the head of the procession the casket would roll down the street. Behind it, in the "first line," a brass band would play mournful tunes, gathering up mourners and friends on the way to the cemetery. These people would form the second line. And on the way back from the cemetery, the band would play upbeat songs to recall the vibrant life of the deceased. The "second line" would take over with their percussion and their dancing.

"My interpretation of the second line [is] that people celebrate death down there in New Orleans," says Zigaboo Modeliste, the drummer for the funk band the Meters, whose signature playing became one of hip-hop's most sampled sounds. "It's designed to say that you've been relieved from the pressures of this ill-fated world. And then they bring you on home one more time."

Hip-hop, in some ways, began as the Bronx answer to a New Orleans street parade. It was a celebration of individuality and community, death and life—all the sad low parts and the joyous highs. And now it was able to speak from the highest platforms to the problems of the world. But would it?

In 2005, Hurricane Katrina hit New Orleans. In the aftermath of the storm, the levees failed and large parts of the city were flooded. White neighborhoods were mostly spared, while Black neighborhoods were extremely hard hit. Rock and roll pioneer Fats Domino's house in the Ninth Ward was flooded and he lost nearly everything, including his National Medal of the Arts. He had to be rescued by helicopter. New Orleans was a city that was two-thirds Black, and had served as American music's wellspring for jazz and rhythm and blues. The post-Katrina man-made disaster played out on television and the internet, as images of people's misery and the government's abandonment revealed the deep divide between Black and white America.

Kanye West was asked to be a part of NBC Universal's fund-raising telethon, "A Concert for Hurricane Relief."[28] He appeared in front of a video screen that showed scenes of a flooded New Orleans with roofs on fire. He stood alongside actor Mike Meyers, who read his canned lines from the teleprompter. Then Kanye departed from the script. With his hands in his pockets, he nervously cleared his throat and with a quiver in his voice, said:

> I hate the way they portray us in the media. If you see a Black family, it says, "They're looting." You see a white family, it says, "They're looking for food." And you know that it's been five days [for the Federal government to go to New Orleans] because most of the people are Black. And even for me to complain about it, I would be a hypocrite—because I've tried to turn away from the TV because it's too hard to watch . . .

His voice sped up as the screen behind him showed a shot of an Army helicopter streaking across the sky. He said, "We already realize a lot of people that could help are at war right now, fighting another way—and they, they've given them permission to go down and shoot us."

The studio had gone completely silent. Myers continued with his lines. Then Kanye said, slowly and deliberately, "George Bush doesn't care about Black people." The producers cut away quickly to Chris Tucker, who looked shocked.

A new generation was telling its truths through hip-hop. What would they have to say about America's original sin—racism?

17

The Great White Hope

In August of 1967, Dr. Martin Luther King, Jr. addressed the National Association of TV and Radio Announcers. He told them that because Black and white kids enjoyed soul music, they had come to know each other better.

"School integration is much easier now that they share a common music, a common language, and enjoy the same dances. You introduced youth to that music, and created the language of soul and promoted the dance which now sweeps across race, class, and nation," he said. "Yes, you have taken the power which Old Sam had buried deep in his soul, and through our amazing technology, performed a cultural conquest that surpasses even Alexander the Great and the culture of classical Greece."[1]

A generation later, Ice-T talked about hip-hop's impact on young whites. "Chuck Berry, Little Richard, Fats Domino weren't loved by everybody in the '50s, either. They called it 'devil music' back then, because it was going to bring the white man down to the level of the Negro. Now a white parent gets all paranoid when his kid says, 'I like Eazy-E, I like Ice-T,'" he told music journalist Greg Kot. "They may have been brought up to think that all Black people are stupid, but on MTV all they see is somebody who looks cool, who talks intelligently."[2]

But what had hip-hop really changed? Most forms of American popular music, like the blues, jazz, soul, and rhythm and blues, began in largely segregated Black communities and crossed over to white communities. Historically, "success" for those Black artists who had pioneered these forms always meant "crossing over," that is, finding acceptance with white audiences. But when Black-originated forms did become popular in white communities, all too often the Black artists, as well as their innovations, were minimized or erased. Instead, white artists who imitated Black styles received acclaim and financial success at the expense of Black artists.

Fletcher Henderson, Count Basie, and Duke Ellington had developed and innovated big-band swing jazz. But white critics anointed Benny Goodman and Paul Whiteman the "Kings of Swing." When pioneering rhythm and blues artists like Little Richard, Etta James, or Big Mama Thornton recorded songs like "Tutti Fruitti," "Roll with Me Henry," or "Hound Dog," record companies sought out white artists like Pat Boone, Georgia Gibbs, or Elvis Presley to redo the songs for white pop audiences.

Even worse, some of those white artists chose to denigrate Black innovators, to insult the very artists whose styles they had tried to imitate. From the birth of American popular culture in the late nineteenth century, white artists had put on blackface while adopting African American songs, then performed minstrelsy, deliberately making Blacks look lazy and stupid. Such stereotypes would be repeated again and again.

After the end of World War II, American society began recognizing a new demographic as a lucrative market—the white American teenager. At the same time, of course, artists were racially segregated. Black artists were played on Black radio stations and their sales were tallied on the "race records," then "rhythm and blues," charts. Pop radio played mostly white artists, who could then make the more heavily promoted pop charts.

But in the early 1950s, radio DJ Alan Freed noticed how many whites were buying rhythm and blues records by Black artists, and gave the sound a new name, "rock and roll." Record producer Sam Phillips, the founder of Sun Records, noted: "If I could find a white man who had the Negro sound and the Negro feel, I could make a billion dollars." When Phillips met Elvis Presley in 1953, he found his man. Presley would eventually be called "The King of Rock and Roll."

By the late 1960s, after the Civil Rights and the Black Power movements, American popular culture had changed dramatically. No white artist would dethrone James Brown as the Godfather of Soul or Aretha Franklin as the Queen of Soul. But white artists were still marketed as acceptable to everyone, while Black artists still had to cross over from Black music to "the mainstream." Then hip-hop arrived, and Black artists insisted that Blackness be respected, and that they receive the recognition and the rewards that they were due.

By the late 1990s, after hip-hop had crossed over to white audiences, Eminem came along and raised many of the old questions about music and race again.

Living on the Other Side

Marshall Mathers III was born in St. Louis, Missouri, and grew up mostly in Detroit, Michigan, two Midwest cities that had long histories of racial segregation. Whites lived in neighborhoods that explicitly prohibited Black and Asian home ownership. For most of the twentieth century, people of color were forced to live in ghettos. By the time Marshall came of age in Detroit, many white families had moved to the suburbs, while the city remained mostly Black.

Marshall's family had a hard time keeping a roof over their heads. His father had left them when the boy was still a toddler. He recalled, "I know my mother tried to do the best she could, but I was bounced around so much—it seemed like we moved every two or three months. I'd go to, like, six different schools in one year. We were on welfare, and my mom never ever worked."[3]

The story of how Eminem became one of hip-hop's biggest stars often emphasizes how he went from rags to riches—a classic Horatio Alger story—that he rose to the top because of his individual genius and hard work. What is less often told is that his success in hip-hop had a lot to do with the fact that he grew up in primarily Black neighborhoods with Black friends and mentors. In one of his earliest interviews, he told music journalist Charles Aaron that he grew up "near 8 Mile Road in Detroit, which separates the suburbs from the city. Almost all the Blacks are on one side, and almost all the whites are on the other, but all the families nearby are low-income. We lived on the Black side."[4]

As a small white kid, he was a minority at most of the schools he attended. He was often bullied. Once he was beaten so bad, he was hospitalized. Another time a group of boys cursed him out, and when he flipped them off, they chased him in their car and fired shots at him. Most of his friends were Black, and hip-hop helped him to find his voice.

He recalled, "There was this mixed school I went to in fifth grade, one with lots of Asian and Black kids and everybody was into breakdancing. They always had the latest rap tapes—the Fat Boys, LL Cool J's *Radio*—and I thought it was the most incredible shit I'd ever heard." Not long after, he heard the Beastie Boys, and decided he could rap, too. By the time he was fifteen, he was doing graffiti and writing rhymes.

He jumped into Detroit's rap battle scene, competing at a spot called the Hip-Hop Shop on 7 Mile Road where his friend and mentor DeShaun "Proof" Holton ran epic freestyle battle sessions. He practiced freestyling until he could understand how to break down a rhyme. He learned how to improvise a phrase, then generate sets of words that rhymed syllable-for-syllable with that phrase. He wasn't great at school, but when he rapped, people began to hear his unique genius.

He became known as a battle rapper and freestyler, but he wanted to become a master storyteller as well. One day, while sitting on the toilet, he came up with a new character through which he could tell his twisted tales. He made a five-song EP named after that character: *Slim Shady*. It didn't sell much but people who heard it liked his fast wit and intricate rhyme styles.

He and his then girlfriend, Kim Scott, were struggling to pay rent and take care of their new baby, Hailie. The three were evicted multiple times. When they did have a spot to stay, their belongings were regularly stolen by crackheads. He was still a poor white man living in a poor Black neighborhood.

One day, he and Kim caught someone breaking into their house for the fifth time. "That day, I wanted to quit rap and get a house in the fucking suburbs. I was arguing with my girl, like, 'Can't you see they don't want us here?'" he recalled. "I just couldn't, though. I'd keep going to the clubs and taking the abuse. But I'd come home and put a fist through the wall. If you listen to a Slim Shady record, you're going to hear all that frustration coming out."[5]

Marshall heard about a freestyle contest called the Rap Olympics in Los Angeles. The night before he flew out for it, he had to break back into a house he had just been evicted from to have a place to sleep. He was broke and homeless. At that contest, he came in second. "The winner of the Rap Olympics got, like five hundred dollars. I could have used that, man," he remembers. "Second place got nothing."

But not long afterward, Dr. Dre heard him freestyling on Sway and King Tech's Wake Up Show, an influential radio show. Then Interscope Records head Jimmy Iovine played Dre the *Slim Shady EP*.

"When I heard it, I didn't even know he was white," said Dr. Dre. "It was incredible, I had to meet him right away."[6]

The two recorded some new tracks for what would become *The Slim Shady LP,* which would showcase Eminem's undeniable rhyme skills, dark sense of humor, and what his critics would call violence, homophobia, and misogyny. There would be many more debates about his lyrics ahead.

But for the bleach-blond rapper, the most difficult interviews were ones in which Black radio DJs and hip-hop journalists asked him about race. When this happened, Eminem bristled and made jokes. He didn't yet know how to talk about it. On the eve of the release of *The Slim Shady LP,* he sat down with Davey D:

DAVEY D: Now let me ask you this. With the whole race thing—the first time that I got a record from you guys, the first thing that came out of the promoter's mouth was: "Yo, this kid is dope. He's a dope white MC." I took offense to it.

EMINEM: Thank you.

DAVEY D: Because, it's like, now it raises the question: Are you being pushed because you're white or are you being pushed because you're good? The perception that a lot of people is having now is that you're gonna blow up, that you're on MTV, that you're getting major radio play . . . because you're a white kid that can rap. And this is the most marketable thing since Elvis.

EMINEM: You know what? Anybody who pulls the race card is gonna get it double back in their face. It's going to backfire right in their face. Anybody. I'm waiting for the race card. I've dealt with the race card all of my life. Where I grew up, how I grew up, where I lived, where I came up at, rhymin', everything. I've dealt with it all my life and I'm telling you, I'm in a boiling point right now in my life where I swear to God that anybody who plays that race card . . .

DAVEY D: See, I understand you don't play that. But what about your label and the marketing machinery behind you that's pushing the race card? They're pushing it heavy: "Look, look, look, man, he's a white MC who can rap."

EMINEM: I don't believe that.

DAVEY D: No, I'm telling you, the first time I got a phone call the promoter was telling me that you were the white dude that raps and I needed to add your record.

EMINEM: Maybe that was the promoter and what he felt. Or maybe that was somebody who individually took it upon himself to think, "Well, maybe this is a plus." I don't feel it's a plus. I don't feel it's a negative. I feel like music is music, and every time someone asked me, "Yo, how do you feel about, like, being a white MC, blah blah blah blah blah?" And then the whole article starts turning into being a white MC. I'm saying, I'm like, "Yo can we get to the music?" . . .

DAVEY D: Well, let's talk about the album . . . What can we expect on the album?

EMINEM: Violins and *NSync on every record.

Eminem knew that he was heralded, in part, because of the novelty of his whiteness. When he battled, his opponents never hesitated to talk about it. He was sometimes booed off stage just because he was white. He was also aware of what he owed his crew members—who were all Black, always had his back, and always had to answer the challenge: "Why you sticking up for the white boy?"[7] It all made him want to work harder—to make his homies proud, to prove to everyone he deserved to hold the mic.

It may have even made him write more outlandish stories and concoct more hilarious disses. "I had to choose between being the class clown and being the shy kid who got the shit kicked out of him," he wrote in his autobiography, *The Way I Am*. "So I had to learn quickly to snap back. And, luckily, snapping on people and being snapped on is something that kind of trains you for hip-hop."[8]

He had met Kim when he jumped up on a lunchroom table and belted out the lyrics to LL Cool J's song "I'm Bad." Battle rhymes always shaded into violent metaphor, and the violence was never far from funny punch lines. "I'm Bad" had included the lines: "I eliminate punks, cut 'em up in chunks" and "Even when I'm bragging, I'm being sincere."

On "'97 Bonnie and Clyde," Slim Shady narrates a story in which he takes his daughter along to dump her mother's body. As he drives to the lake, he raps to his girl in baby talk:

I told you it's okay, Hey-Hey, want to ba-ba?
Take a night-night? Nana-boo, goo-goo ga-ga?
Her make goo-goo ca-ca? Da-da change your dia-dee
Clean the baby up so her can take a nighty-nighty

Dr. Dre, who had stoked controversy before and would regularly provoke Eminem in the studio to be more extreme, defended Em's lyrics as "dark comedy." But not everyone was laughing. Songs like "Guilty Conscience," and later, "Criminal" and "Kill You," would be called misogynistic and homophobic by critics.

Yet Eminem's raps also seemed to speak to the angst of young middle-class white American males, outwardly stable and secure but inwardly paranoid and losing it. Slim Shady was angry, petty, and dangerous. That made him cool to the boys, cute to the girls. But then, just two months after *The Slim Shady LP* came out, two heavily armed white teens stepped into their suburban Colorado high school in Columbine and viciously murdered thirteen people. For decades, hip-hop had given voice to young people at the margins of society. Now it seemed that Eminem had given mainstream white male Americans a voice.

(White) Lies and Allies

Back in the 1980s, the core hip-hop audiences were Black. But Black music had always given people of all cultural backgrounds tools that they needed for hope, expression, and survival. For example, at the Meeting of the Minds gatherings at the Latin Quarter club, Paradise Gray and Afrika Bambaataa influenced kids from all backgrounds to replace the gold chains they wore with Red, Black, and Green medallions in the shape of Africa. As time went on, some fans began to express their own identity, sporting leather medallions with Puerto Rican, Mexican, Filipino, or Irish flags. That was hip-hop's power at its best. Black freedom culture could give voice to those who needed it, that was why it had the power to transform people and society.

At that time there was a group called 3rd Bass, which included a Jewish American rapper named Michael "MC Serch" Berrin, an Irish American rapper named Pete "Pete Nice" Nash, and a Black DJ, Richard "Richie Rich" Lawson. Their two albums, *The Cactus Album* and *Derelicts of Dialect,* would set the bar for authenticity for later white rappers like Eminem, Macklemore, and G-Eazy.

Pete Nice played basketball in New York City and grew up on hip-hop park jam tapes given to him by his ball-playing friends. When he went to Columbia University, he started doing a hip-hop radio show on Monday nights on the school's station, WKCR, with DJ Clark Kent. Pete met MC Serch through X-Clan's founder Lumumba Carson at the Latin Quarter. When MC Serch danced at the club, the crowd would chant, "Go white boy! Go white boy go!" He attended high school in Manhattan with his neighborhood idols, the Kangol Crew, which included Slick Rick, Dana Dane, and Doug E. Fresh. He was mentored by one of hip-hop's first white MCs, a legendary graffiti writer named Blake "Keo" Lethem.

As 3rd Bass, the crew made two gold-selling albums for Def Jam Recordings, and cleared paths for artists like Nas and MF Doom to come into the industry. Serch recalls that when he secured a recording contract for Nas, he refused to take a dime. "I couldn't be that Jew benefitting from the Black man in front of me," he told DJ Vlad. "I wanted him to win."

But some dismissed Serch's high-top fade, Pete Nice's fancy suits and walking cane, and their pro-Black lyrics as if they were "trying to act Black," as if they were trying to be "wiggers." To be sure, there were other whites who might have felt hip-hop was just an opportunity to have fun or be shocking, to put on a costume and disparage Black people, while making lots of money in the process. By the time hip-hop had crossed over in the 1990s, it was impossible for white teens to not be exposed directly to Black artists. But, just as with Elvis, the music industry wanted a white artist who could sound Black and cross the music over to the lucrative white audience.

Not long after 3rd Bass dropped the *Cactus Album,* buzz grew around a new song whose hook was a popular chant used by Alpha Phi Alpha, the oldest and one of the largest Black fraternities: "Ice! Ice Baby!" The song first caught on with Black students in college circles and spread. The artist was a white rapper from Dallas named Vanilla Ice.

No one knew anything about him. One rumor was that he was a member of Alpha Phi Alpha. When the "Ice Ice Baby" video was released, all those rumors were put to rest. The world saw a white guy rocking a pompadour hairstyle, doing the Running Man on the rooftop of a Dallas warehouse with two Black members of his VIP Posse.

As Vanilla Ice's popularity took off, he drew immediate comparisons to MC Hammer, who had a Top Ten hit with "U Can't Touch This." The two went on tour together, with Vanilla Ice opening. But soon Vanilla Ice would surpass Hammer on the pop charts, and began complaining about having to open for Hammer. "Ice Ice Baby" became the first rap song to reach number one on the pop charts.

That's when things turned. He released an autobiography, *Ice by Ice,* in which he claimed he had been in a violent Miami street gang, even though he had grown up in the wealthy Dallas suburbs. The media scrutinized his claims. When he won "Favorite New Pop/Rock Artist" at the American Music Awards, he looked at the camera and said, "To the people that try to hold me down and talk bad about me, kiss my white butt. Word to your mother!"

The next night, he appeared on the *Arsenio Hall Show,* the late-night show that had become hip-hop's nightly town hall. Before the interview was about to start, Vanilla Ice invited Public Enemy's Flavor Flav onstage. But the talk show host was not having it. Arsenio asked Flav to leave, then questioned Vanilla Ice about his American Music Awards appearance the night before. Ice said that for all those who doubted a white person could make it in rap, winning the award was like, "Ha! Right in your face." Arsenio then asked him about all of the media coverage. Ice said, "I am from the streets and if you can't see that I'm from the streets, then you're blind. Because the majority of white people cannot dance."

Arsenio said that a lot of Black rappers were angry because many whites had not been interested in rap music until they saw a "vanilla face." Ice responded that this was not his fault, that their anger was a reflection of their jealousy. Then he mentioned again that he and Flavor Flav were homies. Arsenio asked if he had brought Flavor Flav on to show the world that he had a Black supporter. The audience, which was on Vanilla Ice's side, booed Arsenio for asking the question. But many hip-hop heads saw something different—a white rapper who did not seem to have respect for hip-hop or Black people. After this interview, Vanilla Ice's rap career would never again reach the same heights.

Still, the debate would continue. Would hip-hop help whites better understand Blacks and heal deep historic racial wounds? Or would it be just a new way for whites to exploit Black culture and erase Black artists?

"The King of Hip-Hop"

By the turn of the millennium, hip-hop industry leaders were speaking about how white consumers now made up 70 percent of the rap music market. Eminem's success was perhaps as predictable as it was unparalleled. *The Slim Shady LP* sold 500,000 copies in its first two weeks. His second album, the *Marshall Mathers LP,* sold nearly two million albums in its first week, on its way to selling more than thirty-two million copies and becoming one of the biggest-selling albums of all time. He became the bestselling artist in hip-hop history. In 2011, *Rolling Stone* crowned him "The King of Hip-Hop."

When *The Slim Shady LP* was released, Dre went home to his mansion in the wealthy suburbs of Los Angeles, and Marshall returned to the tiny Detroit 8 Mile trailer park he was living in with Kim and Hailie. The relationship between Dr. Dre and Eminem seemed to reverse the old story in American music. Instead of a wealthy white man finding an undiscovered Black musical genius, it seemed as if a wealthy Black man had found an undiscovered white musical genius.

For some, Dre and Eminem's story seemed an indication that racism was over and that Blacks were now equal to whites. In 2002, with the release of the movie *8 Mile,* which lightly fictionalized his life story, Eminem was portrayed as the hero of a modern-day Horatio Alger story. Alger had been a nineteenth-century author whose novels were about poor boys who overcame intense poverty and insurmountable odds to achieve the American Dream. During the late twentieth century, it had become common to speak of the Horatio Alger myth, the story that anyone could make it in America through hard work and ingenuity. The same myth suggested that people who were poor were that way because they had not tried hard enough, and that histories of racism, racial segregation, and exclusion had nothing to do with racial inequity. The movie also seemed to advance the idea that hip-hop was closed to whites, so that Eminem had somehow overcome not only poverty, but Black antagonism, or what some mistakenly called "reverse racism."

But in Horatio Alger's actual stories, an individual's hard work was never the only factor that propelled the hero from rags to riches. Alger often wrote of rich benefactors who stepped in at crucial moments to give the hero the money and resources he needed. Dr. Dre and Eminem's Black friends had been Eminem's benefactors. They had not only co-signed Eminem in the beginning, they defended Eminem when he became the subject of protests and boycotts. Black fans were the first to launch Eminem's career. While Vanilla Ice reinforced racial stereotypes, Eminem would come to publicly acknowledge the debt he owed his Black benefactors, friends, and fans.

Once Eminem crossed over, his whiteness made the mainstream media take special notice and suddenly, he found himself struggling to talk about race. Two months after *The Slim Shady LP* was released, *Rolling Stone* placed him on its cover, the first of many times. He went on Howard Stern's radio show and got grilled about why he "talked Black." For their part, hip-hop journalists still asked Eminem whether he would be another Vanilla Ice, making a mockery of hip-hop, or an Elvis Presley, erasing hip-hop's Blackness.

Eminem's views about his own whiteness shifted dramatically. Before he found mainstream success, he had talked to Davey D about Vanilla Ice. "He was trying to be something he's not. If you're from the suburbs, say you're from the suburbs. If you want to rhyme, then rap about being from the suburbs," Eminem said. "Be proud of where you came from because nobody on this planet can help what color they are."

But by the time he recorded "Role Model" from *The Slim Shady LP,* he must have thought twice about what it might mean to represent "white pride." Now he rapped how his whiteness made him want to disappear.

> Some people only see that I'm white, ignorin' skill,
> 'cause I stand out like a green hat with an orange bill
> But I don't get pissed, y'all don't even see through the mist
> How the fuck can I be white? I don't even exist

But his ideas continued to evolve. On "The Way I Am," the central track of his next album, *The Marshall Mathers LP,* he wanted to reveal his debts to the Black pioneers of hip-hop. He seemed to want to say to his white fans, don't praise me—look at these greats who have come before me. So he double-tracked his voice like Tupac, rocked the echo machine like Sha-Rock and DMC, and flipped classic Rakim and Chuck D lines to describe how little control he felt he had over his image. "I'm so sick and tired of being admired," he rapped.

> And I just do not got the patience to deal with these cocky
> Caucasians
> Who think I'm some wigga who tries to be Black 'cause I talk
> With an accent and grab on my balls

He also realized that, in his success, he had become the projection of mainstream white America's fears. At the 2000 MTV Video Music Awards, he assembled an army of a hundred Slim Shadys in white tees, jeans, and bleach-blond hair to march in and stand behind him as he rapped, "I am whatever you say I am."

He continued this theme on his 2002 album *The Eminem Show*—an album where, after three years of protests and government hearings against his music, and mounting personal issues, he rapped not as the crazed Slim Shady or the introverted Marshall Mathers, but as the conflicted underdog Eminem. Success had torn his life to shreds. He was on probation for pistol-whipping a man who had kissed Kim, and his ugly feud with his mother spilled into the public.

But he now recognized his whiteness had played a significant role in both his sales success and media attention. On "Without Me," he criticized himself:

> Though I'm not the first king of controversy
> I am the worst thing since Elvis Presley
> To do Black music so selfishly
> And use it to get myself wealthy

He was even more blunt on "White America." He realized that the reason he had become such a huge star was the same reason no one wanted to give him love until Dr. Dre came along: "Look at my sales! Let's do the math. If I was Black, I would've sold half." He told *Rolling Stone,* "In my heart I truly believe I have a talent, but at the same time I'm not stupid."[9]

In the last verse, he portrayed himself as a renegade ringleader of "this circus of worthless pawns," who would lead them to the White House "to burn the flag and replace it with a Parental Advisory sticker, to spit liquor in the faces of this democracy of hypocrisy." In 2004, he released an animated video for "Mosh" that depicted him leading a revolution against President George W. Bush, whom he blamed for plunging the nation into global war.

But he continued to tailspin personally, becoming addicted to drugs. Then *The Source* magazine released two songs he had recorded long before he was famous, one called "Ole Foolish Pride," in which he had dissed Black women, saying they were "dumb" and "only want your money," and another called "So Many Styles" in which he rapped that he wasn't down with big butts and "n---a shit."

For Eminem, who had stated he would never use the n-word in his raps (though he would not stop using the words "b---h" and "f----t"), the moment was devastating. He apologized and sent out a statement: "The tape they played today was something I made out of anger, stupidity, and frustration when I was a teenager. I'd just broken up with my girlfriend, who was African American, and I reacted like the angry, stupid kid I was. I hope people will take it for the foolishness that it was."

The incident made him think about his beginnings as a rapper, and he wrote a song called "Yellow Brick Road," for 2004's *Encore,* one of his most melancholy and nostalgic, especially after the murder of his best friend Proof. On it, he answered his accusers at *The Source,* and recounted his awkward early hip-hop days.

When he first met Proof, he was told that "white rappers don't know how to rhyme." But he won Proof's approval with his "compound syllable rhymes." He rapped about the days when, influenced by X-Clan, he wore an African medallion, and influenced by Flavor Flav, he wore a big clock. Then he told the story of how he started dating a beautiful Black girl to get back at Kim, but was dumped, and wrote the raps that *The Source* surfaced. Hip-hop heads split on whether he could be forgiven.

As he got older, Eminem became more explicit about his support for racial justice. He strongly supported the Black Lives Matter movement and Colin Kaepernick's protest, and called President Trump a racist. In a 2017 BET freestyle, he told Trump supporters:

Any fan of mine who's a supporter of his
I'm drawing a line in the sand, you're either for or against
And if you can't decide who you like more and you're split
On who you should stand beside, I'll do it for you with this:
Fuck you!

Two decades before, before many people knew who he was, the journalist Charles Aaron had asked Eminem whether he thought hip-hop could bring people together.

"I don't know, man," Eminem answered. "Sometimes I feel like rap music is almost the key to stopping racism. If anything is at least going to lessen it, it's gonna be rap. I would love it if, even for one day, you could walk through a neighborhood and see an Asian guy sitting on his stoop, then you look across the street and see a Black guy and a white guy sitting on their porches, and a Mexican dude walking by. If we could truly be multicultural, racism could be so past the point of anybody giving a fuck. But I don't think you or me are going to see it in our lifetimes."[10]

18
All Around the World

Hip-hop took over the world in three phases. In the first phase, from 1979 through the mid 1980s, the old school pioneers ignited hip-hop scenes with their first records and tours to countries like the United Kingdom, France, and Japan. Then movies like *Wild Style* and *Beat Street* sparked more hip-hop outbreaks, even in Communist countries like East Germany. In the second phase, from the late 1980s through the early 1990s, Public Enemy's tours, especially to Black countries in Africa and South America, started the flowering of hip-hop educational programs and hip-hop activism. By the turn of the millennium, hip-hop was the most influential popular youth culture around the world, fueled both by a global market and a network of vibrant local underground scenes.

The first rap record tour came at the end of the 1970s, after thirty-nine-year-old Afro-Filipino musician Joe Bataan first heard rap music. He had been a Latin salsa music superstar and a founder of Salsoul Records, one of the most celebrated record labels of the disco era. But a run of bad luck and business disagreements left him working at a community center in Harlem, far from the musical action—or so he thought. One night some kids rented the hall to throw a party and asked him to collect the money. Joe was stunned when a thousand kids showed up. He looked to the stage and was even more confused.

"I said, 'What the hell's going on here? I don't see no band,'" he recalls. "Then in the middle of the record everybody's clapping, someone's talking on the mic.'"

By the end of the night, he had an idea for a new song. He wrote it and went to two guys he knew from the Harlem World scene, Andre Harrell and Alonzo Brown, who rapped as Dr. Jeckyll and Mr. Hyde. But they stood him up for the recording session. So he recorded "Rap-O Clap-O" and released it himself late in 1979, and was stunned to see the record rise to the top of the charts in

Luxembourg, Belgium, Holland, and France. He toured Europe for six months, the first time people outside the United States were able to see what the kids in New York were doing.

The Sugarhill Gang's "Rapper's Delight" was already a global hit, and the demand for it was more than the small Sugar Hill Records label could handle. Records were being pressed in Sweden, Venezuela, Germany, England, France, Mexico, Spain, Australia, Argentina, Brazil, and Uruguay. Local musicians took the beat and made their own rap versions to it. Cover versions came out where there had been long histories of Black music and oral traditions, like Jamaica and Brazil, and where there had not, like Germany.[1]

In 1982, Afrika Bambaataa and Soulsonic Force's "Planet Rock," musically assembled from German electropop, British rock, and African American disco rap, introduced hip-hop as a new vision for global harmony. The record—and then the crew—stormed the world. Bambaataa and New York's leading rappers, dancers, artists, and DJs went on the first hip-hop tour outside the United States. Bambaataa saw the visits to France and the United Kingdom as a way to expand Universal Zulu Nation and to espouse what he thought of as the core values of hip-hop: peace, unity, love, and having fun. Everywhere he went he planted the seeds for the hip-hop movement in Europe, Africa, and Asia.

After long bus trips broken up only by full-scale tagging and pilfering attacks at the gas stops, the twenty-five-member entourage would head onstage to try to replicate the feel of New York hip-hop for the crowds. "Not too many people showed up to these shows," journalist David Hershkovits, who had come along to document the shows, recalls. "We'd play in some school gymnasium in some town, maybe fifty kids would show up. And the French are not demonstrative, even in Paris where there was a decent turnout. I remember looking at the people and they would just sort of be looking at each other trying to figure out if they should like it or not. They didn't know quite how to react. It was so new."

But in Strasbourg, France, they got a taste of that old Bronx River unpredictability. Crazy Legs recalls, "We did a show and there was these drunk people, and the Double Dutch girls were onstage doing their thing. They threw bottles at them." The music stopped. DJ Grandmixer D.ST armed himself with a broken bottle, graffiti legend PHASE 2 picked up a chair. "Next thing you know, people were backstage talking about, 'We gon' get them!' DONDI led the people out there. DONDI had his belt with his name buckle on and the dudes caught a beatdown. After they got beat down, everybody stepped back onstage, and then the people in the audience started clapping! It went from a show to a brawl to getting applause." Bambaataa went back to playing his records, and their legend was sealed. By the time they reached Paris, the media flocked to meet them.

Not long afterward, many of the same artists went to Japan to introduce the movie *Wild Style*. The crew made quite an impression on the style tribes of Tokyo. "Within three days," director Charlie Ahearn says, "there were people scratch-mixing. Graffiti was popping up in imitated fashions. And by the time we left, they were so excited."

The UK and Japan caught the hip-hop virus. In England, the scene spread quickly. Hip-hop fit in comfortably with British soul, reggae, and dance music. Punk rockers like the Clash and Malcolm McLaren built bridges directly to the scene and made rap records with hip-hop legends. By the early 1980s, there was a legitimate hip-hop scene in Black neighborhoods in London and Bristol. Rappers began rhyming in American accents, but quickly became more comfortable with their own, and by the late 1980s—with artists like Hijack, Rebel MC, and Demon Boyz—were making hip-hop that was as compelling as anything made in the US.

France seemed to take hip-hop the most seriously. In 1984, DJ and television personality Sidney Duteil, one of the first Black hosts on the French airwaves, and a journalist named Sophie Bramly launched a national hip-hop TV show on the TF1 network. Although it only lasted a year, the show sent shockwaves through French youth culture. Before long, French hip-hop had developed a sophisticated network of b-boys and graffiti artists who would influence the rest of Europe and even New York. In 1991, MC Solaar became the first global French rap superstar. Solaar was born in Senegal to parents from Dakar and discovered Zulu Nation and the music of Afrika Bambaataa as a young teenager in Paris. Solaar's multicultural background appealed to youths throughout the Francophone world, which quickly developed into the largest non–English speaking rap market.

Hip-hop had touched down in many unexpected places. In

Germany's East Berlin, still under Communist rule, someone smuggled in a copy of the movie *Beat Street,* and a small scene started to bubble. In New Zealand and Australia, indigenous youths recognized traditions in hip-hop that allowed them to express their Maori and aboriginal identities in new ways. It was the same in South Africa, whose history of Zulu resistance to British colonization, especially the 1906 rebellion led by Zulu leader Bambatha, had inspired Afrika Bambaataa to rename himself and form Universal Zulu Nation.

South African hip-hop pioneer Emile "Emile YX?" Jansen says, "Graffiti and rock art are not different at all. Our ancestors did exactly that. So though we say that we started [doing hip-hop in South Africa] in '82, we reignited what was already inside of us. Our ancestors made a circle, they clapped, they [sang], that's a loop.

"And what you do is you go into trance, do you understand?" he adds. "And when someone in the middle of the circle is dope, we say, 'Fire!' because in the middle of the circle there was a fire."[2]

Jansen grew up in Cape Town and joined the anti-apartheid movement with his Black and Coloured peers. In 1985, when he joined students who were walking out of high schools in the Cape Flats to protest, they were met by the military, tear gassed, and brutally beaten. Through hip-hop, they found a way to both express anger at the racist regime and to find joy in expression.

A Black Planet

The emerging popularity of cable and satellite television throughout the world further spread hip-hop. MTV's *Yo! MTV Raps* became the network's first globally televised show—airing in dozens of countries, first on MTV Europe, and then on MTV Asia and MTV Latino a few years later.

Public Enemy was a group that got a lot of airtime, and, like Afrika Bambaataa, they used it to spread their message of Black empowerment. When their success in the US allowed them to tour around the world, they were excited to visit Brazil, Europe, and Africa, where they met with local artists and activists. They saw their extended world tours as ways to connect Black people around the world. They inspired young artists from Seoul to São Paulo to bend African American hip-hop to their own local languages to voice their own local struggles.

"The [Public Enemy] song 'Don't Believe the Hype' was so important," says legendary Brazilian rapper Eliefi of the hit single that championed Black Power. "We had never seen Black folks in a militant stance before."

Brazil had an urban sound system culture similar to the Jamaican-influenced New York City sound system culture from which DJ Kool Herc had emerged. So when rap records came to Brazil in 1979, they were quickly incorporated. Local rappers adopted New York rap hits into what they called *cantu faladu*, "spoken song" in an urban Brazilian Portuguese dialect. Within a decade, *cantu faladu* had spread from the impoverished neighborhoods of eastern São Paulo into more middle-class venues.

Soon there were hip-hop programs in schools, sponsored by the government and taught by popular local hip-hop artists. Eliefi's militant hip-hop group, DMN, and another popular group, Racionais, visited dozens of schools to do short performances. "This program marked a shift where we realized what we could really do with hip-hop," he recalls.

After each performance, the rappers led passionate discussion forums, where youths spoke about their concerns over racism, police brutality, poverty, and drugs. School administrators became uneasy and national media denounced the programs, believing they were fomenting unrest. But the rappers and community groups continued to conduct the programs independently, helping foster the creation of youth organizations and neighborhood associations.

Such programs spread in other places around the world, especially in places where there were young people who were facing severe conditions. In France and Germany, for instance, young Muslim and Arab immigrants and refugees used hip-hop to describe the racism they faced. In South Africa, as the opposition to apartheid reached a critical point, hip-hop made music that criticized the government and recovered their cultural roots. "As crazy as it sounds, many of us found a new respect for Africa through hip-hop," wrote activist Nazli Abrahams and rapper Shaheen Ariefdien. "For a lot of first-generation [South African] hip-hop heads, hip-hop was African traditions with Japanese technology, processed by kidnapped Africans on stolen land."

Rappers who decried the government received death threats from racist extremists. Graffiti writers piecing political slogans after dark amid curfews risked being shot by government soldiers.[3] Influenced by Public Enemy, Ariefdien, DJ Ready D, and others formed a crew called Prophets of Da City in Cape Town. But when government officials became aware of what they were doing with their music, they were banned from the radio, their shows cancelled, and their recordings confiscated. They were only able to release their record, *Age of Truth,* by smuggling a copy of their master to a label in Britain.

As the country geared up in 1994 for the first elections in which people of all races were allowed to vote, Prophets of Da City played across the country for hundreds of thousands, encouraging them to cast their ballots. Their song, "Understand Where I'm Coming From," became an underground hit, while the video, featuring shots of Black protestors being attacked by the military, was censored. But when Nelson Mandela secured victory in the elections, he invited Prophets of Da City to perform at his first presidential address and his inauguration. The song they sang, "Neva Again," heralded a new era for young Africa. "Ah, excellent! Finally a Black president to represent!" Shaheen rapped, and by the end of the song, the crew had people doing a new dance in tribute to the leader who had brought them to freedom.

The Sound of Money

In 2002, an African American named Dana Burton began an annual rap battle in Shanghai, China, called Iron Mic. Rappers and crews from all parts of China came to compete, often in different accents and dialects. Some rappers rocked in Cantonese, English, and Mandarin in the same verse. Burton, who called himself MC Showtyme, was fluent in Mandarin, conversant in a few other dialects, and intimately familiar with the ambitions and dreams of a new Chinese generation. "I learned it from the streets," he says, through *xi ha,* the Mandarin name for hip-hop.

By the end of the 2000s, Iron Mic had built a national grassroots underground rap scene. Sponsored by Wyborowa vodka, Burton presented 150 shows featuring Chinese rappers, DJs, dancers, and graffiti artists in forty cities. The artists performed a mini-history of hip-hop, from its urban American beginnings to its rise in China. Here was an African American entrepreneur promoting a Polish vodka owned by a French corporation using Chinese performers practicing an Afrodiasporic art form that originated in the inner cities of the United States. By 2017, a streaming show called "The Rap of China" had garnered more than a billion views and became a national sensation. At the end of the decade, 88 Rising, a company started in the US by a group of Asian Americans, was building an online platform for transnational Asian artists from China, Indonesia, Japan, Thailand, Vietnam, South Korea, and the US—including Higher Brothers, Suboi, Rich Brian, Joji, Keith Ape, and Dumbfoundead—while forging ties with the Wu-Tang Clan, Migos, and Travis Scott.

Hip-hop was now at the center of global youth culture. For millions of young people, it had gone beyond just music. Hip-hop influenced the way they dressed, talked, even thought about politics. Young people clung to hip-hop as a pure method of expression and began to connect with each other like they never had before. They came to understand themselves through hip-hop as citizens of the world.

At the same time, corporations saw the power in hip-hop to sell things—not just music, but shoes and clothing, snack crackers and soda drinks, credit cards and jewelry, cars and computers. Annually, hip-hop drove $10 billion worth of business in the United States alone.[4] Commercial rap made in the United States—with its 50 Cent ethic of "get rich or die trying"—displaced local rappers and musicians on the radio and television airwaves in Africa, Asia, the Caribbean, and South America, while serving as the soundtrack for aggressively youth-oriented consumer goods marketing.

In Kenya, for instance, two different kinds of hip-hop competed with each other—hip-hop as a resistance culture oriented toward social justice, the other as a popular culture oriented toward selling commercial products. Young Kenyans, like the pioneering group Kalamashaka, were rapping about joblessness, poverty, and the older generation's failures. They rapped in their own dialect of *Sheng,* a language that includes English, Swahili, and Kikuyu words. One community organization, called Words and Pictures, traveled from Kenya to Ghana, Senegal, South Africa, and Tanzania to connect African hip-hop graffiti and rap artists.

But on the radio, which in some parts of Africa was the primary mass medium, hip-hop from America was the sound. Stations such as Britain's Capital FM and the locally owned KISS-FM preferred to program American artists such as 50 Cent because it helped corporations to sell consumer goods such as cell phones made by Motorola and Nokia. Kenyan rappers complained bitterly about the disappearance of "message music" from their airwaves. Kalamashaka called American rap "white-boy oppressor music," even though the artists were predominantly African American.

"[Hip-hop] is creating opportunities where there were none before," the Nairobi filmmaker Michael Wanguhu said, "but there's no room for that music that is enlightened and empowers people." But he was optimistic about hip-hop's ability to connect young Africans. "Hip-hop in Africa is like the new Pan-Africanism," he says. "It's diffusing all the borders we have."

In 2009, these hip-hop optimists even had a global anthem, Somali-Canadian K'Naan's "Wavin' Flag," which documented the plight of Somali war refugees. "They'll call me freedom," K'Naan rapped, "just like a wavin' flag." The song became a kind of worldwide meme, advancing both community-building and commercial aims at the same time. Among the many more versions of K'Naan's song that were released, one raised funds for Haitian victims of the 2010 earthquake, and one was chosen by Coca-Cola as its theme for the 2010 World Cup.

The Sound of Revolution

Even as hip-hop became mainstream, it remained a voice for the oppressed, and something scary to those in power. All across Europe, hip-hop became the voice of refugees and immigrants to express their feelings about colonization, racism, and poverty. In England, the daughter of a revolutionary from Sri Lanka, Mathangi "Maya" Arulpragasam, remade herself as "M.I.A." As a refugee of war trying to adjust to life in the British housing projects, she said, "My survival technique in Britain was to forget Sri Lanka—completely—and block it out of my mind. Then I thought, 'I know the other side, I've lived through that for ten years, and I have to speak for them at some point.'"

She made music and videos that connected the experiences of poor youths all around the world, whether in Somalia, Trinidad, Brazil, or Burma. Her stories were about kids on the corner selling small amounts of weed to get money for food, about undocumented immigrants trekking across the desert to escape violence and war. She wanted to express the feelings of the forgotten.

Yet, as it had in the United States, hip-hop also caused a backlash. In France, crews like Suprême NTM, Assassin, IAM, and the Ghetto Fabulous Group, made up mostly of immigrants from North and West Africa, rapped about tensions with the government and the police. These tensions boiled over in 2005, when a group of boys running from police hid in an electrical station and two were electrocuted. Three weeks of rioting in over two hundred cities ensued. Two years later, another incident of police brutality touched off a new round of riots across France. Instead of moving to address the government and police violence, two hundred French members of parliament signed a petition to curb hip-hop.

In Britain, when two young Black women were caught in the crossfire of two gangs and killed, British Culture Minister Kim Howells singled out So Solid Crew, and the "hateful lyrics that these boasting macho idiot rappers come up with" that "are glorifying gun culture and violence." Critics clapped back, saying the government leader was racist and anti-immigrant in blaming hip-hop for the women's deaths.

But at the same time Howells tried to censor rappers, Brazil's Culture Minister Gilberto Gil was giving government grants of up to $60,000 to establish hip-hop education programs in schools across the country. Inspired by hip-hop's original "four elements," students work with multimedia technology, read and discuss hip-hop lyrics, run radio stations and write newsletters, organize dance competitions, and create documentaries that have aired on national television. "These [hip-hop] phenomena cannot be regarded negatively, because they encompass huge contingents of the population for whom they are the only connection to the larger world," Gil told the *New York Times*, adding that he saw the program as combating violence and social isolation. "It's a different vision of the role of government, a new role."[5]

In Senegal, the land of griots, young artists and activists took to rap and street protest to confront the oppressive one-party government. Rapping in Wolof, English, and French in the mid 1990s, Positive Black Soul and Daara J became two of the first globally popular African rap crews, using powerful West African beats and political rhymes to urge young people to exercise their democratic rights. Throughout the 2000s, a second generation of rappers continued to mobilize voters to fight the power.

In 2011, young rappers from the popular collective called Keur Gui had formed a movement called Y'en a Marre ("Fed Up") to prevent corrupt officials from stealing a third term. They drove across the country with a sound system installed in a flatbed truck, doing spontaneous rallies and setting up local chapters, until lead rapper Thiat was arrested at a demonstration in Dakar for criticizing the president. He was released only after protestors gathered to demand he be freed. When the president was defeated in free elections, Y'en a Marre was credited with helping ensure his downfall.

In Tunisia, Hamada Ben Amor, who rapped under the name El General, rapped a song called "Rayes Lebled (Head of State)" that criticized the corrupt twenty-three-year rule of Tunisian president Zine El Abidine Ben Ali and the government, and he posted it on his Facebook page. It became the theme song of thousands in the streets protesting the regime. The rapper was jailed. But as many radio stations put "Rayes Lebled" into heavy rotation and young activists spread it on YouTube, the protests culminated in Tunisia's Jasmine Revolution, which, in turn, launched the Arab Spring across Northern Africa and the Middle East. From Tunisia and Libya to Egypt and Syria, rappers made the soundtrack to the revolution, and graffiti muralists painted slogans and visions of democracy on the city walls.[6]

Worldwide Cipher

Every year in Germany, thousands of hip-hop fans from around the world gathered to witness the biggest global breaking competition, the Battle of the Year. First organized in 1990 by German b-boy Thomas Hergenröther as a tiny showcase for a handful of dance crews from Germany and Hungary, the event expanded by the turn of the millennium into the World Cup of hip-hop dance. Elimination competitions were held in twenty countries, including Albania, China, Estonia, Malaysia, New Zealand, Serbia, and South Africa. Dozens of teams featuring two hundred dancers represented their countries on the main stage.

Hip-hop events like Battle of the Year brought people together across the barriers of geography, language, and race. "So many different people came together under the name of hip-hop, that hip-hop changed music, arts completely," said Storm, a German b-boy legend, in Benson Lee's essential b-boy documentary *Planet Rock*. "Hip-hop changed the worldview on how we are together."

The essence of hip-hop is the cipher born—or more accurately *reborn*—in the Bronx, where competition and community feed each other. It's here that hip-hop always returns. For over three decades, Battle of the Year showcased riotous explosions of bodies, as dancers literally burst to the breakbeats, style against style, crew against crew, country against country. The climax of the battle—where two crews from different countries lined up and challenged each other, either one-on-one or "commando style," all at once—was the deepest kind of communication.

"It happens in an exchange," said Storm. "He's giving me something that I can relate to and I have to answer with something that he can relate to so that we can continue this battle." This kind of exchange once used to take place on hard pavement in the streets, parks, and community centers of New York City and now continues daily, among millions, in almost every corner of the world.

The b-boy and b-girl crews gathering at contests like Battle of the Year always represented vibrant cross-sections of their own countries. At one contest in South Korea called R-16, the crew representing Holland, called Funky Dope Manouvres, was as ethnically diverse as Supercrew, the American one. FDM included second-generation kids whose parents came from Brazil, Indonesia, Poland, Ghana, and Surinam. One of the young members, Mahan "King Foolish" Noubarzadeh, was of Iranian and Swedish descent. He literally embodied how hip-hop had brought together Muslims and Christians.

During the 2000s, the country most likely to produce champion breaking crews in international competitions was South Korea. Korean b-boys traced their history to 1997, the year that breaking really jumped off in Seoul. Just four years later, the first year that a Korean crew entered the Battle of the Year competition, the group Visual Shock won "Best Show" honors. Every year for the rest of the decade, a South Korean crew placed first or second. Not long after, the South Korean government began sponsoring R-16, which was broadcast on national television and generated tens of millions of dollars a year.

Filmmaker Benson Lee said of the South Korean breakers, "You see that hunger and that drive." A b-boy or b-girl from the Bronx would have recognized it, too—the kind of desire that comes from wanting to overcome a history of hard times in order to make a name for yourself.

"What happens is they practice on the lowdown until they're up at a level where they can actually come out and shock somebody," said Johnjay Chon, a Korean American b-boy who helped jump-start the movement in South Korea. "They practice in the shadow."

The story of how working-class South Korean b-boys went from battling in the park to becoming global stars was an example of how far hip-hop had come, and of how important hip-hop was for young people who wanted to express themselves.

As recently as the 1980s, the South Korean government had actually banned African American soul and funk music on the radio. As part of what the dictator Park Chung-Hee called a "social purification" campaign, artists, intellectuals, and church leaders were arrested and jailed. Park's censorship committee blocked hundreds of American songs, from "We Shall Overcome" to "Me and Mrs. Jones." Leaders thought the music might give young South Koreans too many ideas about freedom.

"Black music was considered illegal because it was not good for the youth," said Jae Hyun "MC Meta" Lee of the influential Korean rap group Garion. "The music scene itself died. Influential music-makers left the country."

It was not until opposition leader Kim Young-Sam was elected as South Korea's first civilian leader in decades in 1992 that youth culture seemed to flower again. At first, dance-friendly pop imports like Bobby Brown and MC Hammer spawned a host of Korean copies, the foundations of what would become K-Pop. Then, MC Meta said, "The curiosity began and people became hungry for the real thing."

1992 was also the year that riots erupted in Los Angeles after the Rodney King verdict, and Koreatown was burned to the ground. For Korean Americans Johnjay Chon and Charlie Shin, who would become the organizers for South Korea's nationally sponsored and recognized annual R-16 competition, hip-hop was their redemption. "For me, growing up in the states, I had been called all kinds of names," Shin said. Seeing Korean b-boys win respect from others, he said, "kind of dissolved all that racial bullshit I grew up with."

Chon was born in Japan and raised in Seattle. After forming and competing nationally with the Circle of Fire crew, he came to Seoul in 1997 to visit family. Armed with videos and DVDs of dozens of contests, Chon scoured the clubs for b-boys to battle. He met one and gave him a video of a Los Angeles b-boy competition called Radiotron.

"A year later I came back and I just saw there were more b-boys. They were telling me, 'Oh you gotta see this footage,'" Chon said. "I'm watching it and it's the Radiotron [video] that I brought out a year ago. It's been dubbed so many times the screen is shaking."

Hip-hop had taken hold in Seoul. Lively internet groups brought fans together. Hip-hop CDs and videos found their way to South Korea through Tokyo. At the Master Plan club, rap crews like Garion, Artisan Beats & Keeproots, and Drunken Tiger JK pioneered an underground sound which would become commercialized in K-Pop. In Seoul's Taehongno neighborhood, an area of college campuses, nightclubs, galleries, and theaters, b-boys suddenly appeared. They battled all evening in front of the crowds at the popular Maronie Park, then moved to the clubs in the early morning hours. When dawn broke, they headed to school.

Their intensity impressed Chon. "I'm like, 'Okay, how does this work?'" he says he asked the b-boys. "I just sleep in school" was their reply.

The b-boys were often poor kids who felt like outsiders. Shin said, "The minute you're born in Korea, depending on what your economic background is, or who your parents are, what network you're in, what neighborhood you're in, what high school you went to, what college you went to, your life is pretty much decided for you." They danced because it offered freedom from the strict rules governing their lives. But the b-boys knew the freedom would not last.

South Korea was still a country at war. Looming over every young man's life in Korea was mandatory military service. "The service will come up when you're twenty-one, twenty-two. But they can always extend that using some excuse," Chon says. "A lot of the b-boys—now they're like twenty-six, twenty-seven, they haven't gone. They have to go soon." Many of the competitive b-boys had postponed their service or illegally evaded their conscription. Some even mutilated themselves to dodge the army. Hyun-Jin "Bang Rock" Kim of the Rivers Crew said through a translator, "Everyone tries to avoid the service." Then he switched to English for emphasis. "It's like going to hell."

This was why, as C-4, a celebrated b-boy from Rivers Crew, put it, "B-boys in other countries do it as a hobby, but to the Korean b-boys, our life is b-boying."

In 2008, the R-16 battle in Suwon, South Korea, came down to a Russian super group called Top 9 trying to eliminate two of the best Korean crews, Rivers and Gamblerz. On the arena stage in the semifinals, in front of a crowd of tens of thousands, Top 9 lined up across the floor from Rivers, as if across a demilitarized zone turned battleground. Russian b-boy Robin, wearing a brown Yankees hat, oversized polo, and cargo slacks, circled the floor and then taunted the Koreans by pulling back his eyes. The Korean audience gasped at Robin's slant-eye diss. But his subsequent solo dance—featuring a skateboarding-style hand plant and surging rolls broken up with one-armed freezes—was flawless.

Then Rivers launched their commando attack. C-4 dove through two Rivers dancers and leapt straight at Robin, pulling his own eyes back, too. The crowd roared its approval. But as the battle continued, Rivers seemed exhausted while Top 9 gained momentum. In their final routine, Top 9 did some Lindy Hop–style routines, jumping off each other, flipping the other into spins, and forming circles for crewmates to leap through. When Top 9 won, some in the crowd booed.

The finals pitted Top 9 against Korea's Gamblerz crew. As the clock ticked down, Gamblerz b-boy Pop walked a handstand across the stage and balanced on his left hand. Then he arched his body into the heart of the Top 9 line. The Russians tried to strike back but they seemed spent. On Gamblerz's last run, b-boy Sick chased Robin and Top 9 out of the cipher, dropped down for some fleet footwork, then contorted himself into a set of wire-doll freezes in rapid succession. When Gamblerz were announced as the champions, Pop flung his shirt into the crowd and struck a teen idol pose at the edge of the stage. Cameras and cell phones flashed.

"The world is a big place, man, and there's another hungry competitor stepping up," R-16 judge and legendary Rock Steady Crew b-boy Ken Swift said. "It's a cycle, and the cycle is based upon crews like these Korean crews who go out and inspire these new fans. And then five years from now, those new people are going to be saying, 'Okay *we're* the shit now.'"

19
Black Lives Matter

Long ago in the late 1960s in East Oakland, before hip-hop had a name, a young teen named Jerry Rentie watched the Black Panthers marching in the streets and was so moved he was inspired to dance.

Soon he had a nickname, "Worm," after the funk-style dance he had invented. Crossing the city to meet and challenge other street dancers, he became one of the best-known boogaloo dancers in the area. Sometimes people would stop him in the street and ask him to "cut a step." He was always happy to oblige.

"You hit it right there in the crosswalk," he laughs. "What makes us cool is when we make the people standing there watching cool. When you make the crowd cool, they make you cool."

At community gatherings, whether the occasion was a political rally or a concert, when the music began, he and his crew One Plus One started dance ciphers in front of the stage, demonstrating moves they had incorporated from James Brown, tap dancers, even ballet dancers and Disney cartoons.

"You did that to get one thing," he says. "I don't want the crowd to just stand there and go 'ooooh' and 'ahhhh.' I try to make them laugh. I try to make them rock. I try to make them clap. I try to make them get into music, not just me. And when I get that connection, I named it 'a moment of alrightness.'"

"Because for that moment, no matter what happened before, the person next to you is alright. And if you look at it from a crowd sense, then that means the whole crowd is alright. The whole room is alright," he adds. "I'm okay. You're okay. For that moment, the world is alright."

Rentie's idea of alrightness described the power of Black freedom culture to move people together, whether to words and beats or for a social cause. In the moment, that feeling of alrightness connected and sustained a community.

In the late 1990s, as the turn of the millennium neared, a new generation of young people used hip-hop as a way to press for political change. Democratic president Bill Clinton had been a major disappointment. In 1992, a wave of young voters had helped sweep him into office just six months after the Los Angeles riots had ended. But as president, Clinton oversaw the massive expansion of policing and incarceration of people of color. The fact that this had happened at the same time that hip-hop was providing more opportunities for Black people and people of color to impact the popular culture than ever before was not lost on the new generation.

At the end of the 1990s, policies directed at restricting young people of color—like California's Proposition 21—and high-profile police shootings of innocent Black men in New York City—including Amadou Diallo and Patrick Dorismond, as well as the brutal police beating of Abner Louima—spurred hip-hop to action. In California, thousands of young people calling themselves "hip-hop activists" poured into the streets to oppose Proposition 21 and the police killings of Tyesha Miller, Aaron Williams, and Sheila Detoy. In New York City, Rappers Mos Def and Talib Kweli organized a coalition called Hip-Hop For Respect and joined with activists to march on Mayor Rudy Giuliani's home at Gracie Mansion.

A new generation decided it was time to leverage the cultural power they had gained into political power. Mos Def wrote an open letter to fellow rappers, telling them, "We are the Senators and the Congressmen of our communities. We come from communities that don't have nobody to speak for them. That's why they love us. Because we talk about what nobody else will talk about. We represent them. And they need to know that we really represent them."[1]

He added, "Now I'm askin' you and anybody who looks on this letter to come forward and show your heart, to show your love, to love the people who love you back by speaking out against the injustices that they suffer."

As the journalist Mychal Denzel Smith would write, their generational charge was clear: "Despite its undeniable impact, the Civil Rights Movement didn't solve the issue of racial injustice. The world that young Black people have inherited is one rife with race-based disparities. By the age of twenty-three, almost half of the Black men in this country have been arrested at least once, 30 percent by the age of eighteen. The unemployment rate for Black sixteen-to-twenty-four-year-olds is around 25 percent. Twelve percent of Black girls face out-of-school suspension, a higher rate than for all other girls and most boys. Black women are incarcerated at a rate nearly three times that of white women."[2]

In 2003, a group of young organizers—including community activist Baye Adofo Wilson, author Bakari Kitwana, organizer Angela Woodson, former editor of *The Source* James Bernard, community leader Ras Baraka, future Green Party vice presidential candidate Rosa Clemente, and others—began to map out what they called the National Hip-Hop Political Convention. Delegates would qualify by registering fifty people to vote, and would forge the hip-hop generation's first national political agenda. People came from the San Francisco Bay Area, the Twin Cities, Milwaukee, Cleveland, Atlanta, New York, and more. On Tupac Shakur's birthday in 2004, the Convention opened in Newark to six thousand attendees, including some four hundred delegates, from twenty-five states and ten countries. It closed on Juneteenth with the adoption of an agenda meant to take on police brutality, inequitable education, and environmental justice.

By the fall of 2004, Sean P-Diddy Combs's Citizen Change, Russell Simmons's Hip-Hop Action Network, and the grassroots-led Hip-Hop Civic Engagement Project had registered hundreds of thousands of new young voters of color across the United States. On election day, more than four million new voters under the age of thirty showed up, the biggest youth surge since the voting age had been lowered to eighteen. Over half of them were African American or Latinx.

The impact of the Convention was felt for years afterward. Across the country, young activists organized to stop the building of prisons and to overturn the laws—curfews, anti-loitering ordinances, gang injunctions—that filled those prisons. Tens of thousands gathered from across the country to support six Black students in Jena, Louisiana—they came to be known as the Jena 6—who had been the targets of punishment after a series of racial incidents at their high school. The energy continued into the 2006 elections, helping to bring a new group of voices into politics.

The 2008 presidential election was a historic moment for hip-hop activism. Rosa Clemente, one of the original organizers of the National Hip-Hop Political Convention, ran a historic campaign as the Green Party's vice presidential candidate, forming a ticket with the party's presidential candidate, former Democratic congressperson Cynthia McKinney.

"Hip-hop is supposed to be the voice of the voiceless, and I think that post-2001, it has been that voice. But it just keeps being pushed to the underground. There's still a marginalization within hip-hop, especially among women's voices," she said. "Hip-hop is a way for some people to get name recognition, it's a way to get a job, it's a way to get a quasi-celebrity status."

"I always have these moments where I'm like, 'What's the point?'" she continued. But then she recalled when she was at a demonstration against the New York Police Department, whose officers had killed a young Black man named Sean Bell while he was leaving his bachelor party. "I just saw literally thousands of young people from all parts of the city—Black, Latino, Asian, people in gangs. What I saw was that young people have so much fire burning.

"They need that voice that is not a moderate voice," she said. "Every time I think hip-hop is dead, I realize it's not."

A young biracial Black US Senator born in Honolulu, Hawai'i, named Barack Obama also declared his candidacy for president. Obama had grown up between the soul generation and the hip-hop generation, and loved both Aretha Franklin and Public Enemy. At first he was regarded with some skepticism, but by the time 2008 had rolled around, his face was on posters and graffiti murals all around the country—part of an unauthorized underground campaign led by street artist Shepard Fairey and hundreds more. He had the support of rappers like Jeezy, Ludacris, Common, and Queen Latifah. Where Bill Clinton had attacked Sister Souljah and Public Enemy to win white votes, Obama regarded hip-hop's power with much more respect.

"Rap is reflective of the culture of the inner city, with its problems, but also its potential, its energy, its challenges to the status quo. And I absolutely agree my priority as a US senator is dealing with poverty and educational opportunity and adequate health care. If I'm ignoring those issues and spending all my time worrying about rap lyrics then I'm wasting my time," he said.

"On the other hand, I think that there's no doubt that hip-hop culture moves our young people powerfully. And some of it is not just a reflection of reality," he added. "It also creates reality. I think that if all our kids see is a glorification of materialism and bling and casual sex and kids are never seeing themselves reflected as hitting the books and being responsible and delaying gratification, then they are getting an unrealistic picture of what the world is like."

When Election Day came on November 4, 2008, Obama won a record-setting 69 million votes, buoyed into office by the third straight election in which voting by young people had increased dramatically. New young voters of color led the way. Almost three out of every five young Blacks eligible to vote voted for Obama, the highest youth turnout rate for any group ever recorded. Hip-hop had helped elect the first Black president.

A Movement Grows

The election of a Black president was an important threshold for a nation built on slavery and genocide to cross. But still many more things had not changed. Racial inequity persisted, most dramatically in the continuation of racially driven violence.

On January 1, 2009, just weeks before Barack Obama's inauguration, a young Black man named Oscar Grant was shot in the back and killed by a policeman at Fruitvale Station in Oakland, California, while he was handcuffed and face-down on the ground. The murder, which, after eighteen months of protests organized by hip-hop activists, resulted in the officer spending less than a year in jail, reminded the country how African Americans had long been treated differently by police. Then, just three months into Barack Obama's second term, a seventeen-year-old named Trayvon Martin was murdered in cold blood by a Hispanic vigilante named George Zimmerman in Sanford, Florida, a suburb of Orlando. When Zimmerman was acquitted of all charges—in an odd twist, his acquittal came a day after Ryan Coogler's film *Fruitvale Station* about Oscar Grant had opened nationwide—the outrage of a new generation fueled a global movement called Black Lives Matter.

This movement built on the hip-hop activist movement, and generations of Black youth movements before that. It connected issues like anti-Black violence to policing and juvenile justice reform. And it spread virally via social media. A group of young people in Florida calling themselves the Dream Defenders occupied the Florida governor's office in Tallahassee and stayed for a month. And on the other side of the country, three Black women launched the Twitter hashtag #blacklivesmatter.

The idea had come from San Francisco Bay Area organizer Alicia Garza, Los Angeles artist/activist Patrisse Cullors, and New York/Phoenix-based organizer Opal Tometi, all veterans of the "hip-hop activist" generation. After the Zimmerman verdict was announced, Garza quickly posted to her Facebook page, "I can't breathe. NOT GUILTY." Her feed filled up with posts from people who insisted they were not surprised. "That's a damn shame in itself," she responded. "I continue to be surprised at how little Black lives matter." She added, "Black people. I love you. I love us. Our lives matter."

The social media campaign evolved into a national movement a year later, because of the police shooting of another unarmed young Black teenager. In Ferguson, Missouri, a predominantly Black town north of St. Louis, a white police officer shot down an aspiring young rapper named Michael Brown in cold blood at high noon on August 9, 2014. Michael's neighbors gathered to protest the fact that his body had been left in the street for hours in the burning summer sun.

Word of the incident quickly spread all over the country via social media. Some sent photos of Brown's body while others expressed outrage. All eyes turned to Ferguson, Missouri. People wanted information. Why was Brown shot? Was he armed? What did he do? What were the people gonna do? Among the early batches of tweets that came from Ferguson that day were some sent by a young rapper named Kareem Jackson, who went by the name Tef Poe, short for Teflahn Poetix. He tweeted:

> Basically martial law is taking place in Ferguson all perimeters blocked coming and going . . . National and international friends Help!!!

Then:

> 150-200 cops currently riot gear entire neighborhood on lock down no one can enter no one can leave teenager unarmed killed

By dusk, as a full moon rose, police were deploying riot battalions and heavy artillery, including Bearcat tanks, against the residents of the neighborhood. As local artist/activist Elizabeth Vega put it, the murder of Michael Brown was "the collective 'snap of the last straw.'" Daily protests in Ferguson would continue over a year.

Tef was a young rapper on the rise. He had been part of a fourteen-member music collective called Soul Tyde, alongside his older brother Black Spade. The year before, he had been the reigning champion on BET's Freestyle Friday rap battles on the popular *106 & Park* show. His career was about to blow up nationally. But now he decided he had to put those plans on hold. The only thing set to blow up was Ferguson, and Tef Poe would become a frontline figure in the rebellion.

In the weeks that followed, he became a messenger for his community, telling the world what had caused young Blacks to rise up there. He talked about the way that white elites in North St. Louis County deployed police to entangle poor and working-class Blacks in a system of fines and warrants, which in turn paid for their services and salaries.

The way it worked was that police would stop Black people in Ferguson and North County for things like minor auto violations, and issue a ticket for $100, along with a $50 court or processing fee. Even if the ticket was dismissed or overturned, the driver was still on the hook for $50. But as soon as that driver left Ferguson and drove into a neighboring city, they might get pulled over again by the local police there. And so it might go until a driver had amassed three or more tickets on a single trip.

The result was that literally thousands of African Americans in North County owed these local governments. When the fines multiplied and the debts piled up, police issued warrants. The US Department of Justice investigated and found that, in largely Black communities, there were literally more warrants out than people who lived there, an average of three warrants for every household. Tef Poe noted that because so many in Ferguson had a warrant, it gave police an excuse to stop everyone. And they maintained their power this way, too. During elections, he said, police waited near polling places looking for folks who had warrants, threatening them with arrest and discouraging them from voting.

With Michael Brown's death as the spark, young organizers used social media to bring attention to high-profile incidents of violence that were exposed across the country, including the strangling of Eric Garner on Staten Island, the Detroit shooting of Renisha McBride, the beating of Freddie Gray in Baltimore, the killing of Philando Castile in Minneapolis, the hanging of Sandra Bland in Waller County Jail in Texas, and many more. When Trayvon Martin had been killed, the mainstream media had not paid attention for weeks until Black Twitter lifted up the story. But now the young organizers had changed the narrative. They raised the tragic incidents as the starkest examples of the way a racist society devalued Black lives. In this way, they connected the violence of the police with the ways in which Black communities were kept politically and economically disenfranchised.

In communities all around the country, young people, led largely by Black women and queer Blacks, organized themselves and their elders. Alicia Garza says, "Black Lives Matter really is what we called 'a call and response.' It was a response to anti-Black state-sanctioned violence and a call to action for Black people. Part of that call to action is really about expanding our notion of who is Black and also intervening in some of these messages about who is worthy of life and who is worthy of respect and dignity."

The Black Lives Matter movement provided a new platform for young people to be able to express their desires for change. When traditional civil rights leaders like Al Sharpton and Jesse Jackson showed up in Ferguson, they were no longer regarded as legitimate enough to represent the voices in the streets. At one large rally in St. Louis, Tef Poe told the older leaders, "This ain't your grandparents' civil rights movement. Get off your ass and join us!"

Tef had the mic, and he chose to use it for change. Melina Abdullah, a professor at Cal State Los Angeles and a leader of the Black Lives Matter chapter in Los Angeles, says, "Hip-hop was born out of the struggle. Hip-hop was meant to be the voice of Black people who are working class and poor. So if you're going to call yourself a hip-hop artist, I think you're duty bound to represent a certain political perspective. It's not okay for you to just say, 'As long as I get my money, and as long as me and mine are okay, then I'm doing fine.' Because that's not what this particular art is supposed to be."

The New Industry

In the 2000s, the record industry—and the hip-hop industry along with it—collapsed. File sharing and online piracy wreaked havoc on the business. Record sales plunged for over a decade, leaving the industry less than half the size it was at its peak.[3] Thousands in the hip-hop business lost their jobs. Magazines went out of business. Major labels were less effective than ever.

During the peak of hip-hop's success in the 1990s, artists needed to sell hundreds of thousands of albums to debut in the top ten. By the end of the 2010s, rapper A Boogie Wit da Hoodie could hit number one with less than 60,000 "album-equivalent units" sold—equal to 90 million streams, 600,000 song downloads, or 60,000 albums sold.[4] Most of Boogie's units came in the form of streams. He had only sold 823 actual albums that week.

Depending on the service, a song stream garnered anywhere from about two cents down to less than a tenth of a cent per stream in 2018.[5] In the 1990s, an album sold for about $14, the equivalent of about a dollar per song—fifty to a thousand times more. (Artists, then and now, tend to make about 10 percent of total sales.) By all measures, music made a tiny fraction of what it had two decades before.

But locally, all around the world, hip-hop thrived. There was the hyphy movement in the Bay Area, drill in Chicago, snap and trap in Atlanta, grime in London. People were getting crunk across the South. And at that very moment, a new generation of artists was figuring out how to get their music directly to their fans, using the internet to bypass the record industry. They would help create a new consciousness, and, influenced by the Black Lives Matter movement, build a new cultural renaissance.

The "mixtape" was named after the cassette tapes DJs and MCs used to play and sell to get their names known. In the 1970s, the earliest mixtapes were live recordings of DJs and rap crews or special commissioned recordings. From the 1980s into the 1990s, DJs like Kid Capri, DJ Clue, and Ron G made their own DJ mixes and exclusives. Rappers also used mixtapes to quickly release diss tracks, preview new singles, or drop songs for which they could not clear samples. In time many of these recordings were pressed on to CDs to sell on the streets, out of barber shops, or through the internet, but they were still called "mixtapes."

By this time, radio was playing far fewer artists and major record labels were dropping many rappers from their rosters, so mixtapes became the best way for rappers to create a street buzz and build their audiences without any major label support. DJ Drama, who became the mixtape king in the 2000s, said that the mixtapes changed the industry: "Nobody cared about your demo tape anymore, it was like, 'What are you doing with your mixtape, and how are the streets selling it?'"

Artists like 50 Cent, Gucci Mane, Lil' Wayne, and Dipset became known through their mixtapes. But as the record industry continued to collapse in sales, in part because of illegal downloading, some executives blamed mixtapes for bleeding out their profits. In January 2007, Georgia police officers broke into DJ Drama's warehouse and confiscated recording equipment and eighty-one thousand mixtapes, charging him with bootlegging and racketeering. The charges were never pursued. But after this moment, the mixtape would no longer be primarily a DJ showcase. What happened to the mixtape mirrored what happened to hip-hop music when it moved to vinyl records in the late 1970s—the DJ was replaced by the rapper.

Mixtapes allowed artists like Nicki Minaj, Wiz Khalifa, Chief Keef, Meek Mill, Kid Cudi, and Drake to build their fan bases via working largely outside of the traditional record industry systems of radio, clubs, and retail. The internet further changed the game. New mixtapes were increasingly offered free as downloads or streams. Digital platforms—whether blogs, music news sites, or streaming services—allowed rappers a way to bypass record labels to get their music directly to their audiences. Many of these artists were then able to cut better deals with the record labels to release proper albums. In turn, labels benefited from increased demand for the artists. After Wiz Khalifa dropped several well-received mixtapes, his 2011 major-label debut, *Rolling Papers,* went double platinum.

By the mid-2010s, streaming services like Pandora, Spotify, Tidal, and Apple Music were drawing in more and more listeners. Some offered exclusives, as Apple did with Chance the Rapper's *Coloring Book,* and Tidal did with releases from part-owner Jay-Z. Soundcloud allowed artists to upload their own music, spawning its own genre of "Soundcloud rappers."

As hip-hop had done for decades, it was among the first to adapt to new technology in the spirit of using every means to expand its reach. Soon, yet another new generation was building its own cultural renaissance, with its own rich diversity of voices.

A Cultural Renaissance

These digital platforms fostered a new spirit of independence, and a new generation of stars, including Cardi B, Migos, and XXXTentacion. They allowed for more experimentation, and made space for the kind of artists who didn't fit the old music industry–defined idea of what a rapper should be.

For example, the number of women in hip-hop had dropped dramatically after the turn of the millennium as record labels put their money behind male gangster types. But by the late 2000s, Nicki Minaj had built her rep via mixtapes, modeling herself on Lil' Kim (whose look she adapted) and Foxy Brown (with whom she shared a Trinidadian background), showcasing herself as a rapper with ample personality and formidable skills.

On 2009's *Beam Me Up Scotty* mixtape, she dressed up as Wonder Woman, and called herself a "comic-book heroine" come "to save a thing called female rap." In the same breath, she compared herself to Marilyn Monroe and Lauryn Hill, and dissed Def Jam for telling her she would have to choose only to rap or sing. She wanted to do both—her own way. After three mixtapes, followed by two major label albums and one jaw-dropping performance on Kanye West's "Monster," she had transformed the pop landscape. She told MTV News, "Absolutely, I do not see myself as a *female* rapper anymore. I'm sorry. I see myself as a *rapper*."[6]

In 2009, Nicki's Young Money associate, a Canadian actor named Drake, also blew up. His mixtape *So Far Gone* became one of the most successful ever, prompting so much interest that its official re-release became one of the bestselling hip-hop records of the year, and launched a huge career. If Nicki was the center of the party, Drake portrayed himself as the brooding guy in the corner.

In the wake of Kanye West's breakthrough album *808s & Heartbreak,* Drake and other artists like Kid Cudi, Future, and Young Thug went behind the mask of cool to explore melancholy and subvert male gender norms. Young Thug even rocked high-fashion dresses, and did a spot for Calvin Klein in which he said, "In my world, it don't matter, you could be a gangster with a dress or you could be a gangster with baggy pants. I feel like it's no such thing as gender."[7]

Hip-hop reflected changing attitudes in the community. Big Freedia, Young M.A, and Lil' Nas X could be out and proud. Lizzo,

Princess Nokia, and Megan Thee Stallion could be gloriously body positive. All of them could reach levels of success revealing their full selves in ways it had been difficult to do before. At the same time, the Bronx-born-and-raised, hip-hop generation leader Tarana Burke and her #metoo movement brought attention to sexual abuse and assault, which cast new light on the long-buried problem within the hip-hop community and eventually led to the re-evaluation of the legacies of many celebrated icons, including Afrika Bambaataa, Russell Simmons, XXXTentacion, and Crazy Legs. Cardi B, who had also suffered sexual abuse in her personal relationships and her hip-hop career, told Angie Martinez, "When I see the #metoo movement, there's girls from the 'hood I know they went through the same type of treatment . . . It happens every day."

In the same way that the Civil Rights, Black Power, and 1980s and 1990s anti-racism movements had inspired artists to create powerful music, movies, and art, Black Lives Matter pushed a new generation to respond to the community's desire for representation, new images, and progressive ideas. Artists like Noname, Anderson .Paak, and Tierra Whack reflected the shift.

"I have to talk about what's going on with Trayvon Martin and Mike Brown," said the North Carolina rapper Rapsody. "I have a nephew, and he's gonna grow up, and his dad is gonna have to have that hard conversation. I know I'm in a position, whether I want to or not, to be a role model."[8]

In 2019, she dropped an album called *Eve*, naming each of the sixteen tracks after a pioneering Black woman, and rapping about what each represented to her. "I believe the stories that I'm telling and the love and respect I have for Black women," she said. "I want to display that urgency in the music. When they listen to it, I want people to hear that it's honest."[9]

Her friend and regular collaborator Kendrick Lamar represented the pinnacle of the new renaissance. He had been born in the summer of 1987, the moment of Eric B. and Rakim's "I Know You Got Soul," Public Enemy's "Rebel Without a Pause," Eazy-E's "Boyz-N-The Hood," and Ice-T's "6 in the Morning." He rapped with precise aggression in the multisyllabic patterns of pioneering LA stylists the Freestyle Fellowship, and multi-tracked his voice, as Tupac Shakur had, to inhabit different characters—whether a dead gang member or a female prostitute.

His first masterpiece, *good kid m.A.A.d city,* was a semi-autobiographical coming-of-age story set in his native Compton, in which a teen navigates lust, depression, despair, beef, death, and spiritual rebirth in a world of brutal policing and an abundance of guns, lacking educational and economic opportunity. It's a place where, he raps, "Violence is the rhythm." In the end, he is saved by his relationships with older folks—an elderly church lady, his mother and father. "Don't learn the hard way like I did," his father tells him. "Real is responsibility. Real is taking care of your motherfuckin' family. Real is God."

On two more classic records, he developed these themes further. *To Pimp a Butterfly,* which felt like the second part of an autobiography, included meditations on the intergenerational impacts of slavery and racist violence, the links between physical incarceration and being mentally trapped, and the importance of self-love and community identity. On the closer, "Mortal Man," he challenged his own fans to question their loyalties and allegiances—including to him—and whether these were helping them to get free.

And, just as Lauryn Hill had included interludes of Newark community leader Ras Baraka teaching young students about love, Kendrick's imaginary discussion with Tupac represented how hip-hop was a form for knowledge to be passed on from generation to generation:

KENDRICK: In my opinion, only hope we have left is music and vibrations. Lotta people don't understand how important it is, you know? Sometimes I can, like, get behind a mic and I don't know what type of energy I'ma push out, or where it comes from. Trip me out sometimes.

TUPAC: Because it's spirits. We ain't even really rappin'. We just letting our dead homies tell stories for us.

KENDRICK: Damn.

His next album would be called *DAMN.* And it seemed the rest of the world was catching up to his genius. For it, Lamar was recognized with the Pulitzer Prize for music, one of the most prestigious awards in global culture, yet another first for hip-hop.

Yet tragedy was also still around every corner, a reminder of why hip-hop had been necessary in the first place to affirm that Black lives mattered. In 2009, Kendrick Lamar and Nipsey Hussle had been two young artists on the come up, both opening for Los Angeles rapper The Game on his tour. Lamar recalls watching Hussle onstage and how he handled himself with crowds and his entourage and coming to admire him. "My curiosity about who he really was started to grow from that moment in time. Was he a product of Crenshaw and Slauson? Was he a radical? Or was he a thinker? That mystique kept me engaged throughout his life and career."[10]

Hussle was the son of a father who had immigrated from Eritrea and an African American mother whose family had migrated to Los Angeles in the 1930s from Louisiana. He grew up in the Crenshaw District on the Westside of Los Angeles in Rolling 60s Crips territory. By his midteens, he had been courted into the gang, fighting against a group of other gang members all at once until the O.G.'s thought he had shown enough heart. He had always loved music, but he rolled hard for the gang and did time in prison, until, as he put it, "Reality kicked in."[11]

"If you check the stats—the murder rates and incarceration rates in the years I was a teenager in LA—none of my peers survived. None of my peers avoided prison," he said. "So to make it out mentally stable and not in prison and not on drugs, that's a win."[12]

He began focusing on his music instead. And when he was nineteen, his father took him and his brother on a trip to Africa that changed his life. For three months, they stayed in his father's homeland of Eritrea. "At first, I experienced culture shock," he said. "The shit that we rely on here, your cell phone, internet, e-mail, and your females and your daily movement, it's all cut off once you get out there. It's more about the interaction with the people."

There were no Crips or gang wars; instead there was the legacy of a long civil war. And everyone was Black—the leaders, the police, the businesspeople. "It put me in touch with my roots. If you don't know your full-throttle history, the whole story of how you came to where you are, it's kind of hard to put things together," he said. "That filled in a blank spot for me, as far as understanding myself."[13] Now he had a new understanding of his given name—Ermias, which meant, "God is risen." When he came back home he knew exactly what he needed to do for himself and his community.

Working hard on his music, he dropped a series of mixtapes that established him as the heir to Snoop Dogg, who co-signed Nipsey by putting him on his album. The buzz went national in 2010, five years from his first mixtape, when he was named to *XXL*'s Freshmen Top Ten and anticipation built for his major label debut. But when his label experienced money issues, he left and went indie again. He called the rap game a "marathon." He was still grinding three years later, as one of the most popular and respected rappers who hadn't released a major label album, when he decided to put out the *Crenshaw* mixtape, which he sold for a hundred dollars a copy. Jay-Z personally bought a hundred copies, and Nipsey sold all one thousand copies of it in a single day.

Through it all, Nipsey used his creative powers to give back to the community. He partnered with activists and educators to set up STEM programs for Black and Latinx kids. He spoke out against gun violence. He set up a center called Vector 90 to support underrepresented entrepreneurs of color in the Crenshaw area. He invested in an entertainment agency and real estate. And he opened a clothing store called Marathon to give opportunities to area youths, especially those coming back from prison and trying to transition from the violent life toward something more positive.

"I'm not out the game. No, you don't ever get out the game, truthfully. You redirect your energy," he told radio DJ Veda Loca. "I'm not a gangbanger. [But] you don't just hang up your rag and say, 'I'm not from the community no more.' Demonstrations speak louder than conversations. So I ain't in cars going on missions no more. I'm on a radio run, dropping my album, building businesses, employing my homeboys, and paying taxes."

By 2019, he had built the foundations of a thriving platform for educational and business opportunities in his own neighborhood. He titled his major label debut *Victory Lap*. It was recognized as a Los Angeles rap classic and in February, debuted at number four on the Billboard charts. But just six weeks later, Nipsey was shot dead in front of his Marathon store by a man who had just been released from prison, after they had an argument. His murder shocked Crenshaw, the city, and the nation.

Tributes to Nipsey poured in, including ones from Los Angeles mayor Eric Garcetti and former president Barack Obama. Tens of thousands of people filled the streets as his funeral procession wound from the Watts Towers through South Los Angeles to the Staples Center. Just as important, leaders of Crip and Blood gang sets met and declared the biggest gang truce in the city and the country since the peace treaty in April 1992.

In tribute to Nipsey, Kendrick wrote an essay for the funeral program. It concluded:

> A true King will be tested in adversity. To stand in fearlessness in what he believes will impact on the earth, as well as in heaven. So thank you Nipsey the Radical. Nipsey the Thinker. Nipsey the Father. Nipsey the Brother. Nipsey the Husband. Nipsey the Friend. Nipsey the Great. And from now on, Nipsey the Messenger. . . . . . Shalom.

The Power of Hip-Hop

Hip-hop had started out as a pastime for the neighborhood kids that society forgot, a way for them to enjoy themselves and turn their energies from destructive to creative purposes, from dangerous gang warfare to style wars. It had been about battling each other to see whose styles the people loved more. But as it grew, spreading first to other neighborhoods where Black youths had something to express, and then all around the world, it became something bigger.

Scarface of the Geto Boys wrote that hip-hop became "much more about delivering the truth and getting the word out about what was really going on in the streets of America, not just what America wanted you to see . . . Because we were all conversing with each other, and letting everyone know that the shit that they were dealing with in, say, Chicago or LA was the same kind of shit we were dealing with in Houston and the same kind of shit n---as were dealing with in DC. Or New Orleans or Baltimore or Memphis."[14]

People could see each other through hip-hop, recognize what they had in common or learn to empathize with someone who was different from them. It was life-changing, and society-changing. So it made perfect sense that in 2019, Scarface and Willie D, two of the three members of the classic lineup of the Geto Boys, decided to run for Houston City Council. Evolving from young, controversial rappers caught in dust-ups with the law and mainstream authorities to aspiring lawmakers with a desire to help their communities seemed a natural, if unexpected evolution. Hip-hop had always been a way to communicate, and now people were using it to talk about changing their communities and changing the world.

In July 2019, at the Ten Nail Bar in Detroit, a former stripper who was also a former Blood gang member met with a leading presidential candidate. A few days prior, rapper and actor Cardi B had addressed her forty-eight million Instagram followers and asked them to submit questions about the issues that most concerned them. Now US Senator Bernie Sanders was paying tribute to Cardi by sitting for an interview with her.

Once upon a time it would have been deemed political suicide for a senator to sit down with a rapper, perhaps especially one like the unapologetic Cardi B, a proud woman of Dominican and Trinidadian descent from the Bronx who had built her career from nothing. Ten years before, the then nineteen-year-old Belcalis Almanzar was in an abusive relationship marked by domestic violence, trying to find a way to make some money to escape. She started stripping and made enough money to leave her situation and go back to school. She was relentless in her pursuit of turning a bad situation into something good. By 2019, she had become one of the most beloved and influential artists in the world, with a Grammy and seven Billboard Music Awards, and sponsorships with Pepsi, Tom Ford, and Reebok.

Dressed in a conservative green dress, Cardi peppered Bernie Sanders with questions on issues like police brutality, immigration, student debt, and health care. She talked about their shared admiration for Franklin Delano Roosevelt. "I mean, come on now! Like, he did the New Deal, that's the reason why we have Social Security!" she said, as Sanders nodded and smiled. Sanders would tell his staffers that he had been talking about Social Security for decades, but Cardi was making the discussion real to a whole new generation.

She wrapped up the video saying, "I want to tell my millions of followers we're here to educate you guys. I hope your questions have been answered. And let's just get more educated, please. Let's put our focus on this term's elections, because I don't think people understand how serious it is."

The video would be watched twenty-two million times in the following month. For comparison, the most-watched Democratic presidential debate in US history had happened just a month before—and had drawn 18 million people. The balance of power had turned. Although she never brought it up, Cardi B's Instagram following was three times as large as President Trump's, twenty times as large as Bernie's, and also more than all of the twenty-two Democratic candidates combined. When she was invited to interview the eventual Democratic presidential nominee, Joe Biden, she told him, "I want Black people to stop getting killed and no justice for it. I'm tired of it. I'm sick of it." She was determined to leverage her power to, in her own words, "build a movement of young people to transform this country."[15]

Yet another generation was finding its voice. In 2015, after Kendrick Lamar had performed "Alright" on the BET Music Awards, Fox News pundit Geraldo Rivera criticized him, saying that Lamar's line about anger at police violence was sending "exactly the wrong message," and that "hip-hop had done more damage to young African Americans than racism in recent years." Other Fox pundits agreed and suggested his performance would incite violence. Instead, "Alright" became the soundtrack that summer for peaceful Black Lives Matter protests all around the world.

In Cleveland in July, where police had killed thirty-seven-year-old Tanisha Anderson and twelve-year-old Tamir Rice the year before, thousands gathered for a Black Lives Matter convening to set a national agenda to address police violence and call for reparations, economic justice, community control, political power, "investments in education, health, and safety," "divestment from exploitative forces," and "an end to the war on Black people."[16] As the convening let out on a Sunday afternoon, police officers detained a young boy for allegedly having an alcoholic beverage and threw him to the ground. A crowd gathered to protect the boy.

The police called in reinforcements, expecting a riot to break out. Some of them pepper sprayed the crowd. But the crowd remained peaceful and determined to stay until the boy's safety was ensured. Finally, aware that the crowd was not going away, the police released the boy to the care of his mother.

Perhaps they could not ignore the power of what was happening. It had started with just a few people who began chanting. They were quickly joined by dozens more—until hundreds and hundreds were clapping and jumping and dancing in the streets.

In one voice, they were shouting, "We gon' be alright!"

Make This Better

On May 25, 2020, during a warm South Minneapolis evening, a forty-six-year-old Black father named George Floyd stepped into a neighborhood grocery store called Cup Foods. Floyd was a big man—standing six feet, seven inches—and, under the name Big Floyd, had once been a respected rapper with one of Houston's most famous crews, DJ Screw's Screwed Up Click. He had moved to Minneapolis in search of a new life. On this evening, he purchased cigarettes and left.

Cup Foods and its owner, a well-liked Arab American named Mahmoud Abumayyaleh, was known for being fair to customers, who were mostly Black, both US-born and immigrant. But on this evening, a new young clerk grew concerned that the twenty-dollar bill Floyd had handed him was counterfeit. He walked out to Floyd's car to ask him for the cigarettes back. When that failed, he returned to the store and called the police. He did not know Abumayyaleh's policy was never to call police.

Minneapolis had a rep as a liberal city with a flair for music and the arts. It was the home of Prince, Morris Day and the Time, and the legendary independent hip-hop label Rhymesayers Entertainment. It had once been thought of as a Northern city committed to school desegregation. But in recent years, the city had reversed itself dramatically. By the 2010s, Minneapolis had resegregated so severely that its schools now had, one report concluded, "some of the nation's widest racial disparities."[17]

Minneapolis also had a police department that was notorious for its misconduct, paying out $45 million to settle complaints of police brutality between 2003 and 2020, one of the largest amounts of any city.[18] On November 15, 2015, Minneapolis police killed an unarmed Black man named Jamar Clark. In subsequent protests, a group of masked men who were described as white supremacists came to the Black Lives Matter encampment outside a police precinct and shot five demonstrators.

On July 6, 2016, a school worker named Philando Castile was shot at close range by an officer after being pulled over for his car's alleged broken taillight. Castile had told the officer he was armed and had a permit to carry a gun, and the officer yelled for him not to pull out his gun. Castile told him twice he would not. Yet the officer fired seven times at Castile—in front of his partner, Diamond Reynolds, and her four-year-old baby daughter. Reynolds livestreamed the immediate aftermath of the incident on Facebook, and the horror of the shooting resonated nationwide. But the officer was acquitted of all charges. In the aftermath of these tragic killings, organizers in Minneapolis went to work, researching the history of the police and crafting demands for police accountability.

This was the backdrop when George Floyd left the Cup Foods market that warm evening. Not long after, the clerk was calling store owner Abumayyaleh in a panic. "They're killing him," the clerk told him.[19] Abumayyaleh knew Floyd, "a big teddy bear," and said later, "If I would have been here the authorities would not have been called. George Floyd may still be alive."[20]

Minneapolis police had stopped Floyd across the street from Cup Foods, and, almost twenty minutes later, Floyd was facedown on the pavement, unconscious and nearly dead. Police officer Derek Chauvin—whose record included eighteen internal affairs complaints—had kept his knee on Floyd's neck for eight minutes and forty-six seconds, even as Floyd gasped, "I can't breathe, man, please!"—exactly as Eric Garner had—and cried out for his mama. Floyd died shortly afterward.[21]

His close friend from Houston, the NBA basketball star Stephen Jackson, later told marchers at a rally, "Imagine this, a man growing up in an area where the odds are already against him." He continued, "You get an opportunity to move away from the environment that brought you down. You get away. You be successful. You get a job. Your life starts turning in the right direction. You stumble a little bit."

He concluded, "That's not worth your life, though."[22]

Videos of the incident sparked months of protests. In the name of George Floyd and others who had recently been killed by police or white vigilantes, including Breonna Taylor and Ahmaud Arbery, and later, Tony McDade and Rayshard Brooks, marchers took to the streets in over 350 cities.[23] Leaders in Minneapolis and around the country began considering demonstrators' calls to defund and even abolish policing, a demand that had persisted from the days of the Black Panther Party. The Black Lives Matter movement had reached a new level.

These protests took place while many people of color were facing deadly racial inequities in a global pandemic of the novel coronavirus. When the virus, known as COVID-19, began impacting West Coast cities in the early part of 2020, President Donald Trump had dismissed the threat and blamed its spread on China. Violence against Asian Americans spread across the country. Blacks, Native Americans, Latinx people, Asians, and Pacific Islanders were all more likely than whites to be deemed "essential workers" and therefore required to work in public. Infection and death rates for people of color in relation to whites soared.

At the same time, President Trump closed the border and all but stopped immigration, while attacking Black Lives Matter protestors almost daily. At one point, accompanied by leaders of the US military, he had police teargas and beat peaceful protestors outside the White House so that he could stage a photo opportunity at a church. Those who were quarantined could see these horrific moments on their feeds, and many joined the protests for the first time.

As the coronavirus spread, hip-hop legends like Scarface, DJ Jazzy Jeff, and scholar Marc Lamont Hill were among those stricken. British MC Ty and Bronx rapper/DJ Fred the Godson were among the hundreds of thousands whose lives were taken by the virus. Yet the hip-hop community also pulled together. Artists like Anderson .Paak, Rebel Diaz, YG, and Public Enemy released powerful music speaking to what were now called the Uprisings. DaBaby and Roddy Ricch released a moving video for "Rockstar," which restaged the killing of George Floyd. Filipino American DJ Kuttin Kandi and rapper Ruby Ibarra organized Asian Americans and Pacific Islanders to stand up to racism and support Black Lives Matter protests. Instagram became a place to soothe the soul, as D-Nice gathered hundreds of thousands on Instagram for his Club Quarantine, and Timbaland and Swizz Beatz staged Verzuz, a series of events featuring some of the most important artists of the era facing off in old-school-style battles, including DJ Premier vs. RZA, Nelly vs. Ludacris, and Jill Scott vs. Erykah Badu.

The protests moved the nation toward confronting the legacies of its racial past, as protestors pulled down statues of Confederate leaders from Birmingham, Alabama, to Washington, DC. At the largest memorial—Georgia's Stone Mountain, a historic gathering place for the Ku Klux Klan, where a sculpture of three Confederate generals was carved into the quartz rock—Grandmaster Jay led a militia of hundreds of armed Black protestors to call for the removal of the monument. Atlanta—where another Black man, Rayshard Brooks, was chased and shot dead in the back by police—became a frontline for organizing. From his home there, T.I. called out the British company Lloyd's of London for its role in the slave trade and demanded that they pay reparations to the descendants of African slaves.

Four days after George Floyd was killed, as Atlanta was still burning, Killer Mike took a city hall stage alongside T.I. and Mayor Keisha Lance-Bottoms and gave an emotional speech to the young demonstrators. He began by saying, "I didn't want to come here, and I don't want to be here."

He explained, as he choked back emotions, that he came from a family of police officers, and that the first eight Black police officers in Atlanta had been required to suit up in a local YMCA "because white officers didn't want to get dressed with n----rs."

He admitted, "I have nothing positive to say in this moment, because I don't want to be here. But I am responsible to be here, because it wasn't just Dr. King and people dressed nicely who marched to progress this city and so many other cities. It was people like my grandmother and my aunt and uncles who were members of the SCLC [Southern Christian Leadership Conference] and the NAACP."

He told demonstrators, "It is your duty not to burn your own house down for anger with an enemy. It is your duty to fortify your own house so that you may be a refuge in times of organization. And now is the time to plot, plan, strategize, organize, and mobilize."

Then he turned to make a personal plea. "I'm mad as hell. I woke up wanting to see the world burn down yesterday because I'm tired of seeing Black men die," he said, punctuating these last seven words with knocks on the podium. He called the video of Floyd's death "murder porn." "So that's why children are burning it to the ground. They don't know what else to do. And it is the responsibility of us to make this better right now."

Killer Mike had done what he had always done, what hip-hop had always done—he had spoken his truth. And in this moment when a new future was trying to be born, it was clear that the voice of the outcast was also the voice of courage and hope.

How to Flow

Twenty-five years before, when hip-hop had been nearing its global commercial peak, DJ Kool Herc had stepped onto the stage at the *Source* Awards to finally receive his due recognition and to make things right. It had been three years since Tupac had been murdered, two and half since Biggie's death, three years before Jam Master Jay would be killed. Hip-hop had always been there right at the nexus of violence and creativity, a place where young people could choose to continue the divisions and segregation they had inherited or to instead transform their own lives and others, whether the few around them or millions around the world.

At that moment, in a Los Angeles theater, Herc stood tall, flanked by Grandmaster Flash to his right and Jam Master Jay to his left, and received a long-standing ovation.

He said:

> I want to thank God for me being here, alive, drug-free, to live to see this day . . .
>
> Let me set the record straight, it's been twenty-nine years. Got stabbed, nearly got killed in a party, but I didn't give up because the youth was having fun. They said, "Herc, when is the next party?" and that's what kept me going.
>
> 1520 Sedgwick Avenue. My sister was behind me. In the Bronx, y'all, in the Bronx right here is where it started. But it went worldwide. And we give the kids a culture. That's what came up out of it.
>
> . . . Because kids could have been doing something else, but now people living good, having good jobs, an economy . . .
>
> There's a lot of heroes that's not here, that died for this here. Ain't no sense for us to be killing each other over this music. We got to love each other for this, man.
>
> Because I'll tell you one thing, what happened was the gangs back in the days killed it at the Puzzle, the Tunnel, and I'm the one that started to play, and all I asked for was respect . . . It wasn't about me being big and brawn, I never used that over nobody.
>
> I gave respect to give respect and that's how I keep my life flowing.

Reader's Guide

QUESTIONS

- There was a racially segregated social, economic, and political landscape in the South Bronx that led to a cultural reaction centered around music and dance that today we call hip-hop. What are the challenging social, political, and economic conditions that have impacted your community in the past and today? What cultural responses have you seen emerge that can be attributed to those conditions?
- The gangs in New York in the 1970s took it upon themselves to resolve their issues and conflicts and establish a gang truce. What important lessons did we learn from this process that can be applied today?
- In hip-hop, people have been innovative in using existing technologies, building organizations and crews, and thinking about how to approach the world. What key innovations stand out to you from the pioneering days of hip-hop? What kinds of technological and social innovations do we see in hip-hop today?
- The story of DJ Kool Herc brings to light the important contributions immigrants bring to music and cultural movements. What other contributions have immigrants made in hip-hop's evolution?
- Women have shaped hip-hop from before the beginning of the movement. Name some important contributions women made in the early days of hip-hop. Who were some of those key figures? What barriers do women face in hip-hop?
- How important was graffiti or spraycan art in the evolution of hip-hop? Is it an art form or vandalism?
- How important was the b-boy/b-girl in the evolution of hip-hop? What role does the b-boy/b-girl play today in hip-hop?
- How did the Sugarhill Gang's record "Rapper's Delight" change hip-hop when it was released and caught on with mainstream audiences? Was its impact good or bad?

- Many talk about the moment in the early 1980s when the hip-hop scene from uptown and the Bronx met the punk rock/new wave scene from downtown as a special time. What were some of the pros and cons of these two scenes meeting and merging? What kinds of examples can you think of scenes merging now? What can hip-hop history tell us about how to think about these examples?
- What did it mean when hip-hop artists spoke about "crossing over"? Who played key roles in helping hip-hop to cross over? Who benefited and who didn't?
- What is the importance of New York's history in hip-hop? Could hip-hop have started somewhere other than the Bronx? If so, what might it have looked like?
- What do you know about the local history of hip-hop in your city, town, or region? What can the history of hip-hop in your city tell you about your city?
- What was the music, dance, and culture scene like prior to hip-hop emerging on the West Coast? What were the music, dance, and cultural scenes in your area before hip-hop emerged? Did those earlier scenes influence the way hip-hop emerged in your area?
- In what ways has hip-hop and rap music been used to call attention to or heal social, political, and racial issues that needed to be raised? How has hip-hop and rap music explained or exacerbated racial tensions at different moments?
- How have hip-hop artists addressed—or chosen not to address—the issues of sexual harassment, abuse, and assault in their work? How have feminists critiqued hip-hop's treatment of women? Are hip-hop artists better at addressing issues of race and economic class than of gender?
- How would you compare the impact of the gang truce in the Bronx in 1971 with the impact of the gang truce in LA in 1992?
- How has hip-hop shed light on the relationship between communities of color and police and law enforcement? At times, hip-hop artists have argued for alternatives to policing. What might have been the impacts if government had made different choices?
- What were the culture wars hip-hop faced in the '90s and what are some of the reasons they took place? What were the impacts

of these culture wars? What culture wars does hip-hop face today? What steps need to be taken to resolve them?

- Hip-hop has built large businesses and also underground networks. Do you think these distinctions still exist in hip-hop? If so, do you align yourself with one or the other or both? Why?
- Hip-hop has been a powerful force not just in culture but in politics. How do you see hip-hop helping to contribute to social change in communities, countries, and the world?
- What are some of the important lessons we might learn from the story of Tupac and Biggie?
- As hip-hop has evolved we have seen several generations of artists who have ascended to become "Kings" and "Queens" for their day. What makes a hip-hop artist a "King" or "Queen"? Does the definition and criteria change over time? Is it skill set? TV appearances? Album sales? Social media presence? Who are the new "Kings" and "Queens" of hip-hop today?
- Hip-hop has been around for over a half century now. Are white rap artists still a novelty? Should new white artists be judged by the standards that were used to judge Vanilla Ice, 3rd Bass, and Eminem?
- Hip-hop is a global phenomenon. How many artists outside of the United States do you know? Is there a global gap between how much American fans know about non-American hip-hop artists versus how much non-Americans know about American artists? If so, why and how might this gap be closed?
- Our understanding of hip-hop history continues to evolve as we learn more over time. If you were to write this book again now, what would you want to add to the story and why?
- Hip-hop has often spoken to issues that need to be raised, but has also sometimes stayed silent when it needed to speak up. What key issues in society today does hip-hop need to engage? What is the best way for hip-hop to engage?
- A major theme of the book is how young people have often chosen to deal with violence by developing their creativity. How does this theme resonate for you in your life?

Acknowledgments

DAVEY'S ACKNOWLEDGMENTS

This book is dedicated to my late mom, Connie Divack, who always believed in me, taught me how to be resourceful, and encouraged me to write. She encouraged me to keep journals, which I did all throughout the 1970s. She used to say, "Capture those magical and challenging moments on paper. Detail your experiences, good and bad, and revisit them one day to learn about yourself."

My journals as a young kid caught my experience with hip-hop in its infancy. It was a special time. One that could never be replicated. What I wrote helped me hone my craft as a writer and gave me a firm foundation as a historian. I wish she could see this day. I dedicate this to my sister, Robin, who encouraged me after Moms was gone to get the job done.

This is dedicated to Professor Roy Thomas, who was my African American studies professor at Cal Berkeley. He was a godsend to so many of us Black students who came to Cal. He was the first to peep some of the writings in my journals, which came in the form of a term paper, and later became my thesis. Professor Thomas encouraged me to one day put this information in a book. I never forgot his words.

This is dedicated to Chuck D of Public Enemy. His friendship, encouragement, and support are things that words can't capture. He opened doors and helped elevate my writing and, like my mom and Professor Thomas, pushed for me to pen a book.

Lastly, this book is dedicated to my two beautiful kids, Soluna and Akire, and my incredible, supportive, wonderful wife, Erika. They are my anchors. They are my heart and soul. This book was written with my kids in mind. These stories were written for them to pick up and pass along and connect to their own lived experiences and future histories they will one day create. They are hip-hop's next generation. My wife with her quiet strength, patience, understanding, wisdom, and love is why this book was finally able to get done. She is and will always be my inspiration.

One of the most important things we should know about hip-hop is that it did not occur in a vacuum. And while we often focus and uplift key individuals and pioneers, there is no single person who is the totality of this vibrant culture that spans several decades.

Hip-hop is because of the community it emerges from. It's our collective energy. It's our collective expression. It's our collective desires to eradicate troubled times and bring about better tomorrows.

Hip-hop is also a culture steeped in rites of passage. No matter how big one has gotten, no matter how famous one has become, no matter how good one has become, or what skill level one has obtained, all of us involved in hip-hop are there because of those who came before us. Someone before us knocked down doors and blazed a trail for us to follow. That's how we all got put on.

And ideally when hip-hop is at its best, we each blaze trails for the people coming behind us. We pay it forward. Hip-hop is continuously built upon the shoulders we stand on. Shoulders that bore the weight before us.

It's with this in mind that we come to understand why within hip-hop the shout-out and public acknowledgments are so important. Back in the pioneering days, it was important to be publicly acknowledged by the person rocking the mic. It was a big deal to hear the DJ or MC, who was the center of attention, call you out by your name and big up your neighborhood. Listen to any old-school tape and you hear lots of shout-outs.

"Big Jim from Soundview and the Soundview Crew is in the House." "Lil Joe from Edenwald and the Edenwald Crew is in the building." "Sarah Sarah from Monroe is in the building along with her girls, the Sarah Sarah Crew."

The shout-out was the African Oral Tradition being played out. It was call-and-response. It was the concept of saying, "I see you. I hear you. I feel you. We are one."

The shout-out was a way to let people know how you were connected and who were your people. Back in the days it was our way of knowing who was down with us. Did you have juice. Did you roll deep. You were, in a sense, saying you represented whoever you was claiming, which, in turn, meant you had to come correct. You had to do and be at your best. Nobody wanted to be publicly shouted out and your performance was wack. Your triumph was their triumph. Your success was their success. Not everyone got acknowledged. Not everyone got shouted out.

When hip-hop moved to records, the shout-outs weren't always in songs, but instead were shifted to the back of album covers. When a record was released, folks would read the back of album jackets looking to see if their names or the names of people they knew were mentioned. They looked to see if their neighborhood, region, city, or state was acknowledged.

The acknowledgments on the back of albums were a big deal, and some groups like Public Enemy might have as much as two pages. Often those shout-outs had names of people who led you to the library to look them up.

How important were those shout-outs? Public acknowledgment opened doors and affirmed to the world you were down by law. You were important. Chuck D of Public Enemy acknowledged me on several albums. They had my name highlighted on the back of a single, "Revolutionary Generation." Those shout-outs opened doors, helped me get my writing gigs and even radio shows.

So with all that in mind, let's pass the mic and let folks know who I'm down with. Let's note who inspired, who opened doors, and who is my people, my tribe, and my family.

We have to start by shouting out the Boogie Down Bronx. My place of birth. Soundview section. Croes Avenue. Rosedale Avenue. Story Avenue. Parkchester. Shout-out to Riverdale up in the North Bronx section of the Bronx. Skyview, in particular. It was in "The View" where I busted my first rhymes, crafted my first rhyme book, did my first pause-button tapes, and rolled with the Double D Crew.

Shout-out to my childhood friends Mauricio Ospina, Warren Leonard, Henry Mobley, Guy Williams, Marc Price, Bruce Bell, Dave Welch, and Arnold Slappey, who was the one who introduced us all to hip-hop. Shout-out to Avengers Crew, who I rolled with, Jazzy Jay from the Promenade, Arty Art, who lived near Marble Hill. Shout-out to the TDK (Total Def Krew) out of Co-op City, Section 2. Mr. T (Terrai)—who came from a place called Rhodesia when it was colonized and now is called Zimbabwe—was one of the illest on the mic. DJ Gee and Mystery.

Shout-out to Oakland, Cali, and the Bay Area. I was born and raised in New York, but "Tha Town" nurtured me and gave me a voice. It's where my heart and soul are today. Such a vibrant city with a history that is both politically and musically very special. Its contributions to hip-hop are immense and unique all on their own and I'm forever grateful to be part of this city.

In terms of this book, there are some important historians, both within hip-hop and outside, who I ride with and some whose shoulders I stand on. They all were inspirations and constant reminders to try to give voice to forgotten and often erased pasts. They are fellow griots. Mark Skillz, Jay Quan, Zulu King Cholly Rock, Paradise Gray, Dart Adams, Van Silk, Bas-1, Paul Skeeee (Mighty 4 Crew), Troy L. Smith, REFA ONE and Kwadwo Addo Gyan of the Oakland Maroons, Rickey Vincent, Greg Tate, QD III, General Jeff, Kwaku and Rage Souljah of Race for the Times, Sean Kennedy, Chuck Johnson (Soul Beat TV), Byron Hurt, Dan Charnas, Harry Allen the Media Assassin, Red Alert, the late Combat Jack, Traci Bartlow, Dave Paul, Eric K. Arnold, the late DJ Stef, Adisa Banjoko, Donald Lacy, Ernie Paniccioli, Big Jeff and Zulu Nation, Kevin Powell, Jelani Cobb, Lasana Hotep, Medusa, The Poetess, Danyel Smith, Dominique DiPrima, Will Randolph of the Black Resurgents, Boogaloo Dana and Fayzo of Medea Sirkas, BRS Dance Alliance, Sway and King Tech of the Wake Up Show, Bakari Kitwana (Rap Sessions), Jasiri X (1Hood), Paul Porter, the late Kiilu Nyasha, Allen Temple Baptist Church, and the Nation of Islam, Marvin X, Thembisa Mshaka, Professor Tina Bell Wright, Rosa Clemente, Rasheed Shabazz, Bay Area Hip-Hop Coalition (Beni B, KK Baby, Sadiki, Tamu, Kevvy Kev of KZSU, Billy Jam, the Late Nate Copeland, Sleuth Pro, Marcus Clemmons), Alex Mejia, Dawn-Elissa Fischer, the late James Spady, Martha Diaz, Marcyliena Morgan and the Hip-Hop Archives, Dr. Khalid el-Hakim and the Black History Museum, Universal Hip-Hop Museum, the late Natty Prep, CJ Flash and Russell Gatewood, Rich Medina, Dhoruba Bin Wahad, the late Lord Yoda, T-Kash, Qualm Allah, Naru, Barri Scott, Walter Turner, Greg Bridges, Anita Johnson, Cat Brooks, Quincy, and my KPFA Family, Cedric Muhammad, the late Zin and Matt Sonzala of Damage Control, Rico Casanova and The PROs Record Pool, Sarah Allen, Kevin Epps, and Bay Area Black Journalist Association, SF Bayview, SF State Africana and Ethnic Studies Department, and The Old Kan crew (Dug Infinite, Adam Mansbach, Torrance Rogers, Weyland Southon Phraze Vader, Kdub, Bryant Terry).

2020

JEFF'S ACKNOWLEDGMENTS

I want to start by saying it has been a joy to be able to work with a person who has been one of the biggest influences on all my work and writing. I can't express how much Davey D has meant to hip-hop, to me, and to so many of the communities I belong to. I'm incredibly proud of what we were able to do together, and I'm thankful for our friendship.

The original book had four pages of acknowledgments, and I would like to thank each and every one of those folks once again and always.

I wanted to send a shout to the vast crew who made everything that followed the first publication an amazing journey, especially H. Samy Alim, Dave Twombly, Charles Yao, Tom Gagnon, and all of you who have read, shared, and taught this book. I'm full of gratitude.

One more time for the crew that made *Can't Stop Won't Stop* a thing in the first place: Victoria Sanders, Imani Wilson, Bernadette Baker-Baughman, and everyone past and present at VSA, St. Martin's, Picador, and Macmillan, super-designer Brent Rollins, and most of all, Monique Patterson.

And last but always first, my family.

Berkeley and Oakland, California, 2020

Notes

1. Babylon Is Burning

1 Robert Caro, *The Power Broker* (New York: Knopf, 1974), 860.
2 "The Fire Next Door," CBS *Reports,* aired March 22, 1977.
3 *The South Bronx: A Plan for Revitalization* (December 1977). Report prepared by the Office of the Mayor of the City of New York, Office of the Bronx Borough President, Department of City Planning, Office of Economic Development, Office of Management and Budget, Department of Housing Preservation and Development.
4 "Execution in the Bronx," *New York Times* (June 17, 1973).
5 "New York Illustrated: The Savage Skulls with Piri Thomas," produced and written by Abigail Child, aired November 18, 1973, on WNBC.
6 In 2004, Eddie Perez, a former Ghetto Brother from Hartford, Connecticut, became mayor of the city.
7 Gene Weingarten, "East Bronx Story: Return of the Street Gangs," *New York* (March 27, 1972), 35. https://nymag.com/news/features/crime/48271/.
8 Ibid, 34.
9 Jerry Schmetterer, "Trouble Was His Scene," *New York Daily News,* (December 3, 1971), 3.
10 Eric C. Schneider, "Ain't Gonna Eat My Mind" in *Vampires, Dragons and Egyptian Kings: Youth Gangs in Post-War New York* (Princeton: Princeton University Press, 1999), 243–245.
11 Edward Kirkman, "Gangs Hold Rap Session on Cops," *New York Daily News* (December 17, 1971).
12 Aida Alvarez, "Savage Skulls Feared as Worst Bronx Gang," *New York Post* (September 15, 1975), 8.
13 "Execution in the Bronx," *New York Times* (June 17, 1973).
14 *The 51st State: Bronx Gangs,* hosted by Patrick Watson, aired 1972, on WNYC.

2. How DJ Kool Herc Lost His Accent

1 Dmitri Ehrlich and Gregor Ehrlich, "Graffiti in Its Own Words," *New York* (June 22, 2006). http://nymag.com/guides/summer/17406/.
2 Jack Stewart, "Subway Graffiti: An Aesthetic Study of Graffiti on the Subway System of New York City" (Ph.D. diss., New York University, 1989), 148–190. See also Susan A. Phillips, *Wallbanging: Graffiti and Gangs in L.A.* (Chicago: University of Chicago Press, 1999).
3 Stephen Powers, *The Art of Getting Over* (New York: St. Martin's Press, 1999), 10.
4 "TAKI 183 Spawns Pen Pals," *New York Times* (July 21, 1971), 37.
5 Herbert Kohl's great little 1972 book *Golden Boy as Anthony Cool: A Photo Essay on Naming and Graffiti* offers insight on how far Herc had now moved from the gangs: "On gang rosters we sometimes see inscriptions such as 'Clarence as Lefty.' However, they are not common; the 'as' phenomenon is more often found on lists of names of people from the same block or of

boys and girls that 'hang out' together. It is more likely that 'Lefty' would stand alone on the gang roster. The name Clarence, identifying 'Lefty' as the son of his parents, is more thoroughly renounced through gang membership than through becoming part of a more loosely structured and less demanding peer group." Herbert Kohl and James Hinton, *Golden Boy as Anthony Cool: A Photo Essay on Naming and Graffiti* (New York: The Dial Press, 1972), 120.

6 It's interesting that these beats shared the element of cinema or theater. While David Toop believed the Incredible Bongo Band was a Jamaican disco band, they in fact were a band put together by sometime film composer Michael Viner, featuring another soundtrack composer, Perry Botkin Jr., and the formidable bongo playing of King Errisson. Dennis Coffey was a studio musician whose career was furthered by his work for blaxploitation soundtracks. James Brown's "live" record was actually recorded in a studio, and given live audience overdubs. It was later marketed as a performance in his hometown of Augusta, Georgia.

7 Sharon "Sha-Rock" Jackson with Iesha Brown, *Luminary Icon: The Story of the Beginning and End of Hip-Hop's First Female* MC (n.p.: Pearlie Gates Publishing, 2010), 63.

8 Ibid., 62.

9 The Rock Steady Crew's Jorge "Popmaster Fabel" Pabon, a respected hip-hop historian, said in 2001: "The most respected B-Boy crews was the Zulu Kings, the Twins formerly known as the N----r Twins. There was a group that the Twins told me about called the B-Boys. They have a very interesting claim. They say that the word 'b-boys' was really referring to those guys. Like for instance, the lockers. There was a similar argument that came up where one of the Lockers recently [was asked], 'What do you do?' And he said he's a locker. And then some young kid said, 'I'm a locker,' and he looked at him and he said, 'No you're not, *I'm* a Locker.' In other words, it gets into semantics like you know how to lock, okay, but I'm the Locker, I'm one of the original Lockers. And that same argument I heard pop up with b-boying. Where the Twins said, 'Well I don't know why everyone's calling himself a b-boy. Those guys were the B-Boys!' Hey, I have an open mind and it's an interesting concept. I'm not gonna debate it, I don't have any artillery to debate it with!" (Personal interview, November 20, 2001.)

10 Jackson and Brown, *Luminary Icon,* 63.

11 Lessie Sanders, quoted in Robert Jensen, curator, *Devastation/Resurrection: The South Bronx* (New York: Bronx Museum of the Arts, 1980), 64.

12 Ivor L. Miller, *Aerosol Kingdom: Subway Painters of New York City* (Jackson: University Press of Mississippi, 2002), 187–188.

3. Getting It Together

1 The Universal Zulu Nation actually dates its anniversary to November 12, 1973, which is likely the date The Organization came into being. Its Infinity Lesson #3 reads: "The Universal Zulu Nation was founded in the year 1973 but started to come into power in the year 1975 A.D. by a young student at Adlai Stevenson High School named Afrika Bambaataa . . . He also ran the group called The Organization for 2 years and the street gang called the Black Spades for 5 years."

2 Kevin Kosanovich, interview with Lisa Lee Counts (June 11, 2013), William and Mary College Digital Archive. https://digitalarchive.wm.edu/handle/10288/18540.
3 Ibid.
4 Tanya E., "Ladies First: Legendary Zulu Queen Lisa Lee," *Sound O.F.F. Only Fear Fears* podcast (December 5, 2013). https://www.blogtalkradio.com/soundoffonlyfearfears/2013/12/05/ladies-first-legendary-female-mc-zulu-queen-lisa-lee.
5 "Beat This!: A Hip-Hop History," *Arena,* directed by Dick Fontaine, aired 1984, on BBC. https://www.youtube.com/watch?v=tw0uzQM6T5A.

4. Wild Styles

1 Stewart, "Subway Graffiti," 229.
2 Lee Quiñones wrote this in a famous 1978 piece done with BILLY 167, but Henry Chalfant has documented other instances and Jack Stewart dates the slogan to 1974, before Lee was on the trains. Ibid., 475. Another Lee mural, called "Roaring Thunder," has this: "Graffiti is Art, and if Art is a crime, let God forgive all."
3 Phoebe Hoban, *Basquiat: A Quick Killing in Art* (New York: Viking, 1998), 36.
4 *Style Wars,* directed by Tony Silver (1983).
5 Interview by Mandalit Del Barco, "Origins of Breakdancing," aired October 14, 2002, on National Public Radio.
6 Zora Neale Hurston, "Characteristics of Negro Expression," in *Folklore, Memoirs, and Other Writings* (New York: Library of America, 1995), 835. (Originally published in 1934.)
7 Cristina Verán, "(Puerto) Rock of Ages," *Rap Pages* (September 1996), 47.
8 Jackson and Brown, *Luminary Icon,* 102.

5. Hip-Hop Is Dead

1 For a recording of the Flash and the Furious Five's live beatbox routine in its context, including Flash rocking the beatbox, find the version of "Flash It to the Beat" on the Bozo Meko label, an apparently bootlegged tape from the Bronx River Community Center in 1979 or 1980. Bonus: the Furious Five get the crowd going in a frenzied "Zulu! Gestapo!" chant! The flip side features Jazzy Jay cutting up breakbeats on a track entitled "Fusion Beats." The record is absolutely an early classic of the instrumental hip-hop record genre. There is a studio version on Sugar Hill, also a great listen, but it's modified appropriately. In fact, the house band sounds almost anemic, stripped down to a bass, drum, and percussion backbeat.
2 Steven Hager, "Afrika Bambaataa's Hip Hop," *Village Voice* (September 21, 1982), 73.
3 John Leland, *Hip: The History* (New York: Harper, 2004), 5.
4 This story has circulated for a while among hip-hop elders. We give props to Dan Charnas for telling us this version.
5 Peter Scholtes, "Payback Is a Motherland," *City Pages* (July 12, 2006).

6. Zulus Meet the Punk Rockers Downtown

1 Mel Rosenthal, *In the South Bronx of America* (Willimantic, Conn.: Curbstone, 2000), 49.

2 Robert Elms, "Nightclubbing," *The Face One Hundred* (no date), 37.
3 Howard Zinn, *A People's History of the United States, 1492–Present* (New York: HarperPerennial, 1995), 565–6.
4 The National Urban League's "State of Black America," cited in Nelson George, "The Complete History of Post-Soul Culture," *The Village Voice* (March 17, 1992).
5 Rick Hampson, "City's Chronic Teen-Age Jobless Called a Lost Generation by Labor Officials," *Staten Island Advance*, August 1, 1983, as cited in Joe Austin, *Taking the Train: How Graffiti Art Became an Urban Crisis in New York City* (New York: Columbia University Press, 2002), 212.

7. The Big Crossover

1 Cristina Verán, "Breaking It All Down: The Rise and Fall of the B-Boy Kingdom," in *The Vibe History of Hip-Hop*, ed. Alan Light (New York: Three Rivers Press, 1999), 58.
2 Bill Adler, *Tougher Than Leather: Run-D.M.C. Their Whole Uncensored Biography* (New York: New American Library, 1987), 21.
3 From the liner notes to Run-DMC's *King of Rock* (Arista/Sony Legacy, 2005 CD reissue).
4 Michael Diamond and Adam Horovitz, *Beastie Boys Book* (New York: Spiegel and Grau, 2018), 141.
5 Ibid., 211.
6 Sam Roberts, "One Year After Hearings on Police Brutality, Critics Report Some Progress," *New York Times* (July 25, 1984), B1.
7 Isabel Wilkerson, "Jury Acquits All Transit Officers in 1983 Death of Michael Stewart," *New York Times* (November 25, 1985), A1.
8 Adler, *Tougher Than Leather*, 170.
9 Brian Cross, *It's Not About a Salary: Rap, Race and Resistance in Los Angeles* (New York: Verso, 1993), 156–7.
10 Jon Pareles, "Rock: Run-D.M.C. and Beastie Boys at the Garden," *New York Times* (August 19, 1987).

8. Coast to Coast

1 Brad "Scarface" Jordan, *Diary of a Madman: The Geto Boys, Life, Death, and the Roots of Southern Rap* (New York: Dey Street, 2015), 14.
2 Ibid., 15.
3 Ibid., 54.
4 Marvin Dunn, *Black Miami in the Twentieth Century* (Gainesville: University Press of Florida, 1997), 261–278.
5 "Roxanne Shanté on Biopic, KRS-One Beef, Baby Father Abuse (Full Interview)," VladTV (April 9, 2018). https://www.youtube.com/watch?v=utNtvaVR-YQ.
6 "THE REAL ROXANNE SHANTE," Mass Appeal (March 22, 2018). https://www.youtube.com/watch?v=0IRH6RfOsvw.
7 Cristina Verán, "Fly Females Who Rocked the Mic in the '70s and '80s," in *Hip-Hop Divas* (London: Plexus, 2001), 12.
8 Marcus Reeves, "Allah's Messenger," *The Source* (December 1997), 98.
9 Jefferson Mao (Chairman Mao), "The Microphone God," *Vibe* (December 1997), 134.
10 Nick Smash, "The Dollar Sign," *Echoes* (November 21, 1987), 14.

11 Verán, "Fly Females," 11.
12 In 1980, Sugar Hill would rerelease the record under its own imprint.
13 Soren Baker, *The History of Gangster Rap: From Schoolly D to Kendrick Lamar, the Rise of a Great American Art Form* (New York: Abrams, 2018), 3.

9. What We Got to Say

1 Edward Wolff, *Top Heavy: A Study of the Increasing Inequality of Wealth in America* (New York: The Twentieth Century Fund Press, 1995), 2, 17–8.
2 Brian Coleman, *Check the Technique: Line Notes for Hip-Hop Junkies* (New York: Villard, 2007), 78.
3 Ibid.
4 Ibid., 86.
5 Frank Owen, "Wasted in the Zoo," *NME* (September 26, 1987). https://fxowen.wordpress.com/golden-oldies/scott-la-rock-wasted-in-the-zoonme-26-september-1987/.
6 Coleman, *Check the Technique*, 86.
7 For the full story, listen to D-Nice on the *Combat Jack Show* podcast, "The DJ D-Nice Episode" (May 2014). https://soundcloud.com/thecombatjackshow/the-dj-d-nice-episode.
8 National Urban League, *Stop the Violence: Overcoming Self-Destruction,* ed. Nelson George (New York: Pantheon Books, 1990), 12.
9 Michele Kirsch, "Rappers Club Together for Peace," *The Independent* (July 26, 1989).
10 George de Lama, "Reagan: South Africa Reforming, President Says Segregation Over," *Chicago Tribune* (August 27, 1985), C1; Norman D. Sandler, "Washington Window: Reagan on Apartheid: A Potential Problem," United Press International (August 28, 1985).
11 Pauline Baker, *The United States and South Africa: The Reagan Years* (New York: Ford Foundation and the Foreign Policy Association, 1989), 34.
12 Joseph Berger, "Campus Turmoil over South Africa Ties Fades," *New York Times* (December 30, 1987), B8.
13 Scott Minerbrook, "Blacks Locked Out of the American Dream; Real Estate Discrimination," *Business and Society Review* (September 22, 1993), 23; Douglas Massey and Nancy A. Denton, *American Apartheid: Segregation and the Making of the Underclass* (Cambridge, MA: Harvard University Press, 1993), 160–2.
14 Gary Orfield, with Sara Schley, Diane Glass, and Sean Reardon, "The Growth of Segregation in American Schols: Changing Patterns of Separation and Poverty Since 1968," A Report of the Harvard Project on School Desegregation to the National School Boards Association (December 1993), 20, 29.
15 Ibid., 21.
16 Claude "Paradise" Gray and Guiseepe "u.net" Pipitone, *No Half Steppin': An Oral and Pictorial History of New York City Club the Latin Quarter and the Birth of Hip-Hop's Golden Era* (n.p.: Wax Poetics, 2019), 133.
17 Ibid., 139.
18 Robert McFadden, "The Howard Beach Inquiry: Many Key Questions Persist," *New York Times* (December 28, 1986).
19 Jeffrey Page and Victor E. Sasson, "New York Blacks Stage Day of Protest," *The Record* (January 22, 1987).

20 John DeSantis, *For the Color of His Skin: The Murder of Yusuf Hawkins and the Trial of Bensonhurst* (New York: Pharos, 1991), 76.
21 Ibid., 117.
22 "The Jogger and the Wolf Pack," *New York Times* (April 26, 1989).
23 Oliver Laughland, "Donald Trump and the Central Park Five: The Racially Charged Rise of a Demagogue," *The Guardian* (February 17, 2016).
24 Jan Ransom, "Trump Will Not Apologize for Calling for the Death Penalty for the Central Park Five," *New York Times* (June 18, 2019).
25 Laughland, "Donald Trump and the Central Park Five."
26 Frank Owen, "Def Not Dumb," *Melody Maker* (March 21, 1987).
27 Harry Allen, "Public Enemy: Leading a Radio Rebellion," *Black Radio Exclusive* (February 26, 1988), 9–10.
28 James T. Jones IV, "The Big Rap Attack," *USA Today* (August 22, 1989).

10. All About Reality

1 Rennie Harris, interview by the author, September 16, 2003; Rudy Corpuz, interview by the author, 2004. Also read Jorge "Popmaster Fabel" Pabon, "Physical Graffiti," in *Total Chaos: The Art and Aesthetics of Hip-Hop* (New York: Basic, 2006).
2 Brian Cross, *It's Not About a Salary* (New York: Verso, 1994), 180–1.
3 Ibid., 184.
4 Ibid., 201–2.
5 Ibid., 102, 143.
6 Alejandro A. Alonso, "Territoriality Among African American Street Gangs," master's thesis, University of Southern California, Department of Geography (May 1999), 8.
7 Cross, *It's Not About a Salary,* 143.
8 Alonzo Williams, *N.ot W.ithout A.lonzo: Memories of Alonzo Williams, The Roots of West Coast Hip-Hop* (Los Angeles: Lonzo Infotainment Company, 2015), 204.
9 Terry McDermott, "Parental Advisory: Explicit Lyrics," *Los Angeles Times Magazine* (April 14, 2002); Jonathan Gold, "N.W.A.: Hard Rap and Hype from the Streets of Compton," *Los Angeles Weekly* (May 5–11, 1989), 17; Frank Owen, "Hanging Tough," *SPIN* (April 1990), 34. Heller had impressed Dre by securing extra money owed to the Wreckin Cru by the musicians' union, so Dre had told Eazy to get with Lonzo's guy.
10 Gerald Horne, *Fire This Time: The Watts Uprising and the 1960s* (New York: Da Capo Press, 1997), 65.
11 Mike Davis, *City of Quartz* (New York: Verso, 1990), 297–8; Horne, *Fire This Time,* 99.
12 Odie Hawkins, *Scars and Memories: The Story of a Life* (Los Angeles: Holloway House, 1987), 125.
13 Davis, *City of Quartz,* 297.
14 This is according to the Athens Park Blood O.G. named Bone, quoted in the cover story, *F.E.D.S. Magazine* (no date), 79.
15 Ibid.
16 Alonso, "Territoriality Among African American Street Gangs," 90.
17 Ibid., 90–93.
18 Godfather Jimel Barnes in *Uprising: Crips and Bloods Tell the Story of Amer-*

ica's Youth in the Crossfire, ed. Yusuf Jah and Sister Shah'Keyah (New York: Touchstone, 1997), 152.

19 Bone in *F.E.D.S. Magazine;* Leon Bing, *Do or Die* (New York: Harper Collins, 1991), 149–150; Barnes in *Uprising,* 151–2.

20 Alonso, "Territoriality Among African American Street Gangs," 91.

21 Ibid., 7, 97.

22 Ibid., 95.

23 Bone in *F.E.D.S. Magazine,* 82.

24 Alejandro Alonso, "Territoriality Among African American Street Gangs," 98.

25 Bettijane Levine, "An OG Tries to Make Things Right," *Los Angeles Times* (November 24, 1991), E2.

26 Research Group on the Los Angeles Economy, *The Widening Divide: Income Inequallity and Poverty in Los Angeles* (Los Angeles: UCLA Urban Planning Program, 1989), 1.

27 Robin D. G. Kelley, *Race Rebels: Culture, Politics and the Black Working Class* (New York: The Free Press, 1994), 192.

28 Senate Office of Research, *The South-Central Los Angeles and Koreatown Riots: A Study of Civil Unrest* (Sacramento: California State Senate Office of Research, June 17, 1992), 3.

29 Sandy Banks, "Health Center a Vital Aid in Distressed Community," *Los Angeles Times* (January 27, 1985), M1.

30 Michael Krikorian and Greg Kirikorian, "Watts Truce Holds Even as Hopes Fade," *Los Angeles Times* (May 18, 1997), B1.

31 Cross, *It's Not About a Salary,* 197.

32 Gregory Sandow, "What's NWA All About? Anger, Yes. Violence, No," *Los Angeles Herald Examiner* (July 16, 1989), E1, 10.

33 Dave Marsh and Phyllis Pollack, "Wanted for Attitude," *Village Voice* (October 10, 1989), 33.

11. City on Fire

1 Paul Ong and Suzanne Hee, *Losses in the Los Angeles Civil Unrest* (Center for Pacific Rim Studies, University of California, Los Angeles, 1993).

2 Jube Shiver, "Poor Penalized as Food Chains Exit Inner City," *Los Angeles Times* (January 2, 1989).

3 K.W. Lee, "The Haunting Prelude," *KoreAm Journal* (April 2002), 27.

4 "Editorial," *Billboard* (November 23, 1991).

5 James Bernard, "'Death Certificate' Gives Birth to Debate," *Billboard* (December 7, 1991).

6 Quoted in Dennis Hunt, "Outrageous as He Wants to Be," *Los Angeles Times* (November 3, 1991).

7 Dong Suh, "The Source of Korean and African American Tensions," *Asian Week* (February 21, 1992).

8 Sophia Kyung Kim, "Chilling Fields: Ice Cube Rap," *Korea Times* (November 11, 1991).

9 Lynne Duke, "Rapper's Number Chills Black-Korean Relations," *Washington Post* (December 1, 1991).

10 Sophia Kyung Kim, "Ice Cube the Peacemaker," *Korea Times* (May 4, 1992).

11 Ibid.

12 Lou Cannon, *Official Negligence* (New York: Times Books, 1997), 166.

13 Raegan Kelly, "Watts Love: The Truce Is ON!" *URB Magazine* (Vol. 3, No. 6, Issue 30), 1993, 42.
14 Beatriz Johnson Hernandez, "Searching for Inner-City Peace," *Third Force* (June 1996), 18.
15 Multi-Peace Treaty, signed April 29, 1994. The treaty, Sherrills explains, was agreed upon verbally, but not signed until the second anniversary of the rebellion in a formal ceremony at Imperial Courts. The treaty was signed by ex–gang representatives from Hacienda, Imperial Courts, Jordan Downs, and Nickerson Gardens. Also see Jesse Katz and Andrea Ford, "Ex-Gang Members Look to Mideast for a Peace Plan," *Los Angeles Times* (June 17, 1992), B1; Kelly, "Watts Love," 45.
16 Katz and Ford, "Ex-Gang Members Look to Mideast."
17 Ibid.
18 David Whitman, "The Untold Story of the L.A. Riot," *U.S. News and World Report* (May 31, 1993), 34.
19 *Birth of a Nation: 4x29x92*, directed by Matthew McDaniel, 1994.
20 Jim Crogan, "Riot Chronology," in *Inside the L.A. Riots: What Really Happened and Why It Will Happen Again*. Don Hazen, editor. (San Francisco: Institute for Alternative Journalism, 35.
21 Cannon, *Official Negligence,* 322.
22 Ibid., 324.
23 Ibid., 328.
24 Paul Lieberman, "ACLU Lawsuit Charges Riot Curfew Was Illegal," *Los Angeles Times* (June 24, 1992), B1; Ashley Dunn, "Years of '2-Cent' Insults Added Up to Rampage," *Los Angeles Times* (May 7, 1992), A1.
25 Dunn, "Years of '2-Cent' Insults Added Up."
26 Mike Davis, "In L.A., Burning All Illusions," *The Nation* (June 1, 1992), 743; "10 Years After the Riots: In Their Own Words," *Los Angeles Times Magazine* (April 28, 2002).
27 Melvin Oliver, James H. Johnson Jr., and Walter C. Farrell Jr., "Anatomy of a Rebellion: A Political-Economic Analysis," in *Reading Rodney King/Reading Urban Uprising*. Robert Gooding, editor. (New York: Routledge, 1993), 121.
28 Howard Rosenberg, "Medium's Influence Sometimes Warps Our Sense of Reality," *Los Angeles Times* (May 2, 1992), A8.
29 Mike Davis, "Uprising and Repression in L.A.: An Interview with Mike Davis by CovertAction Information Bulletin," in *Reading Rodney King/Reading Urban Uprising*, 145.
30 Louis Sahagun and Patrick J. McDonnell, "Mother Prays, Burns Candles for Disabled Girl Missing in Riot," *Los Angeles Times* (May 7, 1992).
31 Ong and Hee, *Losses in the Los Angeles Civil Unrest,* 12.
32 The Staff of the *Los Angeles Times, Understanding the Riots: Los Angeles Before and After the Rodney King Case* (Los Angeles: *Los Angeles Times,* 1992), 65.

12. New Wars

1 Don Lee, "5 Years Later, a Mixed Legacy of Rebuilding," *Los Angeles Times* (April 22, 1997), A1.
2 Ice-T, as told to Heidi Siegmund, *The Ice Opinion* (New York: St. Martin's Press, 1994), 149–50.

3 Peter Leyden, "Can Gang Members Turn the Tide Toward Peace?" *Minneapolis Star-Tribune* (August 31, 1992), 1A.
4 Sylvester Monroe, "Trading Colors for a Future," *Emerge* (August 1993), 46.
5 Jennifer Rowland, "L.A. Police Say Gang Truce Works," United Press International (June 17, 1992).
6 Russell Ben-Ali, "Deadly Force Wish: Gang Pact: An Uneasy LA Truce," *Newsday* (May 10, 1992), 7.
7 *Larry King Live,* aired May 27, 1992, on CNN.
8 Richard A. Serrano and Jesse Katz, "LAPD Gang Task Force Deployed Despite Truce," *Los Angeles Times* (June 26, 1992), A1.
9 Luis Rodriguez, Cle "Bone" Sloan, and Kershaun "Lil Monster" Scott, "Gangs: The New Political Force in Los Angeles," *Los Angeles Times* (September 13, 1992), M1.
10 Mike Males, *Framing Youth: Ten Myths About the Next Generation* (Monroe, ME: Common Courage Press, 1999), 8.
11 Building Blocks for Youth, from the Center for Children's Law and Policy, *And Justice for Some* (2007). https://www.nccdglobal.org/sites/default/files/publication_pdf/justice-for-some.pdf.
12 Sasha Abramsky, *Hard Time Blues: How Politics Built a Prison Nation* (New York: St. Martin's Press, 2002), 63.
13 Ibid., 71–2.
14 Jason Zeidenburg and Vince Schiraldi, *Cellblocks or Classrooms? The Funding of Higher Education and Corrections and Its Impact on African American Men* (Washington, D.C.: Justice Policy Institute, 2002).
15 James Q. Wilson, "Crime and Public Policy," in *Crime,* ed. James Q. Wilson and Joan Petersilia, (San Francisco: Institute for Contemporary Studies Press, 1995), 507.
16 Tipper Gore, "Hate, Rape and Rap," *Washington Post* (January 8, 1990), A15.
17 Luther Campbell, *As Nasty as They Wanna Be: The Uncensored Story of Luther Campbell of the 2 Live Crew* (New York: Barricade, 1992), 51.
18 Ibid., 72.
19 Steve Huey, "2 Live Crew," allmusic.com (1999).
20 Mak Pankowski, "Seminole Sheriff Raps 2 Live Crew's Music," *Orlando Sentinel* (February 24, 1990), D1; Chuck Philips, "The 'Batman' Who Took On Rap," *Los Angeles Times* (June 18, 1990), F1.
21 Phyllis Pollack, "FBI Hit List Sa Prize Part II," *The Source* (September 1990), 20.
22 David Mills, "Sister Souljah's Call to Arms," *Washington Post* (May 13, 1992), B1.
23 Thomas Edsall, "Clinton Stuns Rainbow Coalition," *Washington Post* (June 14, 1992), A1; *Crossfire,* CNN, aired June 15, 1992.
24 Robert Knight, "Antihero," *Spin* (August 1992), 97.
25 Edsall, "Clinton Stuns Rainbow Coalition."
26 Gwen Ifill, "Clinton Deftly Navigates Shoals of Racial Issues," *New York Times* (June 17, 1992), A22.
27 Chuck Philips, "Police Groups Urge Halt of Record's Sale," *Los Angeles Times* (June 16, 1992), F1.
28 Chuck Philips, "Cop Killer Controversy Spurs Ice-T Album Sales," *Los Angeles Times* (June 18, 1992), F1.

29 Tracey Kaplan and Jim Zamora, "The Heat Turns Out for Ice-T Rap Concert," *Los Angeles Times* (July 25, 1992), B1.
30 "Warner Pulls 'Cop Killer' at Ice-T's Request," United Press International report (July 28, 1992).
31 Ibid.
32 Ice-T, *The Ice Opinion*, 183.
33 Hunter Schwarz, "25 Years Ago, 2 Live Crew Were Arrested for Obscenity. Here's the Fascinating Back Story," *Washington Post* (June 11, 2015).
34 Campbell, *As Nasty as They Wanna Be*, 152–3.
35 Ibid., 154.

13. Ladies First

1 Kathy Iandoli, *God Save the Queens: The Essential History of Women in Hip-Hop* (New York: Dey Street, 2019), 25.
2 Ibid.
3 Ibid., 24.
4 "Roxanne Shanté on How 'Female Rapper' Term Was Created During Her Battle (Part 2)," VladTV (March 27, 2018). https://www.youtube.com/watch?v=KBQ774si6T8.
5 Ibid.
6 Ibid.
7 Harry Allen, "The Queens from Queens," in *Hip-Hop Divas*, 34.
8 Dave Simpson, "How We Made 'Push It,'" *The Guardian* (August 7, 2017). https://www.theguardian.com/culture/2017/aug/07/how-we-made-salt-n-pepa-push-it.
9 Christopher Weingarten, "Salt-N-Pepa: Our Life in 15 Songs," *Rolling Stone* (September 5, 2017).
10 Hattie Collins, "We Thought Tupac Was Mad at Us—A Trip through Hip-Hop History with Rap's Unapologetic Pioneers, Salt-N-Pepa," i-D.com (June 8, 2017). https://i-d.vice.com/en_uk/article/d3p9nv/salt-n-pepa-hip-hop-90s-interview-music.
11 Richard Harrington, "Salt-N-Pepa Taking Control," *Washington Post* (May 27, 1994).
12 Sun Singleton, "Don Divas: MC Lyte, Salt-N-Pepa, and Queen Latifah Put Girls Up Front," *Vibe* (August 2008).
13 "Leading Women: The Story of MC Lyte," aired 2006, on BET, uploaded by Felix Augustine (October 16, 2016). https://www.youtube.com/watch?v=eGfs0BNzswl.
14 Ibid.
15 Coleman, *Check the Technique*, 261.
16 "MC Lyte Talks Marriage, Kids, Female MCs and Rap Beef!" interview by Ebro, Peter Rosenberg, and Laura Stylez, Hot 97 (April 23, 2015). https://www.youtube.com/watch?v=aZ6ZhnXBPAg.
17 Michael Gonzales, "Kickin' 4 Brooklyn," in *Hip-Hop Divas*, 46.
18 Kierna Mayo, "The Last Good Witch," in *Hip-Hop Divas*, 59.
19 Hilary Miller, "Queen Latifah Opens Up About Heartbreak, Alcohol and Using Faith to Grow a Positive Self-Image," Huffington Post (December 12, 2013). https://www.huffpost.com/entry/queen-latifah-alcohol-faith_n_4427337.

20 "Queen Latifah Interview Slammin' Rap Video Magazine," 1990, SlamminVideoMagazine (March 3, 2010). https://www.youtube.com/watch?v=b5GrwZ-PG4k.

21 *My Mic Sounds Nice: A Truth About Women and Hip-Hop,* directed by Ava DuVernay, aired August 30, 2010, on BET.

22 Mayo, "The Last Good Witch," 54.

23 Queen Latifah, *Ladies First: Revelations of a Strong Woman* (New York: William Morrow, 1999), 2.

24 *My Mic Sounds Nice.*

14. Keeping It Real

1 Rob Tannenbaum and Craig Marks, *I Want My MTV: The Uncensored Story of the Music Video Revolution* (New York: Plume, 2012), 167.

2 Paul Grein, "Pop Eye: Rappers Welcome MTV's Enthusiasm," *Los Angeles Times* (June 18, 1989), 64.

3 Janice Simpson, "Yo! Rap Gets on the Map," *Time* (February 5, 1990), 60.

4 "People despise Hammer because he smiled at the world," Danyel Smith wrote. "*If he can smile, why can't you all?* The public Black male smile is a betrayal. People think it should be a secret." Danyel Smith, "MC Hammer," *The Vibe History of Hip-Hop* (New York: Three Rivers Press, 1999), 230.

5 "The Good Life: L.A. Hip-Hop's Untold Story," Hip-Hop Wired (July 7, 2009). https://hiphopwired.com/2734/the-good-life-l-a-hip-hops-untold-story/.

6 The RZA with Chris Norris, *The Wu-Tang Manual* (New York: Riverhead, 2005), 75–6.

7 The RZA, *The Wu-Tang Manual*, 86.

8 Jake Paine, "RZA Explains How His Attempted Murder Case Transformed Him," Ambrosia for Heads (October 6, 2018). https://ambrosiaforheads.com/2018/10/rza-ohio-charge-case-transformation-wu-tang-clan/.

9 Bobbito "The Barber" Garcia, "Street's Disciple: Rrepresenting Queensbridge, New York and the Future of Hip-Hop, Nas Is in His Own State of Mind," in *Born to Use Mics: Reading Nas's Illmatic,* ed. Sohail Daulatzai and Michael Eric Dyson (New York: Basic, 2010), 232. (Originally published in *Rap Pages Magazine,* May 1994.)

10 Ibid., 232–3.

15. Tupac and Biggie

1 dream hampton, "Real N----z Do Die," *Village Voice* (September 24, 1996).

2 Voletta Wallace with Tremell McKenzie, *Voletta Wallace Remembers Her Son, Biggie* (New York: Atria, 2005), 57.

3 "The Final 24: Tupac Shakur," The Final 24 (January 11, 2016). https://www.youtube.com/watch?v=GJ9-ltl0OdU.

4 Tupac Shakur, *Tupac: Resurrection 1971–1996,* ed. Jacob Hoye and Karoyln Ali (New York: Atria/MTV Books, 2003), 14.

5 Connie Bruck, "The Takedown of Tupac," *New Yorker* (June 30, 1997).

6 Ibid.

7 Kevin Powell, "This Thug's Life," in *Tupac Shakur,* the Editors of *Vibe* (New York: Three Rivers Press, 1998), 25. (Originally published in *Vibe,* February 1994 issue.)

8 "Tupac Wishes He Could Have Been a Better Son to His Mother," interview

by Ed Gordon, 1994, BET Networks (September 19, 2016). https://www.youtube.com/watch?v=YyDlOlmku68.
9 Powell, "This Thug's Life," 27.
10 Cheo Hodari Coker, *Unbelievable: The Life, Death, and Afterlife of The Notorious B.I.G.* (New York: Three Rivers Press/Vibe Books, 2003), 26.
11 N.J. Sleuth, *Hip-Hop Tales: From Humpty Dance to Blondie Locks, The Golden Years, 1987–2002* (n.p.: Sleuth Pro Books, 2017), 46–7.
12 Christopher N. Weingarten, "I Get Around: The Oral History of 2Pac's Digital Underground Years," Rollingstone.com (April 6, 2017). https://www.rollingstone.com/music/music-features/i-get-around-the-oral-history-of-2pacs-digital-underground-years-125475/.
13 Ibid.
14 Shakur, *Tupac: Resurrection,* 80.
15 Abby Kearse, "'Tupac Shakur in His Own Words' MTV News 1997," aired 1997 on MTV (October 23, 2011). https://www.youtube.com/watch?v=tHOrL-qcwRU.
16 "The Final 24."
17 Kearse, "Tupac Shakur in His Own Words."
18 "Tupac Shakur: I'm Not a Threat to You Unless You're a Threat to Me," interview by Ed Gordon, aired 1994 on BET Networks (September 19, 2016). https://www.youtube.com/watch?v=u8sy-v1iC1w&t=283s.
19 Larry "The Blackspot" Hester, "Stakes Is High," *Vibe* (September 1996), 100.
20 "Ayanna Jackson on Meeting 2Pac, Sexual Assault, Trial, Aftermath (Full Interview)," interview by DJ Vlad, VladTV (February 13, 2018). https://www.youtube.com/watch?v=0CVBOv9O1GA.
21 "Tupac Shakur: 'God Has Cursed Me to See What Life Should Be Like,'" interview by Ed Gordon, aired 1994 on BET Networks (September 19, 2016). https://www.youtube.com/watch?v=Zll3k9C7HGo.
22 Coker, *Unbelievable,* 135.
23 Kevin Powell, "Ready to Live," in *Tupac Shakur,* 46. (Originally published in *Vibe,* April 1995.)
24 Ibid., 50.
25 "Tupac Shakur Apologizes to Woman He Sexually Abused; Is Sentenced to Four Years in Prison," *Jet* (February 1995); George James, "Rapper Faces Prison Term for Sex Abuse," *New York Times* (February 8, 1995).
26 "Tupac Shakur Apologizes."
27 Powell, "This Thug's Life," 59.
28 Coker, *Unbelievable,* 138–9.
29 Bruck, "The Takedown of Tupac."
30 hampton, "Real N----z Do Die."
31 Hester, "Stakes Is High," 100.
32 Hester, "Stakes Is High," 100, 104.
33 hampton, "Real N----z Do Die."
34 Coker, *Unbelievable,* 197.
35 Ibid., 214.
36 Ibid., 238.
37 James Prince, *The Art & Science of Respect* (Houston: N-The-Water Publishing, 2018), 188.
38 Selwyn Seyfu Hinds, "The Assassination of Christopher Wallace," *The Source* (May 1997), 82.

39 Justin Tinsley, "The Notorious Night Biggie Was Murdered in Los Angeles," *The Undefeated* (March 8, 2017). https://theundefeated.com/features/the-notorious-night-biggie-was-murdered-in-los-angeles/.
40 Letter by Garrett E. Jenkins, *Vibe* (June–July 1997), 43.
41 Snoop went on to give back to the community, by setting up Pop Warner football leagues in Long Beach. In 2005, he hosted his own Peace Summit to unite beefing West Coast rappers.

16. New Queens & Kings

1 Tariq K. Muhammad, "Hip-Hop Moguls: Behind the Hype," *Black Enterprise* (December 1999), 79.
2 *My Mic Sounds Nice*.
3 Preezy Brown, "Foxy Brown's *Ill Na Na* Changed Everything for Her," Vibe.com (November 21, 2016).
4 Joan Morgan, *When Chickenheads Come Home to Roost* (New York: Touchstone Books, 1999), 59.
5 Ibid., 62.
6 Martine Bury, "The Fugees," in *The Vibe History of Hip-Hop*, 378.
7 Thembisa Mshaka, "The Selling of 'The Miseducation of Lauryn Hill,'" Okayplayer.com (September 12, 2018). https://www.okayplayer.com/music/the-making-of-lauryn-hill-the-miseducation-of-lauryn-hill.html.
8 Laura Checkoway, "Inside 'The Miseducation of Lauryn Hill,'" RollingStone.com (August 26, 2008). https://www.rollingstone.com/music/music-news/inside-the-miseducation-of-lauryn-hill-252219/.
9 Joan Morgan, *She Begat This: 20 Years of The Miseducation of Lauryn Hill* (New York: 37Ink, 2018), 120–1.
10 Mshaka, "The Selling of 'The Miseducation of Lauryn Hill.'"
11 Morgan, *She Begat This*, 20.
12 Ibid., 75.
13 Ibid.
14 Rob Marriott, "Outkast. *Southernplayalisticadillacmuzik*," *The Source* (July 1994). https://thesource.com/2015/04/28/record-report-outkasts-southernplayalisticadillacmuzik-review-1994/.
15 "Behind the Music: Missy Elliott," aired June 29, 2011, on VH1.
16 Ibid.
17 "Questlove Speaks on How J Dilla's Death Impacted Him and More at ASCAP 'I Create Music' Expo," Billboard.com (May 4, 2019). https://www.billboard.com/articles/news/8510060/questlove-ascap-expo-2019-j-dilla.
18 Ethan Brown, "Got Beef?" *New York* (December 1, 2003).
19 Jay-Z with dream hampton, *Decoded* (New York: Random House, 2010), 34.
20 Jay-Z, *Decoded*, 33.
21 Elizabeth Méndez Berry, "The Last Hustle," *Village Voice* (November 25, 2003). https://www.villagevoice.com/2003/11/25/the-last-hustle/3/.
22 Jay-Z, *Decoded*, 38–9.
23 Ibid., 43.
24 Ibid., 102.
25 Josh Tyrangiel, "Why You Can't Ignore Kanye," *Time* (August 21, 2005).
26 *My Mic Sounds Nice*.
27 Jay-Z, *Decoded*, 100.

28 Maxwell Strachan, "The Definitive History of 'George Bush Doesn't Care About Black People,'" *Huffington Post* (August 28, 2015, updated September 9, 2015). https://www.huffpost.com/entry/kanye-west-george-bush-black-people_n_55d67c12e4b020c386de2f5e.

17. The Great White Hope

1 "Martin Luther King Speaks to NATRA (full speech-August 1967)," Mr Davey D (January 14, 2012). https://www.youtube.com/watch?v=_wxBCl1RDwA.
For more, see Mr. Davey D, "Dr. Martin Luther King; The Power of Soul Music & the Importance of Black Radio," Hip-Hop and Politics (January 19, 2013). http://hiphopandpolitics.com/2013/01/19/dr-martin-luther-king-the-power-of-soul-music-the-importance-of-black-radio/.
2 Greg Kot, "Rap's Bad Rap," *Chicago Tribune* (April 15, 1990).
3 Charles Aaron, "Chocolate on the Inside," *Spin* (May 1999).
4 Ibid.
5 Ibid.
6 Anthony Bozza, *Whatever You Say I Am: The Life and Times of Eminem* (New York: Three Rivers Press, 2003), 23–4.
7 Aaron, "Chocolate on the Inside."
8 Eminem with Sacha Jenkins, *The Way I Am*. (New York: Plume, 2009), 77.
9 Anthony Bozza, "Eminem: The Rolling Stone Interview," *Rolling Stone* (July 4, 2002).
10 Aaron, "Chocolate on the Inside."

18. All Around the World

1 Johan Kugelbeg, *Born in the Bronx: A Visual Record of the Early Days of Hip-Hop* (New York: Rizzolli, 2007), 139–142.
2 Sabelo Mkhabela, "Emile YX? Shares Some Gems About South African Hip-Hop History, Its Relationship to Capitalism & More," OkayAfrica.com (May 2, 2019). https://www.okayafrica.com/south-african-hip-hop-pioneer-emile-yx/.
3 Cristina Verán, "Soul by the Pound," *One World* (December/January 2003).
4 Jeff Chang, "It's a Hip-Hop World," *Foreign Policy*/Foreignpolicy.com (October 12, 2009). https://foreignpolicy.com/2009/10/12/its-a-hip-hop-world/.
5 Larry Rohter, "Brazilian Government Invests in Culture of Hip-Hop," *New York Times* (March 14, 2007).
6 "The Rap Songs of the Arab Spring," National Public Radio (June 9, 2011). https://www.npr.org/sections/therecord/2011/06/09/137067390/the-rap-songs-of-the-arab-spring.

19. Black Lives Matter

1 Mos Def, "An Open Letter from Mos Def," Hip-Hop and Politics (February 25, 1999). https://hiphopandpolitics.wordpress.com/tag/an-open-letter-from-mos-def-about-amadou-diallo/.
2 Mychal Denzel Smith, "How Trayvon Martin's Death Launched a New Generation of Black Activism," *The Nation* (August 27, 2014).
3 Eric Pfanner, "Music Industry Sales Rise, and Digital Revenue Gets the Credit," *New York Times* (February 26, 2013).
4 Matthew Strauss, "A Boogie Wit Da Hoodie Sold 823 Albums Last Week, Still Goes to No. 1," Pitchfork (January 14, 2019). https://pitchfork.com

/news/a-boogie-wit-da-hoodie-sold-823-albums-last-week-still-goes-to-no-1.

5 Daniel Sanchez, "What Streaming Music Services Pay (Updated for 2019)" DigitalMusicNews.com (December 25, 2018). https://www.digitalmusicnews.com/2018/12/25/streaming-music-services-pay-2019/.

6 Emily Blake, "Nicki Minaj Wants Out of the Female Rapper Category," MTV News (April 24, 2014). http://www.mtv.com/news/1726716/nicki-minaj-wants-out-of-the-female-rap-category/.

7 Sasha Geffen, "Young Thug Breaks Down His Androgynous Style: 'There's No Such Thing As Gender,'" MTV News (July 6, 2016). http://www.mtv.com/news/2901714/young-thug-calvin-klein-gender/.

8 Adam Fleischer, "How Did You End Up Featured on Kendrick Lamar's Album? Rapsody Tells Her Story," MTV News (March 16, 2015). http://www.mtv.com/news/2106673/rapsody-kendrick-lamar-complexion-a-zulu-love-to-pimp-a-butterfly/.

9 Donna-Claire Chesman, "Rapsody Is Happy, She Doesn't Need Your Validation," DJ Booth.net (August 23, 2019). https://djbooth.net/features/2019-08-23-rapsody-eve-interview-legacy-happiness-validation.

10 Noah Yoo,"Kendrick Lamar Writes Tribute to Nipsey Hussle: 'He Was a Vessel from God,'" Pitchfork (April 11, 2019). https://pitchfork.com/news/kendrick-lamar-writes-tribute-to-nipsey-hussle/.

11 Naheem "Farlin Ave" Houston, "Nipsey Hussle Talks What His Real Name Means, Roots in Africa, New Album & More [VIDEO]," 97.9 The Beat (no date, likely 2018). https://thebeatdfw.com/3045593/nipsey-hussle-talks-what-his-real-name-means-roots-in-africa-new-album-more-video/.

12 Rodney Carmichael, "Nipsey Hussle Tells the Epic Stories Behind 'Victory Lap,' Track by Track," National Public Radio (February 16, 2018). https://www.npr.org/sections/allsongs/2018/02/16/586361873/nipsey-hussle-tells-the-epic-stories-behind-victory-lap-track-by-track.

13 "Interview: Nipsey Hussle Talks African Roots, Snoop Dogg Co-Sign, and Rappers Reppin' Gangs," Complex.com (March 31, 2010). https://www.complex.com/music/2010/04/interview-nipsey-hussle-talks-african-roots-snoop-dogg-co-sign-and-rappers-reppin-gangs.

14 Jordan, *Diary of a Madman,* 53–4.

15 Holly Obbertein, "Cardi B Might Be One of Bernie's Most Powerful Allies. Seriously," *Politico* (August 26, 2019). https://www.politico.com/story/2019/08/26/bernie-sanders-cardi-b-friendship-1474249.

16 The Movement for Black Lives, "Platform." https://policy.m4bl.org/end-war-on-black-people/.

17 "Why Are the Twin Cities So Segregated?" Institute on Metropolitan Opportunity, University of Minnesota Law School (February 2015).

18 "Minneapolis Has Paid $45 Million in Police Misconduct Settlements Since 2003," CBSNews.com (June 13, 2020). https://www.cbsnews.com/video/minneapolis-has-paid-45-million-in-police-misconduct-settlements-since-2003/#x.

19 Angelina Chapin, "'If I Would Have Been There, George Floyd May Still Be Alive,'" TheCut.com (June 2, 2020). https://www.thecut.com/2020/06/the-owner-of-cup-foods-speaks-about-george-floyds-death.html.

20 Ibid.

21 "How George Floyd Was Killed in Police Custody," *New York Times*, video (May 31, 2020). https://www.nytimes.com/2020/05/31/us/george-floyd-investigation.html.

22 Charles Holmes, "'He Shook the World': George Floyd's Legendary Houston Legacy," *Rolling Stone* (July 2020), 49.

23 Mohammed Haddad, "Mapping U.S. Cities Where George Floyd Protests Have Erupted," AlJazeera.com (June 2, 2020). https://www.aljazeera.com/indepth/interactive/2020/06/mapping-cities-george-floyd-protests-erupted-200601081654119.html.

Index